# THE ULTIMATE GUIDE TO VINTAGE
# TRANSFORMERS®
## ACTION FIGURES

## MARK BELLOMO

Published by

Krause Publications, a division of F+W Media, Inc.
700 East State Street • Iola, WI 54990-0001
715-445-2214 • 888-457-2873
www.krausebooks.com

To order books or other products call toll-free 1-800-258-0929
or visit us online at www.krausebooks.com

Transformers, all associated character, vehicle, and group names,
and their respective likenesses, are trademarks of Hasbro, Inc.

ISBN-13: 9781440246401
ISBN-10: 1440246408

Cover photography by Kris Kandler
Cover design by Nicole MacMartin
Designed by Nicole MacMartin
Edited by Kristine Manty

Printed in China

10 9 8 7 6 5 4 3 2

Front cover: In the foreground from left are Autobot Commander Optimus Prime and Decepticon
Leader Megatron. In the background, from left, are Autobots Springer, Bumblebee, and Grimlock;
and Decepticons Soundwave and Blitzwing.

Back cover: Autobot Blaster in robot mode and his alternate mode as an AM/FM cassette player.

# ACKNOWLEDGMENTS

As always, there are lots of folks who deserve thanks or this book simply does not exist. First off: My editor, Kristine Manty, who is patient, kind, dedicated, hard working (Did I mention patient? Kind? Hard working?) and a host of other superlatives. Thanks for listening—*truly* listening—to the many suggestions I've made to try and improve this tome. Yours is a rare skill. You're awesome. And by now, you probably actually understand most of the action figure jargon and shoptalk I spout 24-7. I hope we work together for many, many years to come.

Thanks must go to designer Nicole MacMartin for taking my hundreds of ridiculous (and sometimes downright stupid, yet always time-consuming) suggestions with a grain of salt. I push for information and utility; she polishes up a sterile mass of data into a gorgeous package we can actually sell to other human beings. The books you've designed of mine are some of the best I've ever seen in this hobby. Kudos also to Kris Kandler, Krause's in-house photographer, who has been to my home many times to take photos of action figures on my dining room table. We've worked on a host of big, stress-inducing projects together, yet each consecutive book we tackle seems to bring us closer—like compatriots in a foxhole. Our photo sessions last for days on end, twelve-to-fourteen (to sixteen?) hours each: Nobody ever said toys were fun, right?

Then there's the Big Chief: Editorial Director at Krause Publications, Paul Kennedy. I've lost count of the amount of books I've worked on for Krause. Thanks goes to Paul for giving me these opportunities. It's my fondest hope that we can move through all the major toy lines, crafting definitive guides for each and every important franchise: From superheroes to Teenage Mutant Ninja Turtles to He-Man and the Masters of the Universe, Paul and I are always thinking ahead to the next project. Thank you, Mr. Kennedy, for everything.

Gratitude must be given to the following people: The now-defunct Dreamwave Productions for releasing their *Transformers: More Than Meets the Eye* guide books all those years ago which I have referenced liberally, to the online dealers I bought items from at the very last minute, to Delta Star and the rest of the crew at Reprolabels.com for crafting hundreds of dollars of replacement labels for my Transformers samples I owned where their labels were missing or worn (since the first edition was released), to Travis Landry of Bruneau & Co. for providing me with guidance on EVERY SINGLE high-end price in this book (no mean feat, trust me [and check out the book's section on pricing]), to Robert Telleria for his amazing knowledge re: dinosaurs (I'll get back to you when I tackle Dino-Riders next month), to Senior Books Editor Justin Eisinger at IDW Publishing for allowing me to work on the Transformers brand, to Matthew Camaratta at Transformerland.com for the invaluable resource[s] it provides (everything from pricing to pre-production information), and TFWiki.net (the Transformers Wiki) for the vast amount of data available there.

As always, thanks to H.R. Stoneback for showing me the difference between work, dedication, and precision, to my mom and dad for teaching me the value of devoting 12-16 hours a day to a profession I dearly love—and for emotionally supporting me when others viewed my hobby as anathema, and most importantly thanks to the love of my life ... Jessica Rivers-Bellomo. I adore you. Your support of me in the throes of my obsession allows me to continue on, even during long, grueling twenty hour work days. Every January 1st marks another good year in the sun—one where my beloved wife doesn't throw my comics and collectibles into a huge pile on our lawn and set the crap on fire. Burning plastic smells just awful. And the flames would freak out my two cats: Pea-Pod and the Reverend James "Iggy" Caldwell Ignatowski.

– MWB

# CONTENTS

# INTRODUCTION

D ue to the monetary windfall that resulted from the partnership of Marvel and Hasbro for the re-launch of the G.I. Joe brand in 1982, these two companies decided to renew their nuptials (and refill their coffers) with the introduction of another epic toy franchise.

In late 1983/early 1984, they utilized the über-successful three-pronged marketing approach which they devised for G.I. Joe: begin with a monthly Marvel Comic title that was distributed across America, pair the comic with a half-hour animated program constructed by Sunbow Productions that would air every weekday afternoon, and all-the-while employing more traditional modes of advertising (magazine adverts, television commercials, trade show displays, etc.) for an all-out media blitz. Using this trinity of marketing strategies, the new brand's success was inevitable. For the past thirty years, Hasbro's Transformers brand has made hundreds of companies who've licensed their Autobot and Decepticon characters rich beyond imagining. For instance, the worldwide box office gross for the third and fourth *Transformers* films exceeded $1 billion in box office ticket receipts. That's in ticket receipts alone ... for each film.

But what exactly happened behind the scenes at Marvel Comics all those years ago to get the ball rolling? Who were the creative types that struck the initial spark that would eventually conflagrate into this scorching toy line; a brand simply overflowing with characters that reside in toy rooms all around the world? Is there a kid on Planet Earth who doesn't recognize Bumblebee or Optimus Prime or Planet Cybertron? Yet how many of those children know exactly where those names came from?

In the winter of 1983, Marvel Comics' editor-in-chief, Jim Shooter, was handed the reins to develop the back story and characters for the Transformers franchise by Hasbro. Shooter, in an act of good faith, delivered the project to writer/editor Denny O'Neil who was coming off of his revolutionary 1970s run on DC's Green Lantern/Green Arrow and who made his bones at Marvel scripting and editing many of their flagship titles (e.g. *Amazing Spider-Man, Daredevil,* and *Iron Man*). O'Neil chose to work on *Transformers* because the pay for Marvel's toy tie-in projects was usually a bit larger than the rate for standard comic book superhero fare.

However, it appeared that O'Neil didn't "get it." His Transformers back story and the characters he rendered were deemed unacceptable to Shooter, and even though he paid O'Neil for the project, the writer's entire draft was scrapped with the exception of a few minor details. The most important of these lingering details lingered: The heroic Autobots' noble leader was named Optimus Prime.

So then, on the mild afternoon of Friday, November 18, 1983 at Marvel Headquarters—on the weekend before Thanksgiving break—Jim Shooter ran through the corridor that divided Marvel's editorial offices, desperate to find someone to re-create and develop the first series of Transformers characters over the weekend: a project that HAD to be completed by Monday morning. Shooter had taken it upon himself to draft an eight-page treatment that delineated to his chosen writer the canonical back story of the Transformers, and couldn't wait to unload it onto the desk of a willing writer.

As Bob Budiansky recalls, he was the third or fourth choice to tackle the project, but upon asserting to Shooter

Metroplex, alternate "city" mode with Autobot Minicar inhabitants.

———

P. 104

that he could finish the job by Monday morning—and taking advantage of an empty office suite since every other Marvel employee was leaving for Thanksgiving—the staffer wrote like a man possessed. In two short days, Budiansky rendered all of the Transformers' biographical information, authoring those now-iconic "Tech Specs" (Technical Specification[s]) profiles for what would become the first wave of Hasbro's Transformers. Other than retaining Denny O'Neil's moniker for Optimus Prime (and perhaps Prowl as well), it was Bob Budiansky who named the original twenty-eight Transformers and fleshed out their character traits, foibles, and eccentricities.

Although he functioned as the *éminence grise* of the Transformers universe, rendering the Tech Specs bios and packaging "flavor text" for all of Hasbro's Transformers toys from fall 1983 until early 1989, Budiansky's contributions have gone largely unrecognized for developing those memorable, magnificent personalities who occupy a hallowed place in our

"Generation One" canon. Regarding his approach to authoring the original twenty-eight Transformers, Budiansky stated:

*"I knew there was a certain use of language, a certain style of combining words and sounds in their writing [re: Tech Specs] that appealed to me ... Drawing from my knowledge of comic books, science fiction, and my engineering background—I have a B.S. in Civil Engineering, I came up with jargon that I hoped would lend a pseudo-scientific, cool-sounding veneer to the characters."*

Furthermore, if what he wrote inspired a reader to look a word up in the dictionary, "all the better," he claims. Since he grew up reading comics authored by Gardner Fox (herald of the DC Comics' Multiverse) and John Broome (who gave us the S.A. Flash and his rogues), Budiansky reflected their approach to storytelling, since the two writers "...were always introducing science concepts that were new [to him] into their stories," hence readers will notice the scientific, quasi-mechanical bent in Budiansky's Transformers Tech Specs and comic book tales. Yet the writer didn't merely lean on his peers for motivation; he also received stimulation for defining these characters from an often overlooked source:

*"My primary inspiration for the Transformers' characters I created were the toys themselves—what they looked like, what they transformed*

*into, were they good or evil, etc. Once I had that information, I would play word association games in my head to generate possible character names. The names themselves would often suggest personalities. Sometimes I would associate a character with a fictional television or movie character to come up with some personality traits."*

Additionally, if we review the original lineup of Autobots and Decepticons and seriously consider their names—Optimus Prime, Brawn, Bluestreak, Ironhide, Mirage, Megatron, Laserbeak, Skywarp, Thundercracker, Rumble, etc.—it appears that the appellation of every Transformers character functions as a *charactonym*—"an evocative or symbolic name given to a character that conveys his inner psychology or allegorical [emblematic] nature." These names represent their respective character's philosophy of life, and (perhaps) symbolize the character's underlying ideology as well. Therefore, a charactonym is the name of a fictional character that suggests/reflects a distinctive trait of that character.

To that end, the name of the always-impulsive Cliffjumper suggests a character who "looks before he leaps" (i.e. one who *jumps* off of *cliffs*) in order to obtain vengeance against the Decepticons; he leaps into danger before anticipating the scenario or the resulting impact his actions may have upon others. When questioned about the use of charactonyms when he constructed Transformers' Tech Specs, Bob Budiansky stated:

*"I would say that many, if not most, of the names I came up with can be categorized as charactonyms. For example, [take] Ravage—a Decepticon that transforms from a cassette into a jaguar-like creature. The word 'ravage' suggested to me mindless, predatory violence, which I thought was a good fit for a character that looks like a bestial predator and was one of the bad guys."*

The same can be said for Grimlock:

*"I came up with the name Grimlock, and here's how I did it: I wanted a name that had the ring of authority, that sounded dangerous, and that suggested powerful jaws with teeth. Hence, Grimlock ["grim" + "lock"]. Also, since Grimlock was to be the name of the Dinobot leader, I wanted that name to stand apart from the other Dinobots, which all begin with the letter 's'—Swoop, Snarl, Sludge and Slag..."*

Furthermore, according to Budiansky, in many cases a Transformer's name may actually designate a concept larger than the character itself. When involved in the process of naming characters, he played "mental word association games" in order to arrive at a name that "suggested what the character was all about." Often, Budiansky "bestowed a particular personality quirk on the character, and came up with a name for a character based on that quirk. Music-loving Jazz is a good example of that."

With Budiansky developing character bios and Shooter [initially] helming the narrative of Transformers, their treatment was serendipitous to say the least: they struck gold. For if we carefully review the eight-page pitch that Shooter handed to Budiansky to use as a template when the writer began drafting his biographies, readers will be stunned speechless to find that all of Shooter's words and ideas have been followed with stringent exactitude these past thirty-plus years. Whether these ideas have found their way into movie theaters, the small screen, or on the printed page, what was originally slated to be a comic book miniseries had sprawled into something astonishing: a licensed toy property with a rabid fan base that spans multiple generations. What follows is the first paragraph of the original treatment. Nothing has been changed or altered in decades:

*"Civil war rages on the planet Cybertron. Destruction is catastrophic and widespread, and yet no life is lost. None, at least, in the sense that we know life--for the inhabitants of Cybertron are all machines. There is NO 'life' on Cybertron save for mechanical, electronic, 'creatures.' As mankind is first among the organic denizens of Earth, intelligent, sentient robots are the dominant species on Cybertron. Even the planet itself is one vast mechanical construct. Perhaps there was once a 'real' world upon which Cybertron was built on, into, under, and through until no trace of the original planet can be found, but the origin of the planet is unknown, lost in antiquity. Similarly, it is unknown whether the robotic 'life' of Cybertron was originally created by some mysterious, advanced, alien race in the dim, distant past, or whether these strange metallic beings somehow evolved from bizarre, basic life forms beyond human comprehension. What is certain is that the sentient, robotic beings of Cybertron are destroying one another."*

# PREHISTORY

But where did all of these wonderful toy molds that became Hasbro's Transformers originate from? In the early 1980s, successful Japanese toy company Takara, Co. Ltd. (now Takara Tomy) produced two well-designed series of changeable robot toys: Diaclone [ca. 1980-1984/85] and Microman [ca. 1974-1984/85 (and 1998-2007)]. Sales of both lines were waning, so Takara chose to inject new product into these two lines.

Takara's re-engineering of their Diaclone toy line (a portmanteau of "diamond" + "cyclone" [i.e., "strong as a diamond; fast as a cyclone"]) occurred most strikingly in mid/late 1982 when the company devised an all-new series of Diaclone action figures called 'Car-Robots.' This revolutionary toy line offered exotic (yet inanimate) robots that transformed into realistic looking cars whose designs were based on actual automobile models such as the Datsun 280-ZX sports coupe, the Lamborghini Countach LP500S and the sedan type of the Honda City Turbo. These robotic cars were driven/piloted by Diaclone "Inch Man" pilots (standing 1-1/4-inch tall), tiny plastic and die-cast metal figures with magnetized feet that fit into the vehicles' driver seats. The designs for the Diaclone Car-Robots toys were ingenious and would eventually become the templates for many Transformers characters. From a red-colored Sunstreaker to an all-black Ironhide, many Autobot Cars were derived from these marvels of engineering.

The other toy line that Takara revamped was Microman [1974-1984]. The Microman line originally featured an action figure who was a miniaturized [10 cm.] version of Takara's super successful Henshin Cyborg—a toy that, oddly enough, was a Japanese variation on the theme of Hasbro's 12-inch G.I. Joe. [Indirectly then, Transformers' origins are inextricably linked to the G.I. Joe brand.] We would eventually know Microman figures as the famous imported Mego Micronauts brand (1976-1980; i.e. Micronauts' Time Traveler, Space Glider, Acroyear, etc.].

As Microman sales began to decline, Takara developed the 'New Microman: Micro Change' theme in late 1982/early 1983 which featured robots that transformed into realistically detailed household objects: guns, communications devices and 'superdeformed' automobiles. The names given to Micro Change by Takara were ordinary and provincial [i.e., the MC-13 Gun Robo P-38 U.N.C.L.E. or MC-02 Micro Cassette Robo (Jaguar)]—a fact that didn't help kids and collectors suspend

their disbelief and buy into the fiction; hence, these toys lost all their momentum. For although Takara's two toy lines sold well initially, and the company had wanted to amalgamate Microman and Diaclone into one large group of action figures, unfortunately they had no idea how to do this.

Hasbro Incorporated did.

In 1983-84, the licenses to Takara's two toy lines were bought by the American toy giant, and were rebranded and integrated together into one conglomeration, driven by a monumental epic story line to promote their "Transformers" action figure franchise. One day, these generically named toys would become full-fledged animated television stars—a fictional narrative where the Micro Change MC-13 Robot P-38 U.N.C.L.E. was developed into Hasbro's Decepticon Leader, Megatron and the MC-02 Micro Cassette Robo (Jaguar) became Ravage, Decepticon Saboteur. Needless to say, this newly-dubbed Transformers line was a smash success based upon its ingenious back story—one we're all quite familiar with.

Four million years ago, two factions of techno-organic aliens from the planet Cybertron [the Heroic Autobots and the Evil Decepticons] crash-landed on Earth at what

Trypticon,
robot mode.

P. 132

would be the Mount St. Hilary volcano near Portland, Oregon [according to Marvel Comics continuity], in a spacecraft called the Ark. These Cybertronians lay dormant inside the Autobots' Ark, trapped within the side of the volcano for millions of years until awakened in Earth year 1984 by a volcanic eruption that jarred the Ark's supercomputer, Teletraan-1, to life. Teletraan-1 then repaired the Cybertronians, not only fixing the beings' robot modes, but adapting their alternate conversion modes [used for disguise, infiltration, transportation and combat] to mimic Earth life, mistakenly believing the planet's indigenous life forms were automobiles, jets, communications devices and weapons, rather than carbon-based human beings. Unfortunately, the Transformers brought their ages-old conflict to Earth, since their home planet of Cybertron was suffering from a depletion of natural resources. In contrast, Earth had such abundant resources that both factions wanted to obtain these forms of energy; Decepticons desired these resources for conquest and subjugation, while Autobots wished to utilize them

# HOW TO USE THIS BOOK

**1** **"Name"**—As it appears on the Transformer's toy package, Hasbro's original Tech Specs biography card, or Instruction Booklet.

**2** **"Function"**—The character's area of specialization as it appears on the Transformer's Tech Specs.

**3** **"Motto"**—Expression uttered by the character as it appears on the Transformer's Tech Specs dossier.

**4** **"Tech Specs"**—Original Tech Specs biography, the entire text, presented word-for-word.

**5** **"Ability Scores"**—Numbers that indicate a Transformer's various aptitudes as delineated on their Tech Specs biography. This data illustrates: how strong they are [Strength]; how smart they are [Intelligence]; how fast they move, usually in alternate mode [Speed]; how durable/tough they are [Endurance]; their official position in the Autobot or Decepticon army [Rank]; how brave they are [Courage]; how powerful their armaments or energy projection abilities are [Firepower]; and finally, how well they perform their function [i.e. "Warrior," "Leader," "Tactician"] in their respective army [Skill]. Characters that function as a team, i.e. the Air Patrol (1990), have one score overall for: their ability to work together [Teamwork] and their group cohesion [Cooperation]. The combination of these ability scores gives collectors a good idea of a Transformer's relative power and value as a soldier. In some cases, the ability scores do not match the description within their Tech Specs' narrative bio, but that is considered an oversight made during a Transformer toy's lengthy design process.

**6** **"Prices"**—The Transformer's current market value as a loose toy (MLC), packaged toy (MIB), or factory-sealed packaged toy (MISB). For a more detailed explanation of prices, see the "Price Abbreviations" section.*

**7** **"Flavor Text"**—Paragraph describing the Transformers character and/or details about the Hasbro toy itself. Notes on odd facts, back story, variations, etc.

**8** **"Alternate mode"**—The model types for most early-released Transformers toys (ca. 1984-1986) were based on real-world vehicles, weapons, and technological devices. Later on in the line (ca. 1987-1990), the toys' alternate modes became more futuristic and imaginative in design—with peculiar alternate modes that could be loosely identified as "tank" or "race car" or "aircraft."

**9** **"Easily lost weapons and accessories"**—The action figure's loose accessories and removable parts that help to 'complete' the toy are shown here.

**10** **"Images"**—Photos of the Transformers action figure in its **a)** robot mode, **b)** alternate mode—whether vehicle, animal, weapon, etc. (there may be multiple pictures here), and an **c)** image of easily lost weapons and accessories.

---

*Additionally, since this guide does not deal with prices for Tech Specs bio cards, boxed Transformers' Instruction Booklets, Hasbro product catalogs (1984-1990), or other Transformers inserts, accoutrements and ephemera, it is noteworthy that all of these items have value—some more than others. For instance, an Instruction Booklet that came with one of the combiner gift sets (e.g., Devastator, Superion, Menasor, etc.) is quite expensive, selling for $20+ (or more) on the secondary market.

to restore their badly damaged home world. The quest for Energon [the main power source for these Cybertronians] began, and humans were thrust into the middle of this conflict: the epitome of Man versus Machine.

And so was born the "Transformers."

The franchise performed so well in the U.S. that Hasbro then exported the idea of the Autobots and Decepticons back to Japan as the Cybertrons and Destrons, where they flourished as 1985's *Fight Super Robot Life-form: Transformers*, the first of many Japanese iterations of this now-unified toy robot line. Oddly enough, Japanese Transformers eventually outlasted even the American market in terms of endurance, having produced the toy line continually since the introduction of the brand in 1985. Furthermore, since there were certain domestic (North American) Transformers toys manufactured in the U.S., yet not solicited in Japan— there are select Transformers pieces that were exclusively released in Japan that never made it to U.S. shores; Japanese-only Transformers releases are highly prized collectibles and cost a pretty penny today.

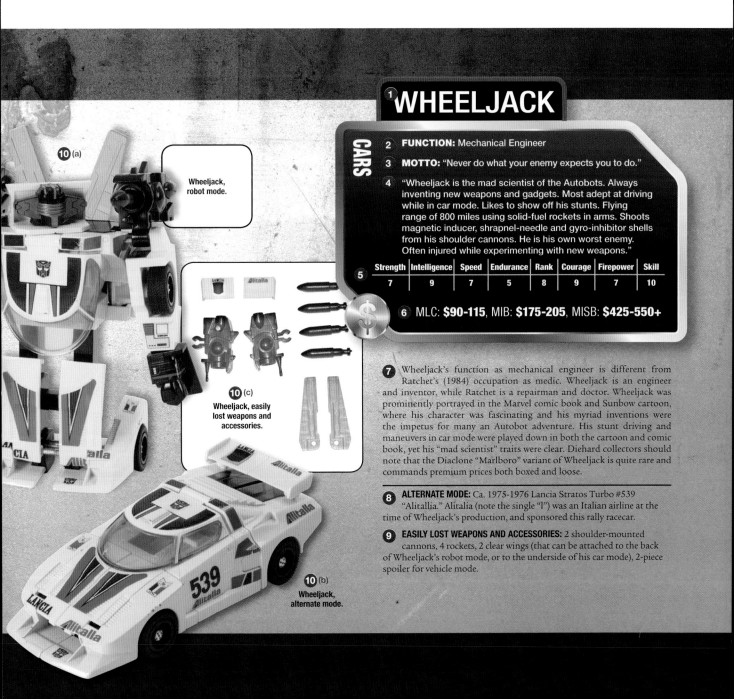

**① WHEELJACK**

**CARS**

② **FUNCTION:** Mechanical Engineer

③ **MOTTO:** "Never do what your enemy expects you to do."

④ "Wheeljack is the mad scientist of the Autobots. Always inventing new weapons and gadgets. Most adept at driving while in car mode. Likes to show off his stunts. Flying range of 800 miles using solid-fuel rockets in arms. Shoots magnetic inducer, shrapnel-needle and gyro-inhibitor shells from his shoulder cannons. He is his own worst enemy. Often injured while experimenting with new weapons."

⑤
| Strength | Intelligence | Speed | Endurance | Rank | Courage | Firepower | Skill |
|----------|--------------|-------|-----------|------|---------|-----------|-------|
| 7 | 9 | 7 | 5 | 8 | 9 | 7 | 10 |

⑥ MLC: **$90-115**, MIB: **$175-205**, MISB: **$425-550+**

⑩ (a) Wheeljack, robot mode.

⑩ (c) Wheeljack, easily lost weapons and accessories.

⑩ (b) Wheeljack, alternate mode.

⑦ Wheeljack's function as mechanical engineer is different from Ratchet's (1984) occupation as medic. Wheeljack is an engineer and inventor, while Ratchet is a repairman and doctor. Wheeljack was prominently portrayed in the Marvel comic book and Sunbow cartoon, where his character was fascinating and his myriad inventions were the impetus for many an Autobot adventure. His stunt driving and maneuvers in car mode were played down in both the cartoon and comic book, yet his "mad scientist" traits were clear. Diehard collectors should note that the Diaclone "Marlboro" variant of Wheeljack is quite rare and commands premium prices both boxed and loose.

⑧ **ALTERNATE MODE:** Ca. 1975-1976 Lancia Stratos Turbo #539 "Alitallia." Alitalia (note the single "l") was an Italian airline at the time of Wheeljack's production, and sponsored this rally racecar.

⑨ **EASILY LOST WEAPONS AND ACCESSORIES:** 2 shoulder-mounted cannons, 4 rockets, 2 clear wings (that can be attached to the back of Wheeljack's robot mode, or to the underside of his car mode), 2-piece spoiler for vehicle mode.

# PRICE ABBREVIATIONS

The prices listed in this guide are the best assessments available based upon the pricing currently realized via a 12-month average "Completed Items Search" on eBay, as well as provided by many prominent retailers across the United States for a period of one full year. Among these retailers, I must mention one above all others: the invaluable assistance I received from the sagacious yet affable Travis Landry and the prices he shared from his tenure at Bruneau & Co. Auctioneers. The data gleaned from Bruneau & Company's finished toy auctions were absolutely essential to constructing all of the high-end prices in this book. It's quite difficult to price sealed pieces, but Travis' assistance made it far easier.

I am compelled to mention that the prices in this tome should be used for reference only—since these estimations may become outdated rather quickly. Therefore, please take the pricing in this book with due deference. The dollar amounts listed in this guide are for NON-AFA GRADED toys, i.e., pieces that have not been professionally assessed and given a grade by the Action Figure Authority. For the purpose of assigning value to the vintage G1 Transformers toys in this reference book, besides loose figures (MLC), there are multiple ways that Hasbro delivered these products for solicitation at retail: Mint On Sealed Card (MOSC), Mint In Box or Mint In Package (MIB/MIP), and Mint In Sealed Box or Mint In Sealed Package (MISB/MISP).

**MLC (Mint, Loose, and Complete):** The toy in question is sold without its original packaging, but retains every single one of its included parts (accessories such as a laser gun, missile[s], or other easily-lost part[s]), yet the specimen is in excellent condition: grading at least an 8.5 out of 10. When grading loose toys, a collectible is only MLC if the toy in question is truly mint, loose, and complete.

Furthermore, many collectors will not purchase a vintage Transformers action figure unless all of its respective labels are applied, in good condition, using the proper placement, and that none are missing: absent stickers will adversely impact the overall appearance of the toy. Labels are of paramount importance to Generation One Transformers, more so than nearly every other vintage toy line.

However, in order to alleviate the stark nature of loose, good condition G1 samples that are missing their essential labels, many collectors choose to utilize high-quality reproduction stickers from the spectacular resource, reprolabels.com. Although the use of "repro" labels rarely impacts the cost of a MLC toy, if you're a dealer or seller, utilizing repro labels should always be mentioned because sometimes label condition (and the use of reproduction labels) may indeed impact value. For instance, a Fortress Maximus MLC with all original labels in mint condition usually holds more value than a Fortress Maximus MLC with newly-applied repro labels. Finally, be careful that all of the accessories you are using to complete a G1 Transformer are originals. There have been a bevy of reissued Transformers released during the past few decades along with commemorative editions and knock-offs of many hard-to-find G1 originals: please educate yourself on telling the difference between the two using respectable I.D. websites.

**MOSC (Mint On Sealed Card):** Next, there are carded items—those vintage Transformers items packaged on a carded bubble—essentially a piece of sturdy chipboard or cardboard (called a "card") with a translucent piece of shaped plastic (called a "bubble") sealed onto said card via glue or paste so that the toy and its requisite accessories are clearly visible to the consumer while said toy hangs on retail pegs.

A Generation One Transformers toy is considered MOSC when the original packaging for the toy in question is completely intact and totally unopened: the translucent bubble is in no way removed (or even slightly separated) from the card, and the action figure and accessories inside are [usually] in C-10, dead mint condition: a solid "10"—on a scale of 1 (the lowest, poorest condition) to 10 (the highest, best condition). Due to the fact that a MOSC package has never been opened and the toy in question has never been exposed to human hands, the toy rates as a "10 out of 10."

Due to the rarity of many MOSC Transformers action figures, some unscrupulous dealers will try and pass off "custom-carded" figures—those toys placed into reproduction packaging—as vintage originals. By using a high-quality printer to replicate an original package's detailed graphics onto cardstock and then constructing custom-made, translucent factory bubbles to match the Hasbro originals, these two reproduction items are then used to mount a vintage figure (and its accessories) onto this reproduction card back. Some sellers—whether intentionally or unintentionally—may try to pass these repro cards off as original MOSC items. If you're in doubt re: whether or not to purchase a MOSC Transformers figure because its provenance is in question, please check with an expert, or compare the packaging to a confirmed original.

**MIB (Mint In Box):** The original box for the toy is intact with nothing cut out or removed (such as a Robot Point[s] proof-of-purchase seal), the box is not factory-sealed with tape or glue, and the package has indeed been opened. Therefore, the toy and all of its elements—in excellent condition—were placed back within the box, along with all of the toy's respective accessories and accoutrements. (Note that some packaged G1 Transformers were sold mounted in a bubble on chipboard and then placed inside of a box; if so, the toy is first positioned within the opened bubble and then is gently fitted inside the box.)

There are a variety of ways for a toy to be considered MIB. For instance, if the box was carefully opened, and the toy is complete—along with all of its packing inserts, unapplied label sheet, protective cardboard dividers, paperwork and inserts—then the toy is considered MIB as well (and not MISB). However, for most collectors and retailers it is not necessary for a MIB toy to include all of the toy's respective paperwork as well (e.g., Transformers product catalog, rub sign explanatory insert, paper promotional material, original shipping bag, etc.).

To wit: If the seal on a box is broken and a mint complete toy is inside, then the toy is MIB.

Furthermore, as with MLC Transformers figures, many collectors will not purchase a vintage G1 Transformers toy designated MIB unless all of its labels were applied and none are missing. Missing labels will adversely affect the toy's aesthetics. When calculating a vintage MIB Transformers item, missing labels should be considered.

**MIP (Mint In Package):** When the original package for the toy is completely intact (nothing has been cut out or removed, etc. [such as a Robot Point[s] proof-of-purchase seal]), but said package is not factory-sealed (with tape, glue, etc.), and the package has indeed been opened. The toy is placed within the package, and is in excellent condition, possessing all of its respective accessories and accoutrements.

There are a variety of ways for a toy to be considered MIP.

For instance, if the package was carefully opened, and the toy is complete—along with all of its packing inserts, protective cardboard dividers (or bubble mounted on chipboard), unapplied label sheet, instructions and paperwork—then the toy is considered MIP (and not MISP). However, for most collectors and retailers and for the grading standards delineated in this guide, it is not necessary for a MIP toy to include all of the toy's respective paperwork as well (e.g., Transformers product catalog, packaging inserts, paper promotional material, etc.). Remember, if the seal on a package is broken, then the toy is MIP.

Throughout this book, a price indicator called **"MIP (opened)"** is used. This descriptor means that a G1 Transformers figure and its accessories are in MINT condition, and that the toy comes with its original, opened package—a card back with its translucent bubble cut open. (Cut either all the way around [where the bubble meets the card], or ¾ of the way, allowing the collector to pop the Transformer into and out of its carded package).

Furthermore, when calculating a vintage MIP G1 Transformers item, missing labels should be considered. Many finicky collectors will not purchase a vintage Transformers toy branded as MIP unless all of its labels are applied and few (or none) are missing.

**MISB (Mint In Sealed Box):** The toy's boxed packaging remains factory-sealed (taped, glued, etc.) while all of its accessories and packaging inserts (unapplied label sheet, instruction sheet, etc.) remain intact and unsullied within its unopened, original box. This is the rarest existing condition for a vintage G1 Transformers toy, and as such, a MISB artifact commands exponentially higher prices than those previously opened, MIB (Mint In Box), non-factory-sealed specimens.

Therefore, MISB samples of vintage Transformers toys are holy grails for many collectors, which is why unscrupulous collectible dealers will try to pass off "re-sealed" MIB items as if they were MISB. So then, please inspect purported MISB toys very carefully to determine their authenticity. If the artifact in question is a considerably rare piece, you should contemplate having the AFA Authority professionally grade the toy.

**MISP (Mint In Sealed Package):** The toy's packaging is factory-sealed (with tape, glue, heat, etc.) while all of its accessories and inserts remain within its unopened, original package (e.g., mailer box, mail-away baggie, etc.). Since this is the rarest condition for a vintage G1 Transformers artifact, MISP items command exorbitantly high prices on the secondary market.

Since MISP samples of vintage G1 Transformers are so very rare, unscrupulous dealers will often try to pass off "re-sealed" items as if they were MISP. Therefore, please inspect your MISP toys carefully to determine their authenticity. Similar to MISB items, if you own a vintage G1 Transformers artifact in MISP condition (usually a mail-away item or promotional toy) and it is a rare piece, you should consider investing some money to have the AFA Authority professionally grade the item.

As a final note, it is imperative that this warning is passed on to Transformers collectors: **Beware of reproduction [and reissued] Generation One Transformers.** Over the past few decades there have been dozens of different reissued Generation One Transformers sold legitimately by Hasbro and Takara—companies that still retain the molds for G1 toys. From 1984's original Optimus Prime to Targetmaster Hot Rod, from a Predaking gift set to a Piranacon/Seacon commemorative exclusive, Hasbro and Takara have expertly capitalized upon the brand's modern popularity to reissue pieces from the original vintage line. However, another gaggle of reproductions are completely unauthorized: including sealed samples of the impossible-to-find MISB Autobot Cars from 1984 & 1985, all five packaged Dinobots, and many, many others—all sold in what looks like factory-sealed, original Hasbro packaging. However, these inexpensive pieces may seem alluring, but they are knock offs, produced in the Pacific Rim and sold at retail for a fraction of the secondary market value of true G1 samples. But, how do you spot a fake? By educating yourself on the difference in date stamps and packaging differences, in color changes and plastic quality, in Country of Origin indicia and accessory variations, and a host of other noticeable dissimilarities. There are many websites online that will help you in your search such as highendtfs.com.

# 1984

## SERIES ①

Hasbro, Inc. quietly infiltrated the toy aisles of 1984 with a series of characters based on the designs of Takara Inc.'s robot toys known as Microman and Diaclone in Japan. These "transformable" robots divided into two factions: Autobots (good) and Decepticons (evil). Like the hugely successful G.I. Joe: A Real American Hero line, the Transformers were introduced into American popular culture via a superb television show by Sunbow/Marvel Productions and an excellent comic book produced by Marvel Comics.

With die-cast metal parts, rubber tires, working action features, and lightly-firing missiles (not Hasbro's fault, but U.S. toy laws), these robots quickly changed to jets, cars, trucks, weapons, or other items, and constructed a foundation for one of the most popular toy franchises of all time. So successful were Hasbro's efforts, that after packaging Takara's creations as Autobots and Decepticons, these originally Japanese-crafted toys were exported back to their home country and refreshed Takara's coffers with Cybertrons (good) and Destrons (evil).

The back story of Marvel Comics' *Transformers* was created by Jim Shooter (treatment), Denny O'Neil (plot), and Bob Budiansky (story—and it was Bob who generated many of the original, and best, "Tech Specs" toy biographies). According to the comic book, and the cartoon that followed suit, Optimus Prime led the heroic Autobots, who were in the midst of fighting an age-old war against their cruel foes, the Decepticons. Commanded by Megatron, this group of ruthless war machines was bent on total conquest of the Transformers' home planet of Cybertron. The conflict between the two factions raged for millions of years, and eventually disrupted the orbit of Cybertron, sending the massive orb hurtling though space. To preserve their world's existence, the Autobots assembled a team for a dangerous mission: guide the planet safely though space and an oncoming asteroid belt. Therefore, Optimus Prime departed from Cybertron on the Autobot spacecraft known as "The Ark," and mid-mission, while the noble Autobots tried to accomplish their dangerous errand, they were attacked by Megatron and his Decepticons aboard their own spaceship, the Nemesis.

Out of sheer desperation, Optimus Prime programmed The Ark to land on a nearby planet, and the large craft crashed on the surface of Earth during what we consider to be pre-historic times—the impact of the landing debilitating all its passengers who would lie damaged and dormant for eons. Four million years later, in 1984, the Ark and its supercomputer, Teletran-1, awoke and repaired the organic robots contained within indiscriminately (in the comic universe; in the animation, the Decepticons were restored first): fixing and repairing Autobots and Decepticons alike to functional status. Sending out a probe to observe the Earth's "inhabitants" circa 1984, the probe transmitted data regarding what it assumed to be native inhabitants back to The Ark: thinking that our mechanical automobiles, jets, and the like were living Earth beings. So instead of their Cybertronian alternate modes, the newly repaired Decepticons converted into recognizable Earth forms such as jet fighters, weapons, and communications devices, while the Autobots became disguised as automobiles.

Recognizing the gravity of their newfound situation, the Decepticons abandoned The Ark while the Autobots established their new base on Mt. St. Hilary. Thus began an epic quest for "Energon," the powerful energy source Cybertronians are dependent upon to survive. The Decepticons realized Earth's readily available natural resources could be converted into Energon, and both factions were inspired to produce Energon, refuel, and strive to return to far-flung Cybertron. Earthlings were therefore thrust into the middle of this great conflict between the Heroic Autobots who needed our help, and the Evil Decepticons who ravaged our planet.

# OPTIMUS PRIME

**COMMANDER**

**FUNCTION:** Autobot Commander
**MOTTO:** "Freedom is the right of all sentient beings."

"Optimus Prime is the largest, strongest, and wisest of all Autobots. Feels his role is the protection of all life, including Earth-life. Fights unceasingly to defeat the Decepticons. Splits into three autonomous modules: 1) Optimus Prime...the brain center known as the Commander; 2) Roller...the Autobot scout car...a spy who operates up to 1,200 miles away; and 3) Autobot Headquarters... the combat deck equipped with a versatile mechanic/artillery robot. Injury to one module is felt by the other two.

| Strength | Intelligence | Speed | Endurance | Rank | Courage | Firepower | Skill |
|----------|--------------|-------|-----------|------|---------|-----------|-------|
| 10 | 10 | 8 | 10 | 10 | 10 | 8 | 10 |

MLC: **$110-120+**, MIB: **$165-220+**,
MIB (sealed contents): **$475-560+**, MISB: **$800-1,000+**

**MOVIE EDITION:** MLC (with paperwork): **$175-210+**, MIB: **$300-400+**,
MIB (sealed contents): **$550-675+**, MISB: **$900-1,100+**

**PEPSI EDITION:** MLC: **$130-175+**, MIB: **$225-300+**,
MIB (sealed contents): **$525-610+**, MISB: **$750-950+**

The compassionate robot formerly known as Orion Pax became Optimus Prime after receiving the legendary Matrix of Leadership. Optimus Prime was known as "Battle Convoy" in Takara's Japanese toy line and cartoons where his Autobots were known as "Cybertrons." Prime is a courageous and valiant leader who uttered many phrases reminiscent of Earth's Eastern philosophers during his long tenure as the beloved Autobot Commander. Voiced by the inimitable Peter Cullen, Optimus Prime's death in the 1987 feature, *Transformers: The Movie*, was an affecting act of tragedy for many young fans. Some suggested that his death drained the cartoon of its sincerity—and so he returned from the dead, albeit too late to prevent the cartoon's demise.

As a figure, he has two major parts: his cab section that transforms into Optimus Prime, and his tractor trailer that converts into a portable Autobot Headquarters/combat deck with repair bay and a "firing" mechanism that launches the speedy reconnaissance scout car, Roller.

There were many different variations in Hasbro's flagship Transformers toy, including black (common) or gray (rarer) missiles for the combat deck robot, raised computer panel plates (rare) instead of stickers inside his trailer, bloated fists and rifle (rare) instead of regular-sized fists and rifle (common), and different colors for Roller: gray (rare), purple (uncommon), or dark blue (common). There is also a smokestack variation on the Prime module itself; long (rare) or short smokestacks.

**ALTERNATE MODE:** (Cab) red and blue post-1973 White Freightliner 96-inch cab WFT cab over engine semi-trailer truck with (trailer) silver high-cube container trailer (unconfirmed).
**EASILY LOST WEAPONS AND ACCESSORIES:** 2 fists, hose, gas pump, gas nozzle, laser blaster, Roller, 4 black rockets, trailer door commonly found missing.

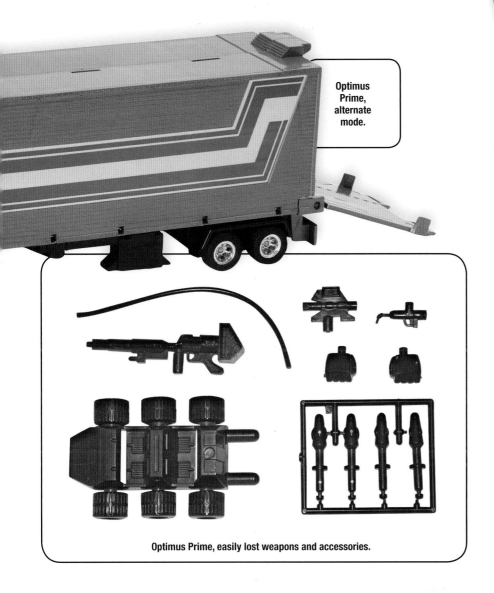

Optimus Prime, alternate mode.

Optimus Prime, easily lost weapons and accessories.

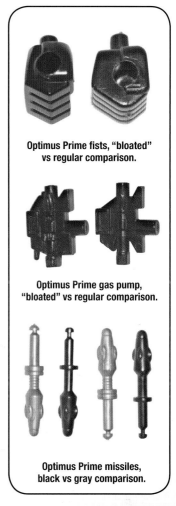

Optimus Prime fists, "bloated" vs regular comparison.

Optimus Prime gas pump, "bloated" vs regular comparison.

Optimus Prime missiles, black vs gray comparison.

Optimus Prime Roller, blue vs purple comparison.

Optimus Prime Trailer, alternate mode with various mechanic/ artillery robot missile and limb variations.

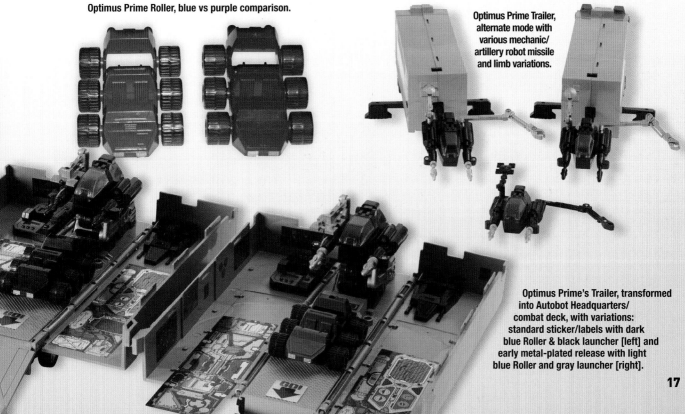

Optimus Prime's Trailer, transformed into Autobot Headquarters/ combat deck, with variations: standard sticker/labels with dark blue Roller & black launcher [left] and early metal-plated release with light blue Roller and gray launcher [right].

## [AUTOBOT]
# MINICARS

The Autobot Minicars were "cute" lower cost alternatives to the much more expensive Autobot cars, and many people purchased these little guys to fill out their Autobot ranks. And why not? Sunbow never shied away from putting members of the Minicars in the forefront of their *Transformers* animated series. With the likes of Brawn, Bumblebee, and Cliffjumper as well-rendered characters, kids couldn't help but pick them up at retail.

Bumblebee, robot mode.

Bumblebee, alternate mode.

## BRAWN

**MINICARS**

**FUNCTION:** Demolitions
**MOTTO:** "Might over microchips."

"To Brawn, Earth is essentially a hostile environment—and he loves it. Strong, rugged, agile—the most macho of all Autobots. Delights in challenges. Sorry for those not as tough as himself. Second strongest (Ark modified) Autobot—can lift 190,000 pounds and knock down a small building with one punch. High resistance to artillery fire. Vulnerable to attack by electromagnetic waves."

| Strength | Intelligence | Speed | Endurance | Rank | Courage | Firepower | Skill |
|----------|--------------|-------|-----------|------|---------|-----------|-------|
| 9 | 3 | 4 | 9 | 5 | 10 | 1 | 4 |

 MLC: **$10-12**, MIP (opened): **$30-32**,
MOC: **$200-300** (with Mini Spy, MOC: **$75-150+**)

By definition, the word brawny means, "having muscular strength and power." This is the perfect encapsulation of Brawn and his personality. His design was taken from the Microman line by Takara, and then given to Hasbro. His 4x4 is fairly detailed for a Minicar (in comparison to the other original five), and his toy manifestation is much different from his cartoon character form. In Sunbow's *Transformers,* Brawn has actual facial features and is "wingless."

Note that as a toy, Brawn's fragile arms have a tendency to be either loose or have come off of the robot altogether, so be careful when transforming this piece. Sadly, Brawn was killed in *Transformers: The Movie* by a Decepticon attack.

Brawn, alternate mode.

Brawn, robot mode.

**ALTERNATE MODE:** British Land Rover Defender 4x4 (aka. Land Rover Ninety [or] Land Rover One Ten).
**EASILY LOST WEAPONS AND ACCESSORIES:** N/A.

Bumblebee, assorted colors, with and without rub signs.

▶ Bumblebee was one of the first Transformers to make contact with humans in both the Sunbow cartoon and Marvel comic book, and was usually the ride of choice for the Autobot's human allies (i.e. Spike, Sparkplug, Buster, etc.). He would later be reincarnated as Goldbug (1988).

As a toy, Bumblebee was available at retail in two different colored versions—red (a bit rarer) and yellow (more common). The yellow is often more popular with casual collectors as it was his "true" color in both the comic book and cartoon. Take a look at his real rubber tires and you'll be amazed that they have the brand "Dunlop" molded onto them!

**ALTERNATE MODE:** Classic Volkswagen Beetle, "superdeformed" (i.e. rendered in a highly exaggerated manner, as are all of the 1984 Minicars).

**EASILY LOST WEAPONS AND ACCESSORIES:** N/A.

## BUMBLEBEE

**MINICARS**

**FUNCTION:** Espionage
**MOTTO:** "The least likely can be the most dangerous."

"Small, eager and brave, Bumblebee acts as messenger and spy. Due to his small size, he dares to go where others can't and won't. He idolizes the bigger Autobots, especially Optimus Prime (1984) and Prowl (1984), and strives to be accepted. He is the most energy efficient and has the best vision of all the (Ark modified) Autobots. He can go underwater for reconnaissance and salvage missions. Although physically the weakest Autobot, his stealth more than compensates for this inadequacy."

| Strength | Intelligence | Speed | Endurance | Rank | Courage | Firepower | Skill |
|---|---|---|---|---|---|---|---|
| 2 | 8 | 4 | 7 | 7 | 9 | 1 | 7 |

**BUMBLEBEE, YELLOW:** MLC: **$25-30+**, MIP (opened): **$45-50**, MOC: **$350-450** (with Mini Spy, MOC: **$200-300**)
**BUMBLEBEE, RED:** MLC: **$24-27**, MIP (opened): **$40-45**, MOC: **$300-400** (with Mini Spy, MOC: **$150-250**)

## CLIFFJUMPER

**MINICARS**

**FUNCTION:** Warrior
**MOTTO:** "Strike first, strike fast, strike hard."

"'Let me at 'em,' is Cliffjumper's motto. His eagerness and daring have no equal. He's driven by a desire to win the battle against the Decepticons. Finds Earth terrain a hindrance. One of the fastest (Ark modified) Autobots. Often uses his speed to draw fire away from others. Shoots 'glass gas,' which makes metal as brittle as glass. His recklessness often leads to actual blow-outs and situations too dangerous for him to handle."

| Strength | Intelligence | Speed | Endurance | Rank | Courage | Firepower | Skill |
|---|---|---|---|---|---|---|---|
| 4 | 4 | 7 | 4 | 5 | 10 | 7 | 5 |

**CLIFFJUMPER, RED:** MLC: **$20-22**, MIP (opened): **$32-38**, MOC: **$200-300** (with Mini Spy, MOC: $100-200)
**CLIFFJUMPER, YELLOW:** MLC: **$15-18**, MIP (opened): **$28-32**, MOC: **$100-200** (with Mini Spy, MOC: **$75-150**)

Cliffjumper, alternate mode.

Cliffjumper, robot mode.

Cliffjumper's cartoon voice was provided by the famous Casey Casem (note the irony when he was using a "countdown" in *Transformers: The Movie*), and his toy was released in both red and yellow colors. Red is the most popular with collectors because it represents the "cartoon appropriate" version of the character. Thankfully, the writer of Sunbow's animated series actually read Hasbro's Tech Specs, and allowed him to use his "glass gas" in the show.
**NOTE:** Hubcap (1986) is a retooling of the Japanese Microman Cliffjumper mold *without* a spoiler and with a different head attached to the toy. The two are *not* from the exact same mold.

**ALTERNATE MODE:** Porsche 944 Carrera GT (ca. 1982), "superdeformed."
**EASILY LOST WEAPONS AND ACCESSORIES:** N/A.

Cliffjumper, different colors, with and without rub sign.

# GEARS

**MINICARS**

**FUNCTION:** Transport/Reconnaissance
**MOTTO:** "Nobody wins a war—somebody loses."

"Gears is anti-social, a self-proclaimed misfit. Finds fault in everything and everyone. Acts this way to help cheer others up as they try to cheer him up. Tremendous strength and endurance. Totes heavy loads long distances. Launches to height of 20 miles, floats down on compressed air. Becomes an easy target due to limited maneuverability. Can detect infrared."

| Strength | Intelligence | Speed | Endurance | Rank | Courage | Firepower | Skill |
|---|---|---|---|---|---|---|---|
| 8 | 7 | 6 | 8 | 6 | 9 | 1 | 7 |

MLC: **$10-12**, MIP (opened): **$27-30**,
MOC: **$200-300** (with Mini Spy, MOC: **$150-200**)

Gears, robot mode.

Gears, alternate mode.

A whole episode of the *Transformer* cartoon was dedicated to Gears and his anti-social tendencies. Note the subtle "M" mounted on his toy's hood that represents the original Japanese Microman line from which he came. Gears became friends with Spider-Man in the Marvel Comics continuity.

As an action figure, be careful of chrome wear to the figure's legs in robot mode: chrome rubbing is a constant concern for Transformer collectors and adversely affects toy values.

**ALTERNATE MODE:** 4WD off road truck [model unknown], "superdeformed."

**EASILY LOST WEAPONS AND ACCESSORIES:** N/A.

# HUFFER

**MINICARS**

**FUNCTION:** Construction Engineer
**MOTTO:** "Molecular structure is the key to success."

"Huffer is cynical, hard-boiled and pessimistic. 'He looks at the world through sludge-colored windshields.' Will complain it can't be built, then builds it anyway. Not too sociable, but absolutely reliable. Arm sensors can test materials for strength, head resistance, elasticity, etc. Extremely strong. Superior mathematical and geometrical abilities. Often unhappy and homesick for Cybertron."

| Strength | Intelligence | Speed | Endurance | Rank | Courage | Firepower | Skill |
|---|---|---|---|---|---|---|---|
| 7 | 8 | 5 | 7 | 6 | 8 | 1 | 9 |

MLC: **$9-11**, MIP (opened): **$30-32**,
MOC: **$200-300+** (with Mini Spy, MOC: **$75-150**)

Huffer, robot mode.

Huffer, alternate mode.

With one of the more interesting voices in the *Transformers* animated series, Huffer is often referred to as a "cute" figure, so we must remember that these Minicars from 1984 were taken from the Microman line in Japan and weren't designed to be authentic looking—they were supposed to simply transform into *toy* trucks and cars. Note the "M" logos on his sides that indicate his affiliation with the Microman line of the early 1980s. Beware of severe chrome wear on Huffer's smokestacks.

**ALTERNATE MODE:** Semi truck cab without trailer; [Ottawa 4x2 off-road terminal tractor], "superdeformed."

**EASILY LOST WEAPONS AND ACCESSORIES:** N/A.

Windcharger, robot mode.

Windcharger, alternate mode.

# WINDCHARGER

**MINICARS**

**FUNCTION:** Warrior
**MOTTO:** "Quick action equals quick victory."

"Windcharger is the fastest (Ark modified) Autobot over short distances. Good in situations requiring fast, decisive action. Enthusiastic but impatient. Short attention span. Casts powerful magnetic field which can attract or repel large metal objects. Smashes them at closer distances. These abilities use up tremendous energy. Often burns himself out due to carelessness."

| Strength | Intelligence | Speed | Endurance | Rank | Courage | Firepower | Skill |
|----------|-------------|-------|-----------|------|---------|-----------|-------|
| 4 | 6 | 8 | 4 | 5 | 9 | 7 | 6 |

MLC: **$10-12**, MIP (opened): **$30-32**, MOC: **$200-300** (with Mini Spy, MOC: **$75-150**)

As an action figure, Windcharger is available in two slightly different shades of red. His character was not used very often in either the cartoon or comic book, yet because of his cool-looking alternate mode (a Pontiac Firebird Trans Am), he was one of the first Minicars snatched up by kids. Unfortunately, Windcharger perished by unknown means in *Transformers: The Movie* when the Decepticons assaulted Autobot City.

**ALTERNATE MODE:** 3rd generation Pontiac Firebird Trans Am (ca. 1982-1992), "superdeformed."
**EASILY LOST WEAPONS AND ACCESSORIES:** N/A.

# BUMPER

**FUNCTION:** - - -
**MOTTO:** - - -

MLC: **$100-120+**, MIP (opened [Bumblebee or Cliffjumper packaging): **$155-165**, MOC (Bumblebee or Cliffjumper packaging): **$625-675+**

Bumper—a shortening of the portmanteau of "Bumblebee" and "Cliffjumper"—was the result of an unintended release of a Transformers Minicar, packaged for sale on either Bumblebee or Cliffjumper packaging. As a character, he was never introduced in the cartoon or comic, but it can be assumed that Bumper is an "Ark modified" Autobot, as his alternate mode suggests that period in Transformers history. Yet, because of his *unintentional* inclusion by Hasbro in their toy selections, he has no tech spec, motto, or even function. He's quite expensive on the secondary market.

Bumblejumper/ Bumper, robot mode.

Bumblejumper/Bumper, alternate mode.

**ALTERNATE MODE:** 2nd generation Mazda 323 [aka. Mazda Familia 1500XG & Mazda Protegé], "superdeformed."
**EASILY LOST WEAPONS AND ACCESSORIES:** N/A.

# CARS [AUTOBOT]

The Autobot cars were the middle-price point items for the good guys in 1984 and 1985, and with the combination of excellent transformation processes, first-rate weapons and accessories, and die-cast metal body parts, they were hard to beat in terms of value and playability on retail shelves. These Autobot cars were the main protagonists throughout the Transformers stories.

Bluestreak, alternate mode.

## BLUESTREAK

**CARS**

**FUNCTION:** Gunner
**MOTTO:** "I never met a Decepticon I didn't dislike."

"Bluestreak often talks incessantly and inanely. Lightens the situation for all Autobots with his good-natured manner. Despite formidable weaponry and blazing speed, he hates war. Haunted by memory of Decepticons destroying his home-city. Fires bombs up to 8.3 miles and lightning-like 80,000-volt beam up to 12 miles of limited accuracy. Often inhibited by his disdain for combat."

| Strength | Intelligence | Speed | Endurance | Rank | Courage | Firepower | Skill |
|----------|--------------|-------|-----------|------|---------|-----------|-------|
| 6 | 6 | 7 | 9 | 5 | 2 | 9 | 7 |

**$** MLC: **$65-78**, MIB: **$120-140**, MISB: **$350-450**

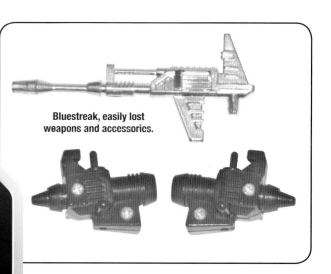

Bluestreak, easily lost weapons and accessories.

Despite what some catalog pictures illustrate, there was never a "blue-streaked" Bluestreak figure solicited to the American marketplace: any samples with a blue stripe are either Diaclone releases or a newer re-release/reproduction, G1 collectors will recall that more than a decade ago, Bluestreak was considered the most expensive packaged Transformer of the 1984 line—perhaps in the whole G1 toy brand. However, due to the exorbitant cost of sealed, boxed vintage Transformers toys, where once this Autobot Gunner existed as a high water mark re: pricing, Bluestreak is now simply one of many rare pieces in an ever-shrinking pool of MISB samples. As a figure, Bluestreak possesses the same brittle, narrow windshield piece as Prowl (1984) and Smokescreen (1985)—since all are based on the same model type. To wit: obtaining Bluestreak with an unrepaired windshield is challenging indeed.

**ALTERNATE MODE:** Datsun 280ZX sports coupe (aka. Nissan S130, Nissan Fairlady Z, Nissan Fairlady 280Z [ca. 1978-1983].

**EASILY LOST WEAPONS AND ACCESSORIES:** 3 incendiary missiles, Electron Rifle [laser gun], 2 missile launchers.

**NOTE:** Although Hasbro used the same mold for all three similarly designed Autobots, Bluestreak's two missile launchers are red in color, Prowl's (1984) are silver, while Smokescreen's (1985) are white.

Bluestreak, robot mode.

Hound, easily lost weapons and accessories.

Hound,
alternate mode.

# HOUND

**CARS**

**FUNCTION:** Scout
**MOTTO:** "Observe everything, remember even more."

"Hound loves the natural wonders of Earth, prefers it to
Cybertron. Brave, fearless, loyal. Secretly desires to be human.
Uses turret gun as radar scope, infrared radiation collector.
Tracks machines as well as humans. Hologram gun projects
3-dimensional grid laser-light topographical maps. Vulnerable to
thermal and electromagnetic interference."

| Strength | Intelligence | Speed | Endurance | Rank | Courage | Firepower | Skill |
|----------|--------------|-------|-----------|------|---------|-----------|-------|
| 5 | 8 | 5 | 7 | 6 | 10 | 3 | 9 |

MLC: **$72-85**, MIB: **$145-160+**,
MISB: **$535-625+**

Hound,
robot
mode.

Although his military motif made Hound one of the most
popular of the 1984 Autobot cars, his poseability as a robot
was extremely limited and sometimes fitting his hologram gun
into his hand was a laborious task. As a toy, please be careful of
chrome wear, and the fragile nature of his side mirrors. In his
Jeep mode, he was well equipped for off-road missions. Hound's
function as a scout was used frequently on the Sunbow cartoon
and in the pages of the Marvel comic book, where he utilized
his hologram gun often, and was amiable with the Autobots'
human compatriots.

**ALTERNATE MODE:** Mitsubishi J59 Jeep; can also form "attack
jeep" with added accessories.

**EASILY LOST WEAPONS AND ACCESSORIES:** Movable machine/
turret gun, spare tire, gas can, shoulder-mounted rocket
launcher, 3 rockets, Hologram Gun.

Ironhide, 2-part robot mode.

## IRONHIDE

**CARS**

**FUNCTION:** Security
**MOTTO:** "High tech circuitry is no replacement for guts."

"'Go chew on a microchip,' is Ironhide's slogan. Prefers action to words. Oldest, toughest, most battle-tested Autobot. Bodyguard to Optimus Prime (1984). In charge of guarding anything of importance. Gruff but kind. Trithyllium-steel skin makes him nearly invulnerable to attack. Shoots variety of liquids from supercooled nitrogen to superheated lead. Has sonar, radar, radiowave detector. Slowest and most fragile of the group."

| Strength | Intelligence | Speed | Endurance | Rank | Courage | Firepower | Skill |
|----------|--------------|-------|-----------|------|---------|-----------|-------|
| 7 | 7 | 3 | 9 | 7 | 10 | 7 | 7 |

MLC: **$50-55**, MIB: **$95-115**, MISB: **$250-350**

Ironhide, alternate mode.

Ironhide, easily lost weapons and accessories.

Ironhide is slow moving, but he is *most certainly not* physically fragile—as both the cartoon and Marvel comic portray this Autobot Security specialist as one of the most durable of all (Ark-designed) Autobots." Regardless, many G1 Transformer fans wish that Hasbro/Takara had released Ironhide and Ratchet (1984) as they looked in the Sunbow cartoon—with bodies that actually have heads, and not semi-passable chrome-sticker faces pasted on the drivers' seats behind their windshields. Ironhide's robot mode is small compared to the other 1984 Autobot cars, but his detachable battle-station with missile launcher somewhat makes up for his "controversial" robot mode. Sadly, the popular Ironhide perished in *Transformers: The Movie* at the hands of Megatron.

**ALTERNATE MODE:** 1980 Nissan Onebox Cherry Vanette.
**EASILY LOST WEAPONS AND ACCESSORIES:** Static Laser Gun (rifle), gun post (almost always found missing in loose samples), 3 missiles.

## JAZZ

**CARS**

**FUNCTION:** Special Operations Expert
**MOTTO:** "Do it with style or don't bother doing it."

"Jazz loves Earth culture. Always looking to learn more. His knowledge of Earth makes him the indispensable right-hand man to Optimus Prime (1984). Takes most dangerous missions. Very cool, very stylish, very competent. Equipped with photon rifle, flamethrower, full-spectrum beacon, 180 db stereo speakers. Creates dazzling, disorienting sound and light shows. Versatile, clever, daring, but prone to be distracted."

| Strength | Intelligence | Speed | Endurance | Rank | Courage | Firepower | Skill |
|----------|--------------|-------|-----------|------|---------|-----------|-------|
| 5 | 9 | 7 | 7 | 8 | 9 | 5 | 10 |

MLC: **$65-70**, MIB: **$170-190**, MISB: **$250-350**
**COOKIE CRISP VARIANT:** MLC (intact labels): **$85-100+**, MIB (w/paperwork): **$115-130+**, MISB (mailer box): **$575-625+**

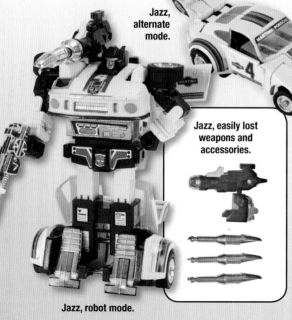

Jazz, alternate mode.

Jazz, easily lost weapons and accessories.

Jazz, robot mode.

Jazz uses his "whale tail" spoiler (the exact name from his model of race car) to glide for a short distance after making jumps in his alternate mode. Jazz is the creative thinker of the Autobots, the Transformer who Optimus Prime (1984) invariably consults regarding popular culture and sociology; he also has an encyclopedic knowledge of intergalactic cultures. As the Autobots' Special Ops Expert, Jazz's speakers and vehicle-mounted light beacon can create a powerful sound and light show.

There was a rare mail away variation of Jazz in 1985, solicited by Ralston Purina's Cookie Crisp cereal. The labels for "Cookie Crisp Jazz" were modified—omitting the "Martinii Porsche" brand on the car's windshield and rear spoiler, and leaving out the word "Martinii" on the doors. As with every sample of Jazz, take care when transforming the toy's thin hood base: It has the tendency to snap off. Finally, Jazz's alternate mode is based upon a 1981 Porsche 935 Turbo, one of the most competitive racecars in motor sports history.

**ALTERNATE MODE:** 1981 Porsche 935 Turbo.
**EASILY LOST WEAPONS AND ACCESSORIES:** Missile launcher (flamethrower), 3 missiles, Photon Rifle.

# MIRAGE

**CARS**

**FUNCTION:** Spy
**MOTTO:** "Who and what I am I hide from the enemy."

"Mirage is not thrilled about being an Autobot freedom fighter. Prefers hunting turbofoxes on Cybertron with his high-priced friends. Effective fighter, more effective intelligence gatherer. Electrodisrupter can cast illusions altering his physical placement and appearance for up to 6 minutes. Expert marksman with armor-piercing rocket-dart hunting rifle. Unsure of Autobot cause...can't fully be trusted."

| Strength | Intelligence | Speed | Endurance | Rank | Courage | Firepower | Skill |
|----------|--------------|-------|-----------|------|---------|-----------|-------|
| 6 | 9 | 7 | 5 | 7 | 5 | 6 | 10 |

**$** MLC: **$60-65**, MIB: **$160-170**, MISB: **$425-550+**

Mirage, easily lost weapons and accessories.

Mirage, alternate mode.

Mirage, robot mode.

Mirage has one of the most complicated personalities of the Earth-bound Autobots: erudite and arrogant, selfish and superior—yet he can be the most valuable of warriors. He uses his Electro-Disruptor to displace the photons around him to make himself invisible (for up to 6 minutes), hence his nickname. In spite of his lack of earnest affiliation to the Autobot cause, his fascinating alternate mode, first-rate accessories (be careful of the spurs on the missile launcher, they break easily), and invisibility power have made him a fan-favorite. It is suggested that Mirage's Formula 1 racecar alternate mode was designed to be used in concert with Optimus Prime's (1984) trailer "launcher."

**ALTERNATE MODE:** Ligier JS-11 Formula 1 Racer.

**EASILY LOST WEAPONS AND ACCESSORIES:** Missile launcher (shoulder-mounted Electro-Disruptor), 3 missiles, Hunting Rifle.

# PROWL

**CARS**

**FUNCTION:** Military Strategist
**MOTTO:** "Logic is the ultimate weapon."

"Prowl will keep at a task for as long as it takes. Strives to find reason and logic in everything. A listener, not a talker. Has most sophisticated logic center of all Autobots. Able to analyze and advise on complex combat situations almost instantaneously. Fires wire-guided incendiary missiles and high-corrosive acid pellets. The unexpected can often scramble his circuits."

| Strength | Intelligence | Speed | Endurance | Rank | Courage | Firepower | Skill |
|----------|--------------|-------|-----------|------|---------|-----------|-------|
| 7 | 9 | 7 | 9 | 9 | 9 | 4 | 9 |

**$** MLC: **$60-65**, MIB: **$155-175+**, MISB: **$400-500+**

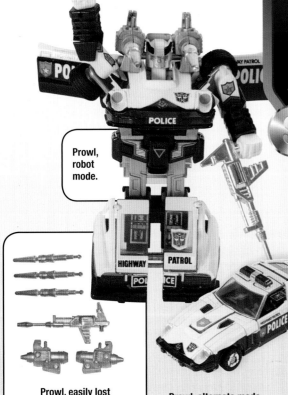

Prowl, robot mode.

Prowl, easily lost weapons and accessories.

Prowl, alternate mode.

Prowl's prototype (non retail-issued) label sheet in his original G1 instruction booklet states the names of many Japanese cities (Tokyo, Sapporo, Osaka, etc.) on stickers that could be peeled off and applied to his toy. He is one of the most demanded of the 1984 Transformers on the secondary market due to his sleek styling as a police car, appropriate accessories, and high Autobot rank.

As a character, it appears Prowl is seen as the logical (if you'll pardon the pun) successor to Optimus Prime (1984), and he functions as his stalwart right-hand-man—but there is always the problem of Grimlock (1985) challenging for authority. As a child, I was stunned to see Prowl killed by Megatron (1984) in the first few minutes of *Transformers: The Movie*.

**ALTERNATE MODE:** Datsun 280ZX police cruiser.

**EASILY LOST WEAPONS AND ACCESSORIES:** 2 missile launchers (shoulder-mounted wire-guided), 3 missiles, Laser Gun.

**NOTE:** The tiny Japanese Police Force Chrysanthemum label/emblem (observe the sixteen petals) on the front hood is a royal emblem—the mark of the Japanese Emperor.

Ratchet,
alternate mode.

Ratchet, 2-part
robot mode.

❶

❷

# RATCHET

**CARS**

**FUNCTION:** Medic
**MOTTO:** "You break it, I'll remake it."

"Ratchet was the best tool-and-die man on Cybertron. In his workbay on Earth he can make anything from a pin to a missile. Repairs injured Autobots, given the right parts. Likes to party, give backtalk, but does any job as well as anyone. Has laser scalpels, arc-welders, electron microscopes, circuit sensors, fluid dispensers at his disposal. Sometimes his having a good time interferes with his effectiveness."

| Strength | Intelligence | Speed | Endurance | Rank | Courage | Firepower | Skill |
|----------|--------------|-------|-----------|------|---------|-----------|-------|
| 4 | 8 | 4 | 5 | 7 | 8 | 3 | 10 |

**$** [Ratchet, no cross]: MLC: **$50-55**, MIB: **$85-110**, MISB: **$400-500;** [Ratchet, with cross]: MLC: **$50-55**, MIB: **$85-110**, MISB: **$300-400**

Ratchet received a lot of page time in early issues of Marvel Comics' *Transformers* series, and beaucoup airtime on the Sunbow cartoon because of his dual status as Autobot doctor and resident party animal. Truly, Ratchet's yearning to have a good time and desire to speak his mind at every turn (to both his peers and his superiors), sometimes interfered with his unparalleled talent as a medic. His toy is constructed from the same mold as Ironhide (1984)—with light modifications for his ambulance's alternate mode. Like Ironhide, Ratchet's toy received the same criticism for its poorly-rendered robot head (essentially a label) and its lack of similarity to his robot mode as portrayed in the cartoon and comic book. Regardless, there are two different versions of Ratchet's toy—one without a red cross label on his roof (slightly more valuable), and one with the red cross (more common).

His toy is constructed from the same mold as Ironhide (1984)—with light modifications for his ambulance's alternate mode. Ratchet's toy, like Ironhide's, has received the same criticisms for the awful robot head and lack of similarity to his cartoon and comic book robot mode. There are two different versions of Ratchet's toy—one with a red cross label on his roof (slightly more valuable), and one without (more common). His Tech Specs picture reflected this interesting variation. In *Transformers: The Movie*, Ratchet was destroyed at the hands of several Decepticons.

**ALTERNATE MODE:** Nissan Onebox Ambulance Vanette.
**EASILY LOST WEAPONS AND ACCESSORIES:** Static Laser Gun (Standard Laser Rifle), gun post (almost always found missing in loose samples), 3 missiles.

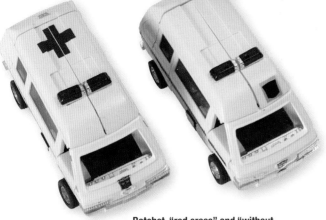

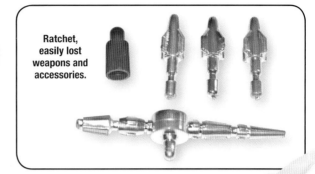

Ratchet, easily lost weapons and accessories.

Ratchet, "red cross" and "without cross" variation comparison.

# SIDESWIPE

**CARS**

**FUNCTION:** Warrior
**MOTTO:** "I don't break rules, I bend them—a lot."

"Sideswipe is nearly the equal of his twin brother, Sunstreaker (1984), in the combat arts, but is less cold-blooded. Relishes a fight to the finish with an opponent. Uses underhanded tactics when absolutely necessary. Arms act as powerful pile drivers. Flies for up to 2 minutes with rocket backpack. Fires flares visible for 18 miles. Rash actions often lead to injuries to himself. Takes them all in stride."

| Strength | Intelligence | Speed | Endurance | Rank | Courage | Firepower | Skill |
|----------|-------------|-------|-----------|------|---------|-----------|-------|
| 7 | 7 | 7 | 7 | 5 | 10 | 3 | 6 |

MLC: **$55-65**, MIB: **$185-205+**, MISB: **$375-475+**

Sideswipe, robot mode.

Many collectors suggest that the Tech Specs for Sideswipe and those of his twin brother, Sunstreaker (1984), were switched well into production. Looking at their "backs" in robot mode, it appears that Sunstreaker is indeed the one with a rocket pack. Sunstreaker also looks like he has "launching flares" from his shoulders.

As brothers (two Transformers who are a result of the splitting of one "spark," the Cybertronian life essence), both Sideswipe and Sunstreaker are Countach Lamborghini models and frequently work together on missions. Sideswipe is kinder than his brother, less ruthless, but a slightly weaker warrior. In the Sunbow cartoon, Sideswipe did indeed use his hands as pile drivers, a useful talent.

**ALTERNATE MODE:** Lamborghini Countach LP500S [a prototype created from the LP400 and LP400S models].
**EASILY LOST WEAPONS AND ACCESSORIES:** rocket launcher (shoulder-mounted), 3 rockets, Laser Gun (Photon Rifle).

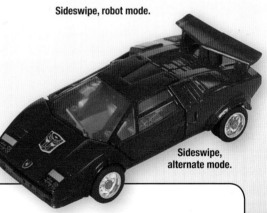

Sideswipe, alternate mode.

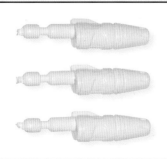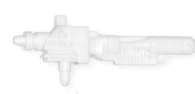

Sideswipe, easily lost weapons and accessories.

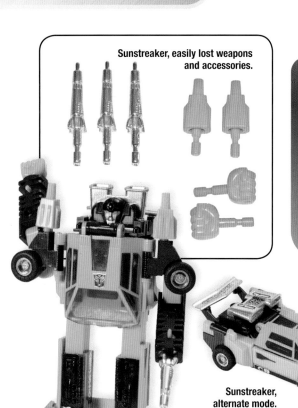

Sunstreaker, easily lost weapons and accessories.

Sunstreaker, alternate mode.

Sunstreaker, robot mode.

# SUNSTREAKER

**CARS**

**FUNCTION:** Warrior
**MOTTO:** "They can't beat the best."

"The complete egotist, Sunstreaker thinks he is the most beautiful thing on Earth. Loves his sleek styling, contemptuous of other Autobot race cars, particularly his twin, Sideswipe (1984). Fires laser-guided ground-to-air rockets and high energy electron pulses at 300 bursts/sec. Tough polymer-steel skin resists artillery. Not a team player. Can be baited into dangerous situations, but is a very calm, competent and ruthless war machine."

| Strength | Intelligence | Speed | Endurance | Rank | Courage | Firepower | Skill |
|---|---|---|---|---|---|---|---|
| 5 | 6 | 7 | 8 | 5 | 7 | 7 | 6 |

**MLC: $75-82, MIB: $175-215, MISB: $375-475+**

Sunstreaker is the twin brother of Sideswipe, and the two share the same Lamborghini model (Countach). It appears the two were switched by Hasbro some time during the production run, as Sunstreaker should have higher Tech Specs numbers across the board if he indeed is the better fighter of the two brothers. Regardless, Sunstreaker is one of the most recognizable and popular of all G1 Transformers—he's a gorgeous automobile, a formidable warrior, and iconic in his own right. When purchasing loose samples make sure that he has all of his easily lost weapons and accessories, and watch for chrome and paint wear.

**NOTE:** 1) "Countach" is an exclamation of surprise in Italian, equivalent to the American "Oh! Wow!" 2) The back half of Sunstreaker's auto body has never been documented as an actual existing racecar, so Takara's Diaclone line may have simply gone off of prototype sketches.

**ALTERNATE MODE:** Lamborghini Countach LP500S "Super Tuning" type with exposed rear engine.

**EASILY LOST WEAPONS AND ACCESSORIES:** 2 rocket boosters, 3 rockets (ground-to-air missiles), 2 fists, spoiler.

# TRAILBREAKER

**CARS**

**FUNCTION:** Defensive Strategist
**MOTTO:** "An Autobot's as good as the fuel in his tank."

"Trailbreaker makes light of any situation, no matter how serious. Practical joker and cheerleader, but considers himself a liability to Autobots since he consumes the most fuel (of the Ark-modified Autobots). Lacks self-esteem and often asks to be left behind. Projects nearly impenetrable invisible force-field. Can jam radio transmissions. Very slow. Often mopes about his handicaps, but his bravery and defensive prowess is unquestioned."

| Strength | Intelligence | Speed | Endurance | Rank | Courage | Firepower | Skill |
|---|---|---|---|---|---|---|---|
| 7 | 6 | 4 | 10 | 7 | 9 | 3 | 7 |

**MLC: $48-60, MIB: $90-115+, MISB: $425-550**

Trailbreaker, alternate mode.

Trailbreaker, like nearly all 1984 Autobot Cars, has many chromed weapons which may suffer from severe playwear over the past 20+ years. It is quite difficult to find loose samples of these chromed weapons in excellent condition. Trailbreaker was dubbed a "camper" on the "set includes" page of his instruction booklet—although going camping in this truck might be a bit prohibitive. As a character, he was not a front line fighter in the comic or on the cartoon, but we did see him using his force field.

**ALTERNATE MODE:** Toyota Hi-Lux 4WD with cab (1979-1980).
**EASILY LOST WEAPONS AND ACCESSORIES:** Radar scanner/force field (head-mounted projector), 2 twin blaster weapons, 2 missiles (high-explosive), 2 fists.

# WHEELJACK

CARS

**FUNCTION:** Mechanical Engineer
**MOTTO:** "Never do what your enemy expects you to do."

"Wheeljack is the mad scientist of the Autobots. Always inventing new weapons and gadgets. Most adept at driving while in car mode. Likes to show off his stunts. Flying range of 800 miles using solid-fuel rockets in arms. Shoots magnetic inducer, shrapnel-needle and gyro-inhibitor shells from his shoulder cannons. He is his own worst enemy. Often injured while experimenting with new weapons."

| Strength | Intelligence | Speed | Endurance | Rank | Courage | Firepower | Skill |
|----------|--------------|-------|-----------|------|---------|-----------|-------|
| 7 | 9 | 7 | 5 | 8 | 9 | 7 | 10 |

$ MLC: **$90-115**, MIB: **$175-205**, MISB: **$425-550+**

Wheeljack's function as mechanical engineer is different from Ratchet's (1984) occupation as medic. Wheeljack is an engineer and inventor, while Ratchet is a repairman and doctor. Wheeljack was prominently portrayed in the Marvel comic book and Sunbow cartoon, where his character was fascinating and his myriad inventions were the impetus for many an Autobot adventure. His stunt driving and maneuvers in car mode were played down in both the cartoon and comic book, yet his "mad scientist" traits were clear. Diehard collectors should note that the Diaclone "Marlboro" variant of Wheeljack is quite rare and commands premium prices both boxed and loose.

**ALTERNATE MODE:** Ca. 1975-1976 Lancia Stratos Turbo #539 "Alitallia." Alitalia (note the single "l") was an Italian airline at the time of Wheeljack's production, and sponsored this rally racecar.

**EASILY LOST WEAPONS AND ACCESSORIES:** 2 shoulder-mounted cannons, 4 rockets, 2 clear wings (that can be attached to the back of Wheeljack's robot mode, or to the underside of his car mode), 2-piece spoiler for vehicle mode.

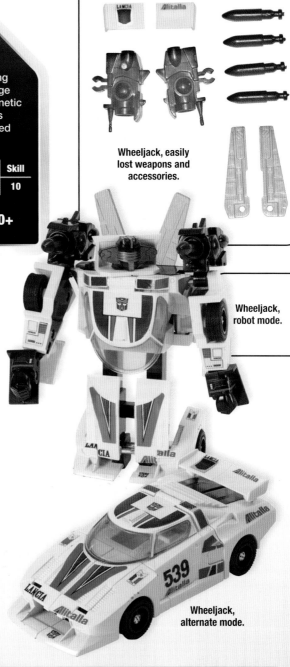

Wheeljack, easily lost weapons and accessories.

Wheeljack, robot mode.

Wheeljack, alternate mode.

Trailbreaker, robot mode.

Trailbreaker, easily lost weapons and accessories.

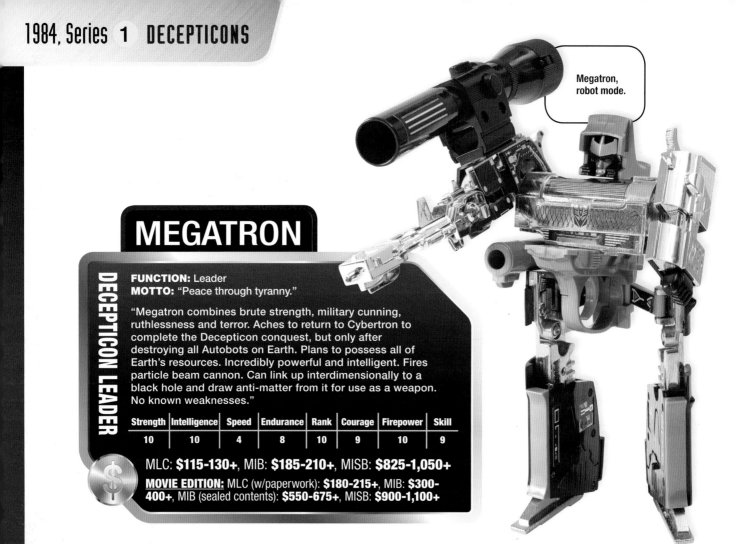

Megatron, robot mode.

## MEGATRON

**DECEPTICON LEADER**

**FUNCTION:** Leader
**MOTTO:** "Peace through tyranny."

"Megatron combines brute strength, military cunning, ruthlessness and terror. Aches to return to Cybertron to complete the Decepticon conquest, but only after destroying all Autobots on Earth. Plans to possess all of Earth's resources. Incredibly powerful and intelligent. Fires particle beam cannon. Can link up interdimensionally to a black hole and draw anti-matter from it for use as a weapon. No known weaknesses."

| Strength | Intelligence | Speed | Endurance | Rank | Courage | Firepower | Skill |
|----------|--------------|-------|-----------|------|---------|-----------|-------|
| 10 | 10 | 4 | 8 | 10 | 9 | 10 | 9 |

MLC: **$115-130+**, MIB: **$185-210+**, MISB: **$825-1,050+**

**MOVIE EDITION:** MLC (w/paperwork): **$180-215+**, MIB: **$300-400+**, MIB (sealed contents): **$550-675+**, MISB: **$900-1,100+**

Evil incarnate, or a Cybertronian bent on righteous conquest? Most would agree that Megatron typifies and embodies the Decepticon ideal—that Cybertronians were destined to conquer the universe by the nature of their powerful robot and alternate modes. As for his character's back story, according to Dreamwave's 2003 *Transformers: More Than Meets The Eye* guide books, it is rumored that a young Megatron rose through the ranks of Cybertron's violent gladiatorial games until he—through his powerful speeches,

and success at brutal personal combat—swayed thousands of disillusioned Cybertronians to his cause in response to a rumored "deception" perpetrated by the reigning Autobots. The purported deception—that the Autobots' (the larger and ruling body on Cybertron) were hiding the Cybertronians' true natural bent toward conquest—rallied many Transformers toward Megatron's cause, and their faction was named the "Decepticons" after the possible Autobot masquerade. Megatron then created a very painful "reformatting" process for the elite members of these Decepticons, who, after undergoing the procedure, found themselves capable of self-propelled flight.

As a toy, Megatron comes with a huge amount of accessories for his robot and Walther P-38 gun mode (originally dubbed the "Microchange Gun Robo Walther P-38" in Japan where he came with firing plastic bullets). With bonus Telescopic Laser Cannon mode and Particle Beam Cannon mode, Megatron is the ultimate Decepticon arsenal. In Megatron's instruction booklet, his gun barrel points forward next to his right hip, instead of straight up as it looks in the Sunbow

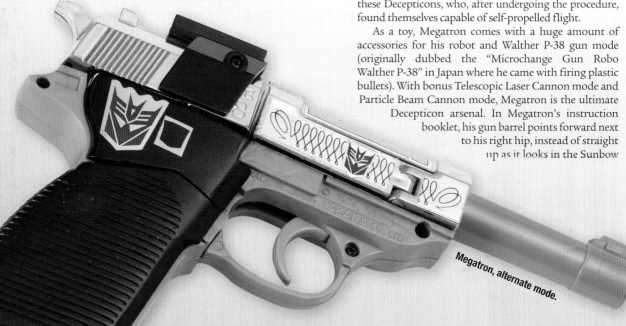

Megatron, alternate mode.

Megatron, full
alternate mode with
all attachments.

Megatron, easily lost weapons
and accessories.

cartoon. On the secondary market, he is always in demand, and sells well in nearly every condition.

Furthermore, Megatron was available as a highly-prized promotional: A mail-away "Movie Edition" of the Decepticon Leader solicited in 1986 to commemorate the release of *Transformers: The Movie*. Hasbro Direct shipped Megatron to your door in a brown mailer box with Styrofoam insert, "Movie Edition Certificate" and small, circular "Movie Edition" label.

**ALTERNATE MODE:** Walther P-38 handgun with and without attachments, particle beam cannon, telescopic laser cannon.

**EASILY LOST WEAPONS AND ACCESSORIES:**
2-piece silencer, 3-piece telescopic sight, 3-piece stock, high-density infrared laser cannon.

Megatron,
particle beam
cannon mode.

Rumble, alternate mode.

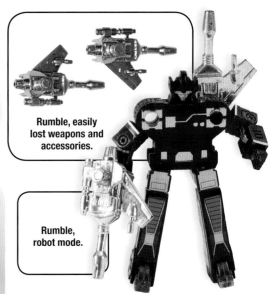

Rumble, easily lost weapons and accessories.

Rumble, robot mode.

## RUMBLE

### CASSETTES

**FUNCTION:** Demolitions
**MOTTO:** "Destroy what's below and what's above will follow."

"Rumble is your basic street punk. Small but always acting tough. Quick temper and mean disposition. Follows Megatron's orders eagerly. Transmits immense low frequency groundwaves to create powerful earthquakes. His small size limits his physical strength, but his ability to shatter the ground makes him difficult to approach in a fight."

| Strength | Intelligence | Speed | Endurance | Rank | Courage | Firepower | Skill |
|----------|--------------|-------|-----------|------|---------|-----------|-------|
| 2 | 5 | 2 | 9 | 5 | 7 | 8 | 5 |

 MLC: **$24-28+**, MIP (opened; two-pack w/ Ravage): **$50-60**, MOC (two-pack w/ Ravage): **$200-300+**

## RAVAGE

### CASSETTES

**FUNCTION:** Saboteur
**MOTTO:** "Today's Autobots are tomorrow's scrap metal."

"Ravage operates best alone. A creature of the night. Craftiest of all Decepticons. Adept at devising deadly new strategies. Remains aloof from others, but his deeds command their respect. Can virtually escape detection—emits an electromagnetic emission shield, has a soundless walk, disappears in subdued light or shadow. Carries 2 powerful heat-seeking missiles. Light-sensitive. Can be blinded."

| Strength | Intelligence | Speed | Endurance | Rank | Courage | Firepower | Skill |
|----------|--------------|-------|-----------|------|---------|-----------|-------|
| 5 | 8 | 5 | 6 | 7 | 4 | 7 | 10 |

MLC: **$24-28**, MIP (opened; two-pack with Rumble): **$50-60**, MOC (two-pack w/ Rumble): **$200-300+**

Ravage, alternate mode.

Rumble and Ravage were available at retail as a popular Decepticon microcassette two-pack. Rumble was prominently featured in the Sunbow cartoon, yet his color was blue as opposed to his toy's red hue, and many die-hard collectors still contend that Rumble is blue, and not red. Regardless, he was a tough-talking minion within the Decepticon ranks. Although small in stature, Rumble's ability to turn his arms into piledriving drums that he punches into the ground (or through vibrational waves in his feet, for a less dramatic effect), creates a devastating effect for his foes.

**ALTERNATE MODE:** Olympus Type IV "Metal" MC60 Microcassette.
**EASILY LOST WEAPONS AND ACCESSORIES:** 2 laser cannons (arm or shoulder-mounted).

The jaguar-like mechanoid known as Ravage has sustained his enormous popularity in the hearts of casual Transformers fans and aficionados alike for the past 20+ years. Although thought by many to be a robot based on a black panther, his Japanese Microman origins' title reads: "MC-02: Jaguar." Ravage symbolizes the Decepticon cause perfectly—he is clever, aggressive, and totally ruthless.

According to Dreamwave Productions' *Transformers: More Than Meets the Eye* guidebook (2003), the "heat-seeking missiles" mentioned in his Tech Specs bio are actually "two proton bombs with a yield of 1 megaton." Ravage is truly a Decepticon to be feared.

**ALTERNATE MODE:** Olympus Type IV "Metal" MC60 Microcassette.
**EASILY LOST WEAPONS AND ACCESSORIES:** 2 proton bombs.

## [DECEPTICON]
# CASSETTES

The gimmick of selling transformable microcassettes that fit into a transformable tape player (Soundwave) was one of the most ingenious toy ideas of the decade. I can't fathom how many units that Hasbro sold, but it had to be astronomical. In the Decepticon hierarchy, it appeared that these cassettes were the minions of Soundwave, and did his bidding without question—at the behest of Megatron, of course.

Ravage, easily lost weapons and accessories.

Ravage, robot mode.

# FRENZY

**CASSETTES**

**FUNCTION:** Warrior
**MOTTO:** "Sow panic and surrender will bloom."

"If Frenzy needed to breathe, war would be his oxygen. He knows no cause, only craves to spread fear and destruction. His efforts are appreciated by other Decepticons. His devotion to warfare makes him hard to deal with on a personal level. Can roll his drums to produce high-pitch, grating sound of 200db (decibels). Disorients and disrupts electrical flow in opponent's circuitry which makes them malfunction. Physically weak. His manic attack can be countered with cool logic."

| Strength | Intelligence | Speed | Endurance | Rank | Courage | Firepower | Skill |
|----------|--------------|-------|-----------|------|---------|-----------|-------|
| 3 | 6 | 2 | 6 | 5 | 10 | 9 | 6 |

**SILVER WEAPONS:** MLC: **$20-25**, MIP (opened; two-pack w/ Laserbeak): **$85-100+**, MOC (two-pack w/ Laserbeak): **$150-250+**
**GOLD OR SILVER WEAPONS, BLACK FEET:** MLC: **$28-36+**, MIP (opened; two-pack w/Ratbat): **$85-100+**, MOC (two-pack w/Ratbat): **$200-300+**

*Frenzy, easily lost weapons and accessories, silver chromed.*

*Frenzy, robot mode.*

*Frenzy, alternate mode.*

Frenzy and Laserbeak were sold carded together as a two-pack, as were most Transformers microcassette tapes, Autobot or Decepticon. Hasbro always molded Frenzy in blue plastic, where Rumble (1984) was cast in red. Most Transformers fans interchange the colors of the two similar toys, as the characters' colors were switched in the Sunbow cartoon (Rumble was blue, Frenzy was red, etc.). In the cartoon, both Frenzy and his "brother" Rumble shared a similar method of dispatching Autobots—transforming their arms into pile drivers to create localized seismic disturbances. However, Frenzy's powers manifested themselves electrically, while Rumble's were seismic in nature.

*Frenzy, easily lost weapons and accessories, gold chromed.*

Frenzy was also released in 1986 in a two-pack with Ratbat, where the character came without leg labels and possessed black plastic feet. He was available for a limited time at retail with "gold chromed" weapons. See Ratbat (1986) for their sealed prices.

**ALTERNATE MODE:** Olympus Type IV "Metal" MC60 Microcassette.

**EASILY LOST WEAPONS AND ACCESSORIES:** 2 laser cannons (arm or shoulder-mounted).

**NOTE:** Later versions of Frenzy (partnered with Ratbat) included the rare gold-plated versions of his laser cannons.

# LASERBEAK

**CASSETTES**

**FUNCTION:** Interrogation
**MOTTO:** "The only point I like in Autobots: melting point."

"Laserbeak takes pleasure in hunting his prey—usually the straggling survivors of a battle. Noticeably not brave. Will run for safety if threatened. Flies at speeds up to 250 mph. Uses two independently targetable laser cannons with extreme precision to get information from captives. Shortage of ruby crystals that powers the lasers can panic his systems into shutting down."

| Strength | Intelligence | Speed | Endurance | Rank | Courage | Firepower | Skill |
|----------|--------------|-------|-----------|------|---------|-----------|-------|
| 5 | 6 | 8 | 5 | 6 | 2 | 8 | 9 |

MLC: **$25-30**, MIP (opened; two-pack w/Frenzy): **$85-100+**, MOC (two-pack w/Frenzy): **$150-250**

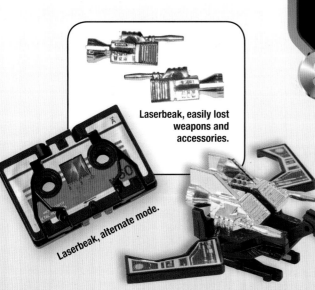

*Laserbeak, easily lost weapons and accessories.*

*Laserbeak, alternate mode.*

*Laserbeak, robot mode.*

Laserbeak was included with Frenzy in a two-pack of Decepticon microcassettes. Laserbeak is red in robot mode, where Buzzsaw is gold, and his condor alternate mode is the more identifiable because of Transfans' inculcation with the *Transformers* cartoon and Marvel comic book. Laserbeak has proven popular with G1 fans over the years because of his similarity to a bird of prey, a likeness that also reduced his speech patterns to simple "squawks" and "caws." His only two weapons, his laser cannons, are smooth along the top ridges in early versions of the weapons, but sharper on later versions. Laserbeak is also renowned for his cowardice.

**ALTERNATE MODE:** Olympus Type IV "Metal" MC60 Microcassette.

**EASILY LOST WEAPONS AND ACCESSORIES:** 2 ruby crystal-powered laser cannons.

Soundwave, alternate mode.

Soundwave, easily lost weapons and accessories.

Soundwave, robot mode.

Soundwave and Buzzsaw, robot modes.

# SOUNDWAVE

**COMMUNICATOR**

**FUNCTION:** Communications
**MOTTO:** "Cries and screams are music to my ears."

"It is said Soundwave can hear a fly sneeze. Uses anything he hears for blackmail to advance his status. Opportunist. Despised by all other Decepticons. Sensors can detect even lowest energy radio transmissions. Able to read minds by monitoring electrical brain impulses. Acts as radio link for others. Locates and identifies Autobots, then informs Decepticons. Carries a concussion blaster gun. Often target of retaliation by his comrades."

| Strength | Intelligence | Speed | Endurance | Rank | Courage | Firepower | Skill |
|----------|-------------|-------|-----------|------|---------|-----------|-------|
| 8 | 9 | 2 | 6 | 8 | 5 | 6 | 10 |

MLC: **$45-60**, MIB (two-pack w/Buzzsaw): **$185-210+**, MISB (two-pack w/Buzzsaw): **$650-850+**

Soundwave's accessories, (those two guns that transformed into "batteries" that could be inserted into his alternate mode's back), the spring-open cassette door, and his sinister monotonic voice on the hit Sunbow cartoon made him one of the most popular Transformers characters. Further endearing him to fans was the fact that he was able to fire Megatron in gun mode at unsuspecting Autobots once in a while. It also helped his reputation—and toy sales—that Hasbro frequently released new Decepticon cassettes to fill Soundwave's ranks of spies and warrior-infiltrators. Soundwave was also unique among Decepticons in that he could create empty energon cube boxes out of his chest; cubes ready to be filled with any crude natural energy source that Megatron ordered the Decepticons to steal. It is also rumored that Soundwave possesses limited telepathic powers—he can read the thoughts of any being within 100 feet of him. Although it may be difficult to hide your feelings from him, he's a first-rate communications officer.

**ALTERNATE MODE:** Walkman-style portable Microcassette recorder, inspired by the blue-and-silver colored Olympus SR-11 (note the "swoosh" stencils on BOTH cassette doors).

**EASILY LOST WEAPONS AND ACCESSORIES:** Rocket launcher, 3 rockets, concussion blaster gun, 2 twin mortar cannons.

**NOTE:** Soundwave is usually not considered "complete" unless his toy is accompanied by the condor/microcassette Buzzsaw (1984).

Soundwave, MIB.

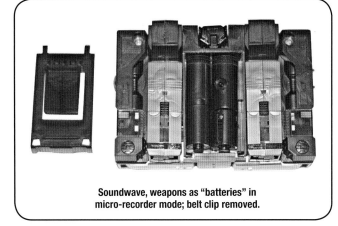

Soundwave, weapons as "batteries" in
micro-recorder mode; belt clip removed.

# BUZZSAW

**COMMUNICATOR**

**FUNCTION:** Spy
**MOTTO:** "My bite is worse than my bark."

"Civil and sophisticated yet very cruel and destructive.
Approaches his lethal tasks like a fine artist. Each deadly
mission is like working on a new masterpiece. Can pinpoint and
photograph a thumbtack from 20 miles away. Flies at 250 mph.
Carries twin mortar cannons. Diamond-hard, micro-serrated beak
can carve up almost any opponent. Due to large ego, will often
sulk rather than proceed if his plans go astray."

| Strength | Intelligence | Speed | Endurance | Rank | Courage | Firepower | Skill |
|----------|--------------|-------|-----------|------|---------|-----------|-------|
| 5 | 8 | 8 | 4 | 6 | 7 | 4 | 9 |

MLC: **$20-25**, MIB/MISB: **N/A**, comes packaged
with Soundwave

Buzzsaw, easily lost weapons
and accessories.

Buzzsaw,
alternate mode.

Buzzsaw,
robot mode.

   Even though his alternate mode is that of an audiocassette, I listed the
cybernetic condor known as Buzzsaw under Soundwave's topical entry instead
of the Decepticon Cassettes, as he was included as a *bonus* Transformer with
the Decepticon Communications Officer. Upon close inspection, it should be
noted that the earliest versions of Buzzsaw and Laserbeak have slightly different
chromed guns (his "twin mortar cannons" and Laserbeak's "ruby crystal-powered
laser cannons") from their later releases where the "fans" on the top of
the cannons are sharper and crisper. Regardless, Buzzsaw is a minor
character in the Transformers canon, and is relegated to a few select
appearances in the comics and cartoon.

**ALTERNATE MODE:** Olympus Type IV "Metal" MC60
Microcassette.
**EASILY LOST WEAPONS AND ACCESSORIES:** 2 twin
mortar cannons.

# PLANES [DECEPTICON]

The Decepticon Planes, or "Seeker Jets" as they are lovingly referred to by Transfans, were the meat of Megatron's army in 1984, and the more formidable members of the original crew of the Nemesis—the spaceship that carried the original thirteen Decepticons who set out from Cybertron to intercept Optimus Prime and his Autobot crew aboard the Ark. Their mold designs (weapons and accessories) are exactly alike, and the only difference between Skywarp, Starscream, and Thundercracker were their colors and label sheets. They were featured prominently in the Sunbow *Transformers* cartoon and the Marvel comic book.

**Starscream, robot mode.**

**Starscream, alternate mode.**

## SKYWARP

PLANES

**FUNCTION:** Warrior
**MOTTO:** "Strike when the enemy isn't looking."

"Skywarp is the sneakiest of all Decepticons. Enjoys playing cruel pranks on fellow Decepticons and appearing out of nowhere to attack Autobots. Not too smart. Would be useless without Megatron's supervision. Top speed of 1,500 mph. Can instantly teleport up to 2.5 miles. Carries heat-seeking missiles and variable-calibre machine guns."

| Strength | Intelligence | Speed | Endurance | Rank | Courage | Firepower | Skill |
|----------|--------------|-------|-----------|------|---------|-----------|-------|
| 7 | 9 | 10 | 7 | 9 | 9 | 8 | 8 |

MLC: **$65-75**, MIB: **$140-160+**, MISB: **$350-450+**

**Skywarp, easily lost weapons and accessories.**

Although each of the Decepticon "Seeker Jets" (1984's Skywarp, Starscream, and Thundercracker; 1985's Dirge, Ramjet, and Thrust) are inherently different characters, they share a similar toy mold based on that of the F-15 Eagle aircraft. When reviewing Skywarp's Tech Specs bio, most fans suggest that his statistics should be switched with Starscream's—note that Skywarp's Tech Specs flavor text states that he is "Not too smart," yet his stats reflect a 9 out of 10 for intelligence. Fans are further puzzled by this comment regarding Skywarp's intelligence, as *none* of the Seeker Jets' Tech Specs ability scores shows a low intellect. Regardless, Skywarp was famous for his power to teleport at will across great distances, always uncannily aware of the best jump location to maximize his destructive potential.

**ALTERNATE MODE:** McDonnel-Douglass F-15C Eagle.
**EASILY LOST WEAPONS AND ACCESSORIES:** 2 wings, 2 rudders, 2 tail fins, 2 missile launchers, 2 missiles, 2 machine guns, 2 fists, landing gear.

**Skywarp, alternate mode.**

**Skywarp, robot mode.**

# STARSCREAM

**PLANES**

**FUNCTION:** Aerospace Commander
**MOTTO:** "Conquest is made of the ashes of one's enemies."

"Seeks to replace Megatron as Leader. Ruthless, cold-blooded, cruel...considers himself the most sophisticated and handsome of Decepticons. Believes Decepticons should rely more on guile and speed rather than brute force to defeat Autobots. Fastest flyer of group, can reach Mach 2.8 and an altitude of 52 miles. Shoots cluster bombs and null-rays which disrupts flow of electricity. Very good at what he does, but sometimes overrates himself."

| Strength | Intelligence | Speed | Endurance | Rank | Courage | Firepower | Skill |
|----------|-------------|-------|-----------|------|---------|-----------|-------|
| 7 | 7 | 9 | 7 | 5 | 8 | 7 | 7 |

**MLC: $75-85+**, **MIB: $150-175+**, **MISB: $600-800+**

It is believed that Starscream's and Skywarp's Tech Specs were switched by mistake, as the Aerospace ("the atmosphere and the space beyond considered as a whole") Commander, should have higher ability scores. The treacherous and powerful Starscream leads the Decepticon air forces, particularly its powerful cluster of F-15 Eagle "Seeker Jets" (1984: Skywarp and Thundercracker; 1985: Dirge, Ramjet, and Thrust). Most fans will remember his ongoing periods of usurpation against Megatron and Galvatron, ultimately resulting in his unfortunate "coronation/destruction scene" in *Transformers: The Movie*. Starscream was cunning and powerful; his sinister machinations reached even beyond the grave.

**ALTERNATE MODE:** McDonnel-Douglass F-15C Eagle.
**EASILY LOST WEAPONS AND ACCESSORIES:** 2 wings, 2 rudders, 2 tail fins, 2 missile launchers, 2 missiles, 2 machine guns, 2 fists, landing gear.

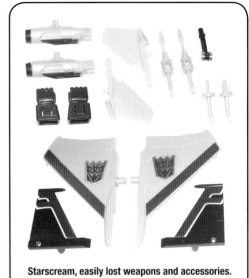

Starscream, easily lost weapons and accessories.

Thundercracker, robot mode.

Thundercracker, alternate mode.

# THUNDERCRACKER

**PLANES**

**FUNCTION:** Warrior
**MOTTO:** "The deadliest weapon is terror."

"Thundercracker is contemptuous of anything that cannot fly. Not totally convinced of the Decepticons' cause, but they've persuaded him to continue battling Autobots. Flies at speeds up to 1500 mph. Produces controlled, deafening sonic booms—can be heard for 200 miles. Equipped with powerful drone rockets and incendiary guns. Doubts about his cause sometimes impedes his effectiveness."

| Strength | Intelligence | Speed | Endurance | Rank | Courage | Firepower | Skill |
|----------|-------------|-------|-----------|------|---------|-----------|-------|
| 7 | 4 | 9 | 7 | 5 | 8 | 7 | 7 |

**MLC: $60-75**, **MIB: $125-145+**, **MISB: $400-500+**

Thundercracker is usually the least in demand of the many Seeker Jets, as his solid blue coloring seemed boring when compared to the designs of Starscream, Thrust (1985), or even Ramjet (1985). His character was fodder for the Decepticon air forces, and he was always seen in the background when more interesting Decepticons were engaging in discussions or even an Autobot assault. He is an example of the effectiveness of Megatron's recruitment process—play on a Transformer's contemptuousness of others, and build on their feelings of superiority—sometimes, though, Thundercracker is not entirely convinced in his leader's propaganda and ruthlessness.
**NOTE:** There are different variants for the fists for the Seeker Jets, the main variant is the "slotted fist" versus "solid fist" variant. The solid fists are the rarer of the two.

**ALTERNATE MODE:** McDonnel-Douglass F-15C Eagle.
**EASILY LOST WEAPONS AND ACCESSORIES:** 2 wings, 2 rudders, 2 tail fins, 2 rocket launchers, 2 rockets, 2 incendiary guns, 2 fists, landing gear.

Thundercracker, easily lost weapons and accessories.

# 1985

## SERIES 2

In 1985, heat-sensitive rub signs were the newest innovation for Generation One Transformers. With the release of Series 2, every Transformer featured either an Autobot or Decepticon square black rub sign sticker. The operating explanation for these heat sensitive stickers appeared in the 1985 Instruction Booklets and in a new brochure that was placed in MISB Transformers that were re-released in 1985 and beyond (those reissued 1984 Autobot Cars, 1984 Decepticon Jets, 1984 Decepticon Leader, etc.). The description read: "Can you find the black square label on your Transformer? Rub the label—Watch the robot face appear! It is your evidence that this robot is a true Transformer!"

These rub signs were a result of inferior bootleg transforming robots that flooded the U.S. market in 1985, and Hasbro wanted to prove to kids and collectors that they were aware of this infringement. The 1984 Transformers released prior to the introduction of these new proofs of authenticity are more rare than their rub sign counterparts and command more money on the secondary market.

In 1985, Autobots and Decepticons received different sub groups: the Autobots "created" the Dinobots and added the mail-away Omnibots from Cybertron to their ranks, while the

Decepticons were affiliated with the Insecticons and Constructicons. Their success led to the annual introduction of various sub groups to the Generation One line, with Autobot sub groups ending with the suffix "–bot," and Decepticon coteries finished with the momentum suffix "–con." The Dinobots sold ridiculously well, as did the Insecticons and Constructicons because of their excellent characterization on the Sunbow animated Transformers cartoon, and the fact that their robot modes derived from their specified function within their sub group.

The Constructicons need to be mentioned in some small detail here, as this is the very first time that a gestalt combiner team was introduced to the Transformers lineup. The popular Constructicons brought new impetus to the idea of "Collect 'Em All," and kids scoured the toy aisles to find the six component characters that formed Devastator. Combiner technology would drive the Transformers line for a long while.

The major packaging promotion for 1985 was the Transformers Mini-spies. The Mini-spies were tiny transformable cars with pull-back motors and either Autobot or Decepticon rub signs. These Mini-spies were sold with late-issue 1985 Autobot Minicars (and only the following Minicars, as they were reissued from the 1984 line up: Bumblebee; Cliffjumper; Huffer; Windcharger; Brawn; and Gears) as an exclusive bonus for either the Autobot or Decepticon armies.

Mini-spies came in 4 different models: [dune] Buggy, Jeep, [Toyota] FX-1, or Porsche [928]—with each model available in three different colors: Blue, white, or yellow. With their working pull-back motors intact, Mini-spies sell for between $8 and $16 each; sometimes a bit more based on condition, and often times faction (Autobot or Decepticon), which—when combined with two different variations of wheel wells (deeply recessed spokes or prominent spokes)—actually comprises 48 different types of Mini-spy.

# BEACHCOMBER

Beachcomber, robot mode.

**MINICARS**

**FUNCTION:** Geologist
**MOTTO:** "Know the conflict within before facing the conflict without."

"No interest in warfare; prefers long, lone trips into deserts and along coasts...only places he feels he can escape to and relax. Cool-headed, low-key, personable—what Earthlings call 'laid-back.' Fights when called upon despite anti-war feelings. Range of 800 miles...can go over very rugged terrain. Sensors can determine chemical composition of land and find needed resources. Susceptible to mental stress."

| Strength | Intelligence | Speed | Endurance | Rank | Courage | Firepower | Skill |
|---|---|---|---|---|---|---|---|
| 3 | 9 | 5 | 9 | 6 | 7 | 1 | 10 |

MLC: **$10-12**, MIP (opened) **$26-28**, MOC: **$200-300**

Beachcomber had the oddest voice of all Transformers: he sounded like he was a throwback from the 1970s from his very first appearance. He was anti-war, and preferred driving, excavating, and exploring to combat, but could always be counted on to return to the good fight.

**ALTERNATE MODE:** 1982 Chenowth FAV [Fast Attack Vehicle].
**EASILY LOST WEAPONS AND ACCESSORIES:** N/A.

Beachcomber, alternate mode.

# COSMOS

**MINICARS**

**FUNCTION:** Reconnaissance and Communications
**MOTTO:** "Reach for the stars, but never leave your friends."

"Lonely in outer space...relieves boredom by scaring humans by hovering over their backyards at night or zig-zagging through meteor showers. Can achieve Earth orbit, even go to Moon and back with enough fuel. Acts as communications satellite...optical sensors can see bicycle at 600 miles. Has pinpoint accuracy, high-powered particle beam. Not well-suited to function on ground as robot."

| Strength | Intelligence | Speed | Endurance | Rank | Courage | Firepower | Skill |
|---|---|---|---|---|---|---|---|
| 2 | 8 | 10 | 6 | 6 | 7 | 6 | 9 |

MLC: **$10-12**, MIP (opened) **$25-30**, MOC: **$150-200**

Cosmos, robot mode.

Cosmos, alternate mode.

A peculiar looking Transformer in his robot mode, Cosmos is short, stout, and colorful. Perhaps this odd appearance adds to his loneliness and discomfort at being in outer space for the majority of his existence, yet even when he returns to Earth and is among friends, he always remembers his responsibility to the Autobots—and returns forlorn to his primary function ... and to the empty void of space.

**ALTERNATE MODE:** Flying saucer (similar to George Adamsky's "Venusian Scout Craft").
**EASILY LOST WEAPONS AND ACCESSORIES:** N/A.

# POWERGLIDE

**MINICARS**

**FUNCTION:** Warrior
**MOTTO:** "To stop me, you have to catch me first."

"A show-off...proud that he's one of the few Autobots that can fly. Incredible maneuverability...delights to display his dazzling aerial virtuosity, to friends or foes...just wants their appreciation of his talent. Cruises at 500 mph...can increase power output and speed to 3200 mph for short periods. Carries small concussion bombs...shoots thermal beam as plane and robot. Gets into more trouble with enemy planes than he can handle."

| Strength | Intelligence | Speed | Endurance | Rank | Courage | Firepower | Skill |
|----------|--------------|-------|-----------|------|---------|-----------|-------|
| 3 | 7 | 8 | 7 | 5 | 8 | 6 | 9 |

**MLC: $10-14,** MIP (opened) **$35-40,** MOC: **$150-200**

Powerglide, robot mode.

Powerglide, alternate mode.

As an Autobot who is not restricted to the confines of the roads, Powerglide's love of the air and pride in his maneuverability shows in his every waking moment. He is armed with bombs and a machine gun in airplane mode, and is sometimes undone by his overconfidence.

**ALTERNATE MODE:** Fairchild Republic A-10 Thunderbolt II "Warthog" Close Air Support Aircraft.
**EASILY LOST WEAPONS AND ACCESSORIES:** N/A.

# SEASPRAY

**MINICARS**

**FUNCTION:** Naval Defense
**MOTTO:** "Be unyielding as the ocean waves and your enemies shall fall."

"Displays a zest for his job unmatched by fellow Autobots. Loves the ocean and its creatures...unhappy when he returns to land and reverts to robot form. Loves the thrill of naval battle. Can go 120 knots, 4,000-mile range. Has sonar radar and underwater and surface-to-air lasers, also used in robot mode. Wheels allow limited land travel. Not too strong or mobile as robot."

| Strength | Intelligence | Speed | Endurance | Rank | Courage | Firepower | Skill |
|----------|--------------|-------|-----------|------|---------|-----------|-------|
| 3 | 8 | 6 | 6 | 6 | 10 | 6 | 7 |

**MLC: $8-10,** MIP (opened) **$30-35,** MOC: **$100-200**

Seaspray, robot mode.

Seaspray had a singular, 'bubbly' voice on the animated program, and functioned as the only aquatic vehicle in the Transformers line as of 1985. As a toy, had a fascinating design, sporting dual spinning propellers and solid primary colors.

**ALTERNATE MODE:** Hovercraft [unknown design].
**EASILY LOST WEAPONS AND ACCESSORIES:** N/A.

Seaspray, alternate mode.

41

# WARPATH

**MINICARS**

**FUNCTION:** Warrior
**MOTTO:** "A good shot is worth more than a good intention."

"Thinks he's more impressive than his comrades do…likes to show off his sharpshooting. Boisterous, loud-mouthed…raucous sense of humor makes him welcome company. Vain—upset by even the smallest scratch to his gun barrel. Can go 30 mph over rough terrain, hit a hex-nut 1.5 miles away. Shoots explosive, thermal, cryogenic, acid, sonic shells. Great strength but helpless if upended."

| Strength | Intelligence | Speed | Endurance | Rank | Courage | Firepower | Skill |
|---|---|---|---|---|---|---|---|
| 9 | 5 | 2 | 8 | 5 | 9 | 7 | 10 |

MLC: **$8-10**, MIP (opened) **$27-32**, MOC: **$100-200**

Warpath, robot mode.

Warpath was the Minibot that every kid wanted. With a great-looking robot mode, a boisterous personality, amazing strength, and a rotating turret, Warpath was a wonderful addition to your Autobot army.

**ALTERNATE MODE:** M551 "Sheridan" Light Tank.
**EASILY LOST WEAPONS AND ACCESSORIES:** N/A.

Warpath, alternate mode.

# TOPSPIN

**JUMPSTARTERS**

**FUNCTION:** Land and Sea Assault
**MOTTO:** "The thrill is in the journey."

"No mountain high enough, no river wide enough to stop this one robot wrecking crew. Has superior mobility due to his Cybertronic vehicular form. Views conquest of rough terrain as much a victory as beating Decepticons. Uses 2 rear jet engines to go 300 mph…goes 80 mph on water with 2 front pontoons…has 2 hi-voltage electric cannons and 2 hand lasers built in…carries a powerful twin ion impulse blaster."

| Strength | Intelligence | Speed | Endurance | Rank | Courage | Firepower | Skill |
|---|---|---|---|---|---|---|---|
| 6 | 6 | 8 | 5 | 6 | 10 | 9 | 8 |

MLC: **$10-12**, MIB: **$20-30**, MISB: **$40-60**

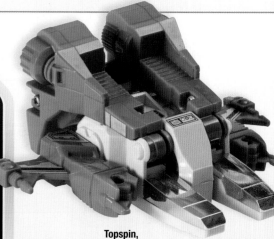

Topspin, alternate mode.

**Twin Twist, robot mode.**

# TWIN TWIST

**JUMPSTARTERS**

**FUNCTION:** Demolitions
**MOTTO:** "War is wherever I want it to be."

"Nothing feels better to him than sinking his drills into a slab of steel. Loves the scrap metal results of his destructive fury and showing off…will attack anything: enemy Decepticon or harmless lamppost. Optimus Prime worries about his uncontrollable nature. Goes 200 mph…has two 6000 rpm diamond-tipped drills…twin ion impulse blaster shoots explosive 100 lb TNT shells. Goes from vehicle to robot in .4 seconds."

| Strength | Intelligence | Speed | Endurance | Rank | Courage | Firepower | Skill |
|----------|--------------|-------|-----------|------|---------|-----------|-------|
| 8 | 4 | 7 | 7 | 5 | 9 | 7 | 6 |

**MLC: $10-12, MIB: $20-30, MISB: $40-60**

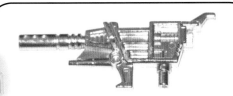

**Twin Twist, easily lost weapons and accessories.**

**Twin Twist, alternate mode.**

The Autobot Jumpstarters Twin Twist and Topspin had a curious switch on the back of their necks that came with the following codicil in their instruction booklet(s): "NOTE: If your Jumpstarter does not stand properly, adjust lever behind robot's head." I tried this and it had little to no effect on how a Jumpstarter would transform on my kitchen floor. They still sold well at retail, however, as they weren't your typical Autobot-to-Earth-vehicle.

**ALTERNATE MODE:** Cybertronian Twin-Drill Tank.
**EASILY LOST WEAPONS AND ACCESSORIES:** Semi-automatic cannon rifle.

**Topspin, robot mode.**

**Topspin, easily lost weapons and accessories.**

The Autobot Jumpstarters were pretty cool toys as they automatically transformed from vehicle to robot mode, and (luck willing) would land upright about 40% of the time. Still, the thought of a toy transforming right in front of your eyes was a pretty interesting concept put forth by Hasbro. Topspin and Twin Twist are common toys to find loose, boxed, and MISB. Alas, they never made it into the Sunbow cartoon.

**ALTERNATE MODE:** Cybertronian Amphibious Vehicle.
**EASILY LOST WEAPONS AND ACCESSORIES:** Particle beam rifle.

## GRAPPLE

CARS

**FUNCTION:** Architect
**MOTTO:** "Beauty is in everything except war."

"On Cybertron, his buildings are considered works of art. On Earth, his ideas are limited by war. Takes pride in his work, prone to severe depression if they're destroyed in battle. As crane, can lift up a 35-ton object and position it with precision and grace. As robot, has high-temperature arc-welder rifle...can launch rockets 4.5 miles from wrist sockets. Prone to breakdowns in vehicle mode."

| Strength | Intelligence | Speed | Endurance | Rank | Courage | Firepower | Skill |
|---|---|---|---|---|---|---|---|
| 8 | 8 | 3 | 4 | 7 | 7 | 7 | 9 |

**MLC: $35-45, MIB: $105-120, MISB: $200-300**

Grapple, robot mode.

Although Grapple was based off of the same mold as Inferno (1985), Grapple maintained an excitement all his own—the fascinating construction crane and its extendable hook. In the Transformers mythos, he is considered to be Cybertron's finest architect (with a bit of vanity splashed into his character), designing building after building for the Autobots until the start of their war against the Decepticons.

As a toy, make sure that loose samples have little to no chrome wear, as Grapple's missiles, wrists, and crane hook are prone to rubbing (and breaking in case of the hook itself).

**ALTERNATE MODE:** Japanese Mitsubishi Fuso Crane [note the "FUSO" logo on the toy's cab front].
**EASILY LOST WEAPONS AND ACCESSORIES:** 2 fists, arc-welder rifle, 3 rockets.

Grapple, alternate mode.

Grapple, easily lost weapons and accessories.

# CARS [AUTOBOT]

Most of the designs for the 1985 Autobot Cars were taken from their previously released 1984 counterparts, or they were based on molds similar to another 1985 Autobot Car. For instance, Grapple (1985) and Inferno (1985) shared the exact same mold (but for some small part replacements); Hoist (1985) and Trailbreaker (1984) had similar truck bodies, yet one possessed a tow hook while the other had a camper top; Red Alert (1985) and Sideswipe (1984) shared precisely the same mold, but were molded in different colored plastic (and, of course, the added emergency lights atop Red Alert's roof). Smokescreen's automobile mold of a Datsun 280ZX was an exact copy of Bluestreak (1984) and Prowl (1984), but with a custom airdam as his front bumper. (Also, Smokescreen does not have the hint of windows on his roof like the other two.)

Note the hidden cockpits located within each one of the Autobot Cars, to allow for their 1.25"-tall Diaclone action figures to sit while "piloting" their vehicles. Remember—in Takara's Diaclone universe before the Transformers were devised, these were robot shells commanded by humans [!].

Hoist, robot mode.

Hoist, alternate mode.

## HOIST

**CARS**

**FUNCTION:** Maintenance
**MOTTO:** "You have to be rolling before you can be fighting."

"'No exceptions!'—All Autobots must submit to his maintenance schedule...knows they must operate at peak efficiency in battle. Jovial, enjoys job and is good at it—will find any problem, from engine overhaul to smallest leaky gasket. As tow truck, hauls 40,000 lbs. As robot, very strong—launches heat-seeking missiles from wrist sockets. Full spectrum multi-sensor behind his head determines an object's composition, density, tensile strength, energy properties."

| Strength | Intelligence | Speed | Endurance | Rank | Courage | Firepower | Skill |
|----------|--------------|-------|-----------|------|---------|-----------|-------|
| 8 | 6 | 3 | 7 | 4 | 8 | 6 | 9 |

MLC: **$40-50**, MIB: **$90-105**, MISB: **$300-400**

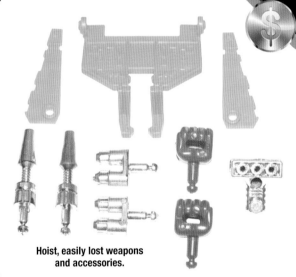

Hoist, easily lost weapons and accessories.

Hoist's design is based on the same model as Trailbreaker (1984), with the exception of his orange tow-truck hook and assembly. Hoist is frequently partnered with Grapple, with Grapple, and their skills are in much demand when it comes to designing and repairing superstructures. Many of the Autobot Cars were designs taken from the Japanese Diaclone toy line that originally had room for their Diaclone drivers or pilots to sit in—as seen in Hoist's flip-up roof with rub sign.

**ALTERNATE MODE:** Toyota N30 HiLux 4x4 pickup [tow truck model].
**EASILY LOST WEAPONS AND ACCESSORIES:** Full spectrum multi-sensor, 2 fists, 2 twin blasters, 2 missiles, 2 radar panels.
**NOTE:** Towing attachment is also removable.

Hoist, towing another Autobot.

# INFERNO

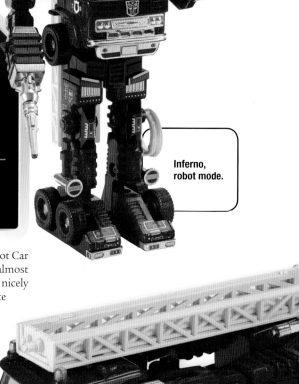

Inferno, robot mode.

**CARS**

**FUNCTION:** Search and Rescue
**MOTTO:** "Where there's smoke, there's me."

"'The hotter things get, the better I like it!'...not only for fires, but battle too. Often distracted from performing his job to engage in combat. Can do anything Earth fire trucks can in vehicular mode. Great strength...ceramic-plated armored skin can take up to 8000°C. Extinguisher rifle shoots flame-suppressing foam and an energy dampening beam to counter other beams. Forearms shoot missiles. Doesn't follow orders well, not very mobile as a robot."

| Strength | Intelligence | Speed | Endurance | Rank | Courage | Firepower | Skill |
|---|---|---|---|---|---|---|---|
| 9 | 6 | 4 | 8 | 5 | 9 | 6 | 6 |

**MLC: $35-45, MIB: $105-120, MISB: $250-350+**

With an alternate mode similar to Grapple's (1985), Inferno was an Autobot Car that most every kid wanted: a big red fire engine with an extendable ladder almost one foot long. He has excellent add-ons including side-attached fire hoses and nicely chromed parts, therefore, loose samples of Inferno are often found incomplete or with a lot of chrome wear or various broken pieces. Inferno is frequently paired with Red Alert (1985) on missions.

**ALTERNATE MODE:** Japanese Mitsubishi Fuso F-series Fire Truck [note the "FUSO" logo on the toy's cab front].

**EASILY LOST WEAPONS AND ACCESSORIES:** 2 hose nozzles, 2 fists, extinguisher rifle, 3 missiles.

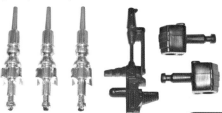

Inferno, easily lost weapons and accessories.

Inferno, alternate mode.

# RED ALERT

Red Alert, alternate mode.

**CARS**

**FUNCTION:** Security Director
**MOTTO:** "Caution can never be overused."

"Nothing escapes his notice, no matter how small. When his sensors are activated, thinks trouble is coming. Edgy... unpopular with comrades, but appreciated. Can trigger alarms in other Autobots. Excellent sensory perception. Fast in vehicular mode. Carries 25-mile range rocket launcher and particle beam rifle. Prone to rash judgments which can lead to injury to himself and comrades."

| Strength | Intelligence | Speed | Endurance | Rank | Courage | Firepower | Skill |
|---|---|---|---|---|---|---|---|
| 5 | 7 | 3 | 5 | 7 | 7 | 7 | 8 |

**MLC: $44-48, MIB: $110-125, MISB: $300-400**

# SMOKESCREEN

Smokescreen, robot mode.

Smokescreen, easily lost weapons and accessories.

**CARS**

**FUNCTION:** Diversionary Tactician
**MOTTO:** "A look can be deceiving; a touch can be lethal."

"Whether engaged in raging battle or friendly conversation, an ulterior purpose usually exists. Job is to lead enemy astray. Sneaky, but charming and affable…considered most devious yet most trusted of Autobots. In car mode, emits thick smoke from tailpipe…attracts to metal. In robot mode, shoots missiles which wreak havoc on enemy aircraft radar and guidance systems… electro-disruptor rifle shorts out electrical targets."

| Strength | Intelligence | Speed | Endurance | Rank | Courage | Firepower | Skill |
|---|---|---|---|---|---|---|---|
| 4 | 9 | 7 | 6 | 6 | 8 | 7 | 9 |

MLC: **$58-75**, MIB: **$155-175+**, MISB: **$300-400**

Smokescreen is one of the more popular Autobot Cars, as his airdam-bumper, excellent color scheme, and spoiler attached to the rear window makes him stand out from the two Autobots who previously shared this mold: Bluestreak (1984) and Prowl (1984). The automobile that Smokescreen was patterned after actually existed: Electramotive's 1979 custom Datsun 280ZX GTU. It was a championship GTO car, winning eight International Motor Sports Association Grand Touring Under Two Liter races in two years.

**ALTERNATE MODE:** [Custom] Nissan Fairlady Z Turbo IMSA car [International Motor Sports Association] with airdam.

**EASILY LOST WEAPONS AND ACCESSORIES:** 2 missile launchers, 3 missiles, electro-disruptor rifle.

Smokescreen, alternate mode.

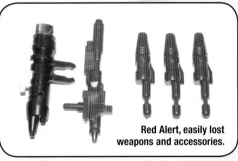

Red Alert, easily lost weapons and accessories.

Red Alert, robot mode.

Red Alert's automobile form is aesthetically pleasing, but one might wonder what fire department would be able to afford a Lamborghini as their fire chief's car? Regardless, as a toy, Red Alert is prone to "yellowing" when exposed to sunlight and heat as his white plastic ages over time. He and Inferno (1985) were used as partners, as they both were emergency vehicles, and their personalities served each other well.

**ALTERNATE MODE:** Lamborghini Countach LP500S [a prototype created from the LP400 and LP400S models] sporting a light bar as a fire chief's car.

**EASILY LOST WEAPONS AND ACCESSORIES:** Shoulder-mounted rocket launcher, 3 rockets, high-energy particle beam rifle.

## SKIDS

Skids,
robot mode.

**CARS**

**FUNCTION:** Theoretician
**MOTTO:** "Deep down, we are more like than unlike humans."

"A daydreamer…often bumps into things at 60 mph while pondering Earth life instead of a Decepticon attack. Considers Earth one vast lab for his research. His findings are often invaluable to fellow Autobots. Enormous memory storage capacity. Carries a liquid nitrogen rifle with 600 foot range. Twin electron blaster of 20,000 volts can short-circuit almost anything. At 60 mph can stop within 25 feet. Not very fast…often in danger due to daydreaming."

| Strength | Intelligence | Speed | Endurance | Rank | Courage | Firepower | Skill |
|---|---|---|---|---|---|---|---|
| 4 | 9 | 5 | 6 | 8 | 7 | 7 | 7 |

MLC: **$38-48**, MIB: **$110-125**, MISB: **$350-450**

With one of the most intricate and delicate transformation modes of all Autobots Cars, Skids is a fairly high-demand piece on the secondary market, particularly MIB or MISB. His toy had a good deal of die-cast metal in it, and captures his model type, a Honda City Turbo, expertly with opening side doors, hood, and trunk. In robot mode, he cannot hold all three of his major weapons at once, as he has no holes in his fists or his shoulder mount.

**ALTERNATE MODE:** Honda City Turbo (AA—sedan type [1982]).
**EASILY LOST WEAPONS AND ACCESSORIES:** Liquid nitrogen rifle, twin electron blaster, rocket pod, 3 rockets.

Skids, easily lost weapons and accessories.

Skids,
alternate mode.

## TRACKS

**CARS**

**FUNCTION:** Warrior
**MOTTO:** "Looking good is what life is all about."

"Called 'lousy Earth-lover' by some fellow Autobots because he prefers sleek Earth car form to original robot form. Thinks they're jealous of his good looks, but they feel struggle against Decepticons should be his top concern. As car goes 280 mph…uses wings under rear fenders for sub-sonic flight. As car or robot uses launcher to fire heat-seeking incendiary missiles 60 miles. Has blinding black beam gun."

| Strength | Intelligence | Speed | Endurance | Rank | Courage | Firepower | Skill |
|---|---|---|---|---|---|---|---|
| 6 | 6 | 7 | 8 | 5 | 6 | 8 | 8 |

MLC: **$45-60**, MIB: **$110-125**, MISB: **$300-400**

Tracks,
alternate mode.

Tracks,
robot
mode.

Tracks had a unique transformation mode among all of the Autobot Cars. Tracks, an instant hit for Hasbro, can also convert to a type of "flying car" where his wings flip out, his missile launcher attaches to a hole in his trunk, and his black beam gun attaches to the bottom of his car mode.

**ALTERNATE MODE:** 1982 Chevrolet Corvette C3, Air Attack Vehicle.
**EASILY LOST WEAPONS AND ACCESSORIES:** Missile launcher mount, 2 missile launchers, 4 missiles, black beam gun.

◀ Tracks, alternate mode, air attack vehicle.

Tracks, easily lost weapons and accessories.

Grimlock, alternate mode.

Grimlock, easily lost weapons and accessories.

Grimlock, robot mode.

# GRIMLOCK

**DINOBOTS**

**FUNCTION:** Dinobot Commander
**MOTTO:** "Among the winners, there is no room for the weak."

"Most fearsome and powerful Dinobot. Although dedicated to the Autobot cause, resents authority. Cold, merciless, but a valiant warrior. Has contempt for the weak, including all humans. Great strength, uses jaws to break almost anything in two. Carries energo sword and galaxial rocket launcher in Dinobot mode. Other than arrogance and lack of speed, has no real weakness."

| Strength | Intelligence | Speed | Endurance | Rank | Courage | Firepower | Skill |
|----------|--------------|-------|-----------|------|---------|-----------|-------|
| 10 | 7 | 3 | 10 | 9 | 10 | 8 | 10 |

**MLC: $70-78+**, **MIB: $135-150+**, **MISB: $500-600**

One of the most popular Transformers characters, Grimlock has been a controversial one as well. His awkward speech pattern, "Me, Grimlock! Me smash Decepti-cons!" was fully explained in Dreamwave's 2003 *Transformers: More Than Meets The Eye* guide books (issue #3). In their analysis of his idiosyncratic phonetic sounds, they resolved that his speech impediment is a result of "...a recurring viral glitch in Grimlock's vocal processors"—some form of Cybertronian anomia or aphasia, perhaps? Therefore, the manner in which Grimlock speaks may actually be an advantage for the most powerful (and most intelligent) Dinobot, as his enemies—whether Decepticon or Autobot—constantly underestimate his cunning and wile (he ranks a 7 out of 10 in his intelligence ability score) while focusing on his child-like way of speaking.

Grimlock and his group of Dinobots are frequently portrayed as the rebels of the Autobot ranks, often called upon as a last wave of defense when the heroes' backs are against the wall. The Dinobots are difficult to control, but they listen well to their military commander Grimlock, who is terribly strong, utterly fearless, and antagonistic to a fault. He has challenged Optimus Prime's (1984) authority on many occasions, he has led his elite cadre of Dinobots away from the Autobots, and sometimes epitomizes altogether different ideals than his faction/ allegiance would allow.

And kids loved Grimlock. But why not? He's a huge robot, with great weapons (his energo-sword is an energon based cutting implement), and he transforms into a T-Rex. What more could you ask for?

**ALTERNATE MODE:** Tyrannosaurus (*Tyrannosaurus Rex*).
**EASILY LOST WEAPONS AND ACCESSORIES:** Energo sword, twin "stunner" lasers, galaxial rocket launcher, 3 rockets.

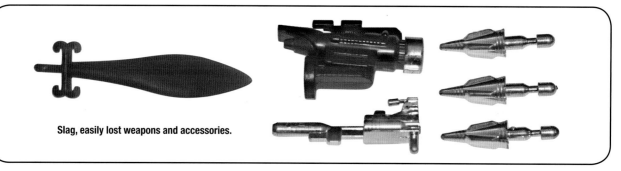

Slag, easily lost weapons and accessories.

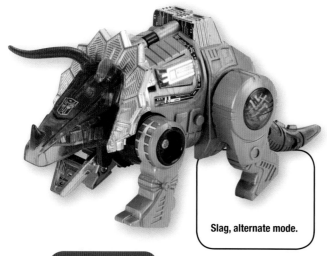

Slag, alternate mode.

## SLAG

**DINOBOTS**

**FUNCTION:** Flamethrower
**MOTTO:** "I have no need for friends, even less for enemies."

"Enjoys melting enemies into pools of liquid metal. Like his fellow Dinobots, resents authority. Disruptive—often brawls with comrades. Shoots 3000°C flame up to 80 feet from mouth. Enormous strength—can shatter a brick building with head. Uses electron blaster in Dinobot mode. Rash, not too bright. Nasty, mean-spirited—often the other Autobots won't help him when he's in trouble."

| Strength | Intelligence | Speed | Endurance | Rank | Courage | Firepower | Skill |
|----------|--------------|-------|-----------|------|---------|-----------|-------|
| 9 | 4 | 3 | 9 | 4 | 7 | 8 | 7 |

MLC: **$65-70**, MIB: **$125-132+**, MISB: **$400-500**

Slag, robot mode.

Originally, Slag was devised as the lone Dinobot flamethrower, yet in later episodes of the animated series, *every* member of the Dinobot team possessed the ability to spit fire. One of the most ill tempered of all the Dinobots, his endless anger manifests itself in combat and in casual conversation. Thankfully, the Decepticons provide Slag with an endless number of adversaries, but if he's not engaged in melee, Autobots should be wary. In toy mode, he has a cockpit in his chest module that opens to allow a Diaclone driver to fit inside—a holdover from his Japanese origins.

He is fairly well-jointed in his triceratops alternate mode: his jaw opens and closes, his front legs move, his rear legs have knee joints, and his two red horns swivel independent of each other. He was a decent looking robot as well, with prominent wings and a good, solid body.

**ALTERNATE MODE:** Triceratops (*Triceratops horridus*).
**EASILY LOST WEAPONS AND ACCESSORIES:** Energo sword, electron blaster, rocket pod, 3 rockets.

**Sludge, alternate mode.**

# SLUDGE

**DINOBOTS**

**FUNCTION:** Jungle Warrior/Demolitions
**MOTTO:** "Stomp your enemy, crush him under your feet."

"Likes to make presence known—a footstep can be heard and felt in a 3-mile radius. Gentle and shy, but terrifying and unstoppable in battle. Like other Dinobots, dislikes authority. Can exert 40,000 psi via feet—enough to shatter a bridge. Immense strength and endurance. Adept at fighting in water, swamp, and jungle. Slow, not too clever—often victim of the calamities he causes."

| Strength | Intelligence | Speed | Endurance | Rank | Courage | Firepower | Skill |
|----------|--------------|-------|-----------|------|---------|-----------|-------|
| 9 | 3 | 2 | 10 | 4 | 9 | 2 | 5 |

💲 MLC: **$65-75**, MIB: **$125-140**, MISB: **$500-600**

Along with Grimlock and Slag, Sludge was one of the three original Dinobots. Sludge is a bashful, unassertive Transformer when not in battle, and can be particularly difficult to motivate. When spurred into combat, he is a fierce and fearless warrior—the second toughest Dinobot next to their leader, Grimlock (1985). Revels in jungle or aquatic environments, and his toy is well-proportioned in either mode.

---

**ALTERNATE MODE:** Brontosaurus [*Brontosaurus excelsus*].
**EASILY LOST WEAPONS AND ACCESSORIES:** Energo sword, electron cannon, rocket pod, 3 rockets.

**Sludge, robot mode.**

**Sludge, easily lost weapons
and accessories.**

Snarl, alternate mode.

Snarl, robot mode.

# SNARL

**DINOBOTS**

**FUNCTION:** Desert Warrior
**MOTTO:** "Only in war is there happiness."

"An unhappy loner of few words and fewer opinions. Finds joy only in battle. Hates his Dinobot form, longs to return to Cybertron. Large golden plates on spinal assembly are solar collectors…strength increases tenfold in sunlight. Tail can shatter 20 foot concrete cube. Armored hide resists most missiles. Vulnerable to nighttime attacks due to his weaker state. Slow… uncooperative nature hinders others from helping him."

| Strength | Intelligence | Speed | Endurance | Rank | Courage | Firepower | Skill |
|----------|--------------|-------|-----------|------|---------|-----------|-------|
| 9 | 6 | 3 | 9 | 4 | 8 | 1 | 4 |

MLC: **$70-80**, MIB: **$125-145+**, MISB: **$600-700+**

Along with Swoop (1985), Dinobot Desert Warrior Snarl was introduced later to the Dinobot lineup. It is suggested that his lack of cooperation to the Autobot cause is because of his dissatisfaction with his alternate mode: one that he personally finds repulsively ugly. It was shown that in stegosaurus mode, when his plates collect sunlight, this solar energy is channeled into powerful blasts through his tail.

As a toy, Snarl appears a bit more "mechanical" than his fellow Dinobots, particularly due to the bevy of stickers of circuits and pistons around his body. Collectors should take care when changing Snarl from stegosaurus to robot, as his lower legs are very weak after repeated transformations.

**ALTERNATE MODE:** Stegosaurus [*Stegosaurus armatus*].
**EASILY LOST WEAPONS AND ACCESSORIES:** Energo sword, electron cannon, rocket pod, 3 rockets.

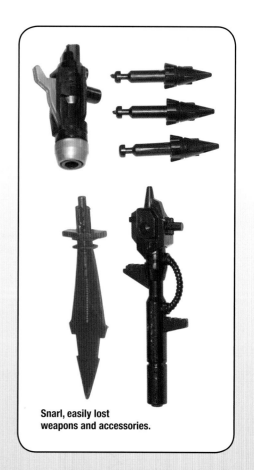

Snarl, easily lost
weapons and accessories.

Swoop, alternate mode.

Swoop, robot mode.

## SWOOP

**DINOBOTS**

**FUNCTION:** Dinobot Bombardier
**MOTTO:** "Fear can hit targets unreachable to bullets."

"Enjoys watching enemies scatter before him as he dives down from the sky…considers spreading fear his greatest weapon. This Dinobot's kind, good-natured side disguised by his horrifying form…even his comrades shy away. Flies at 250 mph…air-to-air missile launcher under each wing fires missiles equivalent of 5000 lbs. TNT, 8 mile range. As robot, uses launchers and 4000°C thermal sword. Fragile wings vulnerable to enemy firepower."

| Strength | Intelligence | Speed | Endurance | Rank | Courage | Firepower | Skill |
|----------|--------------|-------|-----------|------|---------|-----------|-------|
| 6 | 6 | 8 | 9 | 5 | 7 | 7 | 7 |

**MLC: $100-120, MIB: $205-220+, MISB: $600-700+**

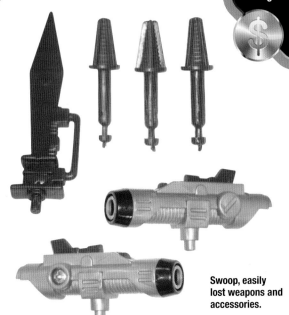

Swoop, easily lost weapons and accessories.

The most expensive of Dinobots on the secondary market (loose or boxed), Swoop has always been in high demand with collectors because 1) he was well designed as a Pteranodon (mistakenly assumed to be a Pterodactyl), and 2) he was one of the few Autobots who could fly. In the cartoon, Swoop seemed to be the most amiable and approachable of the sullen and aggressive Dinobots, yet he used his fearsome alternate mode, missile launchers, and horrifying battle screech to demoralize Decepticon troops from the air.

**ALTERNATE MODE:** Pteranodon [*Pteranodon longiceps*].
**EASILY LOST WEAPONS AND ACCESSORIES:** Thermal sword, 2 missile launchers, 3 missiles.

Roadbuster, alternate mode.

Roadbuster, back view.

[AUTOBOT]
# DELUXE VEHICLES

Very difficult to find at retail, the Autobot Deluxe Vehicles were a nice addition to the Autobot ranks, if you could 1) find them, and 2) use your imagination to incorporate them into your Transformers adventures, as they were never used in the Sunbow cartoon or Marvel comic book. Their designs were intricate and their accessories were appropriate, but somehow they seemed a little out of scale with the rest of the Autobots.

Roadbuster, robot mode.

## ROADBUSTER

**DELUXE VEHICLES**

**FUNCTION:** Ground Assault Commander
**MOTTO:** "War is a dirty business…and I'm as dirty as they come."

"Likes to pass the time 'demolishing Decepticons.' Not happy if not fighting…bores easily, quietest of Autobots when not in battle. Charismatic in combat…inspiring to fellow warriors. Natural leader. Can traverse most terrains as 4-WD, 600 mile range. Carries turret-mounted linear blaster gun…can blow a hole in 2-foot thick concrete. As a robot has laser rifle and shrapnel-missile launcher."

| Strength | Intelligence | Speed | Endurance | Rank | Courage | Firepower | Skill |
|---|---|---|---|---|---|---|---|
| 8 | 7 | 5 | 9 | 8 | 10 | 6 | 7 |

**$** MLC: **$138-155+**, MIB: **$205-235+**, MISB: **$400-550**

Roadbuster's Infrared Range Finder (close-up): Removes from Linear Blaster Gun.

Like Whirl (1985) and Jetfire (1985), Roadbuster's intricate toy mold was borrowed from Takara's competing Japanese toy company Bandai (specifically, the "Mugen Calibur" mecha from the short-lived Dorvack series) and added to Hasbro's Transformers lineup. This wasn't unusual at all, except that Takara was Bandai's competitor in the Japanese market, where the TV cartoon was also being shown. As a result, Roadbuster was never promoted in the cartoon and lost all of his tie-in marketability. Roadbuster has a complex transformation from 4WD vehicle to robot, and a bevy of easily lost weapons and accessories, so finding a loose, complete Roadbuster is quite difficult.

**ALTERNATE MODE:** 4-WD Cybertronian vehicle.
**EASILY LOST WEAPONS AND ACCESSORIES:**
Antenna, Control Pack, handles (2), Infrared Range Finder (NOTE: this is tiny!), laser rifle, Linear Blaster Gun, missiles (5), Power Pack, Shrapnel Missile Launcher, 2 large wheel covers.

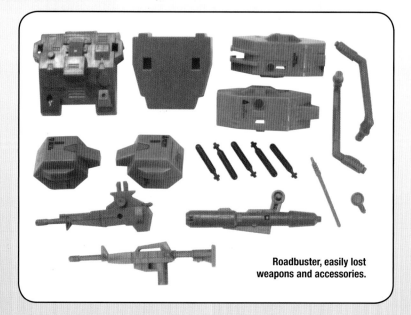

Roadbuster, easily lost weapons and accessories.

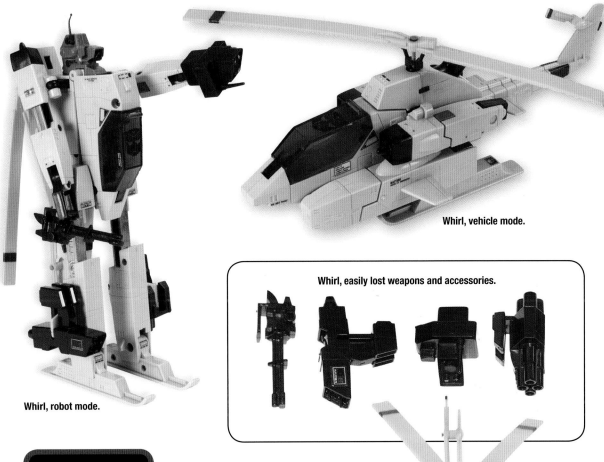

Whirl, vehicle mode.

Whirl, easily lost weapons and accessories.

Whirl, robot mode.

## WHIRL

**DELUXE VEHICLES**

**FUNCTION:** Aerial Assault
**MOTTO:** "If used logically, madness makes a great weapon."

"Loves his job…careens across sky spinning and weaving wild, crazy patterns. Believes enemies are more terrified of him if he acts wild during an attack. Flies at 400 mph, range 1600 miles. Amazing maneuverability…can fly at almost any angle. Carries four incendiary-shell cannons hi-energy photon beam rifle (sic). Great strength as a robot…has null-ray module on hand, paralyzo box on leg. Reckless…prone to rotor blade damage."

| Strength | Intelligence | Speed | Endurance | Rank | Courage | Firepower | Skill |
|----------|-------------|-------|-----------|------|---------|-----------|-------|
| 8 | 8 | 8 | 8 | 6 | 9 | 8 | 8 |

MLC: **$60-72+**, MIB: **$135-155+**, MISB: **$400-500**

Whirl, alternate mode, front view.

Whirl, like Roadbuster (1985), was made from a mold owned by competing toy company Bandai and was based on machines from the Dorvack anime (in this case, the Ovelon Gazzette helicopter mecha). As a result, Takara avoided promoting them in the cartoon, and this combined with his freakish appearance in robot mode gave Whirl fairly low popularity. His alternate mode, inspired by the Bell AH-1 Cobra, is fabulously engineered.

As a toy, sticker wear is usually prominent on Whirl, and his toy is getting more difficult to find in good condition on the secondary market. His antenna in robot mode and his blades in vehicle mode are all very fragile, so be careful to look for mint accouterments with loose Whirl samples.

**ALTERNATE MODE:** [Inspired by the] Bell AH-1 Cobra.
**EASILY LOST WEAPONS AND ACCESSORIES:** Shell Cannon, Paralyzo-box, Null-Ray Module, Photon Beam Rifle.

Blaster, easily lost weapons and accessories.

Blaster, robot mode.

# BLASTER

**COMMUNICATOR**

**FUNCTION:** Communications
**MOTTO:** "When the music is rockin, I'm rollin."

"Finds all Earth music interesting, but it's rock n' roll—good, hard and loud—that really sparks his circuits. In the forefront of any situation he's involved in. As AM/FM stereo cassette player, he can perform as deck plus receive radio signals of all frequencies with power outputs as low as 1/1,000,000 watt. Acts as Autobot communications center...can transmit up to 4,000 miles. Carries electro-scrambler gun that disrupts electrical devices."

| Strength | Intelligence | Speed | Endurance | Rank | Courage | Firepower | Skill |
|---|---|---|---|---|---|---|---|
| 8 | 8 | 2 | 8 | 7 | 9 | 7 | 9 |

MLC: **$45-58**, MIB: **$130-140**, MISB: **$300-400**

Blaster was added to the Autobot roster during the second year of U.S. Transformers releases as a counterpart to the Decepticons' Communicator Soundwave (1984). Unfortunately, as there were no Autobot cassettes created in 1985, he had no reinforcements (and many children fit Decepticon cassettes inside Blaster instead). He transforms into an excellent portable stereo replete with carrying handle. Take care that all four stereo buttons are intact on loose Blaster samples, especially the one on the far left labeled "Eject" since this is most often found broken.

**ALTERNATE MODE:** AM/FM Stereo cassette player.
**EASILY LOST WEAPONS AND ACCESSORIES:** Electro-scrambler gun.

Blaster, alternate mode.

# OMEGA SUPREME

**DEFENSE BASE**

**FUNCTION:** Defense Base
**MOTTO:** "Unyielding resolve has no conqueror."

"The ultimate defensive force. Great strength, even greater courage. Serious, even grim...last line of Autobot defense. Protects the Ark and all else vital to his cause. As robot, can shatter a mountainside, lift 300,000 tons with clawed arm, destroy 12' steel cube with plasma blaster arm...has head-mounted laser cannon. Can transform to laser cannon tank and launching pad with rocket. Rocket can achieve planetary orbit."

| Strength | Intelligence | Speed | Endurance | Rank | Courage | Firepower | Skill |
|---|---|---|---|---|---|---|---|
| 10 | 5 | 3 | 10 | 7 | 10 | 10 | 6 |

MLC: (working electronics) **$125-150+**, MIB: (working electronics) **$210-235+**, MISB: **$500-700**

Omega Supreme, robot mode.

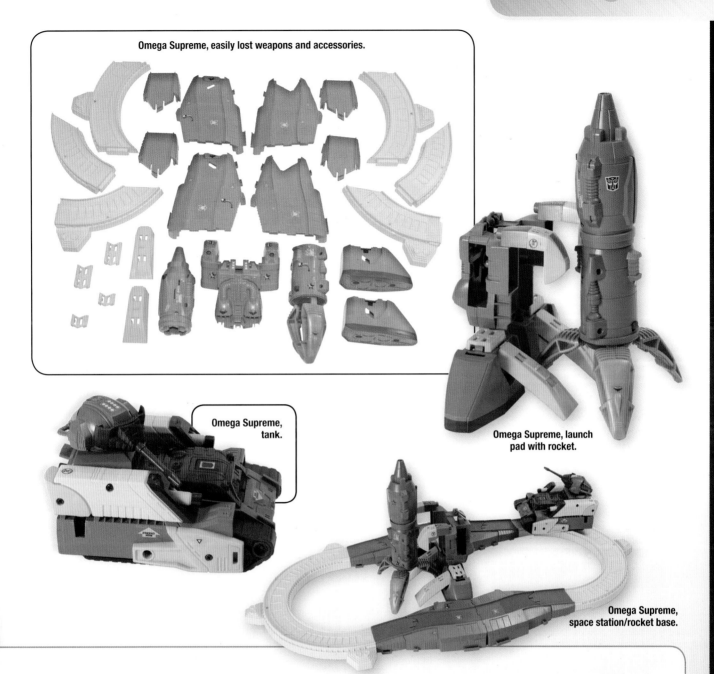

Omega Supreme, easily lost weapons and accessories.

Omega Supreme, tank.

Omega Supreme, launch pad with rocket.

Omega Supreme, space station/rocket base.

At the time of his release, Omega Supreme was the "end all and be all" of Transformers. Frequently hailed as the "last line of defense" for the Autobots, and only called upon when times were dire indeed, many kids didn't feel that way about Omega Supreme, and I'm sure that he was the key Christmas present for Transformers fans back in 1985. As a character, it is rumored that Omega Supreme was the last of the Guardian Robots (according to Dreamwave's 2003 *Transformers: More Than Meets The Eye* guide books). These Guardian Robots, the Omega Sentinels, were mechanical giants designed to oversee the protection of Cybertron's most important natural resources. These fearsome Omega Sentinels were largely without personality or original thought, with the exception of Omega Supreme, who was granted his own "spark" (Cybertronian equivalent of a life essence).

As a toy, Omega Supreme offered "motorized walking action" powered by two AA batteries, and in space station mode, his tank could run the length of his track. Its turret rotated and his cannon moved up and down, all under the glow of a red light. Omega Supreme is a huge toy with many small (and large) pieces, some which command their own special prices on the secondary market. Like Sky Lynx (1986), his toy was originally licensed from the Japanese company Toybox, not Takara, where his original Toybox name was "Super Change Robo Mechabot-1."

**ALTERNATE MODE:** Space Station (rocket base).

**EASILY LOST WEAPONS AND ACCESSORIES:** Tank, 6 pieces of track, rocket with claw, rocket, 2 sets of armor halves (4 pieces total), 2 sets of ankles (4 pieces total), 2 feet, backpack, 6 yellow shields (2 large, 2 medium, 2 small).

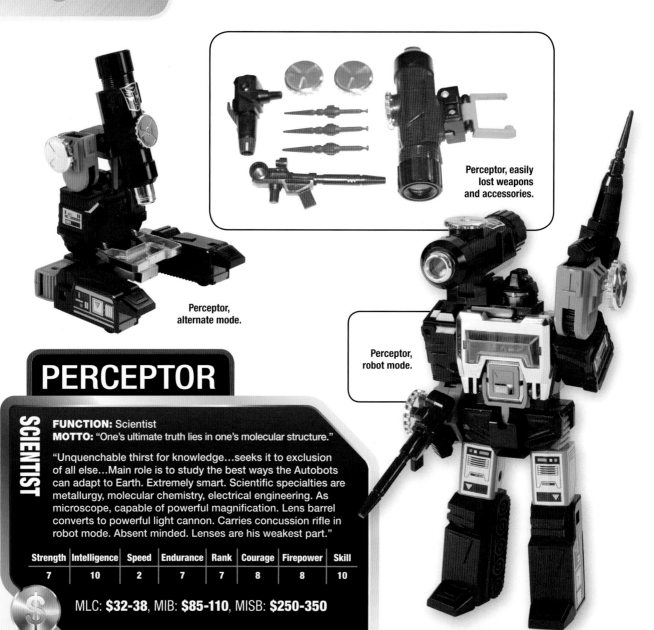

Perceptor, easily lost weapons and accessories.

Perceptor, alternate mode.

Perceptor, robot mode.

# PERCEPTOR

**SCIENTIST**

**FUNCTION:** Scientist
**MOTTO:** "One's ultimate truth lies in one's molecular structure."

"Unquenchable thirst for knowledge…seeks it to exclusion of all else…Main role is to study the best ways the Autobots can adapt to Earth. Extremely smart. Scientific specialties are metallurgy, molecular chemistry, electrical engineering. As microscope, capable of powerful magnification. Lens barrel converts to powerful light cannon. Carries concussion rifle in robot mode. Absent minded. Lenses are his weakest part."

| Strength | Intelligence | Speed | Endurance | Rank | Courage | Firepower | Skill |
|---|---|---|---|---|---|---|---|
| 7 | 10 | 2 | 7 | 7 | 8 | 8 | 10 |

MLC: **$32-38**, MIB: **$85-110**, MISB: **$250-350**

With origins in the same Microman toy line that gave us Soundwave (1984), Blaster (1985), and Megatron (1984) among others, Perceptor was a fun toy because he not only had an excellent robot mode, but his alternate mode provided kids with an actual "working" microscope (magnification 10x). His designs are reminiscent of the Transformers who were released in 1986 with *Transformers: The Movie*, as he had a Cybertronian alternate-mode feel. In the Sunbow cartoon, his character had an excellent voice provided by actor Paul Eiding.

**ALTERNATE MODE:** Desktop microscope.
**EASILY LOST WEAPONS AND ACCESSORIES:**
Concussion rifle, missile launcher, 3 missiles.

Perceptor, mobile laboratory mode.

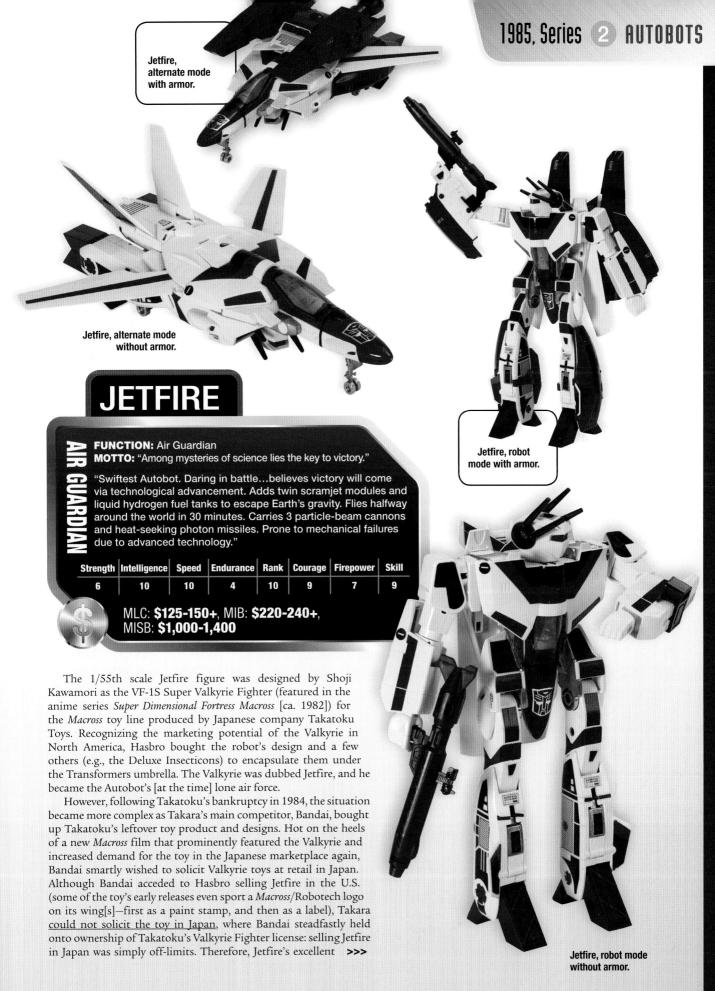

Jetfire, alternate mode with armor.

Jetfire, alternate mode without armor.

Jetfire, robot mode with armor.

# JETFIRE

**AIR GUARDIAN**

**FUNCTION:** Air Guardian
**MOTTO:** "Among mysteries of science lies the key to victory."

"Swiftest Autobot. Daring in battle…believes victory will come via technological advancement. Adds twin scramjet modules and liquid hydrogen fuel tanks to escape Earth's gravity. Flies halfway around the world in 30 minutes. Carries 3 particle-beam cannons and heat-seeking photon missiles. Prone to mechanical failures due to advanced technology."

| Strength | Intelligence | Speed | Endurance | Rank | Courage | Firepower | Skill |
|---|---|---|---|---|---|---|---|
| 6 | 10 | 10 | 4 | 10 | 9 | 7 | 9 |

MLC: **$125-150+**, MIB: **$220-240+**, MISB: **$1,000-1,400**

The 1/55th scale Jetfire figure was designed by Shoji Kawamori as the VF-1S Super Valkyrie Fighter (featured in the anime series *Super Dimensional Fortress Macross* [ca. 1982]) for the *Macross* toy line produced by Japanese company Takatoku Toys. Recognizing the marketing potential of the Valkyrie in North America, Hasbro bought the robot's design and a few others (e.g., the Deluxe Insecticons) to encapsulate them under the Transformers umbrella. The Valkyrie was dubbed Jetfire, and he became the Autobot's [at the time] lone air force.

However, following Takatoku's bankruptcy in 1984, the situation became more complex as Takara's main competitor, Bandai, bought up Takatoku's leftover toy product and designs. Hot on the heels of a new *Macross* film that prominently featured the Valkyrie and increased demand for the toy in the Japanese marketplace again, Bandai smartly wished to solicit Valkyrie toys at retail in Japan. Although Bandai acceded to Hasbro selling Jetfire in the U.S. (some of the toy's early releases even sport a *Macross*/Robotech logo on its wing[s]—first as a paint stamp, and then as a label), Takara <u>could not solicit the toy in Japan</u>, where Bandai steadfastly held onto ownership of Takatoku's Valkyrie Fighter license: selling Jetfire in Japan was simply off-limits. Therefore, Jetfire's excellent >>>

Jetfire, robot mode without armor.

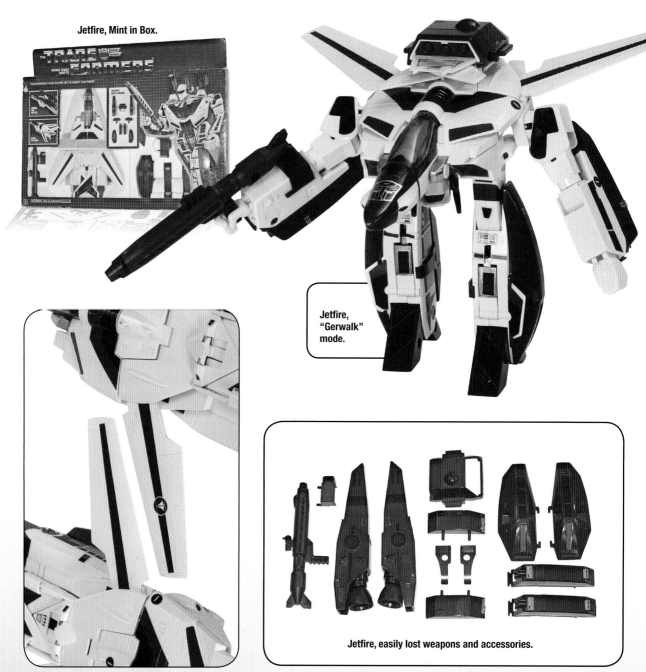

Jetfire, Mint in Box.

Jetfire, "Gerwalk" mode.

Jetfire, wing variations.

Jetfire, easily lost weapons and accessories.

aircraft design was excluded from the *Transformers* animated series as the cartoon was set to be re-released in Japan.

To further complicate the situation, Harmony Gold released the *Robotech* cartoon in the U.S. (America's watered-down, edited version of *Macross*): now children in the United States had the possibility to watch Jetfire on another animated program. But how could children witness Jetfire and his Valkyrie alternate mode on two different U.S. distributed animated programs at the same time? Legally, they couldn't. Therefore, in the Sunbow animation, Hasbro tweaked Jetfire's robot and alternate modes while changing his name to the friendly-faced "Skyfire"— in order for the popular Autobot Air Guardian to appear quite different than that of his *Robotech* counterpart.

Regardless of his storied provenance, Jetfire was equipped to impress with his amazing accessories and armor, gorgeous jet mode, and additional alternate "GERWALK" mode (Ground Effective Reinforcement of Winged Armament with Locomotive Knee-joint) that referred to the Autobot's bizarre-looking third configuration that showcased his protruding legs and arms all-the-while maintaining its winged aircraft appearance.

**ALTERNATE MODE:** Super Jet (license based on the designs of *Macross'* VF-1S Valkyrie).

**EASILY LOST PARTS AND ACCESSORIES:** 11 pieces of battle armor (left and right leg guards, left and right fenders, two leg clips, left and right arm guards, left and right turbo thrusters, back guard), photon missile launcher, mounting pod (sometimes called "gun clip").

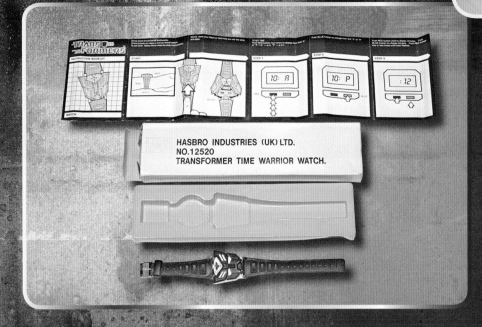

HASBRO INDUSTRIES (UK) LTD.
NO.12520
TRANSFORMER TIME WARRIOR WATCH.

## DIGITAL WATCH
### A.K.A. TIME WARRIOR

Offered for a limited time (for only 5 robot points and $10), the Autobot Watch, the Autobot Watch known as "Time Warrior" is a difficult find in good condition, especially with its spring-loaded ("face-splitting") mechanism intact, its digital LCD ("liquid crystal display") still working, and no paint wear on the Autobot symbol/protective face. It came with an instruction booklet like the rest of the Autobots, and is quite rare on the secondary market. His name, "Time Warrior," was not stated in his instructions, only in the mail-away brochures.

 MLC: **$45-55** (push button & electronics don't work); **$65-85+** (push button and electronics work), MIB (+ Instruction Sheet & Plastic Holder): **$200-225+**, MISB: **$400-500+**

Autobot/Digital Watch, "opened" alternate mode.

# MAIL-AWAYS

Since the beginning of Hasbro's Transformers franchise, the company utilized the concept of direct mailing that they had developed many decades earlier with the original 12-inch G.I. Joe line: as a way to reward devoted fans, Hasbro would solicit exclusive product by mail-order through the G.I. Joe Fan Club. So then, if a consumer bought a boxed Transformers item, a brochure would be placed inside the package that told consumers which Transformers items were available to them and the cost for each item—usually a mixture of a small amount of cash (to cover shipping and handling) and Transformers "Robot Points" (proof-of-purchase seals cut from toy packages).

This aspect of the corporation—known as "Hasbro Direct"—provided the spectacular variety of mail-aways featured on the next few pages. From the Time Warrior LCD watch to the Omnibots (who were developed by Takara in Japan and named the "Double Changers") to the now impossible-to-find S.T.A.R.S. Command Center. By providing this type of service, devoted followers of the brand felt more invested in the franchise and received product that the average consumer simply could not obtain in retail stores.

Later on in the history of the brand, Hasbro would offer standard, retail-released samples (Autobot Cars, Autobot Mini-vehicles, etc.) as mail-away items through their Hasbro Direct mail-order system.

# OMNIBOTS

The three Omnibots were available in one of the first Transformer mail-away offer (for 4 robot points and $5.00 each), and even though their car modes were slightly smaller than the Autobot Cars offered from 1984-1986, the Omnibots were still very well designed. Each Omnibot came without a Tech Spec, therefore the "function" and "motto" information for each is from Dreamwave's 2003 *Transformers: More Than Meets The Eye* guidebooks. However, Hasbro issued the following statement inside the original three Omnibots' instruction booklets: "The Omnibots are special double-change cars that are in the early stages of evolution. Little is known about their true strengths or weaknesses. Tech Specs rating tests have not been completed for this new form of Autobots...The reinforcements from Cybertron have arrived!"

Omnibots, alternate modes with instruction booklets.

Omnibots, alternate "attack" modes.

Camshaft, robot mode.

# CAMSHAFT

**FUNCTION:** Scout
**MOTTO:** "Sometimes you have to be smart enough to know when to run."

MLC: **$24-32**, MISP: **$75-100+**

Each Omnibot had a bonus attack mode ["armored car" mode] that modified the robots' alternate modes. Camshaft's was the most singularly designed of these attack modes, since his robot fists were clearly visible. However, the irony apparent here occurs with Camshaft's name: his alternate mode—the Mazda RX-7 Savanna—possessed a rotary engine. Unlike a piston engine, a rotary engine does not need a camshaft (it has no cam or cam belt). Therefore, Omnibot Camshaft does not possess a ... camshaft.

**ALTERNATE MODE:** Mazda Rx7 Savanna.
**EASILY LOST WEAPONS AND ACCESSORIES:** Neutron blaster, 2 rockets.

Camshaft, easily lost weapons and accessories.

Downshift, easily lost weapons and accessories.

Downshift, robot mode.

# DOWNSHIFT

**FUNCTION:** Security Agent
**MOTTO:** "Nothing is secure as long as there are criminals somewhere."

MLC: **$24-32**, MISP: **$75-100+**

With yet another excellent automobile mode, Downshift is one of the highly detailed Omnibots, new recruitments for the Autobot ranks. Take care to keep Downshift's toy out of direct sunlight, as the white plastic that comprises him fades or yellows over time.

**ALTERNATE MODE:** Toyota Celica XX P-type [the Japanese version of Celica Supra Mark II].
**EASILY LOST WEAPONS AND ACCESSORIES:** rust rifle, 2 magnetic-guided rocket launchers.

Overdrive, easily lost weapons and accessories.

# OVERDRIVE

**FUNCTION:** Strategist
**MOTTO:** "It's always better to think fast rather than last."

MLC: **$26-34**, MISP: **$85-110+**

Overdrive is the most popular of the three Omnibots on the secondary market, as he is 1) a bright shade of red in color, 2) has a great alternate mode, 3) has a decent-looking "attack car" mode with wings, and 4) an excellent robot mode. His weapons, as with all Omnibots, were three chromed silver accessories that were small enough to become quite easily lost.

**ALTERNATE MODE:** Ferrari 512 BB (Berlinetta Boxer).
**EASILY LOST WEAPONS AND ACCESSORIES:** Neutron blaster, plasma beam rifle, twin electron cannon.

Overdrive, robot mode.

# S.T.A.R.S.
## AUTOBOT COMMAND CENTER

This very-difficult-to-find cardboard headquarters was only available as a mail-away through Hasbro Direct. The back story for the S.T.A.R.S. Headquarters is taken from a mail-away brochure packaged in select Transformers products that states: "Our only hope of holding off the Decepticons rests with the (ongoing) S.T.A.R.S.* club (* Secret Transformers: Autobot Rescue Squad)."

For only $6.50 and no Robot Points proof-of-purchases, a S.T.A.R.S. membership allowed collectors to receive the following: 1) Transformers Control Center: Made of sturdy 4-color graphic board. Fits easily on a dresser or book shelf; 2) S.T.A.R.S. (Autobot) Iron-On Patch: Wear it proudly!; 3) Autobot Poster: A bold, full-color action scene; 4) S.T.A.R.S. Membership Card: Check out the unearthly picture that changes from Autobot to Decepticon!; and 5) Autobot Tech Spec Manual: Reveals detailed engineering drawings of all your favorite Autobots, plus secret Cybertron information.

Any collector would be lucky to have this rare mail-away in any condition, as many loose samples are worn or damaged.

ML (playset only): **$55-70+,** MLC (and all paperwork): **$150-175+,** MIP (in mailer pack with all paperwork-unassembled): **$235-250+,** MISB: **425-525+**

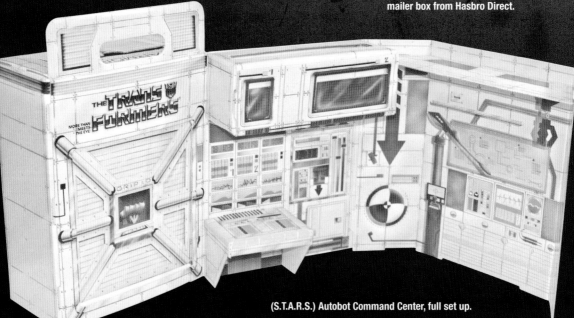

(S.T.A.R.S.) Autobot Command Center, mailer box from Hasbro Direct.

(S.T.A.R.S.) Autobot Command Center, full set up.

(S.T.A.R.S.) Autobot Command Center, tech specs and instruction sheet.

(S.T.A.R.S.) Autobot Command Center, included paperwork.

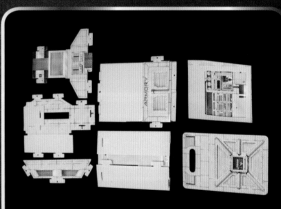

(S.T.A.R.S.) Autobot Command Center, unassembled.

(S.T.A.R.S.) Autobot Command Center, tech spec reader close up.

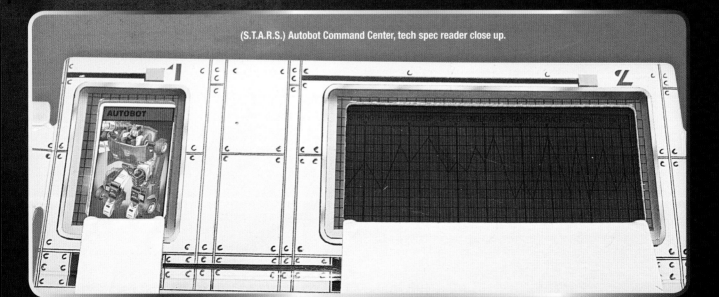

Powerdasher(s), robot modes (jet, car, drill).

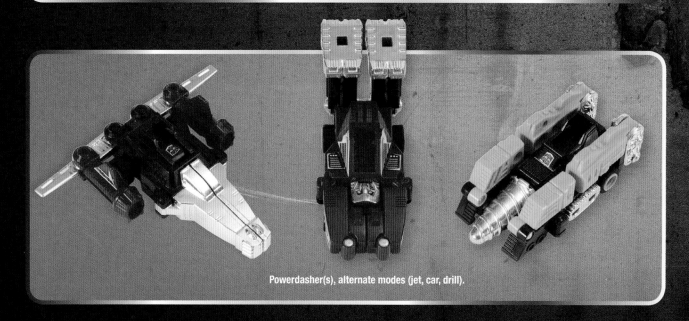

Powerdasher(s), alternate modes (jet, car, drill).

# POWERDASHER(S)

**FUNCTION:** Reinforcements
**MOTTO:** "If it'll help, count us in!"

This Powerdasher is a new form of Autobot. Power is still growing. Fast and skillful. Little is known about its true strengths and weaknesses. Came to Earth to help the Autobots in their cause. Able to take on a variety of shapes and forms. Has the ability to operate at various levels of kinetic energy. Friendly, cheerful and obedient.

"Cromar," Powerdasher Jet (left): MLC: **$18-24**, MISP: **$58-75**
"Aragon," Powerdasher Car (middle): MLC: **$13-18**, MISP: **$54-68**
"Zetar," Powerdasher Drill (right): MLC: **$14-22**, MISP: **$54-68**

Their mail-away brochure, stated: "NOTE: Powerdashers are constantly evolving. The style you get may be different than the one pictured here" (Powerdasher Jet is pictured). Released in three different styles, the Powerdashers were a cheap mail-away alternative to the Omnibots (1985), and only cost $3.00 each plus 2 robot points. The Powerdashers were pretty cool with their pull back action... even without weapons or complex conversions from robot to vehicle.

Bonecrusher, robot mode.

# BONECRUSHER

**CONSTRUCTICONS**

**FUNCTION:** Demolitions
**MOTTO:** "Hit it till it stands no taller than dust."

"Rubble-strewn wasteland is his idea of beautiful landscape. His wild ways create fear and terror. As vehicle, at 30 mph exerts 800,000 psi…has short-range concussion bomb launcher. As robot, carries laser pistol. As left arm module, combines with fellow Constructicons to form giant robot 'Devastator.'"

| Strength | Intelligence | Speed | Endurance | Rank | Courage | Firepower | Skill |
|----------|--------------|-------|-----------|------|---------|-----------|-------|
| 9 | 3 | 2 | 9 | 4 | 8 | 6 | 6 |

MLC: **$14-18**, MIP (opened): **$35-40**, MOC: **$100-175**

Bonecrusher is the strongest of the six Constructicons, and his battle prowess and ability to demolish fortifications [and Autobots] makes him popular among his comrades. While his robot and vehicle forms are excellent, in vehicle mode his extra Devastator parts may be used to create a special "Attack Bulldozer" mode.

**ALTERNATE MODE:** (Generic) bulldozer.
**EASILY LOST WEAPONS AND ACCESSORIES:** Target shooter (Devastator arm), rotor blade, laser pistol, and (Devastator's left) fist.

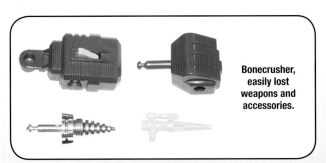

Bonecrusher, easily lost weapons and accessories.

Bonecrusher, alternate mode.

# CONSTRUCTICONS

The Constructicons and their super-robot mode, Devastator, with their bright green and purple colors, smattering of Decepticon logos on their bodies, ample weapons and accessories, and interesting individual robot forms, endure as brisk seller in any condition. Originally produced by Takara for their Diaclone "Construction Vehicle Robo" line, these magnificent toys were created by designer Koujin Ohno. It is worth noting that this was the first assortment of Diaclone toys that the Japanese company produced WITHOUT their requisite 1-1/4-inch tall Diaclone drivers.

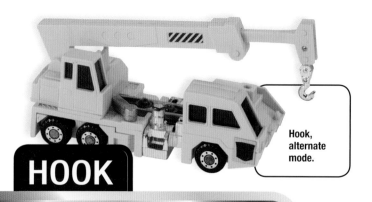

Hook, alternate mode.

Hook, robot mode.

## HOOK

**CONSTRUCTICONS**

**FUNCTION:** Surgical Engineer
**MOTTO:** "Strive for perfection even if others must suffer."

"With the precision of a fine jeweler, performs his job with skill unequalled among The Transformers, whether reconnecting a damaged microchip or setting a two ton girder into place. Snobbish, supercilious, unpopular perfectionist. Lifts 20 tons. As shoulders and head module, combines with fellow Constructicons to form 'Devastator.'"

| Strength | Intelligence | Speed | Endurance | Rank | Courage | Firepower | Skill |
|----------|-------------|-------|-----------|------|---------|-----------|-------|
| 8 | 9 | 3 | 6 | 4 | 6 | 5 | 10 |

MLC: **$40-52**, MIP (opened): **$65-70**, MOC: **$150-250**

While his intelligence and skill are the result of his striving for perfection, Hook won't tolerate unprofessionalism and lack of accomplishment: qualities important for this Decepticon equivalent of a medical doctor and surgeon. As a toy, Hook has a rather difficult series of steps to change him from robot to vehicle, and once again into an "Attack Crane." Furthermore, his importance to the team is most apparent when combining into Devastator where Hook forms the gestalt's head and shoulders.

Hook, easily lost weapons and accessories.

**ALTERNATE MODE:** Nissan Diesel KW-30M with Tadano TL201 crane.
**EASILY LOST WEAPONS AND ACCESSORIES:** laser pistol, (Devastator's head) laser and robot's (Devastator's) head.

## LONG HAUL

**CONSTRUCTICONS**

**FUNCTION:** Transport
**MOTTO:** "A battle front is only as good as its supply line."

"Unhappy with unglamorous role, but understands its importance…helps build Decepticons' massive energy-recovery installations. As vehicle, can carry 90 tons for 1200 miles, use a dual heat-seeking missile mount. As torso module, combines with fellow Constructicons to form giant robot 'Devastator.' Can be goaded into a fight in which he's overmatched."

| Strength | Intelligence | Speed | Endurance | Rank | Courage | Firepower | Skill |
|----------|-------------|-------|-----------|------|---------|-----------|-------|
| 9 | 5 | 2 | 9 | 4 | 8 | 7 | 4 |

MLC: **$25-30**, MIP (opened): **$33-38**, MOC: **$65-70**

Mixmaster, robot mode.

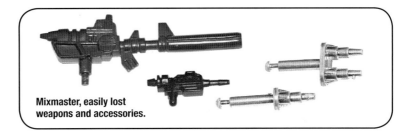

Mixmaster, easily lost
weapons and accessories.

# MIXMASTER

**CONSTRUCTICONS**

**FUNCTION:** Materials Fabrication
**MOTTO:** "How strong the steel, how quick the conquest."

"Nothing is safe from him…he will use anything from unliving rock to living robot in making new materials. Uses acids and bonding agents to reduce and recombine almost anything inside mixing drum…a chemistry lab on wheels. As left leg module, combines with fellow Constructicons to form giant robot 'Devastator.'"

| Strength | Intelligence | Speed | Endurance | Rank | Courage | Firepower | Skill |
|---|---|---|---|---|---|---|---|
| 7 | 6 | 3 | 8 | 4 | 6 | 7 | 9 |

MLC: **$25-30**, MIP (opened): **$33-38**, MOC: **$100-200**

Like his green-and-purple brothers who incorporate Autobot bodies in the creation of new fortresses, Mixmaster prefers to use [functioning or non-functioning] Autobots when rendering a new substance in his drum. Furthermore, Mixmaster's superiors are surprised by the products he can 'magically' procure for these superstructures. Apart from his cement mixer mode, robot form, and ability to form Devastator, Mixmaster has an "Attack Truck" mode.

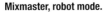

Mixmaster,
alternate mode.

**ALTERNATE MODE:** Nissan Diesel CW 340 cement mixer [or equivalent].
**EASILY LOST WEAPONS AND ACCESSORIES:** (Devastator's) magna laser, twin blaster missiles, and laser pistol.

Long Haul,
alternate mode.

In the Transformers universe, Constructicon Long Haul desires to be a front line fighter instead of a transport specialist since he is the second-strongest Constructicon [see Bonecrusher, 1985]. Regardless, he remains a dangerous adversary due to his ability to carry large loads coupled with the powerful dual heat-seeking missile launcher he wields in "Attack Truck" mode.

**ALTERNATE MODE:** Hitachi DH321 dump truck.
**EASILY LOST WEAPONS AND ACCESSORIES:** Missile mount (missiles are NOT removable), wing, laser pistol.

Long Haul, easily lost weapons
and accessories.

Scavenger, easily lost
weapons and accessories.

## SCAVENGER

**CONSTRUCTICONS**

**FUNCTION:** Mining and Salvage
**MOTTO:** "Everything is worth something, even me."

"Desperately tries to prove his worth to comrades by trying to find things of value—whether by digging up a hillside or a backyard. Only tolerated because of ability to use shovel's magnetic, ionic, electrical, gas sensors to detect presence of fuels, metals, etc. As right arm module, combines with fellow Constructicons to form giant robot 'Devastator.'"

| Strength | Intelligence | Speed | Endurance | Rank | Courage | Firepower | Skill |
|----------|--------------|-------|-----------|------|---------|-----------|-------|
| 7 | 2 | 3 | 6 | 4 | 9 | 6 | 7 |

💲 MLC: **$20-24**, MIP (opened): **$30-35**, MOC: **$100-200**

Scavenger,
robot mode.

Although Scavenger's Tech Spec bio elicits sympathy, the wonderful detail of his vehicle mode does not, thanks to his boom possessing two points of articulation, a pivoting house (the upper platform on an excavator), and a die-cast metal base. Finally, collectors should be careful of the die-cast metal attachment he uses to form Devastator: it is quite fragile.

**ALTERNATE MODE:** [Resembles] John Deere 690D-LC steam shovel.
**EASILY LOST WEAPONS AND ACCESSORIES:** Target launcher (Devastator arm), rotor blade, laser pistol, and (Devastator's right) fist.

Scavenger,
alternate mode.

Scrapper, robot mode.

## SCRAPPER

**CONSTRUCTICONS**

**FUNCTION:** Construction Engineer
**MOTTO:** "My work is a monument to—and of—my enemies."

"A wizard at designing fortresses and energy plants, but modest. Shows his true malevolent genius by incorporating defeated Autobots into his buildings' structures. Shovel can slice through 12 in. thick carbon-steel, lift 30 tons. As right leg and part of torso, combines with fellow Constructicons to form giant robot 'Devastator.'"

| Strength | Intelligence | Speed | Endurance | Rank | Courage | Firepower | Skill |
|----------|--------------|-------|-----------|------|---------|-----------|-------|
| 8 | 8 | 4 | 7 | 5 | 5 | 3 | 9 |

💲 MLC: **$25-30**, MIP (opened): **$33-38**, MOC: **$100-175**

As leader of the formidable Constructicons, Megatron [1984] values Scrapper's ability to organize his unit to assemble nearly any structure the Decepticons require. Scrapper's viciousness toward the Autobots makes him popular among the Decepticons, yet in spite of his acclaim, Scrapper manages to retain a good deal of modesty. In toy mode, Scrapper can convert to a robot, a payloader, and an "Attack Payloader."

**ALTERNATE MODE:** [Generic] payloader.
**EASILY LOST WEAPONS AND ACCESSORIES:** Super wing, laser pistol, and payloader roof.

Scrapper, easily lost weapons
and accessories.

Scrapper,
alternate mode.

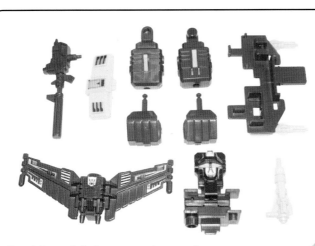

Devastator, easily lost weapons and accessories.

Constructicons, alternate "attack vehicle" modes

Devastator, robot mode.

# DEVASTATOR

**CONSTRUCTICONS**

**FUNCTION:** Warrior
**MOTTO:** "Thinking and winning do not mix."

"Awesome and terrifying, this Decepticon is a bizarre combination of six Constructicons: Scrapper, Scavenger, Bonecrusher, Hook, Long Haul, and Mixmaster. He is pure brutality as his sole purpose is to crush all in his path. His mind is a melding together of his six parts, but he is limited by their competing thoughts. He possesses enormous height and incredible strength—can knock down a bridge with one punch. He carries a 10,000 degree Celsius solar energy beam rifle. Slow, awkward, not too bright."

| Strength | Intelligence | Speed | Endurance | Rank | Courage | Firepower | Skill |
|----------|--------------|-------|-----------|------|---------|-----------|-------|
| 10 | 2 | 1 | 9 | 6 | 10 | 8 | 4 |

Devastator Gift Set (all 6 Constructicons together)
MLC: **$135-120**, MIB: **$215-235+**, MISB: **$700-900**

With the most screen [and page] time of any combiner, Devastator is one of the more powerful gestalts despite his outdated combining technology. Megatron refuses to reinvent the Constructicons regardless of how antiquated the manner in which they merge to form Devastator, since he's afraid that tinkering with the process might cause the super-robot to lose his effectiveness. Furthermore, take note that you cannot switch the Constructicons around like the later "scramble city"-type gestalts, since each member of the team forms his own precise piece of the monstrous Devastator.

71

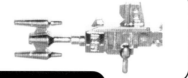

Bombshell, alternate mode.

Bombshell, easily lost weapon.

# BOMBSHELL

**INSECTICONS**

**FUNCTION:** Psychological Warfare
**MOTTO:** "The mind is my playpen."

"Can turn foes into helpless accomplices by injecting cerebro-shells into their head (robot or human) with his stinger…gives him control of their minds…has a cruel sense of humor…arms himself by having his victims debase themselves. In insect mode this Insecticon can fly 5.7 miles. In robot mode wears head-mounted mortar…throws 50 pound explosive shell 8 miles. Cerebro-shells can be used against him if removed from victim's head."

| Strength | Intelligence | Speed | Endurance | Rank | Courage | Firepower | Skill |
|---|---|---|---|---|---|---|---|
| 5 | 8 | 5 | 5 | 6 | 5 | 6 | 9 |

MLC: **$14-18**, MIB: **$35-55**, MISB: **$150-250**

The Decepticon equivalent of a psychologist, the sinister Bombshell treats the universe like one big longitudinal study and every Autobot is in his control group, where his use of "cerebo-shells" was replicated in the Sunbow cartoon. Regardless, Bombshell's peculiar-looking robot mode was taken from Takara's Diaclone designs for their evil Insecter Robo Kabutron.

**ALTERNATE MODE:** [Rhinoceros] beetle [*Dynastinae*].
**EASILY LOST WEAPONS AND ACCESSORIES:** Twin ion impulse blaster.

Bombshell, robot mode

# INSECTICONS

The Insecticons were fascinating Decepticons, utilized frequently in the Sunbow animation. Although they were ravenous—feeding as much as possible off any available energy source—they remained powerful antagonists. It should be noted here that the name of any offshoot of the Decepticons had the prefix of "-con" [e.g., Constructicons (1985), Insecticons, Combaticons (1986), Stunticons (1986), ad infinitum], while Autobot teams held the prefix "-bot" in their names [Dinobots, Protectobots (1986), Aerialbots (1986), Technobots (1987), etc.]. Apparently, the Insecticons and Dinobots started a trend: The creation of specialized groups within their respective affiliations.

Kickback, alternate mode.

Shrapnel, easily lost weapon.

Shrapnel, robot mode.

# SHRAPNEL

**INSECTICONS**

**FUNCTION:** Electronic Warfare
**MOTTO:** "Control electricity and you control the world."

"The noise of war and the scream of his foes are music to this loathsome Insecticon's audio-modules…has piercing battle cry…can be heard 8 miles away. In insect mode, can use antennae to control almost any electrical device. In robot mode, can attract lightning bolts to antennae and shoot them out hands. Grenade launcher shoots 30-pound steel balls that splinter into razor-sharp spikes. Insulation can stop his electrical blasts."

| Strength | Intelligence | Speed | Endurance | Rank | Courage | Firepower | Skill |
|---|---|---|---|---|---|---|---|
| 9 | 6 | 4 | 7 | 6 | 6 | 8 | 9 |

MLC: **$15-20**, MIB: **$35-55**, MISB: **$150-250**

Insecticon leader Shrapnel perfectly exemplified his sub-group's voracious appetite and loose affiliation with the Decepticons. Shrapnel's voice—with its sibilance and repetitive cadence—made him one of the most notorious and ominous of all Decepticons. Tragically, the trio of Insecticons was mortally wounded in *Transformers: The Movie*, and as a result were changed into Cyclonus [1986] and Scourge [1986] by Unicron, the planet-eater.

**ALTERNATE MODE:** Lamellicorn (aka. *Scarabaeoidea*).
**EASILY LOST WEAPONS AND ACCESSORIES:** Gamma ray detonator.

Shrapnel, alternate mode.

# KICKBACK

**INSECTICONS**

**FUNCTION:** Espionage
**MOTTO:** "Friend is another word for fool."

"Charming, but cruelly clever…makes friends so he can influence them to do his bidding by digging up facts he can hold against them. Humans particularly susceptible to this Insecticon. In insect mode can jump 40 ft. for a distance of .1 miles…kick a hole in 1/4 inch steel. In robot mode can fly 30 mph up to 100 miles. Sub-machine gun fires 300 rounds per minute. Very vulnerable as insect and flying in high winds."

| Strength | Intelligence | Speed | Endurance | Rank | Courage | Firepower | Skill |
|---|---|---|---|---|---|---|---|
| 3 | 9 | 4 | 4 | 7 | 6 | 5 | 8 |

MLC: **$14-18**, MIB: **$35-55**, MISB: **$150-250**

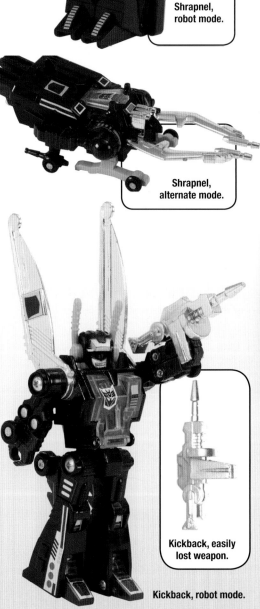

Kickback, easily lost weapon.

Kickback, robot mode.

In the Sunbow cartoon, the Insecticons were able to create clones of themselves to constitute an army: a swarm of robotic insects to overwhelm the Autobots. With impressive-looking robot and alternate modes, collectors should take care with Kickback's wings, since they have a tendency to droop at the joints after repeated manipulations.

**ALTERNATE MODE:** Grasshopper (*Orthoptera*).
**EASILY LOST WEAPONS AND ACCESSORIES:** Electrothermic blast tube.

# TRIPLE CHANGERS

The Triple Changers were one of Shockwave's (1986) more successful experiments with altering a Transformer's alternate mode(s). After the unsuccessful Duocons (1987), Shockwave came to realize that some Cybertronians had a predisposition toward these multiple alternate modes. The result:

Astrotrain and Blitzwing, the Decepticon Triple Changers. Their ability to change from one alternate mode to the other in a fraction of a second makes these Transformers two of the most effective warriors in the Autobot-Decepticon war.

Astrotrain, robot mode.

## TRIPLE CHANGERS

## ASTROTRAIN

**FUNCTION:** Military Transport
**MOTTO:** "In confusion there is opportunity."

"Creating confusion is his specialty. As a Triple Changer, can switch from space shuttle to train to robot almost instantaneously. Thrives on foes' panic and fear. As shuttle, travels at 20,000 mph in orbit, up to 50,000 mph out of orbit… can launch weapons and satellites. Carries cargo. As a train, top speed is 400 mph, range 1700 miles. As robot has great strength, carries powerful ionic displacer rifle."

| Strength | Intelligence | Speed | Endurance | Rank | Courage | Firepower | Skill |
|----------|--------------|-------|-----------|------|---------|-----------|-------|
| 9 | 7 | 10 | 7 | 6 | 7 | 6 | 8 |

MLC: **$28-36**, MIB: **$85-100**, MISB: **$350-450+**

Astrotrain can modify his body into alternate modes that are far larger than seems physically possible. According to Dreamwave's *Transformers: More Than Meets The Eye* guides [2003], in some instances where there is an expansion into a larger alternate mode during transformation, there could be a size or mass change within the robot. For instance, when there is "parts compression," the Cybertronian's body is designed to slide together [or apart] in a tight compression or a shifting expansion. However, when there exists "mass conversion," the subatomic particles of the Cybertronian restructure themselves (!), reconfiguring the Transformer's body "according to a predetermined schematic"—changing to meet the needs of the alternate mode in question.

These two processes explain how Soundwave [1984] and Blaster [1985] can shrink down to human-sized devices, while Autobot Triple Changer Broadside [1986] becomes an aircraft carrier. It appears that Astrotrain uses elements of both approaches to activate his much larger alternate modes of space shuttle and locomotive.

Astrotrain, space shuttle mode.

**ALTERNATE MODE:** Boeing/Rockwell Space Shuttle Orbiter, JNR Class D51 steam locomotive.
**EASILY LOST WEAPONS AND ACCESSORIES:** Ionic displacer rifle.

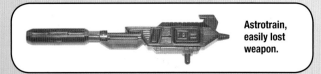

Astrotrain, easily lost weapon.

Astrotrain, train mode.

Blitzwing,
tank mode.

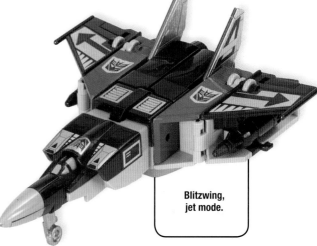

Blitzwing,
jet mode.

Blitzwing,
robot mode.

# BLITZWING

**TRIPLE CHANGERS**

**FUNCTION:** Ground and Air Commando
**MOTTO:** "Destroy first, think later."

"Ability as Triple Changer to rapidly transform makes him one of the most dangerous Decepticons. Cruel sense of humor, loud-mouthed, belligerent, and brash. Flies at Mach 2.7, range 1500 miles, has heat-seeking concussion missiles as plane. As tank, has track-mounted cannon that fires explosive shells 3.5 miles. As robot has electron-scimitar and gyro-blaster rifle. Often gets stuck in mid-transformation."

| Strength | Intelligence | Speed | Endurance | Rank | Courage | Firepower | Skill |
|----------|--------------|-------|-----------|------|---------|-----------|-------|
| 8 | 5 | 9 | 8 | 6 | 7 | 7 | 7 |

MLC: **$36-45**, MIB: **$75-90**, MISB: **$400-500**

Blitzwing was originally designed by Koujin Ohno as "Triple Changer Jet Type" for Takara's Diaclone line. As a Transformer, Blitzwing remains a popular toy on the secondary market due to his character's split-second transformation speed coupled with the fact that both of his alternate modes possess offensive capabilities. Collectors should take care to scrutinize loose samples of Blitzwing since his toy is prone to both 'looseness' and lost parts over time [and many transformations].

**ALTERNATE MODE:** [Russian] Mikoyan-Gurevich MiG-25P "Foxbat" supersonic jet; [Japanese] Mitsubishi Heavy Industries Type 74 Nana-yon M.B.T. [Main Battle Tank].
**EASILY LOST WEAPONS AND ACCESSORIES:** 3 concussion missiles, electron scimitar, gyro-blaster rifle.

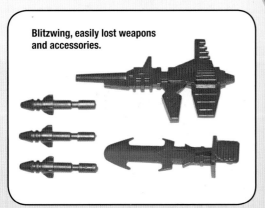

Blitzwing, easily lost weapons and accessories.

# BARRAGE

DELUXE INSECTICONS

**FUNCTION:** Gunner
**MOTTO:** "Nothing left standing means nothing left to change."

"Winning is not enough—this Insecticon's attack continues until the ground is scorched and leveled. Merciless, cruel… believes kindness only stirs hope among the vanquished. Disliked by fellow Decepticons. In insect mode, can shoot non-stop explosive charges from gun mounts, high energy photons from antenna. Flies 15 mph with 400 mile range. Has powerful sonic rifle in robot mode."

| Strength | Intelligence | Speed | Endurance | Rank | Courage | Firepower | Skill |
|---|---|---|---|---|---|---|---|
| 3 | 8 | 3 | 7 | 5 | 10 | 9 | 8 |

MLC: **$40-45**, MIB: **$65-82**, MISB: **$300-400**

Barrage, robot mode.

Barrage, easily lost weapons and accessories.

Although they were not featured in the Sunbow cartoon because of their affiliation with Bandai (Takara's competitor in Japan), the Deluxe Insecticons were still fantastic toys. Barrage is noted for his complex transformation from robot to insect, and his poseable wings and antenna.

**ALTERNATE MODE:** Kabutomushi (Japanese rhinoceros beetle) [*Allomyrina dichotoma*].
**EASILY LOST WEAPONS AND ACCESSORIES:** Electro-sword, sonic rifle.

Barrage, alternate mode.

# CHOP SHOP

DELUXE INSECTICONS

**FUNCTION:** Thief
**MOTTO:** "I take no prisoners, just spare parts."

"Sneakiest of the Insecticons…if it's not bolted to the floor, it's not safe from his greedy grasp. No challenge is too great; the more difficult something is to steal, the more he wants to steal it. As insect, flies 30 mph with two small jets on his back. Pincer-like antennae can slice through 2-inch thick steel. Has twin pinpoint lasers on mouth; can carry 30 tons. As robot has photon cannon."

| Strength | Intelligence | Speed | Endurance | Rank | Courage | Firepower | Skill |
|---|---|---|---|---|---|---|---|
| 7 | 8 | 4 | 5 | 6 | 7 | 6 | 10 |

MLC: **$38-50**, MIB: **$70-85**, MISB: **$300-400+**

Chop Shop, robot mode.

Chop Shop, easily lost weapons and accessories.

Among the legions of Decepticon soldiers, none are more skilled at theft than Chop Shop, who loots and plunders from friend and foe alike. His alternate mode as stag beetle is fascinating, yet it makes his robot mode look very bulky and awkward.

**ALTERNATE MODE:** Stag beetle [*Lucanidae*].
**EASILY LOST WEAPONS AND PARTS:** Vibro-spear, photon cannon.

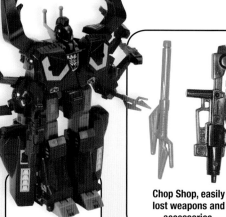

Chop Shop, alternate mode.

# RANSACK

**DELUXE INSECTICONS**

**FUNCTION:** Warrior
**MOTTO:** "The sight of ruin only makes me crave more."

"Unconcerned about safety of innocents…will level an entire town to hunt down an enemy. A tough-talking, straight-to-the-point Insecticon, always looking forward to the next battle. In insect mode, leaps 200 feet at insect size, 1.5 miles normal size. Rear legs can shatter foot-thick steel; their vibrations from rubbing can crumble a brick wall. Antennae shoot 80 kv (kilovolts) electricity. Carries concussion blaster gun in robot mode."

| Strength | Intelligence | Speed | Endurance | Rank | Courage | Firepower | Skill |
|----------|--------------|-------|-----------|------|---------|-----------|-------|
| 8 | 5 | 3 | 8 | 5 | 9 | 9 | 5 |

MLC: **$48-60**, MIB: **$70-85**,
MISB: **$300-400+**

Ransack, robot mode.

Ransack, alternate mode.

Ransack, easily lost weapons and accessories.

Ransack's alternate mode is a locust and this fuels his thirst and single-minded obsession as a Decepticon warrior. His toy is very delicate (as are most of the Deluxe Insecticons), particularly because of his fragile antenna, his delicate wings, and smaller insect legs attached to his robot arms.

**ALTERNATE MODE:** Locust [*Acrdidae*].
**EASILY LOST WEAPONS AND PARTS:** Concussion blaster gun, reflector shield.

# VENOM

**DELUXE INSECTICONS**

**FUNCTION:** Psychological Warfare
**MOTTO:** "Friends are more dangerous than enemies."

"Will use his poisonous talents even on fellow Decepticons because he trusts no one and suspects everyone is trying to usurp his role as leader. His stinger can discharge fluids harmful to mechanical and organic life; corrosive acids, destructive catalysts, paralyzing toxins, and others. Stinger can penetrate 1/4 inch steel, but sometimes gets stuck and breaks off. Flies at 15 mph for 300 miles. Carries electro-blaster in robot form."

| Strength | Intelligence | Speed | Endurance | Rank | Courage | Firepower | Skill |
|----------|--------------|-------|-----------|------|---------|-----------|-------|
| 3 | 9 | 3 | 6 | 8 | 9 | 8 | 8 |

MLC: **$48-55**, MIB: **$70-85**, MISB: **$300-400**

Venom, robot mode.

Venom, easily lost weapons and accessories.

Venom, alternate mode.

If the Deluxe Insecticons were allowed incorporation into the Sunbow cartoon, then Venom would have been the leader of both Insecticon sub-groups. He is aloof and treacherous—aloof because of his imminent fear of blackmail by other Decepticons; treacherous because of what would happen to the offender if Venom let himself become a victim of their extortion. As a character, not the most effective leader, but a fascinating toy with excellent robot and insect modes.

**ALTERNATE MODE:** Insect [cicada (*Cicadidae*)].
**EASILY LOST WEAPONS AND ACCESSORIES:** Battle ax, electro-blaster gun.

Dirge, alternate mode.

## DIRGE

**JETS**

**FUNCTION:** Warrior
**MOTTO:** "Fear is the element that unites all losers."

"The sound of his engines causes petrifying fear in those who hear them. He's a master at handling fear…other Decepticons are put off by his mournful, silent ways. "He gives me the creeps," says Ramjet. He carries two concussion missiles. Needs to control a situation; otherwise, he too falls victim to fear, making him useless as a warrior."

| Strength | Intelligence | Speed | Endurance | Rank | Courage | Firepower | Skill |
|----------|--------------|-------|-----------|------|---------|-----------|-------|
| 7 | 8 | 8 | 6 | 5 | 4 | 8 | 9 |

**MLC: $38-45, MIB: $90-105, MISB: $300-400**

Dirge, robot mode.

Hasbro's six Transformer 'Seeker Jets' have their roots mired in Takara's Diaclone line (ca. 1983). Initially named "Jet Robo F-15 Eagle," the Seekers' core robot and alternate modes were created by Japanese designer Koujin Ohno. However, it was another toy engineer, Takayoshi Doi, that devised DIRGE's unusually long delta wings and concussion missiles—and it was these unusual accoutrements exhibited by the second generation of Seeker Jets that afforded each one the distinction of standing out among his brethren. Yet another major difference between the 1st and 2nd series of Seekers is that Dirge, Ramjet, and Thrust were often portrayed as 'coneheads' in the Transformers canon—with the nosecone of their jet modes pointed straight up to distinguish them from 1984's Skywarp, Starscream, and Thundercracker.

**ALTERNATE MODE:** McDonnel-Douglass F-15C Eagle [modified].
**EASILY LOST WEAPONS AND ACCESSORIES:** 2 wings, front landing gear, 2 concussion missiles, 2 fists.

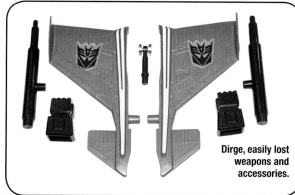

Dirge, easily lost weapons and accessories.

## RAMJET

**JETS**

**FUNCTION:** Warrior
**MOTTO:** "If it flies, crash it!"

"Mid-air collisions are his specialty. It makes little difference if the target is an opponent or not, he'll crash into it just for the fun of bringing terror to the skies. These crashes can take their toll on him, particularly doing damage to his internal mechanisms. 'The skies are my castle and I like to live alone,' he says. His nose module can withstand the impact of three-foot thick concrete at 1500 mph, and he flies as fast as Mach 2.8 while carrying cluster bombs."

| Strength | Intelligence | Speed | Endurance | Rank | Courage | Firepower | Skill |
|----------|--------------|-------|-----------|------|---------|-----------|-------|
| 8 | 5 | 9 | 9 | 5 | 8 | 7 | 6 |

**MLC: $54-62, MIB: $72-85, MISB: $350-450**

Ramjet's origin begins within Takara's Diaclone line (ca. 1983), where his alternate jet mode was designed by Koujin Ohno, while *another* toy engineer (Takayoshi Doi) created Ramjet's distinctive tail fins, unique cluster bombs, and his signature "cranked arrow delta" wings that appear to have been inspired by those of the F-16XL. These unusual accoutrements—along with his sleek, reinforced nosecone and fuselage—made the "cone-headed" Ramjet [see Dirge (1985)] a remarkably effective warrior.

**ALTERNATE MODE:** McDonnel-Douglass F-15C Eagle [modified].
**EASILY LOST WEAPONS AND ACCESSORIES:** 2 wings, 2 tail fins, front landing gear, 2 cluster bombs, 2 fists.

Thrust, alternate mode.

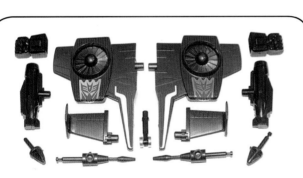

Thrust, robot mode.

## THRUST

**JETS**

**FUNCTION:** Warrior
**MOTTO:** "My engine's roar is my enemies' song of doom!"

"He rattles the air with the roar of his jets…believes half the battle is won if the opponent is 'psyched out' by his mere arrival, so he makes no attempt to be sneaky. Pompous, loud-mouthed braggart and not too brave. Sudden, powerful accelerations can topple nearby buildings. Flies at Mach 2.5, can double speed in 20 seconds for up to two minutes. Carries four air-to-air missiles and two automatic missile launchers in robot mode."

| Strength | Intelligence | Speed | Endurance | Rank | Courage | Firepower | Skill |
|----------|--------------|-------|-----------|------|---------|-----------|-------|
| 8 | 6 | 9 | 6 | 5 | 4 | 8 | 7 |

MLC: **$55-65**, MIB: **$125**, MISB: **$250-350**

The final of the three "coneheads" [see Dirge (1985)], Thrust possessed the most accessories of all the Decepticon Seeker Jets, and therefore is the most difficult to find MLC (Mint, Loose and Complete). His alternate mode is made exponentially more effective thanks to two VTOL (Vertical Take-Off and Landing) turbines incorporated inside his wings. These turbines allow Thrust to insert and extract himself from combat, and expertly complement his blazing [bursts of] speed.

**ALTERNATE MODE:** McDonnel-Douglass F-15C Eagle [modified].
**EASILY LOST WEAPONS AND ACCESSORIES:** 2 wings, 2 tail fins, front landing gear, 4 air-to-air missiles (2 different types), 2 missile launchers, 2 fists.

Thrust, easily lost weapons and accessories.

Ramjet, alternate mode.

Ramjet, easily lost weapons and accessories.

Ramjet, robot mode.

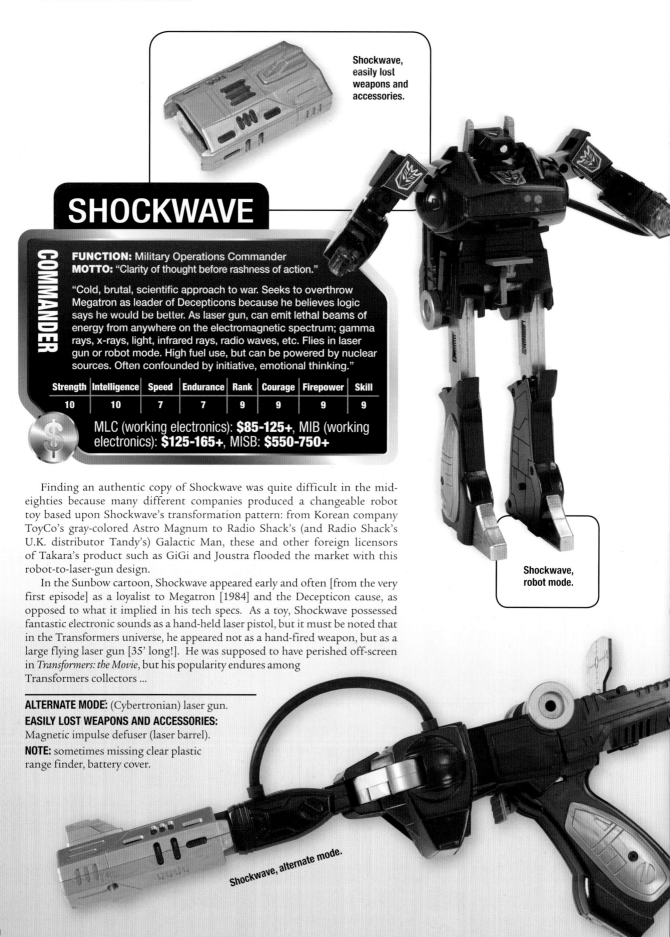

Shockwave,
easily lost
weapons and
accessories.

## SHOCKWAVE

**COMMANDER**

**FUNCTION:** Military Operations Commander
**MOTTO:** "Clarity of thought before rashness of action."

"Cold, brutal, scientific approach to war. Seeks to overthrow Megatron as leader of Decepticons because he believes logic says he would be better. As laser gun, can emit lethal beams of energy from anywhere on the electromagnetic spectrum; gamma rays, x-rays, light, infrared rays, radio waves, etc. Flies in laser gun or robot mode. High fuel use, but can be powered by nuclear sources. Often confounded by initiative, emotional thinking."

| Strength | Intelligence | Speed | Endurance | Rank | Courage | Firepower | Skill |
|----------|--------------|-------|-----------|------|---------|-----------|-------|
| 10 | 10 | 7 | 7 | 9 | 9 | 9 | 9 |

MLC (working electronics): **$85-125+**, MIB (working electronics): **$125-165+**, MISB: **$550-750+**

   Finding an authentic copy of Shockwave was quite difficult in the mid-eighties because many different companies produced a changeable robot toy based upon Shockwave's transformation pattern: from Korean company ToyCo's gray-colored Astro Magnum to Radio Shack's (and Radio Shack's U.K. distributor Tandy's) Galactic Man, these and other foreign licensors of Takara's product such as GiGi and Joustra flooded the market with this robot-to-laser-gun design.
   In the Sunbow cartoon, Shockwave appeared early and often [from the very first episode] as a loyalist to Megatron [1984] and the Decepticon cause, as opposed to what it implied in his tech specs. As a toy, Shockwave possessed fantastic electronic sounds as a hand-held laser pistol, but it must be noted that in the Transformers universe, he appeared not as a hand-fired weapon, but as a large flying laser gun [35' long!]. He was supposed to have perished off-screen in *Transformers: the Movie*, but his popularity endures among Transformers collectors ...

**ALTERNATE MODE:** (Cybertronian) laser gun.
**EASILY LOST WEAPONS AND ACCESSORIES:**
Magnetic impulse defuser (laser barrel).
**NOTE:** sometimes missing clear plastic range finder, battery cover.

Shockwave,
robot mode.

Shockwave, alternate mode.

# 1986

## SERIES ③

"It is the year 2005, the treacherous Decepticons have conquered the Autobots' home planet of Cybertron ... but, from secret staging grounds on two of Cyberton's moons, the valiant Autobots prepare to retake their homeland."

With these few words, the epic 1986 Sunbow film, *Transformers: The Movie*, ushered in a new era of heightened hostility in the aeons-long Autobot versus Decepticons conflict and introduced all-new iconic characters to the Hasbro toy line. Fans were treated to their beloved robots emblazoned on the big screen, and for the first time, many of their favorite Transformers perished during the animated struggle: Autobot and Decepticon alike. In order to "refresh" the ranks, so to speak, Hasbro and Sunbow (their animation studio) created some of the most memorable new Transformer characters and toys ever to grace retail pegs across America.

These new characters were not based on the current automotive and aeronautic designs of 1986, but were fashioned from imagined vehicle forms from the distant future or from the surface of the Transformers' home planet of Cybertron. Space-age race cars, pickup trucks, jet fighters, transports, and other vehicle and creature modes manifested themselves as the groundbreaking designs of the robots' "alternate modes," while the robots themselves smacked of a more colorful, more streamlined perspective—reflecting the anticipated fanciful tastes of the upcoming new millennium.

In the course of the film's narrative, the Autobots

embark on a galaxy-spanning quest to manipulate and wield the Autobot Matrix of Leadership—an artifact passed down from one Autobot leader to the next, holding the combined wisdom of commanders past and present throughout Cybertron's history. During the course of the film, the Matrix was passed on from then Autobot Commander Optimus Prime to Autobot (City) Commander Ultra Magnus, stolen by the new Decepticon (City) Commander Galvatron, and finally given to the youthful Autobot cavalier Hot Rod. When Hot Rod held the Matrix, he was transformed into the Autobots' new head honcho: Rodimus Prime. With the Matrix and its power in his possession, Rodimus opened the device and the Matrix's accumulated wisdom helped the Autobots finally defeat Unicron, the world-eater, as he was about to consume Cybertron. A fascinating story, with remarkable new toys from Hasbro as a result.

Besides the new characters from *Transformers: The Movie*, Series 3 (1986) of Generation One saw the introduction of "scramble city" combiners: the Aerialbots, Protectobots, Stunticons and Combaticons. Comprised of five members on each respective "team," these combiners were different in their designs from the Constructicons (1985) from one year earlier. The larger robot of the team (the leader or commander) always formed the head, chest, and torso of the super robot (whether the super robot is Superion, Defensor, Menasor, or Bruticus). An explanation of the term "scramble city" can be found under the Aerialbots (1986) listing.

[AUTOBOT]

# MINICARS

All new Minicars released in 1985 were re-released MOC with a free promotional iron-on patch included in the package. This does not raise the price of carded specimens (see Autobot Minicars, 1985). These iron-ons sell for $7-12 apiece depending upon the character.

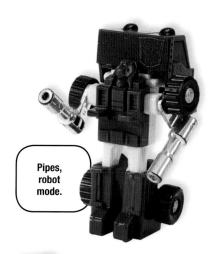

Pipes, robot mode.

## HUBCAP

**MINICARS**

**FUNCTION:** Communications
**MOTTO:** "Weapons can win battles, but words can win wars!"

"Has everybody's friendship, nobody's trust. Affable, witty, generous, and charming, but a true con artist. Living proof of the Cybertronian adage, 'You can't tell an Autobot by its finish.' Head module equipment receives AM and FM, radio shortwave, UHF and VHF television signals as weak as .000001 watts. Maximum speed of 90 mph, range of 1000 miles."

| Strength | Intelligence | Speed | Endurance | Rank | Courage | Firepower | Skill |
|---|---|---|---|---|---|---|---|
| 3 | 9 | 4 | 3 | 6 | 8 | 1 | 9 |

MLC: **$20-24**, MIP (opened): **$40-45**, MOC: **$75-150**

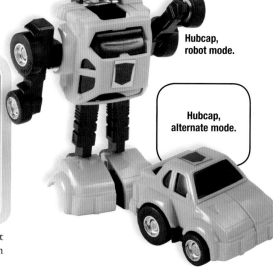

Hubcap, robot mode.

Hubcap, alternate mode.

Hubcap never appeared in the animated series, and even if he had, it appears that he would not have been the most popular of Autobots. His toy is a modified version of Cliffjumper's (1984) vehicle mode with a different head sculpt and no obvious spoiler. Make sure to differentiate between him and yellow versions of Cliffjumper and the very rare Bumper (1984).

**ALTERNATE MODE:** Porsche 944 Carrera GT, "superdeformed."
**EASILY LOST WEAPONS AND ACCESSORIES:** N/A.

## OUTBACK

**MINICARS**

**FUNCTION:** Gunner
**MOTTO:** "Rules are detours on the road of life."

"Thinks going by the book is going the long way. Doesn't follow plans—or roads! Cuts across parking lots, sidewalks, backyards to get where he's going. Travels at 110 mph, range 800 miles, his 4-wheel drive handles roughest terrain, climbs grades up to 50 degrees. Carries turret-mounted mortar cannon that shoots armor-piercing shells."

| Strength | Intelligence | Speed | Endurance | Rank | Courage | Firepower | Skill |
|---|---|---|---|---|---|---|---|
| 4 | 5 | 6 | 5 | 4 | 9 | 6 | 5 |

MLC: **$8-10**, MOC: **$55**

Outback's easily lost weapon.

Outback, alternate mode.

Outback, robot mode.

Outback's action figure is like most of the 1986 Autobot Minicars: modified versions of pre-existing molds and characters. His designs were based on Brawn (1984), and has new arms with actual fists, a new head sculpt, and as an added bonus, a roof-mounted recoilless rifle—making Outback the only Autobot Mini-vehicle to come with an accessory. And that removable weapon was enough to sell him at his price point.

**ALTERNATE MODE:** British Land Rover Defender 4x4 (aka. Land Rover Ninety, [or] Land Rover One Ten).
**EASILY LOST WEAPONS AND PARTS:** Recoilless rifle.

Pipes, alternate mode.

# PIGES

**MINICARS**

**FUNCTION:** Warrior
**MOTTO:** "One being's junk is another's art."

"Fascinated by seemingly worthless Earthen gadgetry—carrot juicers, musical wrist-watches, electrical hair combers, etc. Collects them in unused corner of Ark, creating a mini museum of American consumerism. Travels at 100 mph, range 400 miles, hauls up to 60 tons. Twin exhaust pipes emit corrosive gases that can dissolve (a) 2" thick steel slab in 10 minutes."

| Strength | Intelligence | Speed | Endurance | Rank | Courage | Firepower | Skill |
|---|---|---|---|---|---|---|---|
| 9 | 6 | 4 | 8 | 5 | 8 | 5 | 4 |

MLC: **$18-25**, MIP (opened): **$28-34**, MOC: **$100-200**

Swerve, robot mode.

Swerve, alternate mode.

Pipes' mold is a curious re-tooling of Huffer (1984), as the design of his transformation is completely different from his toy predecessor. The location of his face changed from the underside of his truck mode [as with Huffer], when transformed, Pipes' facial features exist on the top of his truck mode. An interesting-looking, appealing Mini-vehicle, Pipes' character owns a fabulous Tech Spec biography.

**ALTERNATE MODE:** Semi truck cab without trailer; [similar to an Ottawa 4x2 off-road terminal tractor], "superdeformed."

**EASILY LOST WEAPONS AND PARTS:** N/A.

# SWERVE

**MINICARS**

**FUNCTION:** Metallurgist
**MOTTO:** "Molecular structure is the window to understanding."

"If Autobots had driver's licenses, his would have been revoked. A menace on highways. Doesn't pay attention to where he's going or the orders he's being given—easily distracted by anything. Hands' sensors can determine physical and chemical properties of metals. Goes 120 mph, range 500 miles in car mode. Gets into lots of accidents."

| Strength | Intelligence | Speed | Endurance | Rank | Courage | Firepower | Skill |
|---|---|---|---|---|---|---|---|
| 6 | 8 | 5 | 8 | 5 | 6 | 1 | 7 |

MLC: **$7-12**, MIP (opened): **$24-28**, MOC: **$100-200**

# TAILGATE

**MINICARS**

**FUNCTION:** Scout
**MOTTO:** "Let my fellow mechanical beings go!"

"He sometimes has his mind stuck in low gear, believes 55 mph speed limit is infringement on rights of cars. Garages are prisons to him…doesn't understand Earth machines are not alive. Goes 180 mph, range 600 miles. Uses ferrocobalt magnet under hood to be pulled by and within a few feet of other vehicles, reducing his fuel use to near zero. Prone to overheating."

| Strength | Intelligence | Speed | Endurance | Rank | Courage | Firepower | Skill |
|---|---|---|---|---|---|---|---|
| 5 | 5 | 6 | 6 | 6 | 7 | 2 | 7 |

MLC: **$8-12**, MIP (opened): **$30-32**, MOC: **$75-150**

Swerve is one of the more obvious retoolings of the 1986 Minicars: he is a near-exact replica of Gears (1984), albeit with different colors and a new face sculpt. His Tech Spec is interesting, and he would have made an excellent character in Sunbow's animated series—so flawed and chock full of great personality.

**ALTERNATE MODE:** 4WD off road truck [model unknown], "superdeformed."

**EASILY LOST WEAPONS AND PARTS:** N/A.

Another reconstructed Minicar, Tailgate replicates Windcharger's (1984) toy mold with the exception of color and facial sculpt. Most collectors consider his Firebird mold an exceptional one among the Mini-vehicles; they should take care with samples of Tailgate: he is prone to yellowing due to his bright white body. As a character, Tailgate provided the Transformers franchise with one more trooper to swell the Autobot ranks.

**ALTERNATE MODE:** 3rd generation Pontiac Firebird Trans Am (ca. 1982-1992), "superdeformed."

**EASILY LOST WEAPONS AND PARTS:** N/A.

Tailgate, alternate mode.

Tailgate, robot mode.

Wheelie, alternate mode.

## WHEELIE

**MINICARS**

**FUNCTION:** Survivalist
**MOTTO:** "Only the fierce shall live."

"Wheelie is the sole survivor from a party of intergalactic colonists who crash landed on Earth. He's a barbaric little savage who managed to stay alive by cunning, stealth, and fearlessness. Speaks in odd rhyming sentences and despises the Decepticons. Fights only when he's under attack and has to defend himself. Staunch friend to the Dinobots and a reliable ally for Hot Rod and Kup."

| Strength | Intelligence | Speed | Endurance | Rank | Courage | Firepower | Skill |
|---|---|---|---|---|---|---|---|
| 5 | 6 | 8 | 9 | 5 | 9 | 7 | 8 |

**MLC: $8-12, MIP (opened): $32-38, MOC: $100-200**

Autobot Survivalist Wheelie was the only completely new Mini-vehicle sculpt solicited for 1986's third series of Mini-vehicles. Featured prominently in the spectacular *Transformers: The Movie*, debate continues to rage in collectible shops nationwide regarding whether the character is a necessary one due to his loss of re: the Transformers canon. In any case, Wheelie was designed to look stylistically similar to the Autobot Cars [Blurr, Hot Rod, Kup] and the Autobot Heroes [Rodimus Prime, Wreck-Gar] Hasbro released in 1986. Unfortunately, his tech spec has little to do with his characterization in the *Transformers* film.

**ALTERNATE MODE:** Quintessonian car.
**EASILY LOST WEAPONS AND PARTS:** N/A.

Wheelie, robot mode.

## BLURR

**CARS**

**FUNCTION:** Data Courier
**MOTTO:** "The faster it is, the better I like it."

"Blurr is the fastest Autobot on land. He's a close descendant to a thoroughbred Cybertronic race horse, and a superior messenger. He can quickly whisk information from one place to another. In robot mode, he carries an electro-laser that reverses the polarity of an enemy robot's microcircuits and leaves them motionless. Range: 10 miles. In vehicular mode, he can travel faster than the speed of sound, leaving a blurred image in his trail."

| Strength | Intelligence | Speed | Endurance | Rank | Courage | Firepower | Skill |
|---|---|---|---|---|---|---|---|
| 7 | 8 | 10 | 6 | 7 | 8 | 7 | 5 |

**MLC: $65-75, MIB: $75-100+, MISB: $300-400**

Appropriately voiced by Guinness Book of World Record holder John Moschitta (who holds the world record for fastest talker) in *Transformers: The Movie* and the Sunbow animated series, Blurr leaves a fading image in his trail, and is the perfect Autobot courier. According to his entry in the *Transformers: More Than Meets The Eye* (Dreamwave, 2003) guide books, Blurr's hyper-speed is a result of a design quirk and affects and influences his every waking moment. His only flaw: sometimes this ability drains his power reserves faster than he can replace the spent energy. Blurr is a popular figure on the secondary market, and loose toy collectors should note that the pegs that hold his shield/hood in place are often found broken.

**ALTERNATE MODE:** Cybertronian hovercar.
**EASILY LOST WEAPONS AND PARTS:** Hood/shield, electro-laser.

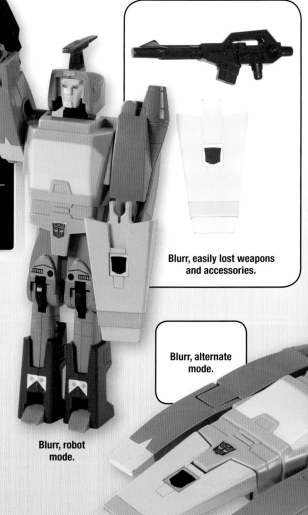

Blurr, easily lost weapons and accessories.

Blurr, alternate mode.

Blurr, robot mode.

[AUTOBOT]
# CARS

In some 1986 boxes, the below figures came with a "free glow-in-the-dark *Transformers: The Movie* poster" (if advertised) in packaged MIB or MISB samples, and you should add $15-25 to the end prices.

Hot Rod, easily lost weapons and accessories.

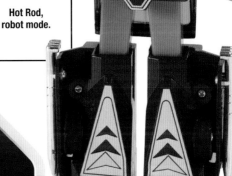

Hot Rod, robot mode.

## HOT ROD

**CARS**

**FUNCTION:** Cavalier
**MOTTO:** "My actions speak louder than words."

"Hot Rod is an all-American-boy Autobot. He's a typical adolescent who dreams of being heroic and important. He tends to follow rules too closely. Although he means well, Hot Rod's impulsive actions often get him into trouble. He carries two photon lasers that temporarily electromagnetize an enemy robot's microcircuits. Speed: 120 mph. Range: 4 miles. He can be hotheaded, but he's always a well-meaning, admirable lad and a brave and honorable fighter."

| Strength | Intelligence | Speed | Endurance | Rank | Courage | Firepower | Skill |
|----------|-------------|-------|-----------|------|---------|-----------|-------|
| 10 | 10 | 9 | 10 | 10 | 7 | 10 | 10 |

**$** (Metal or plastic toes, plastic or rubber tires)
MLC: **$45-55**, MIB: **$105-125**, MISB: **$350-450**

Hot Rod, metal versus plastic toes.

With his earliest toy designs provided by Floro Dery, Hot Rod is the chrysalis form of Rodimus Prime [1986]—the eventual successor to Optimus Prime [1984]. However, his tech spec scores we ludicrously inflated: Hot Rod's average ability score is 9.625 (most aficionados follow his Targetmaster [1987] statistics instead). As an action figure, Hot Rod possesses variations: early releases with rubber tires—later tires used plastic; early releases with metal toes—later toes used plastic. Voiced by Judd Nelson in *Transformers: The Movie*, Hot Rod displayed the impulsiveness found in his tech spec bio. This Autobot Cavalier's was quite popular with Transfans: he is a quick seller on the secondary market.

**ALTERNATE MODE:** Cybertronian racecar.
**EASILY LOST WEAPONS AND ACCESSORIES:**
Two (different) photon lasers.

Hot Rod, alternate mode.

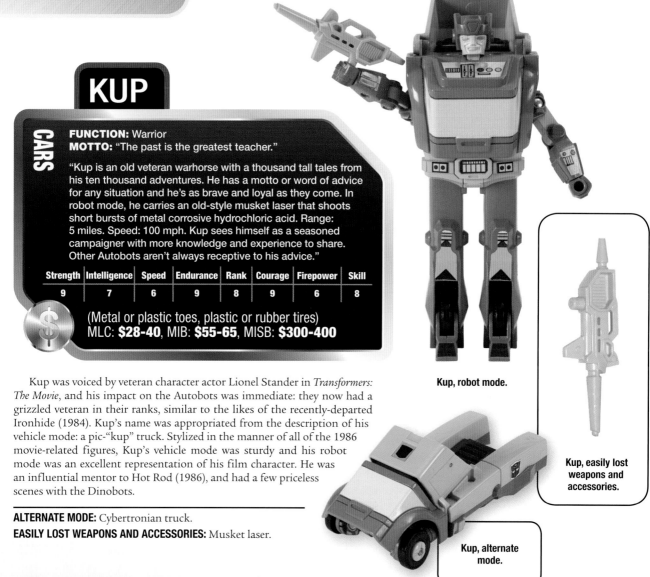

## KUP

**CARS**

**FUNCTION:** Warrior
**MOTTO:** "The past is the greatest teacher."

"Kup is an old veteran warhorse with a thousand tall tales from his ten thousand adventures. He has a motto or word of advice for any situation and he's as brave and loyal as they come. In robot mode, he carries an old-style musket laser that shoots short bursts of metal corrosive hydrochloric acid. Range: 5 miles. Speed: 100 mph. Kup sees himself as a seasoned campaigner with more knowledge and experience to share. Other Autobots aren't always receptive to his advice."

| Strength | Intelligence | Speed | Endurance | Rank | Courage | Firepower | Skill |
|---|---|---|---|---|---|---|---|
| 9 | 7 | 6 | 9 | 8 | 9 | 6 | 8 |

**$** (Metal or plastic toes, plastic or rubber tires)
MLC: **$28-40**, MIB: **$55-65**, MISB: **$300-400**

**Kup, robot mode.**

**Kup, easily lost weapons and accessories.**

**Kup, alternate mode.**

Kup was voiced by veteran character actor Lionel Stander in *Transformers: The Movie*, and his impact on the Autobots was immediate: they now had a grizzled veteran in their ranks, similar to the likes of the recently-departed Ironhide (1984). Kup's name was appropriated from the description of his vehicle mode: a pic-"kup" truck. Stylized in the manner of all of the 1986 movie-related figures, Kup's vehicle mode was sturdy and his robot mode was an excellent representation of his film character. He was an influential mentor to Hot Rod (1986), and had a few priceless scenes with the Dinobots.

**ALTERNATE MODE:** Cybertronian truck.
**EASILY LOST WEAPONS AND ACCESSORIES:** Musket laser.

# AERIALBOTS

The Aerialbots were one of the first "scramble city" combiner teams, a term gleaned from the idea pool of Japanese toy maker Takara. Utilizing a proposed Diaclone series called "Jizai Gattai" ("Free Combination") which was halted due to the success of the Transformers, this concept included all the five-member, interchangeable combiner teams that followed the original six-member Constructicons [1985], but which had a unique design where a team's smaller four members—the gestalt's limbs—were interchangeable.

These new combiner teams [e.g., the Aerialbots] consisted of one [centrally-located] larger team leader [Silverbolt], with four smaller subordinates [Air Raid, Fireflight, Skydive and Slingshot]. When combined in their super-robot mode [Superion], the team leader formed the head and chest, while the four smaller—interchangeable—robots existed as the super robot's limbs, arms or legs.

It should be noted that the Aerialbots do not have "attack modes"—where their robots' weapons and accessories can be mounted to their vehicle/alternate modes. It is assumed that the four smaller fighter planes already possess machine guns and missiles for offensive purposes; while their leader, Silverbolt, fires his electrostatic charge from his undercarriage for an attack. Finally, it is worth mentioning that the Aerialbots were available with either metal (early release) or plastic (later release) parts—since Hasbro was transitioning the removal of die-cast metal out of their toys.

**Fireflight, alternate mode.**

# AIR RAID

**AERIALBOTS**

**FUNCTION:** Warrior
**MOTTO:** "If you look first, you may not leap."

"Prefers streaking into a cluster of Decepticons to shooting at them from long range…says, 'that always sparks their wires a bit.' Tactically, most fearless Aerialbot…just wants to have fun. Flies at Mach 2.5, range 1500 miles. Carries air-to-air heat seeking missiles, uses torque rifle whose beam applies 80,000 psi of rotational force. With fellow Aerialbots forms 'Superion.'"

| Strength | Intelligence | Speed | Endurance | Rank | Courage | Firepower | Skill |
|----------|-------------|-------|-----------|------|---------|-----------|-------|
| 5 | 7 | 9 | 7 | 5 | 10 | 8 | 7 |

MLC (plastic): **$15-20**, (metal): **$20-24**,
MIP (opened): **$40-45+**, MOC: **$200-300**

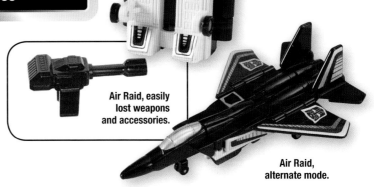
Air Raid, robot mode.

Air Raid is totally fearless and races into battle without hesitation—a tactic that seems to work for the sleek Aerialbot… yet his own reckless behavior may put him in harm's way; past a safe retreat strategy. As a one of the four smaller Aerialbots, Air Raid can form either an arm or leg of Superion.

**ALTERNATE MODE:** McDonnel-Douglass F-15C Eagle.
**EASILY LOST WEAPONS AND ACCESSORIES:** Torque rifle.

Air Raid, easily lost weapons and accessories.

Air Raid, alternate mode.

# FIREFLIGHT

**AERIALBOTS**

**FUNCTION:** Reconnaissance
**MOTTO:** "When I'm flying, no enemy is safe—nor friend."

"If Aerialbots needed pilot's licenses, he'd never have gotten his…a hazard in the skies. Doesn't pay attention to where he's going since he's too busy marveling at scenery. Flies at Mach 2.0, range 1000 miles. Carries flammable 'fire-fog' missiles, uses photon displacer gun that affects sight by distorting light waves. With fellow Aerialbots forms 'Superion.'"

| Strength | Intelligence | Speed | Endurance | Rank | Courage | Firepower | Skill |
|----------|-------------|-------|-----------|------|---------|-----------|-------|
| 7 | 5 | 8 | 8 | 6 | 9 | 7 | 3 |

MLC (plastic): **$15-20**, (metal): **$20-24**,
MIP (opened): **$40-45+**, MOC: **$150-250**

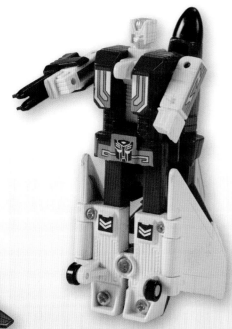
Fireflight, robot mode.

Fireflight, easily lost weapons and accessories.

Unfortunately, Fieflight is the Aerialbot's daydreamer, a hobby he likes to engage in while in mid flight. Therefore, he poses a flight risk to the other members of his Aerialbot team – as they were [nearly, see Jetfire (1985)] the very first Autobots who could fly under their own power.

**ALTERNATE MODE:** McDonnel-Douglass F-4E Phantom II.
**EASILY LOST WEAPONS AND ACCESSORIES:** Photon displacer gun.

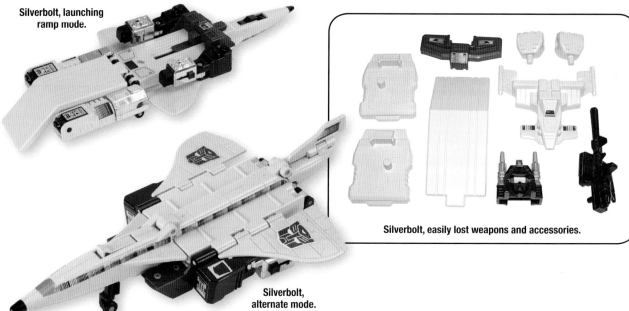

Silverbolt, launching ramp mode.

Silverbolt, alternate mode.

Silverbolt, easily lost weapons and accessories.

## SILVERBOLT

**AERIALBOTS**

**FUNCTION:** Aerialbot Leader
**MOTTO:** "Don't look down, look straight ahead."

"Scared of heights. Brave, grimly determined warrior, but he struggles to maintain that image in order to hide his phobia. Selected by Optimus Prime to command so he'd be too busy worrying about others to worry about himself. In jet mode, speed of Mach 1.9, range 4500 miles. Carries electrostatic battery that releases bolt of up to 150,000 volts through his nose cone. Uses electrostatic discharger rifle in robot mode. Combines with other Aerialbots to form 'Superion.'"

| Strength | Intelligence | Speed | Endurance | Rank | Courage | Firepower | Skill |
|----------|-------------|-------|-----------|------|---------|-----------|-------|
| 6 | 8 | 9 | 8 | 8 | 8 | 8 | 5 |

💲 MLC: **$38-48**, MIB: **$65-85+**, MISB: **$150-250**

Silverbolt, robot mode.

An excellent leader in spite [or perhaps, *because*] of his fear of flying: Silverbolt [named after the discharge of his electrostatic rifle] puts up a false front in order to counteract his debilitating aviophobia. As an alternate transformational mode, Silverbolt can construct a "launching ramp" from out of his airplane form where he may [imaginatively] 'hurl' other Aerialbots into flight. Unfortunately, although it appears Silverbolt did not come with a metal-plated variation, he was utilized as a component of Metroplex's 'super city' mode [re: Metroplex's Japanese Instruction Booklet <u>only</u>].

**ALTERNATE MODE:** Concorde Super Sonic Transport (SST).
**EASILY LOST WEAPONS AND ACCESSORIES:** Robot head (Superion), 2 (Superion) foot stands, electrostatic discharger rifle, 2 (Superion) fists, blast shield, ramp, blast deflector.

Slingshot, alternate mode.

# SKYDIVE

## AERIALBOTS

**FUNCTION:** Air War Strategist
**MOTTO:** "Only by studying the past can we win the present."

"Would rather read about jet fighters than be one…fascinated by the science of aerial warfare. Can, within the limits of his design, duplicate the flying motion of anything he sees… maybe the most skilled flyer of all Transformers. Flies at Mach 2.6, range 1400 miles. Carries laser guided missiles, uses nega-gun that crumbles objects by breaking molecular bonds. Prone to mid-air stalls. With fellow Aerialbots forms 'Superion.'"

| Strength | Intelligence | Speed | Endurance | Rank | Courage | Firepower | Skill |
|----------|--------------|-------|-----------|------|---------|-----------|-------|
| 4 | 10 | 9 | 4 | 7 | 7 | 8 | 10 |

$ MLC (plastic): **$18-24**, (metal): **$23-26**,
MIP (opened): **$48-55+**, MIB: **$200-300**

Skydive, robot mode.

Skydive, easily lost weapons and accessories.

Skydive, alternate mode.

Skydive is one of the most amazing fliers of all Transformers: He can imitate any aerial maneuver he has seen pending that this movement will not destroy his alternate mode due to stress fracturing. As a character, Skydive is a military historian and excellent war strategist who acts modest to the point of diffidence. Unfortunately, he is completely unaware of his value and importance to the integrity of the Aerialbot team. As an action figure, he is quite popular due to his alternate mode's striking "lightning bolt" stickers.

**ALTERNATE MODE:** General Dynamics F-16A Fighting Falcon.
**EASILY LOST WEAPONS AND ACCESSORIES:** Nega-gun.

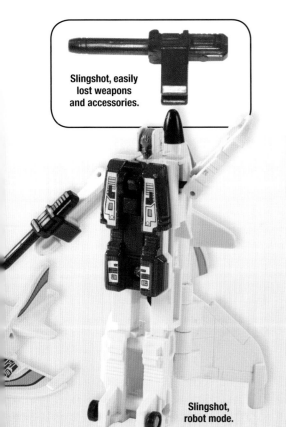

Slingshot, easily lost weapons and accessories.

Slingshot, robot mode.

# SLINGSHOT

## AERIALBOTS

**FUNCTION:** Ground Troop Support
**MOTTO:** "I'm even better than I think."

"He won't ever win a Mr. Popularity contest—incessant braggart, takes credit for exploits of other Autobots. Optimus Prime is supportive since he's hard-working and loyal, but he secretly lacks self-confidence. Vertical-take-off-and-landing aircraft, flies at Mach 1.6, range: 800 miles, extremely maneuverable. Sharpshooter—has twin mortar cannons as jet, neutron rifle as robot. With fellow Aerialbots forms 'Superion.'"

| Strength | Intelligence | Speed | Endurance | Rank | Courage | Firepower | Skill |
|----------|--------------|-------|-----------|------|---------|-----------|-------|
| 6 | 6 | 8 | 4 | 5 | 8 | 8 | 9 |

$ MLC (plastic): **$15-20**, (metal): **$20-24**, MIP (opened):
**$40-45+**, MOC: **$150-250**

Of the four smaller Aerialbots, we must appreciate Slingshot's VTOL capabilities: he can take off and land in places his other team members may find impossible [Silverbolt included], since he does not require a landing strip or field. While Slingshot's personality leaves many Autobots at odds with him since "…he] lacks self-confidence," and this flaw manifests as self-importance. As an action figure—like every Aerialbot—possesses usable landing gear (although his are non-retractable).

**ALTERNATE MODE:** Hawker-Siddeley Harrier GR.3 [VTOL: Vertical Take Off and Landing].
**EASILY LOST WEAPONS AND ACCESSORIES:** Neutron rifle.

Superion, combiner instructions.

# SUPERION

**AERIALBOTS**

**FUNCTION:** Air Warrior
**MOTTO:** "To live is to fight; to die is to stop."

"A fierce and frightful fighting machine. Suppresses thought of the five Aerialbots that comprise him, directs his thinking to one purpose: destruction of Decepticons. Cold, aloof. Flies at 800 mph, range 5800 miles. Can demolish a battleship with one blow. Uses electrostatic discharger rifle. Difficult for him to adapt to new situations or be innovative due to limited mental functions."

| Strength | Intelligence | Speed | Endurance | Rank | Courage | Firepower | Skill |
|----------|--------------|-------|-----------|------|---------|-----------|-------|
| 10 | 3 | 8 | 10 | 5 | 10 | 8 | 7 |

**$ Superion Gift Set (all 5 Aerialbots together)**
MLC: **$95-115**, MIB: **$175-205**, MISB: **$500-700**

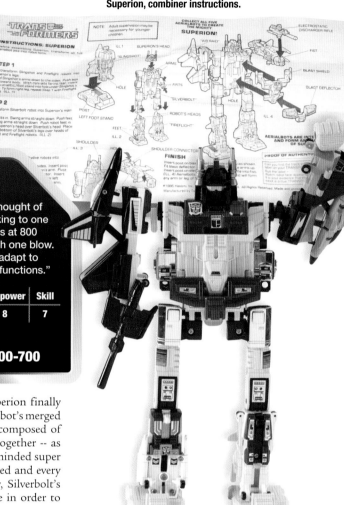

Designed by Koujin Ohno and Kaoru Matsumoto, Superion finally added air power to the grounded Autobot ranks. As the Aerialbot's merged form, Superion is an effective soldier, possessing a mind composed of the team's five disparate personalities that function well together -- as long as their purpose is made clear. Regardless, this single-minded super robot will not cease to fight until all innocents are protected and every Decepticon is destroyed. It should be noted that as a toy, Silverbolt's [1986] legs should be in alternate "launching ramp" mode in order to make Superion stand better.

Superion, robot mode.

# PROTECTOBOTS

The idea of four small rescue vehicles [and one powder-blue fire engine] who transformed into relatively awkward-looking robots may not have appealed to many children in 1986, but on the current secondary market the Protectobots have received their due. Since the other three combiner teams of 1986 were in greater demand (the Aerialbots, Combaticons and Stunticons) due to their more appealing aesthetics, the Protectobots were the easiest combiner team to find at retail in 1986-1987: they were far simpler to complete as a team. However, as time passed, many aficionados grew to love them, their peculiar robot modes, Defensor's powerful projected force field, and Hot Spot's twin fireball cannons— and as such, their gift set and MISB prices reflect the Protectobots' latter-day popularity.

Protectobots in attack mode.

# BLADES

**PROTECTOBOTS**

**FUNCTION:** Air Support
**MOTTO:** "War's a dirty game—and I'm a dirty player!"

"Basically a street fighter—prefers using rotor blades for slashing Decepticons rather than for flying. Considers long-range air attacks unsporting, cowardly. Maximum speed: 400 mph; range 1200 miles. Twin launchers fire 'smart' rockets that seek targets based on encoded computer images. Uses photon pistol. Combines with fellow Protectobots to form 'Defensor.'"

| Strength | Intelligence | Speed | Endurance | Rank | Courage | Firepower | Skill |
|---|---|---|---|---|---|---|---|
| 7 | 6 | 7 | 6 | 5 | 9 | 7 | 7 |

MLC (plastic): **$18-23**, (metal): **$24-28**,
MIP (opened): **$48-55+**, MOC: **$200-300**

Blades, robot mode.

Blades, easily lost weapons and accessories.

It must have been quite difficult for the aggressive Blades to team up with a pacifist [Groove] and an empathic doctor [First Aid]. If only his rotor blades could be removed from his roof and used as weapons—like Combaticon Vortex [1986]. As a smaller combiner released in '86, Blades came with or without a metal chest plate.

Blades, alternate mode.

**ALTERNATE MODE:** Civilian Bell 212 Twin Huey helicopter (aka. Twin Two-Twelve).

**EASILY LOST WEAPONS AND ACCESSORIES:** Photon pistol, twin ("smart rocket") launchers.

# STREETWISE

**PROTECTOBOTS**

**FUNCTION:** Interceptor
**MOTTO:** "You have to know where you are before you know what to do."

"Nothing escapes his notice…amazing capacity to adapt to understand his environment. Clever and determined—nothing deters him from seeking his prey—except an empty fuel tank. As car, has powerful double-mounted air-compressor cannon with 50 mile range; as robot uses blinding photon pistol. With fellow Protectobots forms 'Defensor.' Sometimes overheats as car."

| Strength | Intelligence | Speed | Endurance | Rank | Courage | Firepower | Skill |
|---|---|---|---|---|---|---|---|
| 5 | 9 | 6 | 6 | 4 | 9 | 7 | 7 |

MLC (plastic): **$18-23**, (metal): **$24-28**,
MIP (opened): **$48-55+**, MOC: **$150-250**

Streetwise, alternate mode.

Streetwise, easily lost weapons and accessories.

Streetwise, robot mode.

Early releases of Streetwise's action figure sport a metal torso piece while later released torsos are made of plastic. Similar to his fellow Protectobot First Aid, Streetwise sports a roof cannon that is mounted to his rear fender via a small connector. It is worth noting that Streetwise's connector piece is distinctly different from First Aid's.

**ALTERNATE MODE:** 1983 Nissan 300ZX Turbo police car.
**EASILY LOST WEAPONS AND ACCESSORIES:** Photon pistol, double-mounted air compressor cannon, connector.

First Aid, easily lost weapons and accessories.

# FIRST AID

**PROTECTOBOTS**

**FUNCTION:** Doctor
**MOTTO:** "An ounce of maintenance is worth a pound of cure."

"Hates seeing any machine in pain—even those who don't know it, like a broken street lamp or an overheated car. Compassionate, cautious—will restrict an Autobot to repair bay for faulty directional signal. Carries dual-barreled decrystallizer cannon—weakens metal by disrupting crystalline structure—and photon pistol. Fists shoot laser beams used for welding in surgery. With fellow Protectobots, combines to form 'Defensor.'"

| Strength | Intelligence | Speed | Endurance | Rank | Courage | Firepower | Skill |
|---|---|---|---|---|---|---|---|
| 4 | 9 | 4 | 6 | 6 | 7 | 6 | 9 |

💲 MLC: **$18-23**, (metal): **$24-28**,
MIP (opened): **$48-55+**, MOC: **$150-200**

First Aid, robot mode.

Every [smaller] member of the Protectobots wields a photon pistol as his hand-held accessory, while each of them also possess either a plastic chest (early release [early 1986]) or metal chest (later release [late 1986/1987]). For kids and collector who couldn't find (or afford) Autobot Ratchet [1984] First Aid made an inexpensive alternative.

**ALTERNATE MODE:** Toyota MasterAce Surf Ambulance.
**EASILY LOST WEAPONS AND ACCESSORIES:** Photon pistol, dual-barreled decrystallizer, connector.

First Aid, alternate mode.

# GROOVE

**PROTECTOBOTS**

**FUNCTION:** Scout
**MOTTO:** "War is a problem, never a solution."

"A full tank, clear skies, open road—that's all he wants out of life. Relaxed, easy going, happy wherever he is. Pacifist—difficult for him to accept his role as part of the Protectobot team. Speed: 140 mph, range: 800 miles. Uses twin vaporators, which shoot mists of oxidizing, freezing, and corrosive liquids; and photon pistol. Combines with fellow Protectobots to form 'Defensor.'"

| Strength | Intelligence | Speed | Endurance | Rank | Courage | Firepower | Skill |
|---|---|---|---|---|---|---|---|
| 4 | 9 | 5 | 7 | 6 | 8 | 6 | 8 |

💲 MLC (plastic): **$20-28+**, (metal): **$24-32+**,
MIP (opened): **$48-55+**, MOC: **$100-200**

Groove, robot mode.

Groove, alternate mode.

In combiner mode, Groove comprises an aesthetically-pleasing limb for Defensor—particularly if functioning as the gestalt's arm. Groove is one of the more popular Protectobot acquisitions on the secondary market, while his robot mode's gold chest comes in metal or plastic variations.

**ALTERNATE MODE:** Harley-Davidson FLH Electra Glide 1340 motorcycle (w/1983 Honda Goldwing front fairing).
**EASILY LOST WEAPONS AND ACCESSORIES:** Twin vaporators, photon pistol.

Groove, easily lost weapons and accessories.

Hot Spot, repair bay mode.

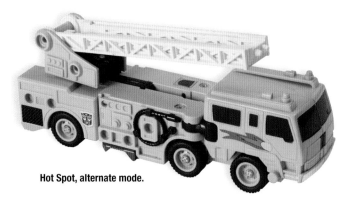

Hot Spot, alternate mode.

# HOT SPOT

**FUNCTION:** Protectobot Leader
**MOTTO:** "Rust never sleeps, and neither do I."

"Likes to be where the action is. Charismatic, inspiring…other Protectobots have trouble keeping up with his non-stop pace. Believes in being maximally operational every moment of one's life. His fire truck hose shoots high-pressure water 1200 feet. As robot, can press 60,000 pounds, uses fireball cannons that shoot bursts of 2000°F blue flame 1.5 miles. With fellow Protectobots, forms 'Defensor.'"

| Strength | Intelligence | Speed | Endurance | Rank | Courage | Firepower | Skill |
|----------|--------------|-------|-----------|------|---------|-----------|-------|
| 9 | 7 | 4 | 9 | 7 | 9 | 7 | 6 |

💲 MLC: **$42-54**, MIB: **$70-82**, MISB: **$200-300**

Hot Spot is a sturdy robot and as impressive fire engine, with an early version of the toy sporting a die-cast metal chest piece; later releases of his chest piece switched to plastic. Hot Spot changed other various modes, as he became 1) the chest and head of Defensor, 2) an 'emergency car carrier' mode to transport smaller Protectobots, 3) a 'repair bay mode' with two mechanical arms, and 4) a component of Metroplex's 'super city mode' [re: Metroplex's Japanese Instruction Booklet <u>only</u>].

**ALTERNATE MODE:** 1983 Mistubishi Fuso The Great (FU) 6x2 fire engine.
**EASILY LOST WEAPONS AND ACCESSORIES:** 2 fireball cannons, hip shield, 2 [Defensor] feet, 2 [Defensor] fists, 2 blast shields, 2 mechanical arms [comprised of 4 pieces total].

Hot Spot, robot mode.

Hot Spot, Emergency Car Carrier Mode.

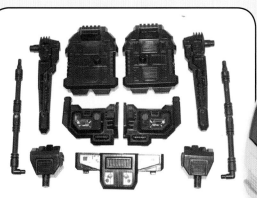

Hot Spot, easily lost weapons and accessories.

Defensor, combiner instructions.

## DEFENSOR

**PROTECTOBOTS**

**FUNCTION:** Super Warrior
**MOTTO:** "As long as one innocent being is threatened, none are truly free."

"Views humans as if they were his own children—will expend his last drop of fuel to protect them. Seeks human friendship, but humans fear his hulking, mechanical form. Can lift 300,000 pounds with one hand. Impervious to most artillery, can surround himself with force field for brief periods. Carries fireball cannon…shoots 2000° bursts of blue fire 1.5 miles."

| Strength | Intelligence | Speed | Endurance | Rank | Courage | Firepower | Skill |
|----------|--------------|-------|-----------|------|---------|-----------|-------|
| 10 | 7 | 2 | 9 | 6 | 10 | 8 | 8 |

💲 Defensor Gift Set (all 5 Protectobots together)
MLC: **$120-135**, MIB: **$175-215**, MISB: **$450+**

As a gestalt, Defensor is an fascinating super robot whose head is not a separate accessory: it flips up as part of Hot Spot's ladder mechanism. With his light blue Hot Spot body and white and red emergency vehicles as limbs, he makes an impressive and [fairly] sturdy robot. Take care to note the condition of the stickers from his component parts, as they are usually found with wear in loose samples.

Defensor, robot mode.

## [AUTOBOT]
# CASSETTES

In 1986, Blaster [1985] finally received micro-cassettes to add to his playability. It appeared that Hasbro somewhat modeled these new cassettes after the original Decepticon cassette offerings: humanoids Rumble [1984] and Frenzy [1984], plus animalistic Ravage [1984] and Laserbeak [1984]. The Autobots followed suit with two humanoid-looking robots, Eject and Rewind, and two animal-themed Transformers: Steeljaw and Ramhorn. Although these toys were solicited at a lower price point alternative when compared to larger Transformers, their articulation and accessories did not disappoint: they are sought after on the secondary market. Furthermore, the earliest versions of these cassettes came with "gold-plated" accessories that are challenging to find; a more expensive alternative to their common, silver-plated guns and missile launchers.

Ramhorn, robot mode.

# EJECT

**CASSETTES**

**FUNCTION:** Electronic Surveillance
**MOTTO:** "Clutch hitting is the key to an effective offense."

"An Earthen sports fanatic…sports clichés clutter his conversation; a surprise attack is a 'fast break,' a victory is a 'touchdown.' Few Autobots understand but they like the enthusiasm with which he says it. Could be a play-by-play announcer, if given the chance. In cassette mode, can monitor and record local radio and TV, decode scrambled signals, tap telephones. In robot mode, uses electrical overload guns. Sometimes his internal tape snaps when he's excited."

| Strength | Intelligence | Speed | Endurance | Rank | Courage | Firepower | Skill |
|----------|--------------|-------|-----------|------|---------|-----------|-------|
| 6 | 6 | 2 | 6 | 6 | 8 | 5 | 8 |

[Gold weapons] MLC: **$24-28**, MIP (opened; 2 pack w/Ramhorn): **$50-60**, MOSC: **$200-300**; [Silver weapons] MLC: **$18-22**, MIP (opened; 2 pack w/ Ramhorn): **$42-48**, MOSC: **$150-200**
NOTE: MOC examples are a two-pack containing Eject and Ramhorn.

Eject, robot mode.

Eject, easily lost weapons and accessories.

◀ Eject, alternate mode.

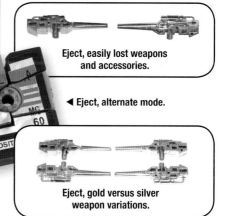

Eject, gold versus silver weapon variations.

Rarely obtaining the same airtime as the Decepticon cassettes, the Autobot Eject was relegated to a few select appearances in 1986, as most cartoon and comic episodes focused on the larger combiner teams and movie-related offerings. If you're interested in seeing these cassette-type characters in animated form, check out episode #78 of the Sunbow animated series titled "Madman's Paradise." Eject was available at retail with Ramhorn (1986) in a cassette two-pack.

**ALTERNATE MODE:** Olympus Type IV "Metal" MC60 Microcassette.

**EASILY LOST WEAPONS AND ACCESSORIES:** 2 thruster guns.

Ramhorn, easily lost weapons and accessories.

Ramhorn, gold versus silver weapon variations.

◀ Ramhorn, alternate mode.

# RAMHORN

**CASSETTES**

**FUNCTION:** Warrior
**MOTTO:** "Flee before me or else you'll fall before me."

"Don't touch him if you value your life, 'cause he'll smash you. Extremely territorial, nasty hair-trigger temper. Best way to deal with him is from a distance. His charge is virtually unstoppable—can knock a train off its tracks or upend an 18-wheeler with one blow. Has two batteries of three laser-guided, heat-seeking missiles that can lock in and hit a target up to twelve miles away. As cassette, can vibrate and destroy any equipment into which he is inserted."

| Strength | Intelligence | Speed | Endurance | Rank | Courage | Firepower | Skill |
|----------|--------------|-------|-----------|------|---------|-----------|-------|
| 8 | 4 | 3 | 9 | 5 | 9 | 3 | 4 |

[Gold weapons] MLC: **$24-28**, MIP (opened; 2 pack w/ Eject): **$54-62**, MOSC: **$200-300**; [Silver weapons] MLC: **$20-24**, MIP (opened; 2 pack w. Eject): **$45-52**, MOSC: **$150-250**
NOTE: MOC examples are a two-pack containing Eject and Ramhorn.

An interesting tech spec, it appears that Ramhorn exhibits social problems: he is irrational, territorial and impulsive. His offensive capabilities [destroying equipment] may manifest themselves out of his adversarial personality, as he is able to effectively resonate and destruct any machinery that he is placed inside. Ramhorn was originally sold with Eject [1986] in a two-pack.

**ALTERNATE MODE:** Olympus Type IV "Metal" MC60 Microcassette.
**EASILY LOST WEAPONS AND ACCESSORIES:** 2 heat-seeking missile batteries.

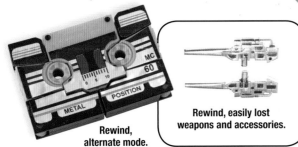

Rewind, robot mode.

# REWIND

**CASSETTES**

**FUNCTION:** Archivist
**MOTTO:** "Too much information is never enough."

"Autobot trivia expert—his memory banks have amazing capacity to store data that is virtually of no use to anyone. Not much help when asked about something important. Internal light-matrix data store system has nearly infinite data storage capacity. Can turn into blinding beacon by releasing some of this light energy. Uses adhesion rifles that shoot unbreakable metal-bonding glue. Prone to severe cerebro-circuit overloads, what Earthlings call 'headaches.'"

| Strength | Intelligence | Speed | Endurance | Rank | Courage | Firepower | Skill |
|---|---|---|---|---|---|---|---|
| 4 | 9 | 2 | 7 | 6 | 7 | 4 | 8 |

[Gold weapons] MLC: **$24-28**, MIP (opened; 2 pack w/Steeljaw): **$50-60**, MOSC: **$200-300**; [silver weapons] MLC: **$18-22**, MIP (opened; 2 pack w/Steeljaw): **$42-48**, MOSC: **$150-200**
NOTE: MOC examples are a two-pack containing Rewind and Steeljaw.

Rewind, alternate mode.

Rewind, easily lost weapons and accessories.

Rewind shared the exact same mold as Eject (1986), with distinct color differences: Rewind was cast in black and gray, while Eject was molded in blue and gray. Rewind was solicited with Steeljaw (1986) in a cassette two-pack. Early versions of this figure and Eject came with gold-plated weapons that are much more difficult to obtain on the secondary market.

**ALTERNATE MODE:** Olympus Type IV "Metal" MC60 Microcassette.
**EASILY LOST WEAPONS AND ACCESSORIES:** 2 thruster guns.

# STEELJAW

**CASSETTES**

**FUNCTION:** Tracker
**MOTTO:** "What the eyes don't see, the nose knows."

"When he's on the hunt, his prey is as good as caught. Determined, tenacious, cooly professional when on a mission. Likely to trace any scent. Range of 800 miles. Super-strong jaws—can snap a foot thick steel cable with one bite. Carries two solar-powered pellet guns that fire 1200 rounds per minute. Lack of sunlight hampers the guns' performance. Can electromagnetize himself in cassette mode. Prone to rusting."

| Strength | Intelligence | Speed | Endurance | Rank | Courage | Firepower | Skill |
|---|---|---|---|---|---|---|---|
| 8 | 8 | 2 | 9 | 6 | 9 | 1 | 9 |

[Gold weapons] MLC: **$24-28**, MIP (opened; 2 pack w/Rewind): **$54-62**, MOSC: **$200-300**; [silver weapons] MLC: **$15-20**, MIP (opened; 2 pack w/Rewind): **$45-52**, MOSC: **$150-250**
NOTE: MOC examples are a two-pack containing Rewind and Steeljaw.

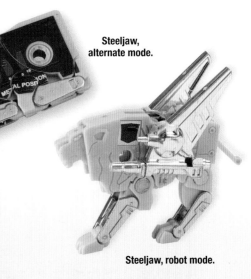

Steeljaw, alternate mode.

Steeljaw, robot mode.

Steeljaw, easily lost weapons and accessories.

Steeljaw, gold versus silver weapon variations.

Of the initial four Autobot Cassettes, Steeljaw is popular with collectors due to his excellent robot mode: a sleek yellow lion. His instructions state that his two weapons are missiles, but his tech spec biography lists them as "solar powered pellet guns." On occasion, loose Steeljaws will be found with gold-chromed accessories, and these are a bit rarer than silver plated versions. Take care when purchasing loose samples to make sure his stickers are in good condition, as they are very delicate—and easily wear off the cassette.

**ALTERNATE MODE:** Olympus Type IV "Metal" MC60 Microcassette.
**EASILY LOST WEAPONS AND ACCESSORIES:** 2 solar-powered pellet guns/missiles (according to instructions).

# BROADSIDE

**FUNCTION:** Air and Sea Assault
**MOTTO:** "I like the sea far away and my feet on the ground."

"Doesn't like transforming into carrier or jet—gets seasick on water, has fear of heights. Effective, valiant warrior, but other Autobots wish he wouldn't gripe so much. Expands to 1200 ft. length as carrier, capable of landing jets and carrying other Autobots. 15,000 mile range, 40 knots maximum speed. Projects 80,000 volt electric field around himself in jet mode. Has high-energy plasma-pulse gun and shattering vibro-ax in robot mode."

| Strength | Intelligence | Speed | Endurance | Rank | Courage | Firepower | Skill |
|----------|--------------|-------|-----------|------|---------|-----------|-------|
| 8 | 8 | 9 | 8 | 6 | 9 | 7 | 7 |

MLC: **$62-80**, MIB: **$110-125**, MISB: **$450-550**

In the Sunbow cartoon Broadside simply stayed large (big enough to fight Devastator [1985]), but his true robot mode is average-sized. To find out how Broadside can transform into his super-huge aircraft carrier mode, please see Astrotrain's (1985) description regarding size/mass change. Although a bit boxy as a robot, he remains a Triple Changer, and sells well on the secondary market.

**ALTERNATE MODE:** Nimitz-Class Supercarrier [aircraft carrier], jet fighter.
**EASILY LOST WEAPONS AND ACCESSORIES:** Plasma-pulse gun, 2 missiles, vibro-axe.

Broadside,
robot mode.

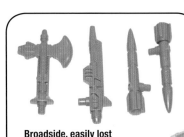

Broadside, easily lost
weapons and accessories.

Broadside, jet mode.

Broadside, aircraft
carrier mode.

## [AUTOBOT]
# TRIPLE CHANGERS

To counterbalance Shockwave's creation of the Decepticon Triple Changers (1985), the Autobot's ranks received Broadside, Sandstorm, and Springer. Although the first two of these were not featured very often in the Sunbow cartoon or Marvel comic book, Springer was a major player in *Transformers: The Movie*.

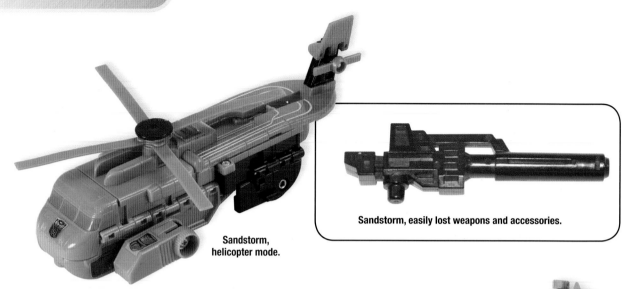

Sandstorm, helicopter mode.

Sandstorm, easily lost weapons and accessories.

## SANDSTORM

Sandstorm, robot mode.

**TRIPLE CHANGERS**

**FUNCTION:** Reconnaissance
**MOTTO:** "When the smoke clears, I've cleared out."

"Always takes death-defying risks. Anything less than dangerous is boring to him. In battle, gets close enough to count the bolts in Decepticon armor plates. As helicopter and buggy, he's adept at using rotors and exhaust to whip up blinding clouds of dust and sand. Extremely maneuverable. Carries sandblaster gun that shoots streams of silicate particles that can erode anything."

| Strength | Intelligence | Speed | Endurance | Rank | Courage | Firepower | Skill |
|----------|--------------|-------|-----------|------|---------|-----------|-------|
| 7 | 9 | 6 | 7 | 6 | 10 | 6 | 9 |

MLC: **$48-55**, MIB: **$85-105**, MISB: **$250-350+**

Sandstorm had a few notable appearances in both the Sunbow cartoon and the modern Dreamwave comics, where he perished escorting Optimus Prime (1984) to a group of Autobot Rebels, but his character's potential remains largely untapped. He is an interesting Triple Changer, as his alternate modes are completely different from one another: a dune buggy and helicopter—it was a singularly difficult task considering Hasbro had to hide two very long rotor blades. Sandstorm is one of the more popular Triple Changers because of his colors and authentic-looking alternate modes.

**ALTERNATE MODE:** Dune buggy, Sikorsky SH-3 Sea King helicopter.
**EASILY LOST WEAPONS AND ACCESSORIES:** Sandblaster gun.

Sandstorm, dune buggy mode.

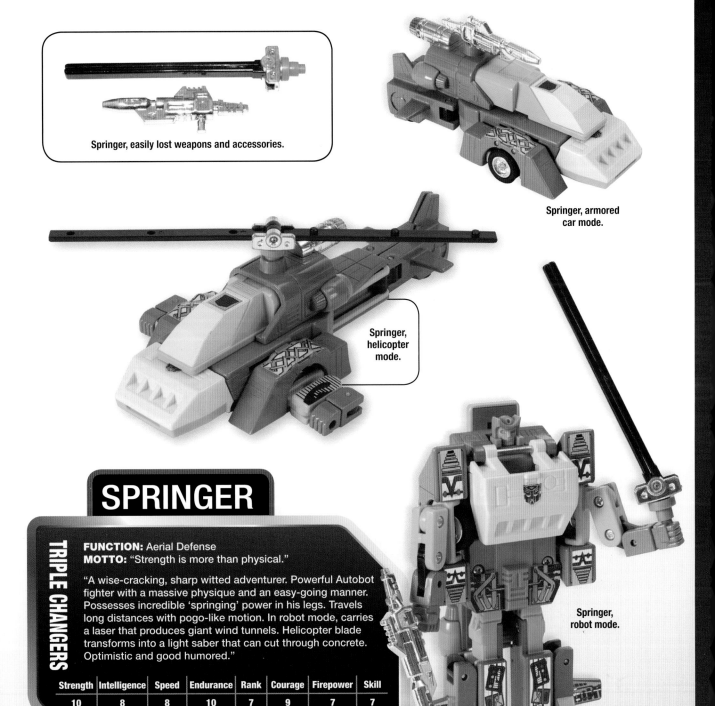

Springer, easily lost weapons and accessories.

Springer, armored car mode.

Springer, helicopter mode.

Springer, robot mode.

# SPRINGER

**TRIPLE CHANGERS**

**FUNCTION:** Aerial Defense
**MOTTO:** "Strength is more than physical."

"A wise-cracking, sharp witted adventurer. Powerful Autobot fighter with a massive physique and an easy-going manner. Possesses incredible 'springing' power in his legs. Travels long distances with pogo-like motion. In robot mode, carries a laser that produces giant wind tunnels. Helicopter blade transforms into a light saber that can cut through concrete. Optimistic and good humored."

| Strength | Intelligence | Speed | Endurance | Rank | Courage | Firepower | Skill |
|---|---|---|---|---|---|---|---|
| 10 | 8 | 8 | 10 | 7 | 9 | 7 | 7 |

MLC: **$50-65**, MIB: **$75-95**, MISB: **$350-450**

Springer is a popular character on the secondary market because of the prominent role he plays in *Transformers: The Movie*—this information combined with the fact that he converts from burly robot to fierce armored car to a wicked helicopter truly helps his cause. As a character, he was incredibly strong and tough, and his tech spec ability scores rival most Autobot Team Leaders. He is quite hard-to-find in mint condition on the secondary market, where chrome and sticker wear plays a large part in his asking price. (There

is another mode indicated in his Instruction Booklet that is worth noting: to form an "Attack Car," simply mount his laser into the hole where his blades mount—yet the laser doesn't fit in this wide space [!].)

**ALTERNATE MODE:** Attack car, armored car, helicopter.
**EASILY LOST WEAPONS AND ACCESSORIES:** Light saber (helicopter blades), laser.

Rodimus Prime, robot mode [left] with mobile defense bay [right].

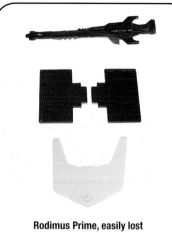

Rodimus Prime, easily lost weapons and accessories.

Rodimus Prime, alternate mode.

# RODIMUS PRIME

HEROES

**FUNCTION:** Protector
**MOTTO:** "Experience is the benchmark of maturity."

"A vanguard for the Autobot ranks. Possesses acute military prowess. Speaks with the savvy of seasoned veteran. Expert tactician with exceptional maneuverability in battle. Can be hot-headed at times. Has a tendency to act first and ask questions later. In robot mode, carries a photon eliminator that shoots high voltage electricity. Range: 500 miles. Speed: 200 mph. Sole purpose is to protect all life. His only weakness is his compassion for other living creatures."

| Strength | Intelligence | Speed | Endurance | Rank | Courage | Firepower | Skill |
|----------|--------------|-------|-----------|------|---------|-----------|-------|
| 10 | 10 | 9 | 10 | 10 | 10 | 9 | 10 |

$ (Metal or plastic toes) MLC: **$50-65**, MIB: **$85-135+**, MISB: **$400-600**

Rodimus Prime was the leader of the Autobots after the death (and before the return) of Optimus Prime, and is the more mature form of the impetuous Autobot Hot Rod (1986), as influenced by the Autobot Matrix of Leadership. The two similar-looking characters (Hot Rod and Rodimus Prime) can be distinguished from one another because of the amount of lines in Rodimus Prime's face, and his slightly taller height. It should also be noted that Rodimus' cab transforms into a "mobile defense bay," similar to Optimus Prime's (1984) trailer cab transforming into "combat deck" mode. Rodimus' Tech Spec ability scores reflect those of an Autobot leader.

**ALTERNATE MODE:** Futuristic (Cybertronian) vehicle.

**EASILY LOST WEAPONS AND ACCESSORIES:** Yellow wing, photon eliminator, 2 blast shields.

Rodimus Prime, mounted on mobile defense bay.

[AUTOBOT]
# HEROES

As a quick note, when the following two Autobot Heroes were packaged with a "free glow-in-the-dark *Transformers: The Movie* poster," add $15-25 to the MIB or MISB prices. Not all samples had this poster.

## WRECK-GAR

**HEROES**

**FUNCTION:** Junkion Leader
**MOTTO:** "Collect and save, collect and save."

"Wreck-Gar leads the Junkions, a race of junk robots. He's made of rusted scraps, chassis bits, manifold parts, and dented odds and ends. A little scatterbrained, he speaks in odd-rhyming, pieced-together sentences. His words are a junkyard collection of broadcast fragments from T.V. commercials and radio jingles. In robot mode, he carries an armor axe and a decelerator laser that inhibits an enemy robot's flow of cerebral impulses."

| Strength | Intelligence | Speed | Endurance | Rank | Courage | Firepower | Skill |
|---|---|---|---|---|---|---|---|
| 8 | 7 | 6 | 10 | 7 | 9 | 7 | 7 |

MLC: **$42-55+**, MIB: **$140-165**, MISB: **$500-700**

The gaggle of scrap-built beings known as the Junkions were fan-favorites in *Transformers: The Movie*. Combine this with fact that their leader, Wreck-Gar, was voiced by the inimitable Eric Idle—the character's quirky personality furthered fans' adoration: the Junkion Leader figure was a resounding triumph. Although in 1986, Transfans wished for a generic Junkion solider toy to complement Wreck-Gar's action figure (or as a troop-builder), they did not get one until Hasbro produced him in deluxe form decades later: 2011's Junkion named "Junkheap." However, when discussing Wreck-Gar, in 1986 Hasbro's concern re: the method for translating a character from the animation into a three-dimensional toy was often challenging—relative to other Transformers, Wreck-Gar's appeared a bit large, while his accessories, robot mode and facial sculpt were all relatively inaccurate.

**ALTERNATE MODE:** Futuristic motorcycle.
**EASILY LOST WEAPONS AND ACCESSORIES:** Decelerator laser, armor axe, front tire.

Wreck-Gar, robot mode.

Wreck-Gar, easily lost weapons and accessories.

Wreck-Gar, alternate mode.

Sky Lynx, dinobird robot mode.

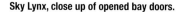

Sky Lynx, close up of opened bay doors.

## SKY LYNX

SPACE SHUTTLE

**FUNCTION:** Lieutenant Commander
**MOTTO:** "The best achievements are worth repeating."

"A powerful fighter. Self-centered and boastful. Fearless, daring, believes himself to be superior to many of his fellow Autobots. Shell-resistant and steel-reinforced hull can withstand enemy bombardment and extreme temperature variations. Possesses solar powered auxiliary engines. Acetylene blaster inside cockpit shoots 3000°C flames. As space shuttle, has interplanetary travel capabilities—maximum speed 30,000 mph, range 40,000,000 miles."

| Strength | Intelligence | Speed | Endurance | Rank | Courage | Firepower | Skill |
|----------|--------------|-------|-----------|------|---------|-----------|-------|
| 10 | 8 | 10 | 10 | 9 | 10 | 7 | 8 |

MLC (non-working electronics: **$45-60**, MIB (non-working electronics): **$90-110**, MISB: **N/A**; (working electronics): **$68-85**, MIB (working electronics): **$140-165+**, MISB: **$350-450**

NOTE: The above figure with a "free glow-in-the-dark *Transformers: The Movie* poster" packaged in a MIB or MISB sample should add $15-25 to the end price.

Motorized via two "AA" Alkaline batteries, Sky Lynx was a fascinating addition to the Autobot ranks. His toy design was concocted by ToyBox, the Japanese company that created Omega Supreme (1985) and Shockwave (1985). There are three different transformational modes for the Autobot Sky Lynx: space shuttle to prehistoric bird (flying dinosaur/dinobird) mode (separate); space shuttle transport to walking lynx mode (separate); and the combined form of his space shuttle and his transport that ultimately transforms into dinobird mode which then attaches to lynx mode: yielding the Sky Lynx super robot, a combination of his two separate components. His motorized feature allows him to walk in Lynx form, or roll in shuttle form.

**ALTERNATE MODE:** U.S. Space Shuttle Orbiter & transporter (aka. crawler pad).

**EASILY LOST WEAPONS AND ACCESSORIES:** N/A.

Sky Lynx, lynx robot mode.

Sky Lynx, alternate mode, space shuttle transport.

Sky Lynx, close up of acetylene blaster.

Sky Lynx, combined robot mode.

Sky Lynx, combined alternate mode.

Sky Lynx, alternate mode, space shuttle.

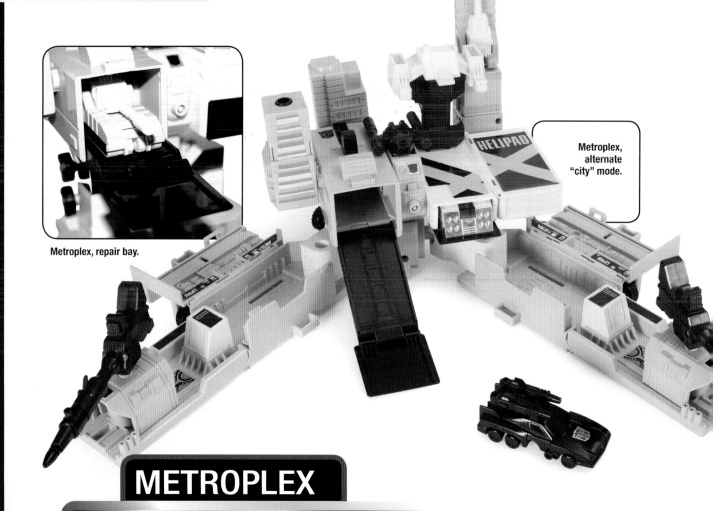

Metroplex, repair bay.

Metroplex, alternate "city" mode.

# METROPLEX

**AUTOBOT CITY**

**FUNCTION:** Battle Station
**MOTTO:** "Vigilance is the foundation on which victories are built."

"Startlingly versatile, staggeringly strong, the Autobots' last line of defense…a mighty instrument of titanic destructive force. Extremely modest about his achievements…berates himself for not doing more. In robot mode, he can lift 70,000 tons, has shoulder-mounted twin high-energy maser cannons and omni-directional receiving and transmitting antenna. In city mode, has helipad and fully equipped repair bays that can handle four vehicles at once. Left rear tower transforms into tank, Slammer, who has rocket-propelled mortar cannon. Scamper is sports car with side mounted electro-blasters; transforms into robot, uses high-energy particle beam pistol. Six-Gun is small robot, has ion-pulse rifles for arms, twin surface-to-air guided missile launchers on back, acetylene pistol. In battle station mode, uses all these weapons and twin disrupter rays, laser lances, powerful anti-matter projectors."

| Strength | Intelligence | Speed | Endurance | Rank | Courage | Firepower | Skill |
|----------|--------------|-------|-----------|------|---------|-----------|-------|
| 10 | 8 | 2 | 9 | 8 | 10 | 10 | 9 |

MLC (plastic tires): **$75-90**, (rubber tires): **$95-120**, MIB: (plastic tires): **$95-115**, (rubber tires): **$140-170+**, MISB: **$800-1,000**
NOTE: A boxed Metroplex with a "free glow-in-the-dark *Transformers: The Movie* poster" packaged in a MIB or MISB sample should add $15-25 to the end price.

Metroplex, "super strong" with added Aerialbots.

Metroplex's robots: Slammer (small tank), Six Gun (red and white), and Scamper (black).

Metroplex, robot mode.

Metroplex, battle station mode.

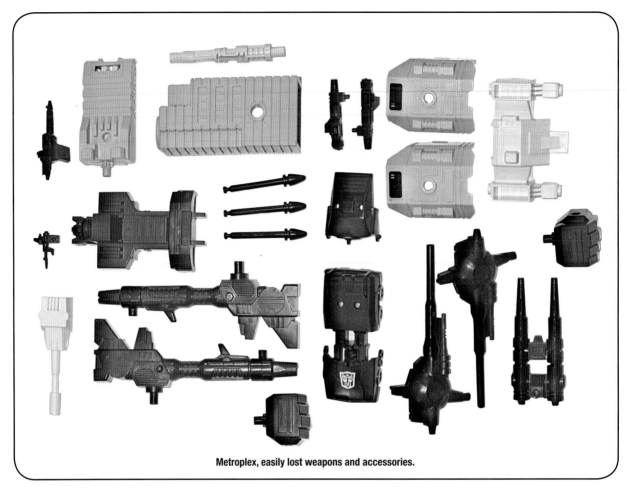

Metroplex, easily lost weapons and accessories.

In 1986's *Transformers: The Movie*, the transformable "Autobot City" we see is reminiscent of Metroplex [note that Slammer is quite visible when he 'transforms'], but still is close in aesthetics and function to suspend the viewers' disbelief. Metroplex is a tremendous Transformer (far bigger than Omega Supreme [1985]), and many kids longed for the super robot because of his vast playability. His accessories were numinous, and the three other robots that were included with him added to the action: Scamper—a small [two-step] transformable race car with removable arms and rifle, Slammer—a non-transforming tank that functioned as his city mode's main tower, and Six-Gun—a robot comprised of six of Metroplex's actual rifles and guns, and a few more parts.

Along with these additional three robots that patrol the perimeter of Metroplex's city mode, the toy also possesses added special features: the back of his legs can open to store unused parts; he manifests a repair bay with an auto-launcher; he exhibits flip-out twin MASER cannons [see Dreamwave's *Transformers: More Than Meets The Eye* guide books (2003), where MASER is an acronym for Microwave Amplification through Simulated Emission of Radiation]; and Metroplex has a 'flip-up' head. He has room for many Autobot Mini-vehicles and small combiner robots; there are removable knee caps; and as an amazing bonus, his instruction booklet also states: "For a 'super strong' Metroplex, team mini-vehicles [Protectobots, Aerialbots] can also be attached" to his shoulders and legs [see pic]; and finally, he had guns sticking out *everywhere*.

Apart from his 'super-strong' robot mode, it is worth mentioning that Metroplex also had a hidden feature— one that was delivered to Japanese consumers, but not to the North American customer. You see, if collectors review Metroplex's Japanese Instruction Booklet, they'll find that each member of the '86 combiner groups' team leaders [Hot Spot, Motormaster, Onslaught, and Silverbolt] can connect to Metroplex in his city mode, to form a far more impressive robotic metropolis—a 'super-city' (!).

Finally, it should be noted that early versions of Metroplex's had the tops of his legs fully chromed and his tires were made of rubber; later versions of the huge toy included chrome silver *labels* to place onto the white tops of his legs, and hard plastic tires instead since they were cheaper to produce that the original rubber.

**ALTERNATE MODE:** Metroplex City, battle station.

**EASILY LOST WEAPONS AND ACCESSORIES:** 2 knee caps, 1 tank/side tower (Slammer), 1 tank/side tower turret (Slammer's), 1 rear tower, 1 small robot body/center tower (Six Gun's), 1 small robot chest/center tower (Six Gun's), 4 accessory cannons (Six Gun's arms and legs), 1 laser pistol (Six Gun's), 1 double barrel cannon (Six Gun's), 1 shoulder antenna, 3 missiles, 2 fists, 2 small cannons/arms (Scamper's), small car/robot (Scamper), 1 small laser pistol (Scamper's).

**NOTE:** With the intricate amount of parts needed to complete a Metroplex, he is a difficult find complete, although he does not command prices as high as the Headmasters Fortress Maximus (1987) or Scorponok (1987).

**Ultra Magnus, robot mode.**

# ULTRA MAGNUS

**CITY COMMANDER**

**FUNCTION:** City Commander
**MOTTO:** "Consistency is victory."

"Ultra Magnus is all soldier. Most comfortable when carrying out Optimus Prime's orders. Possesses magnificent fighting skills, courage, and a gift for battlefield improvisation. Uncomfortable in the mantle of leadership, but presents strong profile as a commander. Carries missile launchers capable of hitting a target 30 miles away. Resolute, fair, and courageous beyond reproach. Ever ready to sacrifice himself for the good of men and mission."

| Strength | Intelligence | Speed | Endurance | Rank | Courage | Firepower | Skill |
|----------|--------------|-------|-----------|------|---------|-----------|-------|
| 9 | 9 | 6 | 8 | 8 | 9 | 6 | 8 |

**$** (Rubber or plastic tires) MLC: **$55-70**, MIB: **$95-120**, MISB: **$500-700**

NOTE: Ultra Magnus with a "free glow-in-the-dark *Transformers: The Movie* poster" packaged in a MIB or MISB sample should add $15-25 to end price.

The foundation of Ultra Magnus' toy [i.e., the cab part of his car carrier] is an all-white molded Optimus Prime figure, yet he includes a fascinating car carrier with many unique touches; Ultra Magnus' car carrier can hold up to four regular-sized Auotobot Cars on two separate levels. When Magnus' cab combines with the carrier to form the Ultra Magnus large-robot—an impressive sight to behold from an engineering perspective. A minor variation note: some super robot Ultra Magnus heads come with or without silver paint.

It is worth noting that when Ultra Magnus was released by Takara, he was a redecoration of a Diaclone toy that the Japanese company named "Powered Convoy" [aka. "Powered (Up) Optimus Prime]—you see, in the Diaclone storyline, Magnus and Prime weren't separate characters, and Optimus Prime was named "Convoy." Oddly enough, the Japanese instructions for the toy provided kids and consumers with quite a few bonus modes—from "Car Carrier" to "Jet Carrier" and from "Repair Bay" to [mini] "Space Shuttle," these interesting alternate modes are very curious indeed [!]

---

**ALTERNATE MODE:** Car carrier.

**EASILY LOST WEAPONS AND ACCESSORIES:** Car carrier/trailer, laser gun, 2 missile holders, 4 red missiles, 2 white cab connectors, 2 small fists, 2 large fists, chest piece, and head.

**Ultra Magnus, alternate mode.**

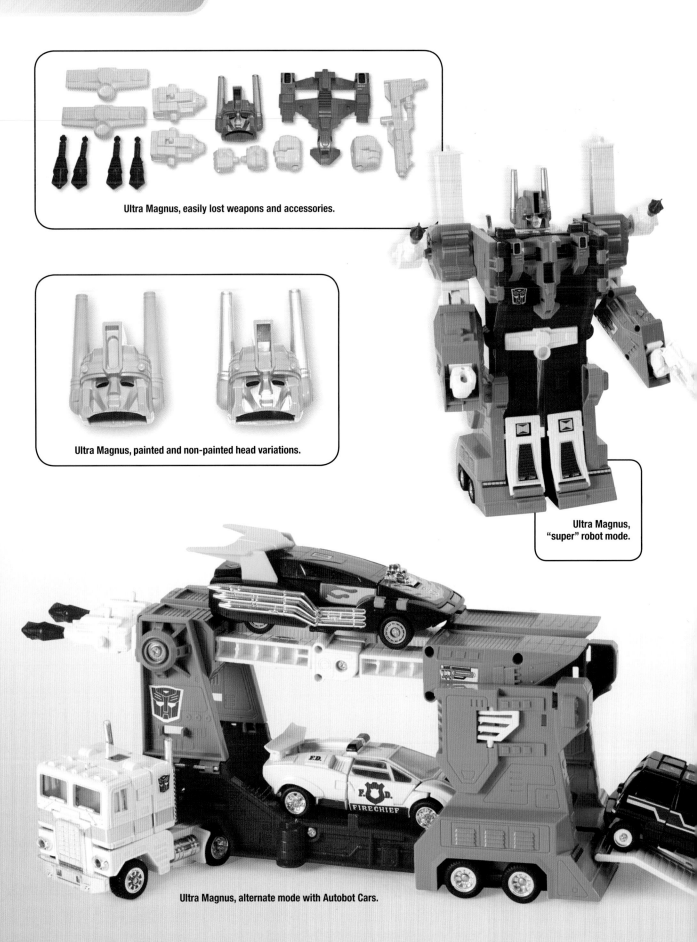

Ultra Magnus, easily lost weapons and accessories.

Ultra Magnus, painted and non-painted head variations.

Ultra Magnus, "super" robot mode.

Ultra Magnus, alternate mode with Autobot Cars.

## [DECEPTICON]
# CASSETTES

Decepticon Cassette Ratbat was released with Frenzy in a 1986 two-pack, yet Frenzy's original entry is found in Series 1, 1984 with notations on his Series 3 incarnation.

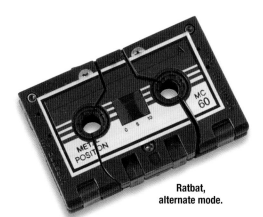

**Ratbat, alternate mode.**

**Ratbat, robot mode.**

**Ratbat, easily lost weapons and accessories.**

**Ratbat, silver vs. gold weapons variations.**

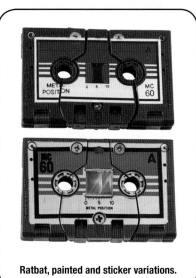

**Ratbat, painted and sticker variations.**

# RATBAT

**CASSETTES**

**PACKAGED WITH FRENZY (1984).**
**FUNCTION:** Fuel Scout
**MOTTO:** "The road is my dinner plate."

"Has no friends, only business partners…his only allegiance is to himself. Refuels by plunging his mecha-fangs into new cars' gas lines—the better made the car, the better the gasoline tastes. Maximum flying speed: 65 mph. Carries two radar-guided, free-electron lasers that detect the presence of an object as small as a fly. Wings contain mechanical sensors for locating fuel sources. Has one foot wingspan that can enlarge to ten feet. Wings are vulnerable to artillery."

| Strength | Intelligence | Speed | Endurance | Rank | Courage | Firepower | Skill |
|---|---|---|---|---|---|---|---|
| 3 | 9 | 4 | 3 | 6 | 7 | 2 | 9 |

[Gold or silver weapons] MLC: **$35-42**, [painted]: **$45-60**, [stickers], MIP (opened; 2 pack w/Frenzy): **$85-100+**, MOSC: **$200-300+**
NOTE: MOC examples are a two-pack containing Ratbat and Frenzy.

Ratbat rivals Ravage in terms of popularity as a Decepticon cassette on the secondary market. His fragile (and oft-missing) ears, his complex transformation from bat to cassette, the chance of paint or sticker wear (he came with either stamped paint applications or stickers), and his two easily lost accessories make him a very desirable and coveted toy to Transformers collectors, particularly in mint or near-mint condition.

**ALTERNATE MODE:** Olympus Type IV "Metal" MC60 Microcassette.
**EASILY LOST WEAPONS AND ACCESSORIES:** 2 free-electron lasers/missiles.

# JETS [DECEPTICON]

Like all boxed (MISB—Mint in Sealed Box) Transformers, the versions of the following two figures that came with a "free glow-in-the-dark *Transformers: The Movie* poster" packaged in MID or MISD samples should add $13-23 to the end price. It is curious to note that Scourge is not really a "jet" per se: yet his price point and basic structure warranted his being packaged with Cyclonus in Decepticon Jet cases.

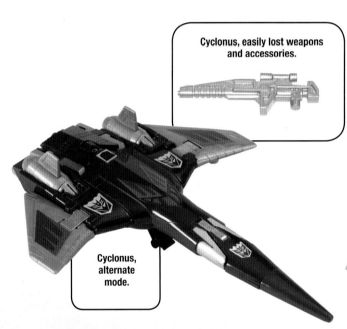

Cyclonus, easily lost weapons and accessories.

Cyclonus, alternate mode.

Cyclonus, robot mode.

## CYCLONUS

**JETS**

**FUNCTION:** Saboteur
**MOTTO:** "Compassion is the Autobots' downfall!"

"Cyclonus is a huge and emotionless air warrior. He has vast resources of power and can draw strength in direct proportion to his need. Cyclonus is equipped with nuclear-powered turbine engines which enable him to reach speeds greater than Mach 2. In robot mode, he carries an oxidating laser that fuses an enemy robot's internal mechanisms. Cyclonus has no weaknesses and no interests other than conquest."

| Strength | Intelligence | Speed | Endurance | Rank | Courage | Firepower | Skill |
|---|---|---|---|---|---|---|---|
| 8 | 8 | 9 | 8 | 9 | 9 | 8 | 8 |

**$** MLC: **$45-58**, MIB: **$75-95**, MISB: **$300-400**
(Blue-eared variant) MLC: **$80-90**, MIB: **$135-145**,
MISB: **$425-550+**

A spawn of the all-powerful world-eater Unicron, Cyclonus is a reformatted and recreated version of the injured Seeker Jet Skywarp (1984; or some claim Bombshell, 1985), and has functioned as Galvatron's (1986) lieutenant. Although not as powerful as Galvatron, it is suggested that Cyclonus is infinitely stronger than his Seeker Jet origins (in light of this, ignore a comparison of the data to the Tech Spec readouts for Skywarp). There are other members of Cyclonus's "armada" that serve the same function as the original: they are his clones. It should be noted that a 'blue-eared' variant version of Cyclonus can bring more money to loose and MIB collectors.

**ALTERNATE MODE:** Swept-wing space fighter.
**EASILY LOST WEAPONS AND ACCESSORIES:** Oxidating laser.
**NOTE:** His arms are fragile so be careful of loose samples.

Scourge, easily lost weapons and accessories.

Scourge, robot mode.

## SCOURGE

**JETS**

**FUNCTION:** Sweep Leader
**MOTTO:** "Desolation follows in my trail."

"Scourge is a fearsome, merciless and implacable hunter. Created from Decepticon wreckage, he leads 'The Sweeps,' a wolf pack of tracker-terminators designed to hunt down and eradicate Autobots. Scourge possesses powerful high-tech scanning equipment and a disintegrator ray that can cut through solid rock. In robot mode, he carries a laser blaster that shoots short bursts of intense heat. Scourge's only weakness is his arrogance."

| Strength | Intelligence | Speed | Endurance | Rank | Courage | Firepower | Skill |
|----------|--------------|-------|-----------|------|---------|-----------|-------|
| 8 | 8 | 9 | 8 | 9 | 9 | 8 | 8 |

$ MLC: **$50-65+**, MIB: **$85-115**, MISB: **$400-500**

Created by Unicron out of the wreckage of Seeker Jet Thundercracker [1984], Scourge and his group of look-alike clone/soldiers known as the "Sweeps" have gained popularity *Transformers: The Movie*. It should be noted that on early versions of Scourge, his toy's disintegrator ray arrived in two pieces: the rear tip was removable–like a missile. Later issues of this ray were solicited as one whole piece. Furthermore, early releases of Scourge were manufactured with a blue plastic hood for the raised region on his hull (plus additional blue paint), while later releases simply had blue colored labels [barely] representing this area.

Scourge, alternate mode.

**ALTERNATE MODE:** Space hovercraft.
**EASILY LOST WEAPONS AND ACCESSORIES:** Distintegrator ray (early versions disassemble into two pieces), laser blaster.

Breakdown, alternate mode.

# STUNTICONS

The Stunticons were the first "scramble city" type combiner introduced to the Decepticon lineup. Many kids and collectors marveled at their introduction to the Sunbow cartoon, as Motormaster and his wild charges challenged the Autobots to ownership of the roads. Although a bit simplistic in design when looking at the other combiner teams, the Stunticons were still an interesting departure from the aircraft and weapons that filled the ranks of the Decepticons.

Breakdown, robot mode.

Breakdown, easily lost weapons and accessories.

# BREAKDOWN

**STUNTICONS**

**FUNCTION:** Scout
**MOTTO:** "Keep your optical sensors to yourself."

"Thinks everyone is staring at him, even Earth cars and stop lights. His self-consciousness hurts his performance. Finds heavy traffic nerve-wracking. Would prefer to be human so he could fit in better. In car mode, engine emits vibrations that cause mechanical failures in other vehicles; prone to leaky fuel pump. In robot mode, carries a concussion rifle which also causes mechanical failures. Combines with fellow Stunticons to form 'Menasor.'"

| Strength | Intelligence | Speed | Endurance | Rank | Courage | Firepower | Skill |
|----------|--------------|-------|-----------|------|---------|-----------|-------|
| 6 | 7 | 7 | 5 | 6 | 8 | 6 | 6 |

(Plastic or metal variations) MLC: **$18-25**, MIP (opened): **$42-50+**, MOC: **$200-300**

Breakdown was an easy sell for the Stunticons because of his sleek alternate mode as a Lamborghini. His Tech Spec suggests that his self-consciousness is debilitating as he pursues his function as Decepticon Scout, to the extent that he'd like to be re-created as an unassuming human being. Like all of the four smaller Stunticons, he came with either metal or plastic chest variations.

**ALTERNATE MODE:** Lamborghini Countach LP500s race car.
**EASILY LOST WEAPONS AND ACCESSORIES:** Concussion rifle, plasma-energy blaster (with attached connector).

# DEAD END

**STUNTICONS**

**FUNCTION:** Warrior
**MOTTO:** "We are all just food for rust."

"Sullen, fatalistic, sees little reason to continue Transformers' war. Motivating him to fight is always a problem. Vain—spends most of his time shining himself. In car mode, goes 220 mph. Radar scan covers 200 mile radius. In robot mode, has a compressor-air gun that shoots a 40,000 psi blast of air. Combines with fellow Stunticons to form 'Menasor.'"

| Strength | Intelligence | Speed | Endurance | Rank | Courage | Firepower | Skill |
|----------|--------------|-------|-----------|------|---------|-----------|-------|
| 7 | 6 | 7 | 7 | 5 | 9 | 5 | 7 |

(Plastic or metal variations) MLC: **$18-25**, MIP (opened): **$42-50+**, MOC: **$200-300**

Dead End, robot mode.

Dead End, easily lost weapons and accessories.

Dead End, alternate mode.

As a toy, Dead End shares the same conversion design with Breakdown [1986], while loose collectors should take note of the condition of the long yellow label running the length of his body, for this is frequently damaged. Like all of the four smaller Stunticons, Dead End came with either metal or plastic body variations. Furthermore, although at first glance it appears his connector accessory is exactly the same as Wildrider's this is untrue: when placed side-by-side, Dead End's connector has three circles on it that are a bit smaller than Wildrider's.

**ALTERNATE MODE:** 1985 Porsche 928S racecar.
**EASILY LOST WEAPONS AND ACCESSORIES:** Compressor-air gun, plasma-energy blaster, connector.

# DRAG STRIP

**STUNTICONS**

**FUNCTION:** Warrior
**MOTTO:** "The first one to cross the finish line LIVES."

"Nasty, underhanded, loves to gloat over his victories. Would rather be scrapped than lose. Prone to overheating. Megatron would sooner melt him than talk to him, but knows he's even worse company for the Autobots. In car mode, has a plasma-energy blaster. Carries a gravity-enhancing gravito-gun. Combines with fellow Stunticons to form 'Menasor.'"

| Strength | Intelligence | Speed | Endurance | Rank | Courage | Firepower | Skill |
|----------|--------------|-------|-----------|------|---------|-----------|-------|
| 6 | 7 | 7 | 4 | 5 | 8 | 7 | 6 |

(Plastic or metal variations) MLC: **$20-26**, MIP (opened): **$42-50+**, MOC: **$100-200**

Drag Strip, easily lost weapons and accessories.

Drag Strip, robot mode.

Drag Strip, alternate mode.

Drag Strip has a unique transformation mode, as his engine flips up to form his gleaming chestplate in robot mode. His alternate six-wheeled racecar mode is based on the innovative design of the Tyrell P34, one of the most recognizable Formula-1 cars in world motor sport history, with its reduced-diameter wheels. As a character, Drag Strip hates losing under any circumstances and goes to great lengths to "win" in combat.

**ALTERNATE MODE:** 1976 Tyrrell-Cosworth P34 [six wheeler] Formula-1 racecar.
**EASILY LOST WEAPONS AND ACCESSORIES:** Gravito gun, plasma-energy blaster (with attached connector).

# WILDRIDER

**STUNTICONS**

**FUNCTION:** Terrorist
**MOTTO:** "Either you're out of my way or you're out of luck."

"Look out motorists—he exults in the accidents he causes! Drives recklessly, screaming and laughing. Some comrades think it's an act, others really know he's as nuts as he appears. Fears quiet, prone to tire blow-outs. In car mode goes up to 250 mph with amazing maneuverability. In robot mode, his scattershot gun sprays laser beams over wide areas. Combines with fellow Stunticons to form 'Menasor.'"

| Strength | Intelligence | Speed | Endurance | Rank | Courage | Firepower | Skill |
|----------|--------------|-------|-----------|------|---------|-----------|-------|
| 6 | 6 | 7 | 6 | 5 | 8 | 7 | 6 |

(Plastic or metal variations) MLC: **$18-25**, MIP (opened): **$42-50+**, MOC: **$200-300**

Wildrider, robot mode.

Wildrider, easily lost weapons and accessories.

Wildrider, alternate mode.

As a toy, Wildrider has a simple and straightforward transformation from robot to vehicle, but loose collectors should take care that his side stickers on his arms are intact. Similar to his fellow three smaller Stunticons, he came with either metal or plastic body variations. Furthermore, although at first glance it appears his connector accessory is exactly the same as Dead End's that's not true: when placed next to each other, Wildrider's connector has three circles on it that are a bit larger than Dead End's.

**ALTERNATE MODE:** 1984 Ferrari 380 GTS QV.
**EASILY LOST WEAPONS AND ACCESSORIES:** Scattershot gun, plasma-energy blaster, connector.

# MOTORMASTER

**STUNTICONS**

**FUNCTION:** Stunticon Leader
**MOTTO:** "These wheels are made for crushing."

"No one on the road is colder and crueler. Shows no mercy to Autobots who happen to be on the highway with him. Seeks to destroy Optimus Prime so he can claim to be 'King of the Road.' Can survive a collision with anyone, except Optimus Prime. Reaches a top speed of 140 mph and can shatter a 20-foot concrete block. Uses a 400 mph wind producing cyclone gun. Forms robot 'Menasor' with fellow Stunticons."

| Strength | Intelligence | Speed | Endurance | Rank | Courage | Firepower | Skill |
|----------|--------------|-------|-----------|------|---------|-----------|-------|
| 9 | 6 | 5 | 10 | 7 | 9 | 7 | 4 |

**$** (Plastic or metal variations) MLC: **$42-58**, MIB: **$60-75**, MISB: **$200-300**

Motormaster, easily lost weapons and accessories.

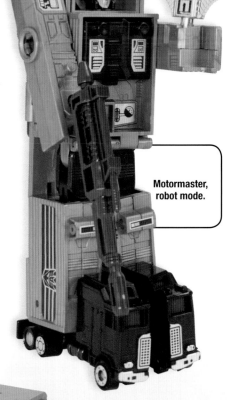

Motormaster, robot mode.

The often peculiar scale of Transformers action figures applies to Motormaster. Since the Stunticon Leader's alternate mode (and purple-striped labels) was clearly intended to mimic Optimus Prime's substantial tractor trailer (and Prime's prominent blue stripes), then why couldn't Hasbro allow Motormaster to replicate Prime's size? Regardless, it should be noted that besides Motormaster's robot form, he could also convert into his 1) alternate vehicle mode, 2) the head and torso of Menasor, 3) a "ramp" mode for his roller car accessory, 4) an expanded 'ramp' to Trypticon's Decepticon City mode, or 5) a component of Metroplex's 'super city' mode [re: Metroplex's Japanese Instruction Booklet <u>only</u>].

**ALTERNATE MODE:** Kenworth K100 Aerodyne with High Cube Trailer.
**EASILY LOST WEAPONS AND ACCESSORIES:** Roller car, blast deflector, ionizer sword, 2 (Menasor) fists, 2 (Menasor) foot stands, cyclone gun, (Menasor) robot head.

Motormaster, "ramp" mode.

Motormaster, alternate mode.

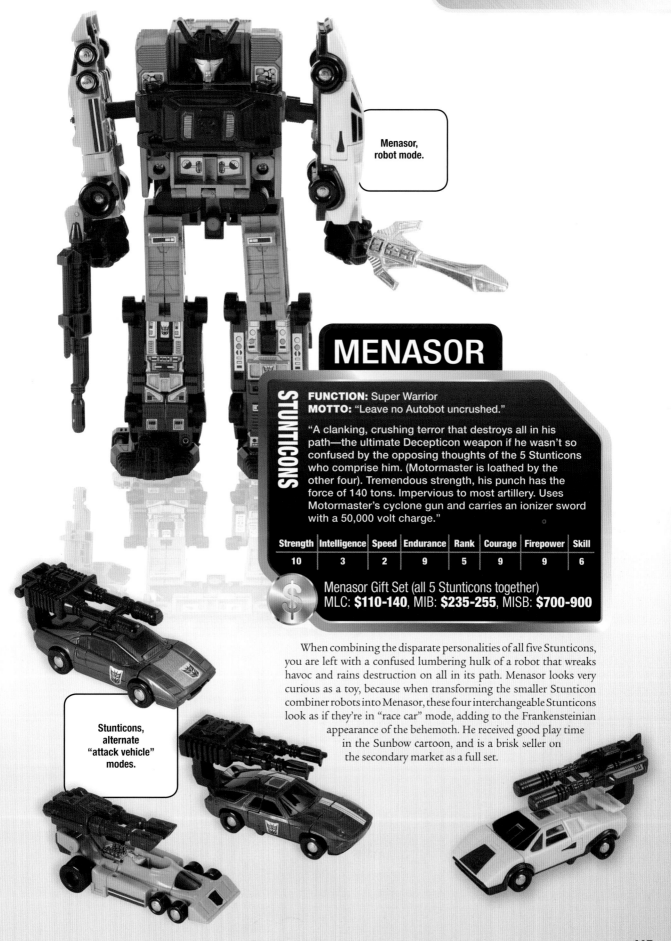

Menasor, robot mode.

# MENASOR

## STUNTICONS

**FUNCTION:** Super Warrior
**MOTTO:** "Leave no Autobot uncrushed."

"A clanking, crushing terror that destroys all in his path—the ultimate Decepticon weapon if he wasn't so confused by the opposing thoughts of the 5 Stunticons who comprise him. (Motormaster is loathed by the other four). Tremendous strength, his punch has the force of 140 tons. Impervious to most artillery. Uses Motormaster's cyclone gun and carries an ionizer sword with a 50,000 volt charge."

| Strength | Intelligence | Speed | Endurance | Rank | Courage | Firepower | Skill |
|----------|--------------|-------|-----------|------|---------|-----------|-------|
| 10 | 3 | 2 | 9 | 5 | 9 | 9 | 6 |

**$** Menasor Gift Set (all 5 Stunticons together)
MLC: **$110-140**, MIB: **$235-255**, MISB: **$700-900**

Stunticons, alternate "attack vehicle" modes.

When combining the disparate personalities of all five Stunticons, you are left with a confused lumbering hulk of a robot that wreaks havoc and rains destruction on all in its path. Menasor looks very curious as a toy, because when transforming the smaller Stunticon combiner robots into Menasor, these four interchangeable Stunticons look as if they're in "race car" mode, adding to the Frankensteinian appearance of the behemoth. He received good play time in the Sunbow cartoon, and is a brisk seller on the secondary market as a full set.

# COMBATICONS

As with the rest of the 1986 combiner teams, you will be able to find both types of Combaticon variations on the secondary market (for the four smaller team members): those with early released die-cast metal [chest] pieces, and those with later-released plastic [chest] pieces, and those without— there is no difference in the price for these action figures.

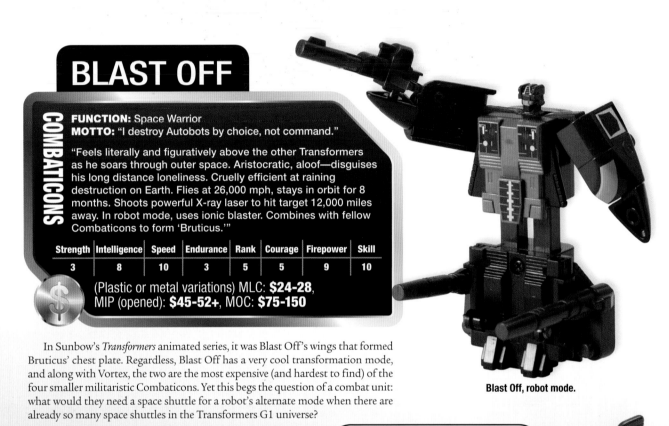

## BLAST OFF

**COMBATICONS**

**FUNCTION:** Space Warrior
**MOTTO:** "I destroy Autobots by choice, not command."

"Feels literally and figuratively above the other Transformers as he soars through outer space. Aristocratic, aloof—disguises his long distance loneliness. Cruelly efficient at raining destruction on Earth. Flies at 26,000 mph, stays in orbit for 8 months. Shoots powerful X-ray laser to hit target 12,000 miles away. In robot mode, uses ionic blaster. Combines with fellow Combaticons to form 'Bruticus.'"

| Strength | Intelligence | Speed | Endurance | Rank | Courage | Firepower | Skill |
|----------|--------------|-------|-----------|------|---------|-----------|-------|
| 3 | 8 | 10 | 3 | 5 | 5 | 9 | 10 |

(Plastic or metal variations) MLC: **$24-28**, MIP (opened): **$45-52+**, MOC: **$75-150**

Blast Off, robot mode.

In Sunbow's *Transformers* animated series, it was Blast Off's wings that formed Bruticus' chest plate. Regardless, Blast Off has a very cool transformation mode, and along with Vortex, the two are the most expensive (and hardest to find) of the four smaller militaristic Combaticons. Yet this begs the question of a combat unit: what would they need a space shuttle for a robot's alternate mode when there are already so many space shuttles in the Transformers G1 universe?

**ALTERNATE MODE:** Boeing/Rockwell Space Shuttle Orbiter.
**EASILY LOST WEAPONS AND ACCESSORIES:** Ionic blaster, dual sonic cannons.

Blast Off, easily lost weapons and accessories.

Blast Off, (alternate) attack mode.

# BRAWL

**COMBATICONS**

**FUNCTION:** Ground Assault
**MOTTO:** "I was built to be wild."

"Noisy, irritates all nearby. Hair-trigger temper, blusteringly belligerent…a terrifyingly effective warrior. Enormously strong, resistant to most conventional artillery. As tank, goes 45 mph, range 600 miles. Turret mounted gun shoots 200 lbs TNT-equivalent shells, twin sonic cannon shoots powerful, ear-splitting 300-decibel bursts of concentrated sound energy in stereo. In robot mode, has 10-megawatt electron gun. Combines with fellow Combaticons to form 'Bruticus.'"

| Strength | Intelligence | Speed | Endurance | Rank | Courage | Firepower | Skill |
|---|---|---|---|---|---|---|---|
| 8 | 2 | 4 | 9 | 5 | 9 | 8 | 7 |

(Plastic or metal variations) MLC: **$24-28**, MIP (opened): **$45-52+**, MOC: **$150-250**

Brawl, robot mode.

Brawl, easily lost weapons and accessories.

Brawl, (alternate) attack mode.

Although Brawl is a fairly rugged looking combat tank (based on NATO's famous workhorse, the Leopard-1 Main Battle Tank), his robot mode is a bit disappointing, as his tank turret seems to stick out like a sore thumb from the robot's back. He was an important cog in any Transformer fan's Decepticon armada, however. If you find one of his earlier die-cast metal variations, he did not follow standard Combaticon protocol: it was not his chest plate that was comprised of die-cast metal, but his rear tank treads.

**ALTERNATE MODE:** Leopard 1A5 M.B.T.
**EASILY LOST WEAPONS AND ACCESSORIES:** Electron gun, twin sonic cannon.

# ONSLAUGHT

**COMBATICONS**

**FUNCTION:** Combaticon Leader
**MOTTO:** "The mind is the greatest weapon."

"Believes the key to a mission's success lies in the perfection of its planning. Prefers devising sinister schemes to actual combat, but a relentless, furious fighter when stirred into action. As a missile trailer, Onslaught is capable of launching 6,500-mile range photon missiles, each equivalent to 3000 tons of TNT. Accuracy of missiles is hampered by electromagnetic interference. Uses powerful sonic stun gun in robot mode. Joins with fellow Combaticons to form robot 'Bruticus.'"

| Strength | Intelligence | Speed | Endurance | Rank | Courage | Firepower | Skill |
|---|---|---|---|---|---|---|---|
| 8 | 8 | 3 | 7 | 7 | 8 | 8 | 9 |

MLC: **$40-58**, MIB: **$65-82**, MISB: **$200-300**

Onslaught, robot mode.

Onslaught, battle station mode.

117

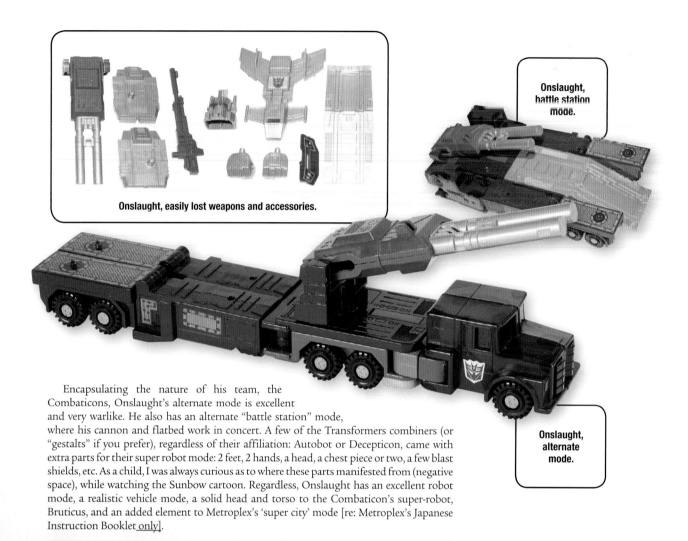

Onslaught, easily lost weapons and accessories.

Onslaught, battle station mode.

Onslaught, alternate mode.

Encapsulating the nature of his team, the Combaticons, Onslaught's alternate mode is excellent and very warlike. He also has an alternate "battle station" mode, where his cannon and flatbed work in concert. A few of the Transformers combiners (or "gestalts" if you prefer), regardless of their affiliation: Autobot or Decepticon, came with extra parts for their super robot mode: 2 feet, 2 hands, a head, a chest piece or two, a few blast shields, etc. As a child, I was always curious as to where these parts manifested from (negative space), while watching the Sunbow cartoon. Regardless, Onslaught has an excellent robot mode, a realistic vehicle mode, a solid head and torso to the Combaticon's super-robot, Bruticus, and an added element to Metroplex's 'super city' mode [re: Metroplex's Japanese Instruction Booklet only].

**ALTERNATE MODE:** U.S. Army Flatbed Truck TMT-18420 (modified).

**EASILY LOST WEAPONS AND ACCESSORIES:** 2 (Bruticus) fists, 2 (Bruticus) feet, sonic stun gun, ramp, large body shield, robot head (Bruticus), chest shield, double barrel missile launcher.

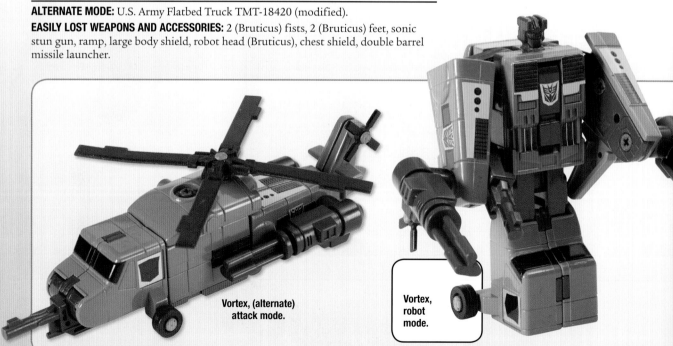

Vortex, (alternate) attack mode.

Vortex, robot mode.

Swindle,
robot mode.

# SWINDLE

**COMBATICONS**

**FUNCTION:** Munitions Expert
**MOTTO:** "Make deals, not war."

"Easy-going and good natured, but within him beats the fuel pump of the most greed-driven street hustler. Thrives on wheeling and dealing, works for his own personal material advancement. A one-robot 'black market.' Uses a scatter blaster that sprays explosive pellets, gyro gun that disrupts Transformers' balance center. Combines with fellow Combaticons to form 'Bruticus.' Prone to overturning on sharp turns."

| Strength | Intelligence | Speed | Endurance | Rank | Courage | Firepower | Skill |
|----------|--------------|-------|-----------|------|---------|-----------|-------|
| 5 | 9 | 5 | 6 | 6 | 5 | 7 | 10 |

$ (Plastic or metal variations) MLC: **$14-20**, MIP (opened): **$28-35**, MISB: **$75-150**

Swindle, easily lost weapons and accessories.

Swindle is an excellent example of a Transformer whose Tech Specs were actually used to influence his personality on the animated Sunbow program. His 4-WD vehicle mode looks sharp, but his robot mode is a bit short, stout, and boxy. He is a simple Transformer to find on the secondary market, and his metal variation is his chest piece.

**ALTERNATE MODE:** FMC XR 311 Combat Support (4-WD) Vehicle.
**EASILY LOST WEAPONS AND ACCESSORIES:** Gyro-gun, scatter blaster.

Swindle,
alternate mode.

# VORTEX

**COMBATICONS**

**FUNCTION:** Interrogation
**MOTTO:** "I'm Vortex, fly me—if you dare!"

"Gives a ride to remember—in your nightmares! Takes Autobots on dizzying, death-defying flights to scare information out of them. As helicopter, goes 300 mph with a range of 1200 miles. Whirls rotor blades to create 200-300 mph wind funnels. Uses semi-automatic glue gun. Combines with fellow Combaticons to form 'Bruticus.'"

| Strength | Intelligence | Speed | Endurance | Rank | Courage | Firepower | Skill |
|----------|--------------|-------|-----------|------|---------|-----------|-------|
| 4 | 9 | 6 | 5 | 6 | 7 | 7 | 8 |

$ (Plastic or metal variations) MLC: **$18-25**, MIP (opened): **$50-55**, MISB: **$150-250**

Vortex, alternate
mode.

Vortex, easily lost weapons and accessories.

Vortex is the hardest to obtain of the smaller Combaticons because of his easily lost parts and fragile rotor blades. His Tech Spec suggests his love of flight and joy riding with Autobot passengers—all part of his interrogation techniques, of course. He is very maneuverable in vehicle mode. Like nearly every "scramble city" combiner, each member of the Combaticons has an alternate "attack mode" to their vehicles.

**ALTERNATE MODE:** Kaman Aerospace HH-2C Super Seasprite helicopter.
**EASILY LOST WEAPONS AND ACCESSORIES:** 2 side-mounted cannons, semi-automatic glue gun, removable rotor blades (1 pc.).

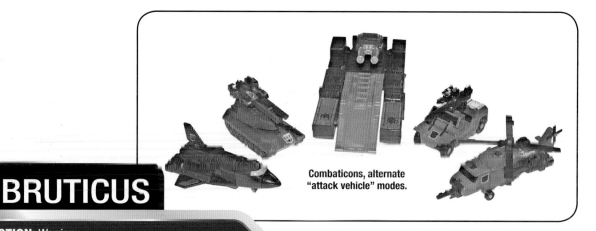

Combaticons, alternate "attack vehicle" modes.

## BRUTICUS

**COMBATICONS**

**FUNCTION:** Warrior
**MOTTO:** "The road to conquest is paved with Autobot wrecks."

"Bruticus transforms into the five Combaticons. Can destroy his enemies with ultrasonic waves and smash metal bridges with a single chop of his hand. Cold blooded, likes nothing more than destroying Autobots. Once he starts running wild, he is unstoppable. Has small brain circuits, making him simple-minded. Carries a sonic stun gun and a missile cannon. (Translated from the original Japanese Tech Spec with his quotation taken from Marvel Comics' *Transformers Universe* comic book)."

| Strength | Intelligence | Speed | Endurance | Rank | Courage | Firepower | Skill |
|----------|--------------|-------|-----------|------|---------|-----------|-------|
| 10 | 3 | 1 | 9 | 5 | 10 | 8 | 8 |

Bruticus Gift Set (all 5 Combaticons together)
MLC: **$115-135**, MIB (foreign-made only): **$310-330**,
MISB (foreign-made only): **$400-600**

Bruticus' actions reflect his brutish namesake: cruel, carnal, bestial; like that of an animal. He is barbarous and destructive, and difficult to control when he's on a rampage of terror. This antagonistic personality is a result of the merging of the sinister criminal minds of all five Combaticons. He follows orders well...perhaps too well, as he revels in the annihilation he causes.

Bruticus, robot mode.

# PREDACONS

The Predacons were considered one of Hasbro's finest achievements within the G1 Transformers franchise, for not only were they large, colorful robots that converted into fierce beasts, they also functioned as a massive combiner team—much larger than the standard gestalt—that merges to form the super warrior, Predaking. Since the price points of the Predacons were quite high (roughly $12.99 each), and the odds of finding all five at retail at the same time was a challenge (consumers nabbed Razorclaw and Divebomb first), the collector who possessed all five of these robots back in 1986 was truly lucky indeed.

Furthermore, although they are a combiner team, they did not follow the popular "Scramble City" designs: they could only swap an arm for an arm (Divebomb and Rampage were interchangeable as Predaking's left arm or right arm), or a leg for a leg (Headstrong and Rampage were interchangeable as a left or right leg)—they simply couldn't function in the same way as the smaller combiner teams.

Regarding prices, Predacons either came with a smattering of die-cast metal parts or are rendered fully in plastic parts—but these different parts variations make no difference in price on the secondary market.

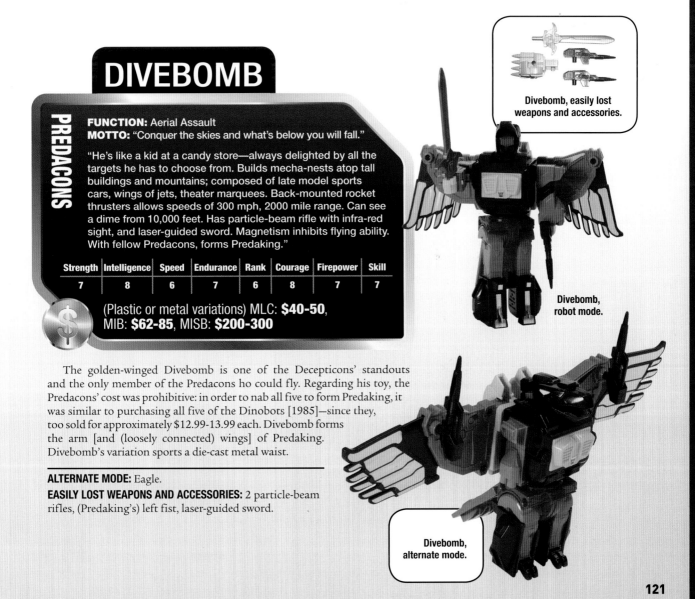

Divebomb, easily lost weapons and accessories.

## DIVEBOMB

**PREDACONS**

**FUNCTION:** Aerial Assault
**MOTTO:** "Conquer the skies and what's below you will fall."

"He's like a kid at a candy store—always delighted by all the targets he has to choose from. Builds mecha-nests atop tall buildings and mountains; composed of late model sports cars, wings of jets, theater marquees. Back-mounted rocket thrusters allows speeds of 300 mph, 2000 mile range. Can see a dime from 10,000 feet. Has particle-beam rifle with infra-red sight, and laser-guided sword. Magnetism inhibits flying ability. With fellow Predacons, forms Predaking."

| Strength | Intelligence | Speed | Endurance | Rank | Courage | Firepower | Skill |
|----------|-------------|-------|-----------|------|---------|-----------|-------|
| 7 | 8 | 6 | 7 | 6 | 8 | 7 | 7 |

(Plastic or metal variations) MLC: **$40-50**, MIB: **$62-85**, MISB: **$200-300**

Divebomb, robot mode.

The golden-winged Divebomb is one of the Decepticons' standouts and the only member of the Predacons ho could fly. Regarding his toy, the Predacons' cost was prohibitive: in order to nab all five to form Predaking, it was similar to purchasing all five of the Dinobots [1985]—since they, too sold for approximately $12.99-13.99 each. Divebomb forms the arm [and (loosely connected) wings] of Predaking. Divebomb's variation sports a die-cast metal waist.

**ALTERNATE MODE:** Eagle.
**EASILY LOST WEAPONS AND ACCESSORIES:** 2 particle-beam rifles, (Predaking's) left fist, laser-guided sword.

Divebomb, alternate mode.

# TANTRUM

PREDACONS

**FUNCTION:** Fueler
**MOTTO:** "Anger gets me running better than any other fuel."

"Prefers brute force over reason. Steam comes from his nasal ducts when he's enraged. Smashes head-first into highway trestles and small buildings to relieve his aggression. Always feels better afterwards. Carries 4 exterior fuel tanks, capacity: 1600 gallons, as a reserve for himself and his comrades. His horns shoot bolts of 20,000 volt electricity. Carries a catalytic carbine that shoots destructive chemicals, and an electro-sword. Combines with fellow Predacons to form Predaking."

| Strength | Intelligence | Speed | Endurance | Rank | Courage | Firepower | Skill |
|---|---|---|---|---|---|---|---|
| 8 | 4 | 3 | 8 | 5 | 9 | 8 | 7 |

$ (Plastic or metal variations) MLC: **$40-55**, MIB: **$62-82**, MISB: **$200-300**

In his alternate mode, possesses qualities similar to a real buffalo bull, with smoke issuing from his nostrils, a propensity to charge, etc. As a toy, Tantrum possesses a curious design—as a Decepticon Fueler, his four gray-colored, exterior-mounted fuel tanks can be easily observed while in alternate mode. Tantrum forms a leg of Predaking. In earlier-released versions of Tantrum, his die-cast metal variation is found in his two hip plates.

**ALTERNATE MODE:** Buffalo.
**EASILY LOST WEAPONS AND ACCESSORIES:** 2 catalytic carbines, electro sword, cannon [Predaking's foot].

Tantrum, easily lost weapons and accessories.

Tantrum, robot mode.

Tantrum, alternate mode.

# HEADSTRONG

PREDACONS

**FUNCTION:** Ground Assault
**MOTTO:** "The best advice is not to listen to advice."

"Doesn't listen to anyone, particularly his friends. Smug, arrogant. Puts up a stubborn front to hide deep-rooted insecurities. More vulnerable to psychological rather than physical attacks. In rhinoceros mode, his horn can puncture 3-foot thick steel, release corrosive acid. Uses plasma-sphere shooter that emits explosive energy balls; has light distorting diffraction sword. Combines with fellow Predacons to form Predaking."

| Strength | Intelligence | Speed | Endurance | Rank | Courage | Firepower | Skill |
|---|---|---|---|---|---|---|---|
| 7 | 5 | 4 | 7 | 5 | 6 | 8 | 6 |

$ (Plastic or metal variations) MLC: **$42-55**, MIB: **$68-85**, MISB: **$200-300**

Headstrong, robot mode.

Headstrong, alternate mode.

Rampage, easily lost weapons and accessories.

# RAMPAGE

**PREDACONS**

**FUNCTION:** Gunner
**MOTTO:** "Those who conquer, act; those who are conquered, think!"

"Barrels through life with an uncontrolled fury. Has difficulty talking coherently for more than a few seconds before violently lashing out at anything near him, friend or foe. TV calms him...stares at rock music videos for hours. As tiger, can leap 300 ft. in height, 500 ft. in length. A kick from his foreleg can crumble a cinder block well. As robot, carries 60,000 volt lightning rifle, 5000°F thermosword. Combines with fellow Predacons to form Predaking."

| Strength | Intelligence | Speed | Endurance | Rank | Courage | Firepower | Skill |
|----------|--------------|-------|-----------|------|---------|-----------|-------|
| 8 | 3 | 5 | 6 | 5 | 9 | 9 | 6 |

(Plastic or metal variations) MLC: **$35-45**, MIB: **$62-74**, MISB: **$200-300**

Rampage, alternate mode.

With an alternate mode similar to Predacon Leader Razorclaw [1986], Rampage changes into a spectacular tiger with good poseability. As a character, television quiets and placates Rampage: particularly reality TV [according to the *Transformers: More Than Meets The Eye* (2003) guide books]. He is fiercely strong and is a Decepticon who believes that actions speak volumes. Furthermore, Rampage forms an arm of Predaking, while his metal part[s] variation is his red-painted die-cast metal waist.

**ALTERNATE MODE:** Tiger.
**EASILY LOST WEAPONS AND ACCESSORIES:** Right fist (Predaking), thermo sword, 2 lightning rifles.

Rampage, robot mode.

Other smaller combiner teams have a team commander or team leader that usually came with the [extra] accessories needed to complete the group's super-robot. Not so with the Predacons, as each of the five individually-packaged robots included parts to form Predaking. Headstrong came with Predaking's foot, and utilized it in his attack mode. Headstrong forms a leg of Predaking, and his die-cast metal variant sports a metal back plate.

**ALTERNATE MODE:** Rhinoceros.
**EASILY LOST WEAPONS AND ACCESSORIES:** Diffraction sword, cannon [Predaking's foot], 2 plasma sphere shooters.

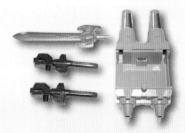

Headstrong, easily lost weapons and accessories.

Razorclaw, alternate mode.

Razorclaw, robot mode.

## RAZORCLAW

**PREDACONS**

**FUNCTION:** Predacon Leader
**MOTTO:** "All good things succumb to those who wait."

"All business. Hates waste in any form…won't burn an extra drop of fuel unless he's certain the results will be worth the effort. Long stretches of inactivity often mistaken for laziness. Explodes into furious, ferocious action when it's time to strike. As a lion, can leap distances as long as a football field. Claws can rip through foot-thick steel. Has twin concussion blasters and sonic sword. Combines with fellow Predacons to form Predaking."

| Strength | Intelligence | Speed | Endurance | Rank | Courage | Firepower | Skill |
|----------|-------------|-------|-----------|------|---------|-----------|-------|
| 8 | 9 | 4 | 9 | 8 | 10 | 7 | 7 |

(Plastic or metal variations) MLC: **$40-55**, MIB: **$68-85**, MISB: **$200-300**

Razorclaw, easily lost
weapons and accessories.

Predacon Leader Razorclaw acts precisely as a manifestation of his alternate mode: that of a lion. He carefully watches and waits for the perfect moment to strike against his enemies; he is a furious and relentless fighter. When selecting a Razorclaw toy for your collection, make sure that on loose samples, his 'mane' labels are intact and carefully applied, or Razorclaw [and Predaking (1986), for that matter (Razorclaw's head and mane are prominent in the gestalt)] won't look quite right. Razorclaw forms the head, chest and torso of Predaking. On his metal variation, his die-cast piece is his waist.

**ALTERNATE MODE:** Lion.
**EASILY LOST WEAPONS AND ACCESSORIES:** Twin concussion blaster, (Predaking's) robot head, sonic sword.

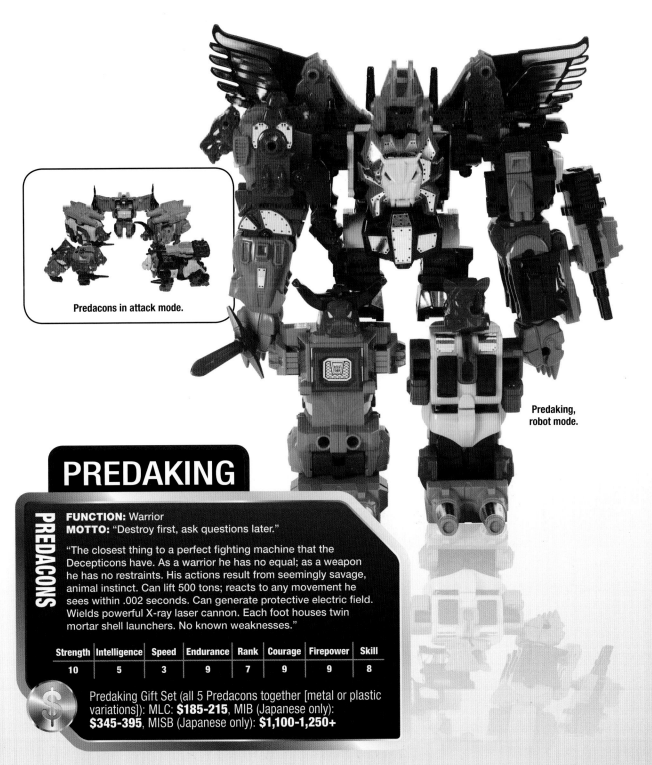

Predacons in attack mode.

Predaking, robot mode.

# PREDAKING

**PREDACONS**

**FUNCTION:** Warrior
**MOTTO:** "Destroy first, ask questions later."

"The closest thing to a perfect fighting machine that the Decepticons have. As a warrior he has no equal; as a weapon he has no restraints. His actions result from seemingly savage, animal instinct. Can lift 500 tons; reacts to any movement he sees within .002 seconds. Can generate protective electric field. Wields powerful X-ray laser cannon. Each foot houses twin mortar shell launchers. No known weaknesses."

| Strength | Intelligence | Speed | Endurance | Rank | Courage | Firepower | Skill |
|---|---|---|---|---|---|---|---|
| 10 | 5 | 3 | 9 | 7 | 9 | 9 | 8 |

**$** Predaking Gift Set (all 5 Predacons together [metal or plastic variations]): MLC: **$185-215**, MIB (Japanese only): **$345-395**, MISB (Japanese only): **$1,100-1,250+**

A magnificent combiner, the super articulated Predaking is one of the most effective of all the gestalts. Rarely do combiner team members share a similar opinion, much less a parallel though process—this is untrue with Predaking, who moves and fights with lightning-fast, primal, animalistic self-assurance. It should be noted that Predaking's component parts may *not* be rearranged [like most "scramble city" combiners: the Predacons may only swap an arm for an arm (Divebomb and Rampage were interchangeable as arms), or a leg for a leg (Headstrong and Rampage were interchangeable as legs). Furthermore, please note that Predaking's X-Ray laser cannon is a reconfigurable weapon [it is Razorclaw's twin concussion blaster transformed].

## [DECEPTICON]
# TRIPLE CHANGERS

One of Shockwave's more successful experiments, and the only Decepticon Triple Changer to be introduced to the line in 1986 [as opposed to the three Autobot Triple Changers in 1987: Broadside, Sandstorm and Springer] Octane is very popular on the secondary market, and is an excellent complement to 1985's Blitzwing and Astrotrain.

## OCTANE

**TRIPLE CHANGERS**

**FUNCTION:** Fueler
**MOTTO:** "He who has fuel, has power."

"A greedy, mean-spirited bully. Enjoys watching fellow Decepticons become painfully inoperative from lack of fuel. Forces Autobots off roads and Aerialbots to abort landings just for fun. Crashes make him laugh. In jet mode: range 700 miles, maximum speed 750 mph. In tanker mode: range 65,000 miles, maximum speed 90 mph, carries 10,000 gallons of fuel. Carries fuel-powered flamethrower and deflecto-shield."

| Strength | Intelligence | Speed | Endurance | Rank | Courage | Firepower | Skill |
|----------|--------------|-------|-----------|------|---------|-----------|-------|
| 6 | 6 | 7 | 4 | 7 | 3 | 4 | 6 |

MLC: **$58-75**, MIB: **$95-120**,
MISB: **$300-400**

Octane, robot mode.

Since Octane has a complex conversion mode [from robot to tanker truck to passenger airplane], the labels applied to certain areas will rub off and wear with ease. Further, be careful of chrome wear on his tanker truck cover/shield and wings, as it vanishes and rubs away quickly. As a Triple Changer, Octane is different from 1986's Autobot Triple Changers, since there are no apparent offensive capabilities for either alternate mode. (In comparison, Sandstorm [1986] changed into alternate modes that were aggressive—a rugged dune buggy and fierce combat helicopter.) Octane is challenging to find MISB because of his toy's delicate nature and his popularity. One thing that must be noted about his character is the fear he manifests because of the potentially explosive fuel he carries: One good hit or laser blast could mean his untimely demise ...

**ALTERNATE MODE:** Fuel tanker truck, Boeing 767-200 wide-body passenger airplane.

**EASILY LOST WEAPONS AND ACCESSORIES:** Flamethrower, tail rudder/deflector shield, tanker truck cover.

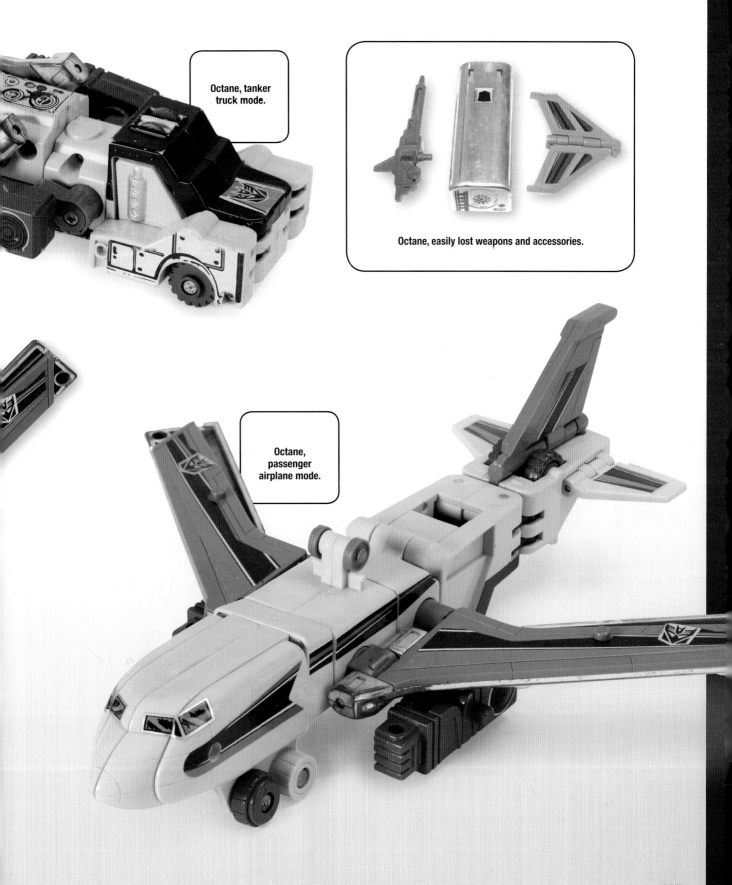

Octane, tanker truck mode.

Octane, easily lost weapons and accessories.

Octane, passenger airplane mode.

Runabout, alternate mode.

Runabout, easily lost weapon.

# RUNABOUT

**BATTLECHARGERS**

**FUNCTION:** Shock Trooper
**MOTTO:** "A pretty car makes an even prettier wreck."

"Likes to watch things blow up—the bigger the explosion the better. Uses parked cars and gas station fuel pumps for target practice. Usually very busy as a Battlecharger, but terrified of boredom. Maximum speed 185 mph. Range: 550 miles. Has high-energy particle beam rifle. Easily distracted by a beautiful car—because he wants to destroy it, not admire it."

| Strength | Intelligence | Speed | Endurance | Rank | Courage | Firepower | Skill |
|---|---|---|---|---|---|---|---|
| 5 | 6 | 7 | 7 | 6 | 7 | 7 | 7 |

MLC: **$12-15**, MIP (opened): **$25-35**,
MOC: **$100-150**

Similar in function to the Autobot Jumpstarters, Topspin (1985) and Twin Twist (1985), the Decepticon Battlechargers have "pull back and go" action that automatically transforms them from vehicle to robot. Runabout is the more fragile of the two Transformers toys however, as his red line-detail stickers are often found missing or torn off.

**ALTERNATE MODE:** Lotus Turbo Esprit.
**EASILY LOST WEAPONS AND ACCESSORIES:** High-energy particle-beam rifle.

Runabout, robot mode.

# RUNAMUCK

**BATTLECHARGERS**

Runamuck, easily lost weapon.

Runamuck, robot mode.

**FUNCTION:** Shock Trooper
**MOTTO:** "The road is my playpen, cars are my toys."

"Cackling like a mechanical wildman, this Battlecharger is a twirling, tumbling two-lane terror. Spreading fear is his favorite pastime. Admires junkyards like humans admire art museums. Maximum Speed 180 mph. Range: 600 Miles. Uses friction rifle that increases kinetic energy of its target's molecules for 5 minutes. Even the slightest movement results in tremendous friction, causing flames and melting. Afraid of heights."

| Strength | Intelligence | Speed | Endurance | Rank | Courage | Firepower | Skill |
|---|---|---|---|---|---|---|---|
| 6 | 6 | 7 | 7 | 6 | 5 | 7 | 8 |

MLC: **$12-15**, MIP (opened): **$25-35**,
MOC: **$100-150**

Runamuck, alternate mode.

With motorized, pull back "pop up action," the Decepticon Battlechargers were a bit of an improvement over their Autobot Jumpstarter counterparts, and, like them, their weapons had to be added on after their automatic conversions took place. Although the automobile modes of the Battlechargers appear to be based on the same automotive model, they are indeed different.

**ALTERNATE MODE:** Pontiac Firebird Trans Am (3rd generation).
**EASILY LOST WEAPONS AND ACCESSORIES:** Friction rifle.

[DECEPTICON]

# BATTLECHARGERS

With their simple (yet automatic) transformations, cool automobile modes, and great Tech Spec descriptions, the Decepticon Battlechargers were a nifty (and relatively inexpensive) introduction to the 1986 lineup. Their instructions were simple: "To transform into robot, grasp racecar from rear of body. Hold bottom of racecar against floor or other flat surface. Pull racecar backwards about 6 inches...Let it run!"

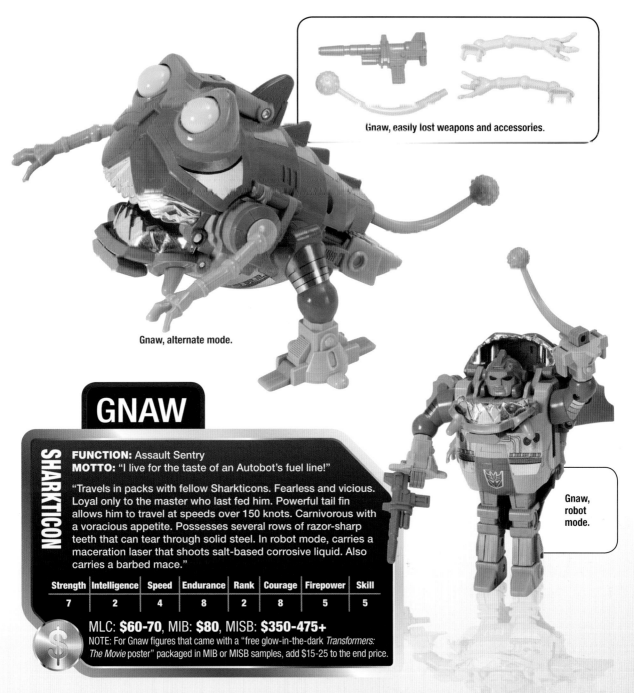

Gnaw, easily lost weapons and accessories.

Gnaw, alternate mode.

Gnaw, robot mode.

# GNAW

**SHARKTICON**

**FUNCTION:** Assault Sentry
**MOTTO:** "I live for the taste of an Autobot's fuel line!"

"Travels in packs with fellow Sharkticons. Fearless and vicious. Loyal only to the master who last fed him. Powerful tail fin allows him to travel at speeds over 150 knots. Carnivorous with a voracious appetite. Possesses several rows of razor-sharp teeth that can tear through solid steel. In robot mode, carries a maceration laser that shoots salt-based corrosive liquid. Also carries a barbed mace."

| Strength | Intelligence | Speed | Endurance | Rank | Courage | Firepower | Skill |
|----------|--------------|-------|-----------|------|---------|-----------|-------|
| 7 | 2 | 4 | 8 | 2 | 8 | 5 | 5 |

**MLC: $60-70, MIB: $80, MISB: $350-475+**
NOTE: For Gnaw figures that came with a "free glow-in-the-dark *Transformers: The Movie* poster" packaged in MIB or MISB samples, add $15-25 to the end price.

Here we should take note that there are different types of servant-level guards for the Quintessons portrayed in *Transformers: The Movie*. The first contingent that Hot Rod [1986] and KUP [1986] encountered on the planet of Quintessa—immediately before our two Autobot Heroes were captured, tried, and found "guilty"—were a breed of enforcers named the Allicons. The second gaggle of troopers they meet, we witnessed them swimming like fierce piranhas in an aquatic pit within the Quintessons' judgment chambers: the swarm of fearsome Sharkticons. Gnaw is a lone member of the latter group, a ravenous lunkhead who would eventually re-appear in Dreamwave's *Transformers* comic, where he partnered with [the almost universally reviled] Autobot Survivalist, Wheelie [1986]. Gnaw's alternate mode is difficult to pin down: it manifests as a type of bipedal, amphibious, futuristic, techno-organic frog-shark. Whose sense of loyalty and camaraderie is simple: Gnaw is devoted to the individual who fed him last.

**ALTERNATE MODE:** Bipedal techno-organic frog-shark [!].
**EASILY LOST WEAPONS AND ACCESSORIES:** Maceration laser, tail/mace, 2 arms (left and right).

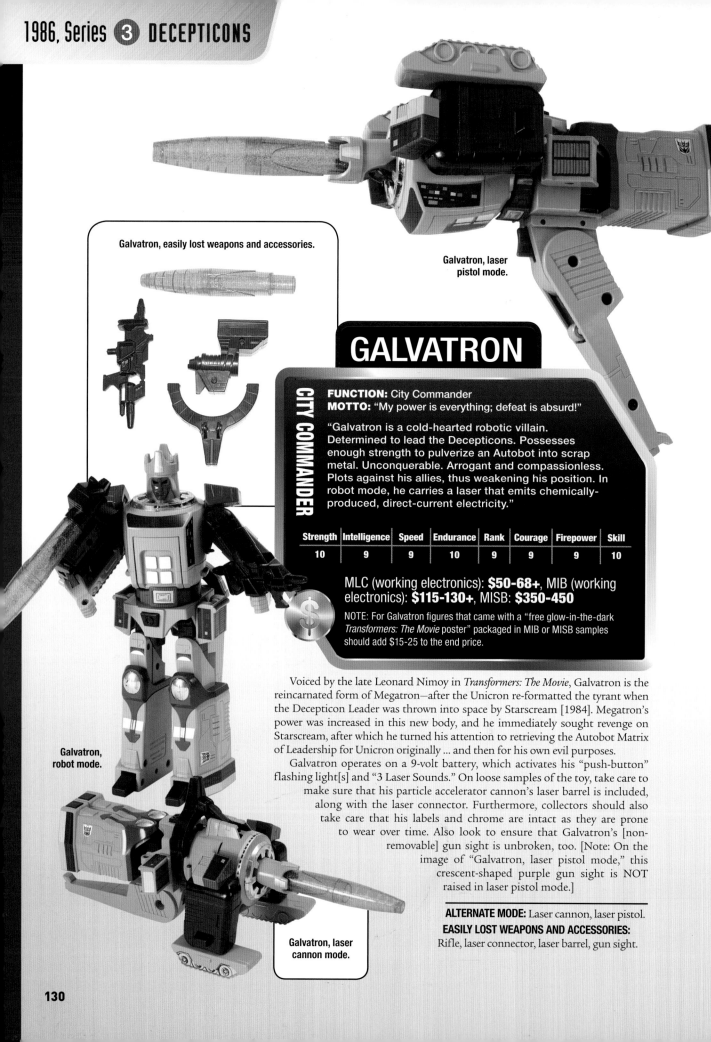

Galvatron, laser
pistol mode.

Galvatron, easily lost weapons and accessories.

# GALVATRON

**CITY COMMANDER**

**FUNCTION:** City Commander
**MOTTO:** "My power is everything; defeat is absurd!"

"Galvatron is a cold-hearted robotic villain. Determined to lead the Decepticons. Possesses enough strength to pulverize an Autobot into scrap metal. Unconquerable. Arrogant and compassionless. Plots against his allies, thus weakening his position. In robot mode, he carries a laser that emits chemically-produced, direct-current electricity."

| Strength | Intelligence | Speed | Endurance | Rank | Courage | Firepower | Skill |
|----------|--------------|-------|-----------|------|---------|-----------|-------|
| 10 | 9 | 9 | 10 | 9 | 9 | 9 | 10 |

MLC (working electronics): **$50-68+**, MIB (working electronics): **$115-130+**, MISB: **$350-450**

NOTE: For Galvatron figures that came with a "free glow-in-the-dark *Transformers: The Movie* poster" packaged in MIB or MISB samples should add $15-25 to the end price.

Galvatron, robot mode.

Voiced by the late Leonard Nimoy in *Transformers: The Movie*, Galvatron is the reincarnated form of Megatron—after the Unicron re-formatted the tyrant when the Decepticon Leader was thrown into space by Starscream [1984]. Megatron's power was increased in this new body, and he immediately sought revenge on Starscream, after which he turned his attention to retrieving the Autobot Matrix of Leadership for Unicron originally ... and then for his own evil purposes.

Galvatron operates on a 9-volt battery, which activates his "push-button" flashing light[s] and "3 Laser Sounds." On loose samples of the toy, take care to make sure that his particle accelerator cannon's laser barrel is included, along with the laser connector. Furthermore, collectors should also take care that his labels and chrome are intact as they are prone to wear over time. Also look to ensure that Galvatron's [non-removable] gun sight is unbroken, too. [Note: On the image of "Galvatron, laser pistol mode," this crescent-shaped purple gun sight is NOT raised in laser pistol mode.]

Galvatron, laser cannon mode.

**ALTERNATE MODE:** Laser cannon, laser pistol.
**EASILY LOST WEAPONS AND ACCESSORIES:**
Rifle, laser connector, laser barrel, gun sight.

Reflector, alternate mode combined.

Reflector, robot modes (Clockwise: Spyglass, Viewfinder, Spectro).

# REFLECTOR
### [SPECTRO, SPYGLASS, VIEWFINDER]

**CAMERA**

**FUNCTION:** Reconnaissance
**MOTTO:** "See and you can know, know and you can destroy."

"Loves to observe things: vegetation, architecture, Earthen topography, and particularly comrades' mistakes. Likes to blackmail his associates and is impressed with his own ability. Has highly-developed infra-red vision that can record images in darkness, through camouflage and at great distances. In camera mode, can emit powerful flash explosion that leaves enemy blind and disorientated for up to 15 seconds."

| Strength | Intelligence | Speed | Endurance | Rank | Courage | Firepower | Skill |
|----------|--------------|-------|-----------|------|---------|-----------|-------|
| 7 | 8 | 2 | 6 | 6 | 7 | 6 | 9 |

MLC: **$150-175**, MIP: **$225-250+**, MISB: **$500-700**

The Decepticon team known as Reflector is made up of three uniquely different robots, each of which comprises one third of their alternate camera mode: Spyglass–the blue robot, the eager strong arm of the team; Viewfinder–the team leader, whose talent for blackmail and keen visual acumen is unmatched; and Spectro–the red robot, the dullest and most disloyal of the three. Reflector was introduced in Sunbow's animated series from the very first episode until the end of the first season, and as a character each member of the triad spoke in concert and looked exactly like a clone of Viewfinder. As a toy, Reflector was only available as a mail-away, and is highly prized and desirable on the secondary market for his intricate transformation mode and difficulty to find complete, whether mint-in-mailer-box, or mint, loose and complete.

**ALTERNATE MODE:** Vintage SLR (single lens reflex) 35 mm camera.
**EASILY LOST WEAPONS AND ACCESSORIES:** Lens laser, shutter gun, opto blaster, 3 missiles, telephoto lens, flashcube.

MAIL AWAY

Reflector, easily lost weapons and accessories.

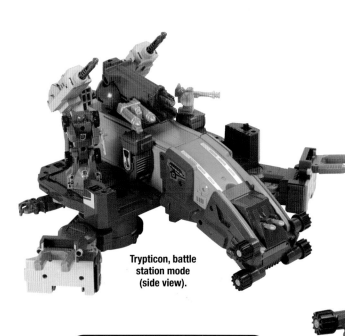

Trypticon, battle
station mode
(side view).

Trypticon,
robot mode.

# TRYPTICON

**DECEPTICON CITY**

**FUNCTION:** Assault Base
**MOTTO:** "Total victory requires total destruction."

"Doesn't stop blasting until he's hip-deep in smoking rubble.
Completely without mercy. The most lethal fighting machine
devised by the Decepticons. In dinosaur mode, jumps 20 miles
with rocket backpack. Shoots heat-seeking plasma bombs from
mouth and mind-controlling hypno-beam from optical sensor.
As city, has landing and repair bays, communications center and
rotating scanners. In mobile station mode, has laser cannon,
rotating blasters, destructo-beams and dual photon launchers."

| Strength | Intelligence | Speed | Endurance | Rank | Courage | Firepower | Skill |
|----------|-------------|-------|-----------|------|---------|-----------|-------|
| 10 | 7 | 8 | 10 | 9 | 10 | 10 | 8 |

MLC (working electronics): **$185-235,**
MIB (working electronics): **$335-360+,**
MISB: **$1,000-1,200**

Trypticon, mind-controlling hypno-beam close up.

As a toy, Trypicon electronically runs on two "AA" batteries
(for his laser cannon) and two "C" batteries (for his dinosaur's
walking motion). He transforms from dinosaur mode to city
mode, and also to battle station mode—although on Sunbow's
animated program, the last of these two alternate modes
were rarely seen. Trypicon is very difficult to find mint, loose,
and complete, and commands high prices in good condition
(particularly boxed) due to his bevy of small parts. Although his
Tech Spec meter reads an intelligence of 7, he was portrayed as a
dimwit on the animated program (one of the flaws in translating
a toy's biography into a character). Trypticon has two other
"helpers" in city mode: Brunt, the five-part tank, and Full-Tilt,
the transformable rocket car. With side ramps, helipads, and
way too many accessories, this Decepticon is highly popular and
prized in many Transformers collections.

In Decepticon City mode, Trypicon also has an "optional
transformation" that includes either Combaticon Leader
Onslaught's (1986) battle station mode or Stunticon Leader
Motormaster's (1986) ramp mode for added play value, and
Trypicon's "connectors" are used for this.

**ALTERNATE MODE:** Dinosaur, battle station mode, [optional]
expanded city mode.

**EASILY LOST WEAPONS AND ACCESSORIES:** 2 loading ramps
(right and left: note that these are different from each other!),
small tower, large tower, 2 tank treads, laser cannon, 2 blaster
stands (different), double barreled blaster, single barreled
blaster, 2 (different) scanners, 2 connectors (for optional
transformation), Full Tilt car, electro-disruptor (Full-Tilt's).

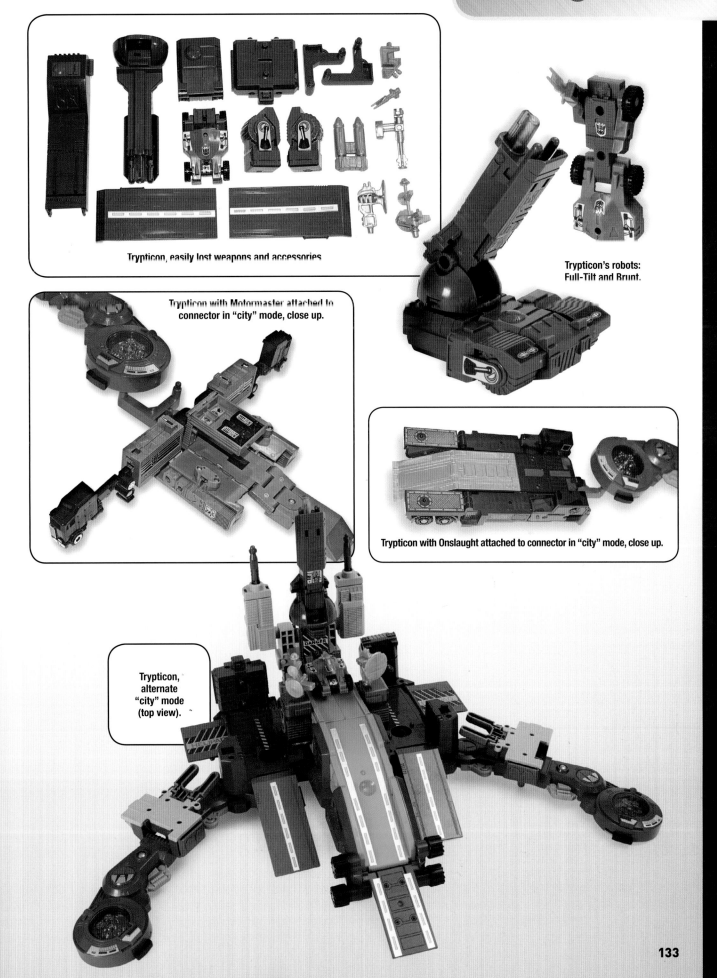

Trypticon, easily lost weapons and accessories

Trypticon's robots: Full-Tilt and Brunt.

Trypticon with Motormaster attached to connector in "city" mode, close up.

Trypticon with Onslaught attached to connector in "city" mode, close up.

Trypticon, alternate "city" mode (top view).

# 1987

## SERIES 4

The creativity of Transformers offerings in 1987 was unparalleled. Headmasters and Targetmasters led the pack and featured Nebulan drivers, pilots, and trainers that merged with Transformers to act as the robots' heads or weapons. These two ingenious sub-groups of Autobots and Decepticons command very high prices on the secondary market, whether loose or packaged. One particular stand out of 1987 is the 2' tall Autobot Headmaster Base: Fortress Maximus, who collectors consider to be the "Holy Grail" (the most oft-requested and desirable Transformer) of the line.

The Technobots and Terrorcons became the last of the "scramble-city"-type combiner teams issued. Other innovations to the 1987 line-up included the Autobot and Decepticon Clones, whose robots modes looked almost alike, but their alternate modes differed entirely; the Autobots' Monsterbots, who remarkably mimicked Decepticon alternate modes; and the ultimate Transformer—the Decepticon Six Changer Six Shot, who had a challenging "sealed" instruction booklet and could transform into six different modes!

Transformers decoys were the new promotional items for 1987. The decoys were small rubber Transformers figures packaged randomly into both newly released and re-released MOC (*not* MISB) Transformers. Autobot decoys were cast in red, while Decepticon decoys were crafted in purple (note that some early issue Decepticon decoys are also cast in red and are very hard to find). The decoys' back story was illustrated in a tiny fold-out comic that came with carded figures, and stated (via a comic strip) that they functioned to "draw Decepticon fire" so Blurr (1986, 1987) and Hot Rod (1986, 1987) could retrieve the captured Creation Matrix (The Autobot Matrix of Leadership).

These non-poseable rubber toys were randomly inserted onto carded Transformers, so it is quite difficult to obtain a complete collection of decoys (which could run upward of $160-200+). Most decoys sell for $4-10 each when you can find them, while more popular Autobot characters, i.e. the Dinobots (1985), Sunstreaker (1984), Optimus Prime (1984), etc., and later Decepticon decoys (#'s 33-52). However, red-colored Decepticons in particular fetch far more money (think $10-45+ per decoy). Each decoy is individually-numbered, and this tiny raised number can be found somewhere on the back of each decoy itself.

## CHASE

**THROTTLEBOTS**

**FUNCTION:** Scout
**MOTTO:** "Hunters drive; targets park."

"Impatient, overeager, usually ten miles down the road before other Throttlebots have shifted into gear. Likes to brag about past exploits and future conquests. Very popular. In car mode, can cruise at 240 mph. Excellent vision—can see long distances in three directions at the same time. Possesses an array of radar dishes positioned under roof in car mode. Prone to drive shaft and transmission problems."

| Strength | Intelligence | Speed | Endurance | Rank | Courage | Firepower | Skill |
|---|---|---|---|---|---|---|---|
| 4 | 6 | 6 | 4 | 6 | 9 | 1 | 8 |

MLC: **$6-10**, MIP (opened): **$24-30**, MOC: **$75-150**

Chase, robot mode.

Chase, alternate mode.

Chase, with his pull-back action and red color is a relatively bland addition to the Throttlebots, yet aptly fills the holes of Autobot Mini-cars. His transformation sequence is simple, and he does not retail for much on the secondary market.

**ALTERNATE MODE:** Ferrari Testarossa.
**EASILY LOST WEAPONS AND ACCESSORIES:** N/A.

# THROTTLEBOTS

The Throttlebots were a low-price point addition to the Autobots army in 1987. Taking the place of the Autobot Mini-cars from 1984-1986, the Throttlebots were essentially a step up in quality, as they had pull-back action and were not as "superdeformed" as the earlier Takara constructed mini-car designs. But they were official Transformers, and they were inexpensive at retail.

## Transformers Decoys: 1987 pack-in promotional (#s 1-52)

**AUTOBOTS:**
[01] Grimlock
[02] Snarl
[03] Swoop
[04] Sludge
[05] Slag
[06] Ratchet
[07] Ironhide
[08] Smokescreen
[09] Grapple
[10] Trailbreaker
[11] Sunstreaker
[12] Skids
[13] Jazz
[14] Inferno
[15] Tracks
[16] Red Alert
[17] Hound
[18] Sideswipe

**AUTOBOTS** *cont.*
[19] Prowl
[20] Mirage
[21] Hoist
[22] Wheeljack
[23] Bluestreak
[24] Brawn
[25] Windcharger
[26] Bumblebee
[27] Huffer
[28] Cliffjumper
[29] Blaster
[30] Perceptor
[31] Optimus Prime

**DECEPTICONS:**
[32] Megatron
[33] Skywarp
[34] Thundercracker

**DECEPTICONS** *cont.*
[35] Starscream
[36] Soundwave
[37] Blitzwing
[38] Astrotrain
[39] Kickback
[40] Shrapnel
[41] Bombshell
[42] Hook
[43] Scavenger
[44] Bonecrusher
[45] Long Haul
[46] Mixmaster
[47] Scrapper
[48] Devastator
[49] Ravage
[50] Frenzy
[51] Shockwave
[52] Reflector

# FREEWAY

**THROTTLEBOTS**

**FUNCTION:** Saboteur
**MOTTO:** "Words can cut deeper than steel."

"The Throttlebots' self-appointed comedian. Specializes in insulting others, but gets angry when others make fun of him. His car radio intercepts and decodes enemy radio broadcasts, transmits erroneous ones instead. Uses sonic land mines, magnetic homing grenades, rusting agents, etc. for sabotage. At times he laughs so hard at his jokes he blows internal circuits and disables himself."

| Strength | Intelligence | Speed | Endurance | Rank | Courage | Firepower | Skill |
|----------|--------------|-------|-----------|------|---------|-----------|-------|
| 3 | 6 | 4 | 6 | 6 | 8 | 3 | 9 |

MLC: **$6-10**, MIP (opened): **$24-30**, MOC: **$75-150**

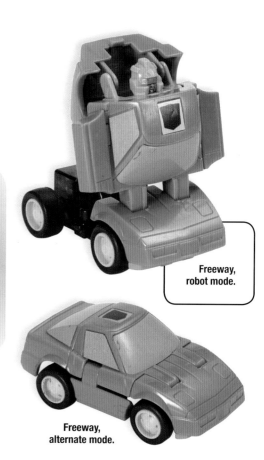

Freeway, robot mode.

Freeway had a nice-looking alternate mode, yet because of his simple transformation, he is not one of the more popular Autobots. He is readily available on the secondary market.

**ALTERNATE MODE:** Chevrolet Corvette.
**EASILY LOST WEAPONS AND ACCESSORIES:** N/A.

Freeway, alternate mode.

# GOLDBUG

**THROTTLEBOTS**

**FUNCTION:** Espionage Director
**MOTTO:** "To know others you must know yourself first."

"Has the mind of the Autobot Bumblebee, but a new, improved body. More serious, assertive, mature than he was. Realizes what others think of him isn't nearly as important as what he thinks of himself. Excellent fuel efficiency; 2-1/2 times better than the next best Throttlebot. Adaptable to underwater, cold and hot environments. Can withstand temperatures from 150 to 180 degrees Fahrenheit."

| Strength | Intelligence | Speed | Endurance | Rank | Courage | Firepower | Skill |
|----------|--------------|-------|-----------|------|---------|-----------|-------|
| 9 | 8 | 4 | 8 | 8 | 10 | 1 | 7 |

MLC: **$8-16**, MIP (opened): **$28-35**, MOC: **$75-150**

Goldbug, robot mode.

Goldbug is often the most in-demand of the Throttlebots on the secondary market, as he is the reincarnated form of Bumblebee (1984), except exponentially stronger, smarter, and tougher. Any fan of the Autobots' most underrated espionage agent was almost forced to pick him up in his new form.

**ALTERNATE MODE:** Volkswagen Beetle.
**EASILY LOST WEAPONS AND ACCESSORIES:** N/A.

Goldbug, alternate mode.

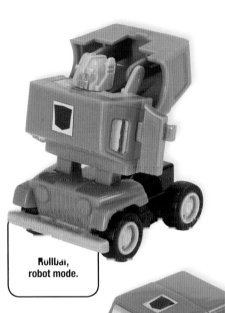

Rollbar,
robot mode.

Rollbar,
alternate mode.

# ROLLBAR

### THROTTLEBOTS

**FUNCTION:** Tracker
**MOTTO:** "When the going gets tough, the tough get driving."

"Impulsive, loves to take chances, put his life on the line. Speaks in corny, macho clichés, which unintentionally elicits laughter from the other Throttlebots. Extremely agile in jeep mode; can go into flips and rolls with very little loss in speed. Has built-in chemical sensors, radiation detectors, audio and video recorders to assist his tracking."

| Strength | Intelligence | Speed | Endurance | Rank | Courage | Firepower | Skill |
|---|---|---|---|---|---|---|---|
| 5 | 7 | 4 | 7 | 6 | 10 | 1 | 9 |

MLC: **$8-12**, MIP (opened): **$24-30**, MOC: **$75-150**

Because Rollbar's alternate mode is that of a Jeep 4x4, he will always be one of the more popular of smaller Transformers, and his excellent characterization on his Tech Spec bio encourages some productive role play well after ripping him out of his package.

**ALTERNATE MODE:** 4x4 Jeep Wrangler.
**EASILY LOST WEAPONS AND ACCESSORIES:** N/A.

# SEARCHLIGHT

### THROTTLEBOTS

**FUNCTION:** Surveillance
**MOTTO:** "Seeing is, by itself, not enough for believing."

"A creature of the night. Cruises the Earth with the curiosity of a cat. Nothing is too insignificant or irrelevant to escape his notice. Quiet, serious; a loner. Top row of headlights equipped with stereoscopic digital video cameras, spectroscopic chemical analyzer, and radiation detector. Bottom lights can produce strobe effect, full color spectrum with blinding 10,000 watt brightness."

| Strength | Intelligence | Speed | Endurance | Rank | Courage | Firepower | Skill |
|---|---|---|---|---|---|---|---|
| 3 | 7 | 5 | 8 | 6 | 4 | 1 | 9 |

MLC: **$6-10**, MIP (opened): **$24-30**,
MOC: **$75-150**

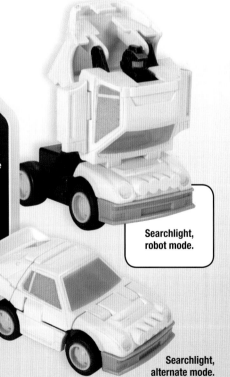

Searchlight,
robot mode.

Searchlight,
alternate mode.

The strange Tech Spec description of Searchlight almost belies his physical form. He's bright white, has light-blue colored windows and a nice powder-blue bumper. If there ever were a misnomer among the Transformers, this is the one.

**ALTERNATE MODE:** Ford RS200.
**EASILY LOST WEAPONS AND ACCESSORIES:** N/A.

# WIDELOAD

**THROTTLEBOTS**

**FUNCTION:** Materials Transport
**MOTTO:** "Look good and you'll have the world in your pocket."

"Usually he's so dirty you'd think he sweated grease, but he's a neatness fanatic. Vain and superficial—judges others on appearances. Uses spare time to work on his polish. Can haul up to 1,000,000 pounds. Uses hands and tires' sensors to find new sources of raw materials. Unusually susceptible to rust, an embarrassment given his pride in his appearance."

| Strength | Intelligence | Speed | Endurance | Rank | Courage | Firepower | Skill |
|----------|--------------|-------|-----------|------|---------|-----------|-------|
| 9 | 4 | 2 | 9 | 5 | 7 | 1 | 5 |

MLC: **$6-10**, MIP (opened): **$24-30**, MOC: **$75-150**

Wideload, robot mode.

As a bright orange and blue dump truck, he was an odd standout among the other more tamely designed Throttlebots such as Searchlight, Chase, and Rollbar, yet there was something about him (well, he is a construction vehicle) that still keeps him in demand. Pull him back, and let him go.

**ALTERNATE MODE:** Caterpillar 777 Dump Truck.
**EASILY LOST WEAPONS AND ACCESSORIES:** N/A.

Wideload, alternate mode.

Cloudraker, robot mode.

# CLOUDRAKER

**CLONES**

**FUNCTION:** Sky Fighter
**MOTTO:** "Gravity is the chain that binds us all."

"Often acts frustrated, can't reach escape velocity and achieve orbit. Extreme claustrophobe—feels the sky isn't big enough for him. Usually flies as high as he can. Terrified of being on the ground. In vehicle mode, uses 2 gravity-rod rifles to cause objects to float away or crash to the ground. Clone brother is Fastlane."

| Strength | Intelligence | Speed | Endurance | Rank | Courage | Firepower | Skill |
|----------|--------------|-------|-----------|------|---------|-----------|-------|
| 6 | 6 | 8 | 6 | 5 | 7 | 6 | 6 |

MLC (Cloudraker only): **$20-28**, MLC (set w/ Fastlane): **$38-42**, MIB (set w/Fastlane): **$42-58**, MISB (pair): **$125-250**

**ALTERNATE MODE:** Futuristic jet.
**EASILY LOST WEAPONS AND ACCESSORIES:** 2 gravity-rod rifles.

Cloudraker, easily lost weapons and accessories.

Cloudraker, alternate mode.

Fastlane and Cloudraker, together.

Fastlane, easily lost weapons and accessories.

Fastlane, alternate mode.

## FASTLANE

**CLONES**

**FUNCTION:** Warrior
**MOTTO:** "Either you're out of my way or out of luck."

"A bit immature, sometimes acts like a thrill-seeking show-off, enjoys looking for new ways to get his kicks. Usually makes reckless driving a way of life. In vehicle mode, reaches maximum speed of 220 mph; maximum speed with booster jets: 550 mph (for no more than 5 seconds). Range: 350 miles. In robot mode, carries 2 sonic boom rifles; one blast can shatter foot-thick steel. Clone brother is Cloudraker."

| Strength | Intelligence | Speed | Endurance | Rank | Courage | Firepower | Skill |
|----------|-------------|-------|-----------|------|---------|-----------|-------|
| 6 | 3 | 6 | 6 | 5 | 9 | 7 | 7 |

(Fastlane only): **$20-28**, MLC (set w/Cloudraker): **$38-42**, MIB (set w/Cloudraker): **$42-58**, MISB (pair): **$125-250**

**ALTERNATE MODE:** Futuristic dragster.
**EASILY LOST WEAPONS AND ACCESSORIES:** 2 sonic boom rifles, spoiler.

Fastlane, robot mode.

[AUTOBOT]

# CLONES

A new and fascinating concept of design, the Autobot and Decepticon "Clones" were intriguing because the robots looked nearly identical, but they transformed into entirely different vehicles.

It is rumored that the Clones were a failed experiment by Shockwave, but how Cloudraker and Fastlane then joined the Autobot cause is a mystery (see Decepticon Clones, 1987). As for the toys, in addition to their heat-sensitive faction stickers, the Autobot and Decepticon Clones each came with an extra rub sign that indicated what mode they would be transforming into: Cloudraker's extra heat sensitive label was that of a jet, while Fastlane's rub sign revealed a dragster.

# DOUBLESPY

Punch/Counterpunch was the one Transformer that every collector desired due to his function as Autobot Double Agent—and the toy's ability to transform into both an Autobot and a Decepticon (he comes with both factions' hidden rub signs). Many Transformers play room adventures revolved around this fascinating toy because "[Punch/Counterpunch] can disguise himself as a Decepticon and infiltrate their [enemy] forces."

Punch, Autobot robot mode.

## PUNCH/ COUNTERPUNCH

**DOUBLESPY**

**FUNCTION:** Double Agent
**MOTTO:** "In my business, there are no friends, only suspects."

"Punch, the Autobot, transforms into Counterpunch, the Decepticon, to infiltrate enemy installations. Cool-headed, a robot of few words, reveals little of his true self to either side. Maximum car mode speed: 160 mph. Uses twin mortar launcher in Autobot mode, photon cannon in Decepticon mode."

| Strength | Intelligence | Speed | Endurance | Rank | Courage | Firepower | Skill |
|---|---|---|---|---|---|---|---|
| 6 | 9 | 4 | 6 | 7 | 10 | 6 | 9 |

MLC: **$55-68**, MIB: **$110-135**, MISB: **$200-300+**

Counterpunch, Decepticon robot mode.

Punch/ Counterpunch, easily lost weapons and accessories.

Punch/ Counterpunch, alternate mode.

The Autobot Double Agent Punch/Counterpunch had a realistic vehicle mode that transformed into a robot that owed his allegiance to the Autobots, yet was able to convert into an "alternate" robot mode whose appearance was that of a Decepticon. It was an excellent attempt at creating a fascinating toy.

As a character, Dreamwave Comics suggested in their 2003 *Transformers: More Than Meets The Eye* guide books that Punch/Counterpunch is the victim of a dissociative identity disorder, where, the patient "suffer(s) from (the) alternation of two or more distinct personality states with impaired recall among personality states of important information." Autobot Punch has been undercover as Decepticon Counterpunch for so long, that his original benevolent personality is losing its frequency, becoming buried under his merciless faux identity: he is frequently blacking out for days, with no memory of where he's been, or what he's done.

**ALTERNATE MODE:** Pontiac Fiero.
**EASILY LOST WEAPONS AND ACCESSORIES:** Photon cannon, twin mortar launcher.

# TECHNOBOTS

Ascribing to the "scramble city" concept of Transformers combiners (where the four smaller members of the team can form interchangeable limbs for their gestalt), the Technobots were the answer to the question: Can any Transformers combiner team think efficiently as a super robot? Computron was the most effective thinker of all gestalts, although it took him a bit of time to reach a decisive thought. The Technobots are some of the more popular of the combiners, commanding good prices on the secondary market, and decent sales as a set.

Afterburner, robot mode.

## AFTERBURNER

**TECHNOBOTS**

**FUNCTION:** Gunner
**MOTTO:** "Following leaders leads nowhere."

"Quick to anger, even quicker to attack. Defiant, uncooperative, nasty tempered. Hates authority. In vehicle mode, uses solid rocket fuel packs to boost speed to 450 mph. Tires secrete adhesive that enables him to drive up most walls. Carries 2 laser-guided incendiary missiles, rapid-fire plasma pulse cannon. In robot mode, uses semi-automatic sonic blaster pistol. Combines with fellow Technobots to form Computron."

| Strength | Intelligence | Speed | Endurance | Rank | Courage | Firepower | Skill |
|---|---|---|---|---|---|---|---|
| 7 | 6 | 6 | 6 | 5 | 9 | 7 | 7 |

MLC: **$20-25**, MIP (opened): **$40-45**, MOC: **$100-200**

Afterburner, easily lost weapons and accessories.

Afterburner's vehicle design seem to be patterned after the "light cycles" from the Disney movie *Tron*, and this, coupled with his imagined ability to climb most walls, made him a pretty popular Autobot. Take care when you find loose samples of Afterburner on the secondary market, as the two stickers near his front wheel in vehicle mode are prone to rubbing off.

**ALTERNATE MODE:** Sonic blaster pistol, pulse cannon, missiles/missile rack.
**EASILY LOST WEAPONS AND ACCESSORIES:** Sonic blaster pistol, pulse cannon, missile bracket.

Afterburner, alternate mode.

# LIGHTSPEED

**TECHNOBOTS**

**FUNCTION:** Data Processor
**MOTTO:** "Space travel is the only flight to freedom."

"He longs to be reconstructed into an interstellar spacecraft so he can explore the vast gulfs of space, feels he's a prisoner of gravity in his present form. In jet car mode, goes from 0 to 500 mph in 8 seconds. Cruising speed: 300 mph. Has twin infra-red scope missile launchers. In robot mode has blinding light-burst gun. Combines with fellow Technobots to form Computron."

| Strength | Intelligence | Speed | Endurance | Rank | Courage | Firepower | Skill |
|---|---|---|---|---|---|---|---|
| 6 | 8 | 5 | 6 | 6 | 8 | 7 | 8 |

**$** MLC: **$20-28**, MIP (opened): **$42-55+**, MOC: **$175-300**

Lightspeed, robot mode.

Technobot Lightspeed's excellent characterization on his Tech Spec biography makes his toy really come to life as an Autobot car that wishes he were soaring through the heavens. However, his dedication to the Autobot cause allows him to subdue this impulse. As a toy, he shares a problem similar to Scourge (1986) and Afterburner (1987): two of his stickers (on the side of his vehicle mode) can be damaged when transforming the toy from car to robot.

Lightspeed, alternate mode.

**ALTERNATE MODE:** Futuristic jet car.
**EASILY LOST WEAPONS AND ACCESSORIES:** Light-burst gun, 2 infra-red missile launchers.

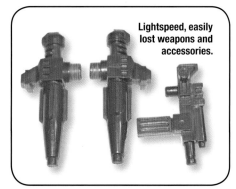

Lightspeed, easily lost weapons and accessories.

# NOSECONE

**TECHNOBOTS**

**FUNCTION:** Assault Vehicle
**MOTTO:** "It's not who's the fastest; it's who reaches the finish line."

"He makes enemy fortifications look like walls of Swiss cheese by the time he's finished with them. Slow and methodical—weathers artillery fire with the same calm he endures criticism of his apparent laziness. In vehicle mode, durabyllium-steel alloy drill can pierce almost any material; 2 rocket-propelled missiles use vidicon cameras to lock onto targets. In robot mode, has X-ray laser pistol. Combines with fellow Technobots to form Computron."

| Strength | Intelligence | Speed | Endurance | Rank | Courage | Firepower | Skill |
|---|---|---|---|---|---|---|---|
| 7 | 6 | 3 | 9 | 5 | 8 | 7 | 7 |

**$** MLC: **$20-25**, MIP (opened): **$40-45**, MOC: **$100-200**

Nosecone, robot mode.

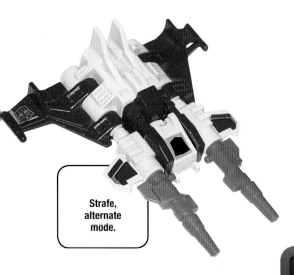

Strafe, alternate mode.

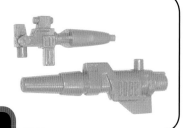

Strafe, easily lost weapons and accessories.

## STRAFE

**TECHNOBOTS**

**FUNCTION:** Aerial Gunner
**MOTTO:** "Shoot everywhere—since that's where the enemies are."

"He never looks at his targets before he shoots since he never aims—he just sprays artillery in all directions as soon as he arrives. High-strung, unnerved by quiet, expert marksmen. Lightning fast reflexes. In vehicle mode, maximum ground speed: 250 mph; maximum air speed: 580 mph. Carries twin automatic light-pulse blasters. In robot mode, uses heat-ray rifle. Combines with fellow Technobots to form Computron."

| Strength | Intelligence | Speed | Endurance | Rank | Courage | Firepower | Skill |
|---|---|---|---|---|---|---|---|
| 5 | 6 | 6 | 7 | 5 | 8 | 7 | 4 |

MLC: **$20-25**, MIP (opened): **$40-45**, MOC: **$100-200**

Strafe, robot mode.

Strafe has the distinction of being one of the few Transformers whose weapons in robot mode are imperative in establishing the integrity of his vehicle mode: to wit, he needs his 2 light-pulse blasters to form part of his rocket plane's wings. He is one of the more popular Technobots because of his alternate mode's appearance, and sells briskly on the secondary market.

**ALTERNATE MODE:** Futuristic rocket plane.
**EASILY LOST WEAPONS AND ACCESSORIES:** Heat-ray rifle, 2 light-pulse blasters.

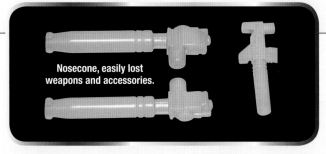

Nosecone, easily lost weapons and accessories.

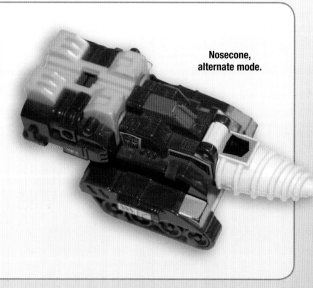

Nosecone, alternate mode.

Although he is usually the least in-demand of the Technobots on the secondary market, Nosecone's vehicle mode is still colorful and team-appropriate. Nosecone's rifle can fit in his right hand's side peg mount, or in a mount underneath the hand, and like every other Technobot, they can utilize their robot's weapons to form attack vehicle modes.

**ALTERNATE MODE:** Excavation vehicle.
**EASILY LOST WEAPONS AND ACCESSORIES:** X-ray laser pistol, 2 rocket-propelled missiles.

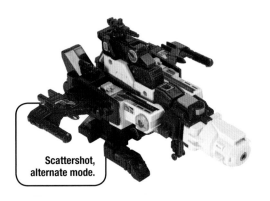

Scattershot, alternate mode.

# SCATTERSHOT

**TECHNOBOTS**

**FUNCTION:** Technobot Leader
**MOTTO:** "Decepticons are like rust spots—they're ugly and they can pop up anywhere."

"A brawling, bragging berserker…he wades into a Decepticon patrol with all barrels blazing, doesn't stop until he's out of ammo. Calls those who disapprove of his methods 'tinplated bucketheads.' Rude, gruff, and direct. In vehicle and battle station modes, has electron pulse cannon in nosecone; array of sonic, thermal and artillery shell guns. In robot mode, has 500 rounds-per-minute automatic acid-pellet gun. Combines with fellow Technobots to form Computron."

| Strength | Intelligence | Speed | Endurance | Rank | Courage | Firepower | Skill |
|----------|-------------|-------|-----------|------|---------|-----------|-------|
| 8 | 7 | 7 | 8 | 8 | 9 | 8 | 6 |

MLC: **$48-65**, MIB: **$80-105**, MISB: **$300-450**

Scattershot, robot mode.

As leader of the sophisticated and intelligent Technobots, one would assume that Scattershot would be methodical and precise when carrying out his assigned duties. However, his personality is contrary to this assumed belief. As a toy, Scattershot sports many fine and gross details, but is a little "boxy looking" as a robot. Scattershot can transform into a strange-looking rocket launcher mode in addition to his standard attack jet alternate form.

**ALTERNATE MODE:** Futuristic attack jet, rocket launcher.
**EASILY LOST WEAPONS AND ACCESSORIES:** 2 artillery guns, acid pellet gun, 2 (Computron) foot stands, 2 large (Computron) fists, (Computron) robot head, (Computron) chest shield/base.

Scattershot, easily lost weapons and accessories.

Scattershot, rocket launcher mode.

Computron, combiner instructions.

Technobots in attack mode.

Computron, robot mode.

## COMPUTRON

**TECHNOBOTS**

**FUNCTION:** Super Warrior
**MOTTO:** "Complete data analysis is essential for the synthesis of successful strategy."

"He always makes the right choice…but takes several minutes to make it, since he first completely analyzes input from the 5 Technobots who comprise him. Has great strength, equipped with data processing, communications, radar equipment. Uses Scattershot's automatic acid-pellet gun. Chooses his words with great care and precision—when Computron talks, everyone listens."

| Strength | Intelligence | Speed | Endurance | Rank | Courage | Firepower | Skill |
|---|---|---|---|---|---|---|---|
| 9 | 10 | 2 | 8 | 7 | 10 | 7 | 9 |

Computron Gift Set (all 5 Technobots together)
MLC: **$125-165+**, MIB: **$325-340+**, MISB: **$600-900**

Computron is unique among combiner characters, because his intelligence is actually *raised* by the merging of his component parts—the perfect definition of a gestalt! His appearance defines who the Technobots are, and his analytically-visaged head sculpt, bright colors, and futuristic-looking component parts make him one of the most popular and sought after "scramble city" combiners on the secondary market. Like all combiners, finding Computron in his gift set box is extremely rare.

Doublecross, alternate mode.

Doublecross, easily lost weapon and accessory.

# DOUBLECROSS

**MONSTERBOTS**

**FUNCTION:** Supply Procurer
**MOTTO:** "Decepticon destruction is my favorite sport… and mine, too."

"Can't be depended on—can't even depend on himself, since he has two minds and they never agree on anything. A deal made with one mind won't necessarily bind the other to act accordingly. Ferocious, savage, hisses when he talks. In creature mode, flies at 80 mph, has razor-sharp teeth. In robot mode, uses rust-ray rifle to corrode enemy robots."

| Strength | Intelligence | Speed | Endurance | Rank | Courage | Firepower | Skill |
|---|---|---|---|---|---|---|---|
| 1 | 6 | 2 | 10 | 6 | 9 | 6 | 7 |

MLC: **$48-65+**, MIB: **$60-75+**, MISB: **$200-300**

With "Spark-shooting action!!!" coming out of his chest, the undependable and contradictory Doublecross is not a favorite in the Autobot ranks, yet his ferocity and ability to fly (fairly quickly) makes him a desirable warrior to have on your side in combat. In action, Doublecross exemplifies his appellation. Many unfamiliar collectors incorrectly identify the three Monsterbot toys as Decepticons because of their frightening alternate modes, but Autobots they are at heart. Note: The buzzsaw that covers Doublecross's spark opening actually moves when his spark button is depressed.

**ALTERNATE MODE:** Two-headed dragon.
**EASILY LOST WEAPONS AND ACCESSORIES:** Rust-ray rifle.

Doublecross, robot mode.

# GROTUSQUE

**MONSTERBOTS**

**FUNCTION:** Military Strategist
**MOTTO:** "If it ain't fun to do, it ain't worth doing."

"He says that nothing frightens him, except when he looks in the mirror. He thinks that everything is a big joke and acts accordingly, even during battle. Goofy, irreverent, sometimes annoying…but a top-notch warrior. In robot mode, wields a vaporator which gassifies a target's fuel, leaving it inoperable. In creature mode, has indestructible tusks. Flies at 45 mph, can leap 3 miles at a time."

| Strength | Intelligence | Speed | Endurance | Rank | Courage | Firepower | Skill |
|---|---|---|---|---|---|---|---|
| 7 | 9 | 4 | 6 | 8 | 10 | 7 | 10 |

MLC: **$48-65+**, MIB: **$60-75**, MISB: **$200-300**

Grotusque, robot mode.

The fire-breathing monster Grotusque (a pun on the grotesqueness of his appearance combined with the two large tusks that protrude from his monster mode's mouth) is a valuable warrior in the Autobot army. He is a skilled military tactician with very high intelligence, impeccable expertise,

# MONSTERBOTS

When released in 1987, the Monsterbot commandos confused many devoted collectors based upon the similarities these Transformers shared with the fearsome Decepticons (aggression, bloodthirstiness, belligerence, etc.). Yet Autobots they were ... usually called upon to perform tasks that most heroic do-gooders would scoff at entirely. With their "fire breathing" push button action and fairly intricate transformation sequences, the Monsterbots were first-rate additions to the Autobot ranks.

Repugnus, easily lost weapon and accessory.

Repugnus, alternate mode.

Repugnus, robot mode.

## REPUGNUS

**MONSTERBOTS**

**FUNCTION:** Counter-Intelligence
**MOTTO:** "No job is too disgusting to disgust me."

"He has a personality as repellent as his looks—been kicked out of the Autobots many times for insubordination only to be asked back since he's always willing to undertake missions too low-down and dirty for anyone else to consider. In robot mode, carries venom laser that slows cerebro impulses and paralyzes on impact. In creature mode, has infra-red and X-ray vision; can emit colors and stroboscopic effect with eyes. Claws contain chemical, electromagnetic and audio sensors; can rip through almost any substance."

| Strength | Intelligence | Speed | Endurance | Rank | Courage | Firepower | Skill |
|---|---|---|---|---|---|---|---|
| 5 | 9 | 2 | 9 | 6 | 10 | 2 | 10 |

MLC: **$42-60+**, MIB: **$54-68+**, MISB: **$175-265**

The amoral Repugnus is truly the Autobots' last hope when called upon to perform the more despicable tasks of war; and they are usually reluctant to call upon his questionable services. Regardless, as interrogator, assassin, or fearless warrior, Repugnus is a formidable force, and has always fascinated me. As with all of the Monsterbots, you can push their respective buttons, and "flames shoot!" As for his alternate mode, the only direction that his instruction booklet provides is that he is an "insect."

**ALTERNATE MODE:** Insect monster.
**EASILY LOST WEAPONS AND ACCESSORIES:** Venom laser.

Grotusque, easily lost weapons and accessories.

and limitless courage. Sadly, Grotusque despises his hideous appearance, but makes light of it to cheer up the troops that depend on him for guidance on the battlefield. His toy is one of the more curious and unidentifiable of all Transformers: a winged sabertooth tiger.

**ALTERNATE MODE:** Winged sabertooth tiger.
**EASILY LOST WEAPONS AND ACCESSORIES:** Vaporator, two wings.

Grotusque, alternate mode. **147**

[AUTOBOT]

# TARGETMASTERS

Targetmasters were a fascinating new addition to both factions of the Transformers. According to the back story, Targetmasters are Nebulan [humanoid] aliens who paired up with Cybertronian Transformers – where these Nebulans would undergo a process by which they would be able to change into the Transformers' weapon of choice.

Therefore, when a Transformer was not using his Targetmaster weapon, the gun/laser/launcher would exist as a humanoid companion. And what kid wouldn't want a Transformer whose gun could also have an alternate mode? Hasbro's introduction of the Targetmasters also allowed them to re-use the molds of some 1986 characters [Blurr, Hot Rod, Kup, and Decepticons Cyclonus and Scourge – with some minor changes to their hand pegs and vehicle-weapon mounts] and re-introduce these popular Transformers as ... bum-bum-bum: Targetmasters!

## HOT ROD

**TARGETMASTERS**

**FUNCTION:** Cavalier
**MOTTO:** "My actions speak louder than words."

"He dreams of great heroics, but he acts like an immature adolescent. Impulsive, friendly, not to good at following orders. Often goes off on his own adventure with Firebolt, his electrostatic discharger rifle, who led a quiet scholarly life as Nebulan's top atomic physics scientist until he became the thrill-seeking Hot Rod's partner. Firebolt is excited, but nervous, about the prospect. In vehicle mode, maximum speed: 330 mph, range: 150 miles."

| Strength | Intelligence | Speed | Endurance | Rank | Courage | Firepower | Skill |
|----------|-------------|-------|-----------|------|---------|-----------|-------|
| 6 | 5 | 6 | 8 | 5 | 10 | 7 | 6 |

MLC: $70-85, MIB: $95-135+, MISB: $350-500+
NOTE: Even though 'Targetmaster Hot Rod' was re-released by Takara in 2002, there are differences in the mold of both the released Targetmaster Hot Rod and his partner Firebolt from this, the original.

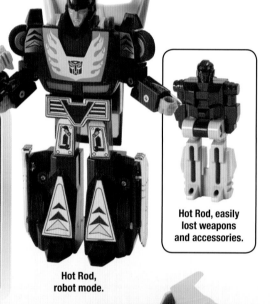

Hot Rod, easily lost weapons and accessories.

Hot Rod, robot mode.

Hot Rod's (1986) original Tech Spec meter contained much beefier stats than Targetmaster Hot Rod. How do you become a Targetmaster and have your firepower rank decrease? One explanation was that when originally released, Hasbro felt that their *Transformers: The Movie* version of Hot Rod (1986) was far too powerful, so they adjusted his statistics when they could—one year later during his Targetmaster re-release. Regardless, Targetmaster Hot Rod is one of the most expensive and challenging of all Transformers to find in any condition.

Note that Targetmaster Hot Rod's hands have been re-molded to accommodate for his partner, Firebolt, instead of his former photon lasers. His hood peg has also been modified for the same purpose. For a more complete bio, see Hot Rod (1986).

Hot Rod, close up of inner racecar seats.

**ALTERNATE MODE:** Cybertronian car.
**EASILY LOST WEAPONS AND ACCESSORIES:**
Firebolt figure/electrostatic discharger rifle.

Hot Rod, alternate mode with attached Targetmaster.

Hot Rod, Targetmaster hand hole vs. non-Targetmaster hand hole comparison.

# BLURR

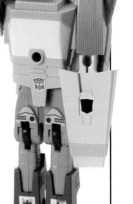

Blurr, robot mode.

**TARGETMASTERS**

**FUNCTION:** Data Courier
**MOTTO:** "The faster it is, the better I like it."

"The fastest Autobot land vehicle—and he talks even faster; often has to be told to slow down so he can be understood. Nervous, high-strung, loyal, determined. Paired with Haywire, excitable Nebulan teenager whose impulsiveness makes him a chancy electro-laser cannon, at best. In vehicle mode, maximum speed: 750 mph, range: 1500 miles."

| Strength | Intelligence | Speed | Endurance | Rank | Courage | Firepower | Skill |
|---|---|---|---|---|---|---|---|
| 5 | 7 | 7 | 4 | 5 | 9 | 7 | 7 |

**MLC: $65-82, MIB: $110-125, MISB: $200-300**

As per usual, any of the re-released Targetmasters characters from Sunbow's *Transformers: The Movie* are more difficult to find in their 1987 incarnation with Nebulan partner. Blurr is no exception. His hand holes and hood mount (along with a larger peg on his hood/shield) have been made larger in order to accommodate Haywire (instead of his 1986 accessory, a simple black colored electro-laser). For a more complete bio, see Blurr (1986), and note the differences in his ability scores.

**ALTERNATE MODE:** Futuristic hover.

**EASILY LOST WEAPONS AND ACCESSORIES:** Haywire figure/electro laser cannon, shield/hood.

Blurr, easily lost weapons and accessories.

Blurr, alternate mode with attached Targetmaster.

# CROSSHAIRS

Crosshairs, alternate mode with attached Targetmaster.

**TARGETMASTERS**

**FUNCTION:** Weapons Supervisor
**MOTTO:** "Don't shoot until you see the wires in their eyes."

"Meticulous, cautious, some would say overcautious—won't take a shot unless he's sure he can't miss…won't waste ammo. Pinpointer, his dual rocket-propelled grenade launcher, can lock on target in less than .0003 seconds, but usually trusts Crosshairs to decide when to shoot. In vehicle mode, maximum speed: 160 mph, range: 750 miles; built for traversing rough terrain."

| Strength | Intelligence | Speed | Endurance | Rank | Courage | Firepower | Skill |
|---|---|---|---|---|---|---|---|
| 6 | 7 | 4 | 8 | 6 | 8 | 7 | 9 |

**MLC: $45-62, MIB: $75-100, MISB: $200-300**

All Targetmasters (both "larger" ones in 1987 and the "smaller" releases in 1988) have "attack vehicle" modes, where their Targetmaster Nebulan partners can be mounted on their roof or hood. Crosshairs's Targetmaster partner, Pinpointer, has a fairly simple transformation from Nebulan to grenade launcher with joints existing between Pinpointer's top half, hips, and laser barrels. Crosshairs is a colorful Transformer with an excellent alternate mode. As a character, has the tendency to be overly cautious.

**ALTERNATE MODE:** Armored vehicle.
**EASILY LOST WEAPONS AND ACCESSORIES:** Pinpointer figure/grenade launcher.

Crosshairs, easily lost weapons and accessories.

Crosshairs, robot mode.

Kup, Targetmaster partner
shown lengthwise.

## KUP

TARGETMASTERS

**FUNCTION:** Warrior
**MOTTO:** "The past is the greatest teacher."

"A grizzled veteran with 10,000 tall tales from his 1,000 adventures—has advice for his pals in any situation, whether they want to hear it or not. Recoil, his Nebulan partner, is an old style musket laser and former all-world prismaball (most popular sport on Nebulos) player. In vehicle mode, maximum speed: 100 mph, range: 800 miles."

| Strength | Intelligence | Speed | Endurance | Rank | Courage | Firepower | Skill |
|----------|-------------|-------|-----------|------|---------|-----------|-------|
| 8 | 5 | 2 | 9 | 5 | 10 | 5 | 8 |

MLC: **$46-64**, MIB: **$70-95**, MISB: **$200-300**

Kup was reintroduced as a Targetmaster in 1987 with the likes of his *Transformers: The Movie* compatriots Blurr and Hot Rod. He is one of the more common Targetmasters to find in various conditions on the secondary market, yet his popularity from his appearances in *Transformers: The Movie* and the Sunbow cartoon make him a fairly brisk seller. It should be noted that are a few differences between his initial release (1986) and re-introduction as a Targetmaster: his hand holes are larger, and the bed of his truck now includes a mounting post for Recoil, without his previous incarnation's vaned sticker. For a more complete bio, see Kup (1986).

**ALTERNATE MODE:** Cybertronian pickup truck.
**EASILY LOST WEAPONS AND ACCESSORIES:** Recoil figure/musket laser.

Kup, alternate
mode with attached
Targetmaster.

Kup, robot mode.

Kup, easily lost
weapons and
accessories.

## POINTBLANK

TARGETMASTERS

**FUNCTION:** Enforcer
**MOTTO:** "Be brief of speech and long on action."

"He's a somber, no-nonsense sort, weary from millions of years of war on Cybertron. Believes words can do more harm than weapons, so he has few to offer. Understands the reason for the Autobot-Nebulan alliance, but disapproves of it. Peacemaker, his stereophonic sonic blaster, is a Nebulan law enforcement official who's trying, but failing, to persuade Pointblank to be more accommodating."

| Strength | Intelligence | Speed | Endurance | Rank | Courage | Firepower | Skill |
|----------|-------------|-------|-----------|------|---------|-----------|-------|
| 6 | 7 | 4 | 7 | 8 | 10 | 6 | 8 |

MLC: **$46-65**, MIB: **$75-115**, MISB: **$200-300**

Pointblank,
robot mode.

Sureshot, alternate mode with attached Targetmaster.

Sureshot, easily lost weapons and accessories.

## SURESHOT

**FUNCTION:** Sharpshooter
**MOTTO:** "Believing in yourself improves your aim better than target practice."

"His confidence borders on arrogance—can hit targets blindfolded, from memory. Resents his twin laser cannon, Spoilsport, since he needs no help from Sureshot to shoot, and never asks for any. Spoilsport likes to shoot and show off on his own. The two only cooperate when their lives depend on it. In vehicle mode, Sureshot's maximum speed: 290 mph, range: 1200 miles."

**TARGETMASTERS**

| Strength | Intelligence | Speed | Endurance | Rank | Courage | Firepower | Skill |
|----------|--------------|-------|-----------|------|---------|-----------|-------|
| 6 | 7 | 6 | 7 | 6 | 8 | 7 | 10 |

MLC: **$36-48**, MIB: **$60-78**, MISB: **$200-300**

Sureshot, robot mode.

One of the more gifted sharpshooters of the Autobot Targetmasters, Sureshot's arrogance may be well-founded, for it is assumed that when he and Spoilsport actually cooperate, there isn't a target that they can miss—but they simply can't get it together. Sureshot's robot mode is uniquely well-designed (as are all of the "larger" Autobot Targetmasters), and his futuristic dune buggy mode is also quite aesthetically pleasing.

**ALTERNATE MODE:** Dune buggy.
**EASILY LOST WEAPONS AND ACCESSORIES:** Spoilsport figure/laser cannon, [removable] orange rear spoiler.

With enormous shoulders, a lean waist, great colors, a spoiler in vehicle mode and a chilling name, Pointblank is one of the most aesthetically pleasing of the Autobot Targetmasters. Although his weapon/companion Peacemaker doesn't have one of the most complex transformations, he still achieves an excellent overall effect.

**ALTERNATE MODE:** Race car.
**EASILY LOST WEAPONS AND ACCESSORIES:** Peacemaker figure/sonic blaster, shield/spoiler.

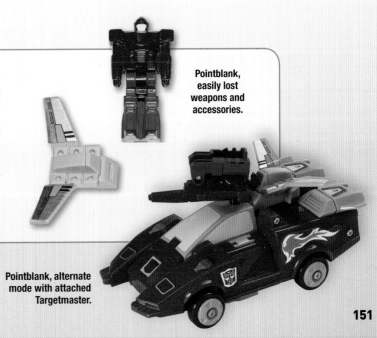

Pointblank, easily lost weapons and accessories.

Pointblank, alternate mode with attached Targetmaster.

Brainstorm, alternate mode.

# BRAINSTORM

**HEADMASTERS**

**FUNCTION:** Biomechanical Engineer
**MOTTO:** "The strongest tyrant cannot crush freedom of thought."

"So full of ideas that he often begins disclosing a new one before he finishes explaining an old one. Worked with the mysterious Nebulan medical doctor, Arcana, to whom he's binary-bonded, to devise new technology that created the Headmasters. In jet mode, maximum speed: 5200 mph. Range: 8000 miles. In robot mode, carries high-energy photon pulse cannons. Sometimes overheats and shorts out sections of his cerebro-circuitry."

| Strength | Intelligence | Speed | Endurance | Rank | Courage | Firepower | Skill |
|---|---|---|---|---|---|---|---|
| 5 | 8 | 9 | 6 | 7 | 9 | 7 | 8 |

MLC: **$75-115**, MIB: **$125-155**, MISB: **$200-300**

Brainstorm's cannons can be mounted on the underside of his jet's cockpit in vehicle mode, and these weapons look as if they're precisely part of his design. It is refreshing to see the Autobots with air vehicles again, as Headmasters Brainstorm and Highbrow (1987) are both futuristic looking jets/spacecrafts. Regardless, Brainstorm is popular on the secondary market, and his design is excellent. Be careful not to transform and move the fins on his robot shoulders too often, as they are frequently found very loose and drooping.

**Brainstorm, easily lost weapons and accessories.**

**ALTERNATE MODE:** Futuristic jet.
**EASILY LOST WEAPONS AND ACCESSORIES:** Arcana pilot/robot head, 2 high-energy photon pulse cannons (left and right).

**Brainstorm, robot mode.**

[AUTOBOT]
# HEADMASTERS

Hardhead, alternate mode.

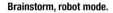

The Headmasters are one of the more fascinating toy concepts ever produced for retail. Here again, the Transformers and Nebulan aliens were binary-bonded to each other. Each Nebulan alien donned an armored transformable suit and changed into the robot's head, thus influencing the robot's attributes. The impact on their strength, intelligence, and speed attributes was observed by flipping open a panel on each robot's chest where a "Built In Tech Specs Meter" provided a colorful readout. These Nebulan heads then became the drivers/pilots of the Transformers' alternate modes (whether vehicle or animal), fitting in an empty compartment somewhere on their respective Transformer. Headmasters, particularly those from 1987, are highly prized by collectors.

# CHROMEDOME

**HEADMASTERS**

**FUNCTION:** Computer Programmer
**MOTTO:** "A battle plan is only as good as its programmer."

"Spent several thousand years crunching numbers at Cybertron's Institute for Higher Programming before a Decepticon attack reduced it to a pile of smoking microchips. Binary-bonded to Stylor, an egotistical Nebulan more concerned with personal appearance than warfare. In car mode, maximum speed: 478 mph. Range: 630 miles. Hood-mounted infra-red range finder automatically targets roof-mounted dual lasers."

| Strength | Intelligence | Speed | Endurance | Rank | Courage | Firepower | Skill |
|----------|--------------|-------|-----------|------|---------|-----------|-------|
| 6 | 9 | 6 | 6 | 7 | 6 | 7 | 9 |

MLC: **$85-115**, MIB: **$140-165+**, MISB: **$300-400**

*Chromedome, robot mode.*

It is suggested that Chromedome was named after his silver-streaked hood, and his vehicle mode stands as one of the most interesting of all Transformers. Although he is one of the easier first generation Headmasters (1987) to find, Chromedome still has a very compelling vehicle mode where both of his lasers can mount on his roof. His robot mode is a bit simplistic and boxy, yet is fairly poseable—even without proper hands.

**ALTERNATE MODE:** Futuristic stock car.

**EASILY LOST WEAPONS AND ACCESSORIES:** Stylor driver/robot head, dual lasers.

*Chromedome, alternate mode.*

*Chromedome, easily lost weapons and accessories.*

# HARDHEAD

**HEADMASTERS**

**FUNCTION:** Ground Assault
**MOTTO:** "It's either MY way—or NO way!"

"The only way to get him to follow advice is to persuade him to come up with the idea himself. Stubborn, doesn't talk much. Binary-bonded to Duros, a Nebulan who loves who loves a battle as much as he does. In tank mode, maximum speed: 155 mph. Range: 450 miles. Has 120mm laser-guided gun that shoots incendiary, sonic and explosive shells. In robot mode, has 2 shatterblasters that shoot diamond-hard shards."

| Strength | Intelligence | Speed | Endurance | Rank | Courage | Firepower | Skill |
|----------|--------------|-------|-----------|------|---------|-----------|-------|
| 10 | 6 | 5 | 9 | 5 | 10 | 8 | 6 |

MLC: **$75-100**, MIB: **$120-145+**, MISB: **$300-400**

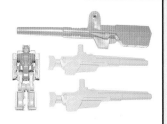

*Hardhead, easily lost weapons and accessories.*

As a strange looking futuristic tank with four treads instead of two, Hardhead is a fine addition to the Autobot ground forces. Stubborn and intractable, Hardhead's strength, endurance, and courage more than surpass those deficiencies. On Hardhead's toy, his shoulder cannon is not *meant* to be removed, yet some collectors force the issue.

**ALTERNATE MODE:** Futuristic tank.

**EASILY LOST WEAPONS AND ACCESSORIES:** Duros tank commander/robot head, 2 shatterblasters, shoulder cannon.

*Hardhead, robot mode.*

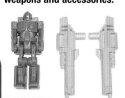

Highbrow, easily lost weapons and accessories.

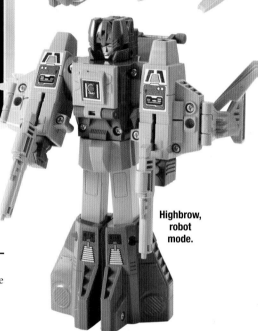

Highbrow, close up on Headmaster in cockpit.

Highbrow, alternate mode.

Highbrow, robot mode.

## HIGHBROW

**HEADMASTERS**

**FUNCTION:** Electronic Warfare
**MOTTO:** "War is the playground of the ignorant."

"To him, warfare is barbaric, worthy of only the most primitive… thinks differences need to be talked about, which he does endlessly. Uses big words no one else understands. A self-righteous snob. Binary-bonded to Gort, a cheerful, courageous young Nebulan. In helicopter mode, maximum speed: 1200 mph; equipped with radioactive jammers, target-indicating radar, magnetic, infra-red, and audio sensors. In robot mode, uses 2 corrosive acid rainmaker rifles."

| Strength | Intelligence | Speed | Endurance | Rank | Courage | Firepower | Skill |
|----------|--------------|-------|-----------|------|---------|-----------|-------|
| 7 | 7 | 7 | 6 | 6 | 6 | 6 | 10 |

MLC: **$92-125+**, MIB: **$150-165**, MISB: **$300-500**

One of the most wonderfully-crafted of all vehicles, Highbrow's helicopter mode allowed him to wield both rainmaker rifles underneath the wings of vehicle mode, or just one under his cockpit. His conversion from futuristic helicopter to robot is relatively simple. As a character, his friends are concerned that his intellectual condescension may be detrimental to Autobot morale, yet they understand that Highbrow's elitism is a result of his doubt about the Autobot-Decepticon conflict.

**ALTERNATE MODE:** Futuristic helicopter.
**EASILY LOST WEAPONS AND ACCESSORIES:** Gort pilot/robot head, 2 corrosive acid rainmaker rifles.

## FORTRESS MAXIMUS

**HEADMASTER CITY**

**FUNCTION:** Headmaster Leader
**MOTTO:** "Prepare for war, but strive for peace."

"Valiant, courageous, a warrior without peer…but peace is his most fervent wish. Fights only out of necessity; believes all violence is ultimately pointless and counterproductive. Transforms to battle station and city modes. Armed with twin laser-guided mortars on legs, heat-seeking dual laser blasters, and fusion-powered photon rifle. Has communications, detection, and repair equipment. Controls two armored vehicles, Gasket and Grommet, which combine to form Cog. Head transforms to semi-autonomous Cerebros, who is binary-bonded to the Nebulan leader, Spike."

| Strength | Intelligence | Speed | Endurance | Rank | Courage | Firepower | Skill |
|----------|--------------|-------|-----------|------|---------|-----------|-------|
| 10 | 10 | 10 | 9 | 10 | 10 | 10 | 9 |

MLC: **$575-650**, MIB: **$750-1,150+**, MISB: **$2,000-3,000+**

The holy grail of the Transformers G1 toy line, Fortress Maximus stands two feet tall and has sixteen different cannons and weapons dotting the landscape of his body. This is unusual because his character is a near-pacifist, and along with Ultra Magnus (1986), he inherited the shared mantle of Autobot Leadership on Cybertron after the disappearance of Optimus Prime and his command team of Autobots on the Ark spacecraft. After millions of years of conflict and hundreds of missions, Fortress Maximus has ultimately resolved that war is not the answer.

As a toy, Fortress Maximus has a wide variety of play features. With a rotating sensor array, launching ramps, a working elevator, jail cell, communications room, command center, helipad with double

Fortress Maximus, Mint in Box.

Fortress Maximus, battle station mode.

Fortress Maximus, robot mode.

lasers, and a control seat, Fortress Maximus is an astonishing achievement for Hasbro. As Headmaster Leader, Fortress Maximus comes replete with five other robots: Cerebros, Spike, Gasket and Grommet, and Cog.

His head can transform into Autobot Cerebros, who is the largest of the supplementary five robots included with the toy and is equipped with small rifle. As a character, Cerebros is fairly independent from "Fort Max," and functions as the super-robot's Headmaster and alternately, as his communications room. Hasbro ingeniously made Cerebro's head removable as well, and this piece converts into the smaller of the two Headmasters included in the set: Spike Witwicky, the most famous human friend and ally of the Autobots (who was prominently featured on the Sunbow animated series). Therefore, Fort Max is a Headmaster with a removable head (Cerebros) that transforms into a robot with a removable head (Spike) that transforms into its own robot!

Two of the other small robots are Gasket (reconnaissance/attack vehicle) and Grommet (armored vehicle); these are outfitted

maintenance vehicles that combine, along with a small right laser arm and small left laser arm and a small rifle, to form the *final* of the five small robots: Cog, who monitors on-site battles as Fort Max's replacement while in city mode.

Fort Max is *always* in demand on the secondary market, where collectors and dealers have a tendency to parcel out the large robot and his accessories into "piecemeal"—piece-by-piece, part-by-part, a relatively popular way of selling larger Transformers.

In Japan, Fortress Maximus came equipped with a Master Sword added to his list of accessories, and was featured prominently in the Japanese exclusive cartoon, *Transformers: Headmasters*.

**ALTERNATE MODE:** City, battle station.

**EASILY LOST WEAPONS AND ACCESSORIES:** Spike Headmaster mini figure/robot head, Cerebros Headmaster robot/robot head, photon rifle, Gasket recon/attack vehicle, Grommet armored vehicle, 2 laser arms, dual laser blaster, Cerebros's mini-laser rifle, Cog's laser, radar scope, 2 side ramps, 2 forearm compartment doors, control center door.

Fortress Maximus, city mode top view.

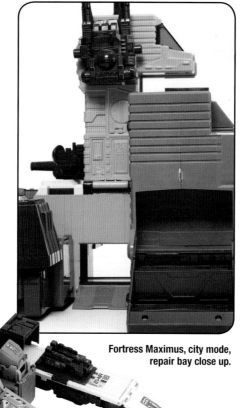

Fortress Maximus, city mode, repair bay close up.

Fortress Maximus, city mode, side ramp close up.

Fortress Maximus, city mode.

Fortress Maximus, city mode, towers close up.

Fortress Maximus, Cerebros as Headmaster with mini-laser rifle.

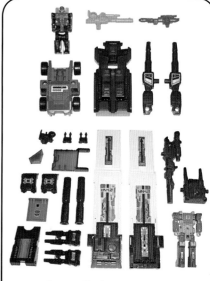

Fortress Maximus, easily lost weapons and accessories.

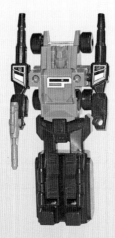

Fortress Maximus, Gasket and Grommet with Cog's laser.

Fortress Maximus, Cog's combined form.

Fortress Maximus, Cerebros in robot mode with Headmaster Spike separate.

Fortress Maximus, Headmaster Tech Specs readout.

[DECEPTICON]

# CASSETTES

These additional cassettes [and the others released in 1988] should be used to assist Decepticon Communications officer Soundwave, yet they came <u>after</u> his solicitation at retail. Yet even without a micro cassette deck to use, these two dinosaurs appealed to Transfans everywhere.

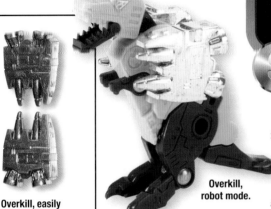

Overkill, easily lost weapons and accessories.

Overkill, robot mode.

## OVERKILL

**CASSETTES**

**FUNCTION:** Warrior
**MOTTO:** "Too much destruction is never enough."

"Whether talking, terrifying, or attacking, he does everything to excess. So busy proving how tough he is by snapping cars in half between his jaws, that he forgets his mission. Can record data as a cassette, rip open the hull of a battleship as a tyrannosaurus. Armed with 2 batteries of motion missiles—each reacts to any moving object bigger than a baseball and explodes on contact."

| Strength | Intelligence | Speed | Endurance | Rank | Courage | Firepower | Skill |
|----------|--------------|-------|-----------|------|---------|-----------|-------|
| 8 | 5 | 2 | 8 | 5 | 6 | 5 | 5 |

MLC: **$20-25**, MIP (opened; two-pack w/Slugfest): **$45-50**, MOC: **$200-300** (two-pack with Slugfest sealed on card)

With a Ceratosaurus (note the small horn) as his robot mode, the feisty Overkill epitomizes his moniker: his overzealousness toward everything is his undoing. His toy's colorful alternate mode—combined with the fact that he is a dinosaur—makes him a popular pick up on the secondary market. Originally sold as a two-pack set with Slugfest.

**ALTERNATE MODE:** Olympus Type IV "Metal" MC60 Microcassette.

**EASILY LOST WEAPONS AND ACCESSORIES:** 2 (braces of motion) missiles.

Overkill, alternate mode.

## SLUGFEST

**CASSETTES**

**FUNCTION:** Messenger
**MOTTO:** "Expect betrayal and your friends won't disappoint you."

"He's as slow and stupid as he looks. Plays back the messages he carries, thinks others are talking about him, goes into violent rages. End result is usually destruction of messages and nearby small towns that get in his way. In stegosaurus mode, plates on back, like teeth on a chainsaw, cut through almost any substance; carries 2 solar-powered vibro-cannons."

| Strength | Intelligence | Speed | Endurance | Rank | Courage | Firepower | Skill |
|----------|--------------|-------|-----------|------|---------|-----------|-------|
| 9 | 2 | 1 | 7 | 4 | 8 | 5 | 4 |

MLC: **$20-25**, MIP (opened; two-pack w/Overkill): **$45-50**, MOC: **$200-300** (two-pack with Overkill sealed on card)

Slugfest, easily lost weapons and accessories.

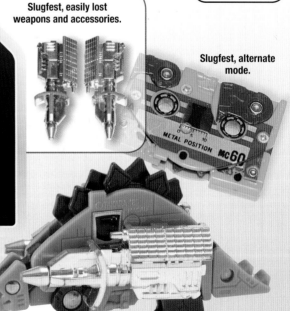

Slugfest, alternate mode.

Sold in a Decepticon cassette two-pack with Overkill, the stegosaurus-inspired design of Slugfest was cool looking enough to warrant the pair's quick purchase at retail. Slugfest's Tech Spec bio inspires pity, however, as sadly, his paranoia seems ill-founded if he is as powerful as he suggests.

**ALTERNATE MODE:** Olympus Type IV "Metal" MC60 Microcassette.
**EASILY LOST WEAPONS AND ACCESSORIES:** 2 solar-powered vibro-cannons.

Slugfest, robot mode.

# DUOCONS

The Duocons were rumored to be the result of one of Shockwave's (1985) failed experiments to create robots with the ability to change between more than one alternate mode and their robot form. Sadly, this nascent attempt resulted in a Transformer comprised of two robots with distinctly different personalities, yet whose personalities were split (and fractured) between their two separate robot modes.

Battletrap, robot mode.

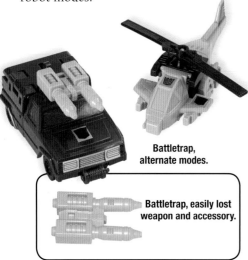

Battletrap, alternate modes.

Battletrap, easily lost weapon and accessory.

## BATTLETRAP

### DUOCONS

**FUNCTION:** Assault Team
**MOTTO:** "We're only halves of a whole, but double the trouble."

"He's the wrestling tag team of robots. Likes to trap his foe between his jeep and helicopter vehicles and have 'fun' with him—knock him back and forth a bit—before finally destroying him. Jeep maximum speed of 90 mph, range 600 miles. Helicopter maximum speed of 780 mph, range 1200 miles. In robot mode, carries double-barreled assault missile launcher with leaf-imaging for night-firing capability."

| Strength | Intelligence | Speed | Endurance | Rank | Courage | Firepower | Skill |
|----------|--------------|-------|-----------|------|---------|-----------|-------|
| 7 | 3 | 6 | 8 | 5 | 6 | 7 | 7 |

MLC: **$12-18**, MIB: **$35-48**, MISB: **$75-150**

## FLYWHEELS

### DUOCONS

**FUNCTION:** Assault Team
**MOTTO:** "Believe in yourself, but only if you both agree."

"Split personality—fights himself more often than his foes. Each half of him is jealous of the other. Often heard arguing with himself, even when unified in robot mode. Tank has maximum speed of 75 mph, range 350 miles. Jet has maximum speed of 1300 mph, range 1800 miles. In robot mode, carries a laser cannon with infra-red sensors for heat-seeking capabilities."

| Strength | Intelligence | Speed | Endurance | Rank | Courage | Firepower | Skill |
|----------|--------------|-------|-----------|------|---------|-----------|-------|
| 7 | 4 | 7 | 7 | 6 | 8 | 8 | 6 |

MLC: **$12-18**, MIB: **$35-48**, MISB: **$75-150**

Of the two Duocons, Battletrap is the better adjusted of the pair: he gleefully functions as a sinister adversary who engages in a dangerous game of cat and mouse. The toy is ingeniously designed, as Battletrap's spring-loaded inner mechanism allows his helicopter to land on his jeep and "transform" the two halves into his robot mode. A pretty neat trick... and easy find on the secondary market.

**SEPARATE ALTERNATE MODES:** Helicopter, jeep.
**EASILY LOST WEAPONS AND ACCESSORIES:** Double-barreled assault missile launcher.

The more confused of the two Duocons, Flywheels' dissociative episodes inhibit his optimal functioning. His alternate modes (fighter jet and assault tank) are considerably more military-based than Battletrap, and therefore his toy is a bit more popular than his Duocon partner.

**SEPARATE ALTERNATE MODES:** Jet, tank.
**EASILY LOST WEAPONS AND ACCESSORIES:** Laser cannon.

Flywheels, alternate modes.

Flywheels, easily lost weapon.

Flywheels, robot mode.

Pounce, easily lost weapons and accessories.

Pounce,
alternate mode.

## POUNCE

**FUNCTION:** Infiltrator
**MOTTO:** "Terror is the stage on which I perform."

"Sly, silent, and savage. The right machine for the right job. Often ignores his victims' pleas for mercy. In puma mode, can leap .7 miles. Possesses superior eyesight and sense of smell. In robot mode, laser range finder in optical sensors provides 99.4% accuracy with twin anti-personnel missile launching bayonets. Clone brother is Wingspan."

| Strength | Intelligence | Speed | Endurance | Rank | Courage | Firepower | Skill |
|---|---|---|---|---|---|---|---|
| 5 | 7 | 4 | 5 | 6 | 8 | 7 | 10 |

MLC (Pounce only): **$20-28**, MLC (set w/Pounce): **$38-46**, MIB (set w/Wingspan): **$60-95+**, MISB (pair): **$175-300**

Although a fascinating concept, the Transformer Clones (both Autobot and Decepticons) are sometimes criticized by G1 aficionados as being "all about the robots" with not enough concentration on the design of their alternate modes. Pounce is cited as an example of a clone's alternate mode looking a little weak: note his tiny head, stick-like legs, and stiff tail. Regardless, the idea was innovative, even if the delivery was a little off.

**ALTERNATE MODE:** Puma.
**EASILY LOST WEAPONS AND ACCESSORIES:** 2 anti-personnel missile launching bayonets.

Pounce,
robot mode.

## [DECEPTICON]
# CLONES

Dreamwave's *Transformers: More Than Meets The Eye* (2003) guide book (#8) explains that the Cybertronian cloning process was an experiment in creating new Transformer life through artificially separating/splitting the life essence of a single Transformer (a "spark": the Transformers' version of a soul) into two tubes. The two new tube-filled essences are then used to "construct the beings to match (i.e.

robot or alternate modes) on a pre-programmed set of variables." The result: Decepticon Clones Pounce and Wingspan. As for the toys, in addition to their heat-sensitive faction stickers, the Decepticon and Autobot Clones came with extra rub signs that indicated what mode they would be transforming into: Pounce's was that of a puma, while Wingspan's revealed a hawk.

# WINGSPAN

**CLONES**

**FUNCTION:** Data Processor
**MOTTO:** "Knowledge is the most deadly weapon of all."

"Always poking his beak where it doesn't belong. Nosey. Voracious appetite for new data to analyze. Looks in people's windows as readily as he spies on enemy troops. In hawk mode, has superb vision. Chemical and infra-red sensors collect and analyze geographical data, locate resources. In robot mode, has two electro-burst rifles. Clone brother is Pounce."

| Strength | Intelligence | Speed | Endurance | Rank | Courage | Firepower | Skill |
|----------|--------------|-------|-----------|------|---------|-----------|-------|
| 5 | 9 | 6 | 5 | 6 | 7 | 7 | 9 |

**$** MLC (Wingspan only): **$20-28**, MLC (set w/Pounce): **$38-46**, MIB (set w/Pounce): **$60-95+**, MISB (pair): **$175-300**

Wingspan, alternate mode.

With the interesting alternate mode of a hawk (in contrast to his brother's puma mode), Wingspan is a little boxy, as his robot arms are quite visible as a bird of prey. Take care to make sure loose samples of Wingspan actually have his two large purple wings, as these accessories can cost as much as the robot himself.

**ALTERNATE MODE:** Hawk.
**EASILY LOST WEAPONS AND ACCESSORIES:**
2 electro-burst rifles, two large purple wings

Wingspan, easily lost weapons and accessories.

Wingspan, robot mode.

Blot, robot mode.

Blot, easily lost weapons and accessories.

# BLOT

**TERRORCONS**

**FUNCTION:** Foot Soldier
**MOTTO:** "I'm not as bad as I look—I'm worse."

"The most disgusting of all Transformers. Wherever he goes, he leaves a trail of foul-smelling lubricant which is oozing out of several different joints at any given moment. Dumb, brutish, but loyal. In creature mode, claws allow him to climb any wall. Breathes fire. In robot or creature modes, uses slime gun to shoot stream of corrosive liquid. Combines with fellow Terrorcons to form Abominus."

| Strength | Intelligence | Speed | Endurance | Rank | Courage | Firepower | Skill |
|----------|--------------|-------|-----------|------|---------|-----------|-------|
| 9 | 2 | 2 | 10 | 4 | 10 | 6 | 5 |

**$** MLC: **$15-22**, MIP (opened): **$32-40**, MOC: **$75-100**

# TERRORCONS

The Terrorcons' combined mode of Abominus, although a "scramble city" combiner (where the four smaller robots are interchangeable for all intents and purposes) looks somewhat different from the other gestalts. Is it Abominus' colors, or the odd alternate monster modes of his component parts? Indeed, the Terrorcons were the Decepticons' horrifying answer to the Autobots' intellectually superior combiner team of Technobots and their gestalt: Computron.

Cutthroat, alternate mode.

## CUTTHROAT

**TERRORCONS**

**FUNCTION:** Shock Trooper
**MOTTO:** "Compassion is the currency of losers."

"Not a trace of mercy can be found among his microchips. Insatiable lust for destruction. In battle, lashes out with wings, beak, and claws to cut everything to ribbons. In creature mode can leap 4 miles in one jump, breathes flame. In robot mode, carries double-barreled magnetizer that oppositely charges any metal target so it tears itself apart. Combines with fellow Terrorcons to form Abominus."

| Strength | Intelligence | Speed | Endurance | Rank | Courage | Firepower | Skill |
|---|---|---|---|---|---|---|---|
| 8 | 4 | 4 | 9 | 5 | 8 | 7 | 7 |

MLC: **$10-18**, MIP (opened): **$28-32**, MOC: **$75-150**

Cutthroat, robot mode.

A well-constructed figure, Cutthroat's hawk mode had poseable legs, movable wings, and a swiveling head. His coloring was not as outrageous as most of the Terrorcons, and with the double-barreled magnetizer mounted on a hole in his back, Cutthroat looked almost formidable.

**ALTERNATE MODE:** Hawk.
**EASILY LOST WEAPONS AND ACCESSORIES:** Double-barreled magnetizer.

Cutthroat, easily lost weapon and accessory.

Apart from his Tech Spec that describes Terrorcon Blot as an exponentially detestable sentient life form, his alternate mode as an unidentifiable monster-creature and his truly abhorrent robot mode design adds to my fascination of this odd little Transformer. As a robot, he looks like a purple box with a big proboscis. Yet this is forgivable, as on the Sunbow cartoon whenever he was incited to violence, he would yelp, "Blot! Blot!!!"

**ALTERNATE MODE:** Monster.
**EASILY LOST WEAPONS AND ACCESSORIES:** Slime gun, laser mount.

Blot, alternate mode.

# SINNERTWIN

Sinnertwin, robot mode.

## TERRORCONS

**FUNCTION:** Sentry
**MOTTO:** "The sound of ripping metal is music to my audio modules."

"Prowls the perimeter of the Terrorcons' lair looking for trouble—and hoping to find it! Then he can show off his razor-sharp teeth, piercing pronghorns, and steel-shredding claws. Has flame cannon and flame breath in creature mode, armor-piercing rocket-grenade launcher in robot mode. Combines with fellow Terrorcons to form Abominus. Unnerved by small creatures like mice, insects, and mini-droids."

| Strength | Intelligence | Speed | Endurance | Rank | Courage | Firepower | Skill |
|---|---|---|---|---|---|---|---|
| 8 | 6 | 3 | 9 | 5 | 5 | 6 | 7 |

**$** MLC: **$14-24**, ; MIP (opened): **$32-40**, MOC: **$100-200**

With another odd-looking alternate mode, Terrorcon Sinnertwin has a standard transformation and is an easy pick up on the secondary market.

**ALTERNATE MODE:** Two-headed monster.
**EASILY LOST WEAPONS AND ACCESSORIES:** Flame cannon, rocket grenade launcher.

Sinnertwin, alternate mode.

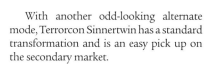

Sinnertwin, easily lost weapons and accessories.

# RIPPERSNAPPER

## TERRORCONS

**FUNCTION:** Terrorist
**MOTTO:** "Autobots are an error I intend to correct."

"Any organic creature whose status on the evolutionary scale ranks higher than a slime mold, particularly Autobots, sends him into a ferocious frenzy. Hates the smell of carbon-based life forms. In creature mode, claws and teeth can slice through almost any substance. Has twin, ground-to-air, voice-guided missile launchers. In robot mode, has cyclone gun. Combines with fellow Terrorcons to form Abominus."

| Strength | Intelligence | Speed | Endurance | Rank | Courage | Firepower | Skill |
|---|---|---|---|---|---|---|---|
| 3 | 5 | 5 | 9 | 6 | 8 | 8 | 6 |

**$** MLC: **$14-24**, MIP (opened): **$32-40**, MOC: **$100-200**

Of all of the alternate modes of the G1 Transformers, Rippersnapper, his fellow Terrorcon Blot (1987), and the Pretender Monsters (1989) have some of the most unidentifiable alternate modes ever witnessed. Is Rippersnapper a shark? A lizard? A dinosaur? Whatever he may be, his odd appearance must fuel the belligerent and jealous personality documented on Rippersnapper's Tech Spec bio: he hates any and all carbon-based life forms.

**ALTERNATE MODE:** (Bipedal) lizard.
**EASILY LOST WEAPONS AND ACCESSORIES:** Twin missile launcher, cyclone gun.

Rippersnapper, robot mode.

Rippersnapper, easily lost weapons and accessories.

# HUN-GURRR

**TERRORCONS**

**FUNCTION:** Terrorcon Leader
**MOTTO:** "Eat only what you need—destroy the rest."

"He has two mouths to feed—his own—and spends most of his time doing it. Since his mouth is usually full, his orders are usually misinterpreted. Prefers eating non-living to living things… doesn't like anything that might still be wriggling about after he swallows it. Can refashion digested materials and spit them out as crude missiles. Has powerful sonic stun gun in robot mode. Combines with fellow Terrorcons to form Abominus."

| Strength | Intelligence | Speed | Endurance | Rank | Courage | Firepower | Skill |
|----------|--------------|-------|-----------|------|---------|-----------|-------|
| 10 | 8 | 3 | 10 | 9 | 10 | 9 | 6 |

MLC: **$28-42**, MIB: **$58-68**, MISB; **$300-450**

On the Terrorcon Leader's instruction sheet, his name reads "Hun-Gurr", yet on his Tech Spec it states: "Hun-Gurrr." Curious. In any case, Hun-Gurrr is one of the most poseable of all combiner team leaders, as his two multi-jointed monster/dragon necks transformed into his legs in robot mode. As an added bonus, his arms were jointed, and his head even swivelled! His Tech Spec scores are ridiculously high, and place him as one of the most powerful team leaders. Oddly enough, Hun-Gurrr does not have any other transformation modes except for two-headed monster and robot, unlike nearly every other gestalt team leader. See the other modes of Hot Spot (1986), Onslaught (1986), Silverbolt (1986), Motormaster (1986), and Scattershot (1987).

**ALTERNATE MODE:** Two-headed monster.

**EASILY LOST WEAPONS AND ACCESSORIES:** Sonic stun gun, 2 large (Abominus) fists, (Abominus) chest shield, (Abominus) robot head, 2 (Abominus) foot stands.

Hun-Gurrr, robot mode.

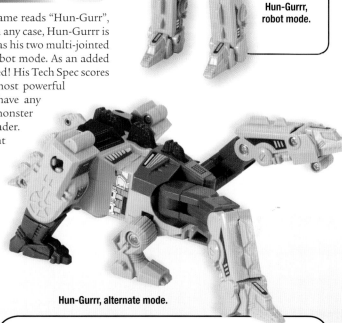

Hun-Gurrr, alternate mode.

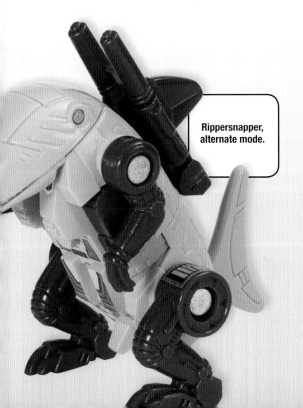

Rippersnapper, alternate mode.

Hun-Gurrr, easily lost weapons and accessories.

Terrorcons, alternate "attack creature" modes.

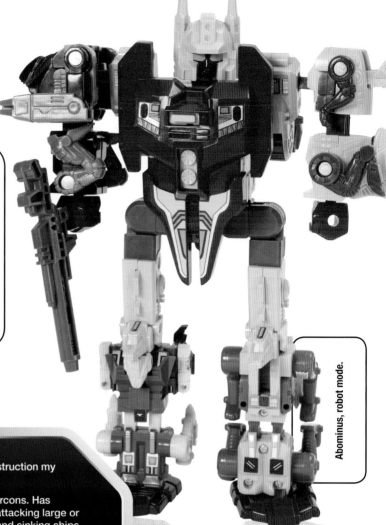

Abominus, robot mode.

## ABOMINUS

**TERRORCONS**

**FUNCTION:** Super Warrior
**MOTTO:** "Chaos is my only ally, and destruction my only friend."

"Abominus transforms into the five Terrorcons. Has overwhelming destructive power. Likes attacking large or moving objects, climbing tall buildings, and sinking ships. Has no heart/soul and is nothing more than a killing machine. Abominus carries a sonic concussion blaster."

| Strength | Intelligence | Speed | Endurance | Rank | Courage | Firepower | Skill |
|----------|--------------|-------|-----------|------|---------|-----------|-------|
| 10 | 1 | 3 | 10 | 5 | 10 | 8 | 4 |

Abominus Gift Set (all 5 Terrorcons together) MLC: **$80-85**, MIB (Japanese only): **$375-575+**, MISB: **$1,400-1,650**

The Tech Spec is translated loosely from Abominus' Japanese bio, as the Terrorcons were never released in a deluxe boxed gift set in the U.S. Strange, as their Autobot counterparts, the Technobots were. Abominus' motto is taken from Dreamwave's 2003 guide book, *Transformers: More Than Meets The Eye.*

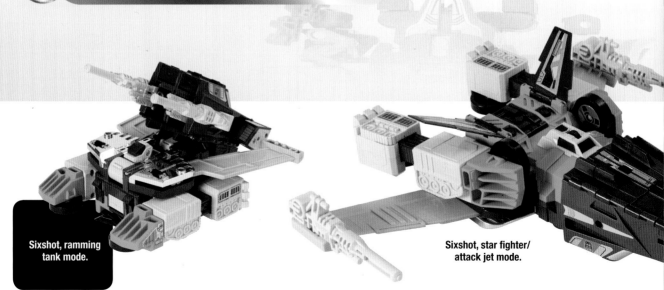

Sixshot, ramming tank mode.

Sixshot, star fighter/ attack jet mode.

Sixshot, armored
(car) carrier mode.

Sixshot,
wolf mode.

Sixshot, easily lost
weapons and accessories.

# SIXSHOT

**SIX CHANGER**

**FUNCTION:** S.T.A.G. (Solo Transformer Assault Group)
**MOTTO:** "Life is worth living only as long as there are
enemies worth destroying."

"A vile, nasty murderous sort who carries out his job with ferocious
intensity. Only redeeming quality is he speaks well of those he's sent
to 'the great junkyard in the sky,' his phrase for destruction. Has 6
forms: robot, armored carrier (with twin laser batteries), ramming-
tank (with infra-red rangefinder and target tracker), jet-propelled
laser pistol, star fighter (maximum speed: 80,000 mph; range: .8
million miles), and wolf-creature modes. Only the wolf creature has
no need for Sixshot's 2 hypersonic concussion blasters, the wolf
mode prefers to rip apart enemy Autobots with his razor fangs."

| Strength | Intelligence | Speed | Endurance | Rank | Courage | Firepower | Skill |
|----------|--------------|-------|-----------|------|---------|-----------|-------|
| 10 | 9 | 4 | 9 | 7 | 8 | 9 | 8 |

MLC: **$50-65+**, MIB: **$85-125+**, MISB: **$200-350**

Sixshot, robot mode.

Sixshot is a fascinating offensive arsenal for the Decepticons. As a toy, his
instruction booklet came sealed and touted him as "The Ultimate Transformers
Challenge!" Furthermore, the instructions directed collectors to, "Before opening
the instructions, challenge your skill! See if you can transform Sixshot into all 6
devastating modes!" His toy is very well-constructed and durable, and his colors
and fierce appearance make him very popular on the secondary market.

---

**ALTERNATE MODE:** Robot, armored carrier, ramming-tank, jet-propelled
laser pistol, star fighter, and wolf.
**EASILY LOST WEAPONS AND ACCESSORIES:** 2 hypersonic blasters.

Sixshot, jet-
propelled laser
pistol mode.

Sixshot's super-thick
instruction booklet
(it came sealed).

**TRANSFORMERS**

IT'S
THE ULTIMATE
TRANSFORMERS CHALLENGE!

Before opening the instructions,
challenge your skill! See if
you can transform Sixshot
into all 6 devastating modes!
(Hint: Look at the package for clues.)

**DECEPTICON®** SIXSHOT

165

Cyclonus, easily lost weapons and accessories.

## CYCLONUS

**TARGETMASTERS**

**FUNCTION:** Saboteur
**MOTTO:** "Compassion is the Autobots' downfall."

"An emotionless marauder whose single-minded purpose is to destroy the Autobots. Incapable of fear. Paired with Nightstick, a Nebulan master criminal who doubles as a blinding, corroding black-beam gun. In space jet mode, has nuclear-powered turbine engines that allow him to cruise at Mach 2 in suborbital altitudes and achieve escape velocity for interstellar space travel."

| Strength | Intelligence | Speed | Endurance | Rank | Courage | Firepower | Skill |
|----------|--------------|-------|-----------|------|---------|-----------|-------|
| 8 | 8 | 10 | 6 | 7 | 10 | 5 | 6 |

MLC: **$95-120**, MIB: **$175-230+**, MISB: **$300-500**

Reformatted to become a Targetmaster, Cyclonus is one of the rarer of the 1987 figures, as he drops his oxidating laser in lieu of a new Nebulan Targetmaster accomplice, Nightstick. Part of his toy's reformatting process is the enlargement of his robot's hand-holes, and a new peg added onto the roof of his jet, in order for Cyclonus to mount his partner/black beam gun. For a more complete bio, see Cyclonus (1986).

**ALTERNATE MODE:** Swept-wing space fighter.
**EASILY LOST WEAPONS AND ACCESSORIES:** Nightstick figure/black beam gun.

Cyclonus, robot mode.

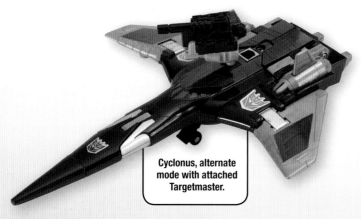

Cyclonus, alternate mode with attached Targetmaster.

Misfire, alternate mode with attached Targetmaster.

## [DECEPTICON]
# TARGETMASTERS

The Decepticon Targetmasters afforded Transfans some of the finest toy sculpts of the G1 canon. Although Cyclonus and Scourge are rereleases and were reformatted from their original 1986 versions, Misfire, Slugslinger, and Triggerhappy were spectacular products and flew off of retail shelves. All five Decepticon Targetmasters command high prices on the secondary market.

Scourge, alternate mode with attached Targetmaster.

Misfire, easily lost weapons and accessories.

Misfire, robot mode.

# MISFIRE

**TARGETMASTERS**

**FUNCTION:** Interceptor
**MOTTO:** "Keep shooting, eventually, you're bound to hit something."

"When Misfire shoots, his fellow Decepticons run for cover. Has terrible aim, but he says he's improving. No one else shares his confidence. Paired with the cowardly Nebulan, Aimless, a former construction engineer who had one too many buildings collapse due to poor design; now he doesn't care enough about anything to even bother aiming when he shoots as an ion particle blaster. Maximum speed: 1600 mph."

| Strength | Intelligence | Speed | Endurance | Rank | Courage | Firepower | Skill |
|----------|--------------|-------|-----------|------|---------|-----------|-------|
| 7 | 8 | 7 | 8 | 8 | 4 | 7 | 2 |

MLC: $95-115 **MID: $100-165+**, MISD: $300-500

Misfire has one of the more sophisticated conversions from robot to vehicle of all Targetmasters. He is a fantastic-looking spacecraft in vehicle mode, and his colors, although bright, seem somewhat appropriate for his alien/Cybertronian look and feel. His partner, Aimless, has a very simple "flip-his-legs-up" transformation from Nebulan partner to ion particle blaster, and like every Targetmaster, he can be mounted on Misfire's roof in the larger robot's vehicle mode.

**ALTERNATE MODE:** Cybertronian jet.
**EASILY LOST WEAPONS AND ACCESSORIES:** Aimless figure/ion particle blaster.

Scourge, easily lost weapons and accessories.

Scourge, robot mode.

# SCOURGE

**TARGETMASTERS**

**FUNCTION:** Tracker
**MOTTO:** "Desolation follows in my trail."

"Merciless, fearsome—only his extreme hatred of Autobots prevents him from attacking his Nebulan allies. The Nebulan is a high-temperature incendiary cannon with a volatile temper to match. In vehicle mode, Scourge is a hunter-destroyer, land-scouring vehicle. Equipped with optical and heat sensors for detecting and eliminating enemies. Maximum speed: 260 mph, range 800 miles."

| Strength | Intelligence | Speed | Endurance | Rank | Courage | Firepower | Skill |
|----------|--------------|-------|-----------|------|---------|-----------|-------|
| 7 | 9 | 6 | 6 | 8 | 8 | 7 | 7 |

MLC: $175-225, MIB: $275-325+, MISB: $600-900+

Scourge is the rarest of all Decepticon Targetmasters and is difficult to locate in any condition. Although this Targetmaster version shares a [relatively] similar mold to the original Scourge release [see 1986], it should be noted that the *hull* of TM Scourge is most similar to the hull of the original Scourge's latter variation. You see, TM Scourge's blue hood only exists as a LABEL on the hull; the original release of '86 Scourge's possessed a *molded plastic hood* on the hull. Fracas, Scourge's TM partner, is quite expensive, commanding ludicrously high prices in mint, *unbroken* condition—since many of the leg tabs on Targetmaster partners are found chipped or missing altogether. For a larger biography, see Scourge, 1986.

**ALTERNATE MODE:** Space hovercraft.
**EASILY LOST WEAPONS AND ACCESSORIES:** Fracas figure/incendiary cannon, rocket booster [does not separate into two pieces as did early variations of his 1986 release].

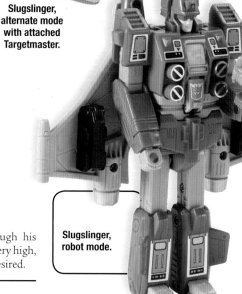

Slugslinger, easily lost weapons and accessories.

Slugslinger, alternate mode with attached Targetmaster.

## SLUGSLINGER

**TARGETMASTERS**

**FUNCTION:** Air Defense
**MOTTO:** "The only way to survive a duel with me is to not show up."

"A brawling, swaggering braggart, claims he'll challenge anyone to a duel, but prefers sneaking up and shooting enemies in the back. When his ammunition runs out, so does his courage. Paired with Caliburst, one-time Nebulan leading actor who only does this for the money. As an automatic machine gun, Caliburst can shoot armor-piercing shells at 1200 rounds per minute. In jet mode, maximum speed: 2400 mph."

| Strength | Intelligence | Speed | Endurance | Rank | Courage | Firepower | Skill |
|----------|--------------|-------|-----------|------|---------|-----------|-------|
| 6 | 8 | 8 | 7 | 6 | 3 | 8 | 9 |

MLC: **$85-115**, MIB: **$135-165+**, MISB: **$300-500**

Slugslinger, robot mode.

Slugslinger is another one of my all-time favorite Transformers because of his excellent transformation, and great vehicle and robot modes. Couple this with the fact that his Nebulan partner, Caliburst, has the added bonus of a removable barrel (hard to find on loose samples); and that his twin-nosed Cybertronian jet's light gray plastic is prone to "yellowing" over time, and you've got one very collectable Transformer. Although his character's skill and intelligence are very high, his courage leaves something to be desired.

**ALTERNATE MODE:** Cybertronian jet.
**EASILY LOST WEAPONS AND ACCESSORIES:** Caliburst figure/machine gun, blaster (attaches to Caliburst).

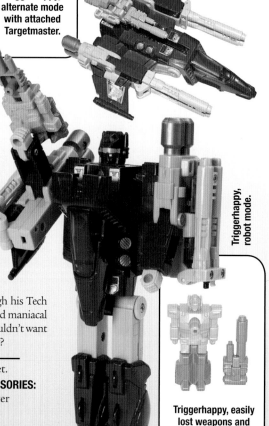

Triggerhappy, alternate mode with attached Targetmaster.

## TRIGGERHAPPY

**TARGETMASTERS**

**FUNCTION:** Gunner
**MOTTO:** "Have gun, have fun!"

"Usually too busy laughing uncontrollably and drooling out oil to look where he's shooting. Loves the sound of his guns blasting away. Wild and unpredictable. Paired with Blowpipe, a powerful compressed-air cannon who is also the conniving, envious brother-in-law of Lord Zarak, the Nebulan leader of the Decepticon Headmasters. In jet mode, has side-mounted, rapid-fire photon-pulse guns. Maximum speed: 1,980 mph."

| Strength | Intelligence | Speed | Endurance | Rank | Courage | Firepower | Skill |
|----------|--------------|-------|-----------|------|---------|-----------|-------|
| 7 | 7 | 7 | 7 | 5 | 9 | 8 | 6 |

MLC: **$75-115**, MIB: **$125-150+**, MISB: **$300-500**

Triggerhappy, robot mode.

The impulsive Triggerhappy is as well designed as any Transformer, and, as with most large Targetmasters from 1987 (Autobot or Decepticon), he commands big money on the secondary market, in any condition. The design of his Nebulan partner, Blowpipe, is similar to Caliburst (see Slugslinger, 1987): the figure folds together to form the main body of the weapon, and then a removable barrel is added to complete the conversion. Although his Tech Spec shows him to be overzealous and maniacal when firing his weapon, what kid wouldn't want a crazy gun-toting robot as a bad guy?

**ALTERNATE MODE:** Cybertronian jet.
**EASILY LOST WEAPONS AND ACCESSORIES:** Blowpipe figure/air cannon, blaster (attaches to Blowpipe).

Triggerhappy, easily lost weapons and accessories.

Mindwipe, robot mode.

## MINDWIPE

**HEADMASTERS**

**FUNCTION:** Hypnotist
**MOTTO:** "Just one look from me and you've lost."

"A mystic; spends most of his time trying to contact the electromagnetic essences of long-dead Decepticons than talking to live ones. Binary-bonded to Vorath, former Nebulan Minister of Science, expelled from office as a result of an illegal experiments scandal. In bat mode, has hypnotic stare, flies at 700 mph. In robot mode, uses vipor (sic) pistol—shoots streams of neuro-circuitry paralyzing liquid."

| Strength | Intelligence | Speed | Endurance | Rank | Courage | Firepower | Skill |
|----------|--------------|-------|-----------|------|---------|-----------|-------|
| 8 | 6 | 7 | 5 | 6 | 8 | 7 | 9 |

**MLC: $75-105, MIB: $120-145, MISB: $200-300**

Mindwipe, easily lost weapons and accessories.

One of the more high-demand large Headmasters, Mindwipe's popularity endures because of his wicked-looking alternate mode, subdued colors, and the fact that his Nebulan companion Volrath transforms into his robot's head. As a hypnotist, it is assumed that his suggestive messages are "projected" out of the two speaker-like appendages protruding from his chest in bat mode.

**ALTERNATE MODE:** Bat.

**EASILY LOST WEAPONS AND ACCESSORIES:** Volrath trainer/robot head, viper pistol.

Mindwipe, alternate mode.

Skullcruncher, alternate mode.

Weirdwolf, alternate mode.

## [DECEPTICON]
# HEADMASTERS

Similar in nature to the Autobot Headmasters, their ranks were fewer (only 3, compared to the Autobots' 4) yet these three Decepticon Headmasters seemed more interesting, if not more powerful. Using animals as their alternate modes instead of the good guys' vehicles, the Decepticon Headmasters are very popular on the secondary market and command high prices.

## SKULLCRUNCHER

**HEADMASTERS**

**FUNCTION:** Swamp Warrior
**MOTTO:** "Autobots are like bad fuel—weak and greasy."

"Has a habit of grinding his teeth before he strikes—annoying his friends and tipping off his enemies. Binary-bonded to Grax, a Nebulan industrialist who's joined up to eliminate his competition. In robot mode, uses softening ray run—gives metal the consistency of rubber, making his enemies easier to chew when he reverts to alligator mode."

| Strength | Intelligence | Speed | Endurance | Rank | Courage | Firepower | Skill |
|---|---|---|---|---|---|---|---|
| 10 | 8 | 3 | 10 | 5 | 9 | 5 | 6 |

**MLC: $75-105, MIB: $135-175, MISB: $300-500**

Skullcruncher, easily lost weapons and accessories.

Skullcruncher, robot mode.

Like Terrorcon Hun-Gurrr (1987), it appears that the odd-colored Headmaster Skullcruncher enjoys tearing Autobots apart with his teeth and swallowing them up. Oddly enough in Skullcruncher's case, his Nebulan Headmaster partner, Grax, rides inside his mouth in his alligator/alternate mode—seems kind of dangerous.

**ALTERNATE MODE:** Alligator.
**EASILY LOST WEAPONS AND ACCESSORIES:** Grax trainer/robot head, ray gun, tail/laser.

## WEIRDWOLF

**HEADMASTERS**

**FUNCTION:** Tracker
**MOTTO:** "My pleasure with my enemy's pain comes."

"Cruel, vicious, but apparently built with a few wires crossed. Talks to himself in a sing-song backward way: 'Destroy the Autobots I shall. Tear them to scrap I will.' Binary-bonded to Monzo, a brutish, professional hyper-wrestler-turned-underworld nightclub owner. In robot mode, uses photon pistol and thermal sword. In wolf mode, nose module is equipped with various tracking scanners. Can leap .8 miles."

| Strength | Intelligence | Speed | Endurance | Rank | Courage | Firepower | Skill |
|---|---|---|---|---|---|---|---|
| 6 | 10 | 6 | 10 | 6 | 9 | 5 | 6 |

**MLC: $71-105, MIB: $135-175, MISB: $300-500**

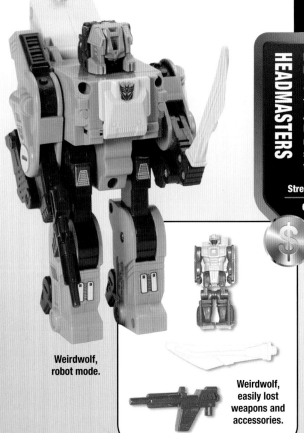

Weirdwolf, robot mode.

Weirdwolf, easily lost weapons and accessories.

Weirdwolf's alternate mode is precisely what his name describes: he *is* a funny looking lupine. This peculiar appearance results from his odd colors, his prominent sword-like tail, and his bright red cockpit that houses his Nebulan partner Monzo, when the humanoid is not acting as Weirdwolf's head. However, the hidden missile racks that flipped up from his shoulders in either wolf or robot mode appealed to my sense of adventure. He was one neat toy.

**ALTERNATE MODE:** Wolf.
**EASILY LOST WEAPONS AND ACCESSORIES:** Monzo trainer/robot head, photon pistol, tail/robot sword.

Apeface, alternate
jet mode.

Apeface, easily
lost weapons and
accessories.

## APEFACE

**HEADMASTER** Horrorcons

**FUNCTION:** Saboteur
**MOTTO:** "Obnoxiousness is not a problem, it is an art."

"Thoroughly obnoxious—pounds loudly on his chest plates, insults everyone he talks to, knocks over anyone in his way, never changes his lubricant so he smells like a grease-encrusted turboworm, and spits fuel in public. Binary-bonded to the nervous, insecure Nebulan Spasma. In jet mode, maximum speed: 3250 mph, emits powerful jamming frequencies. In ape mode, has super-agility. In robot mode, carries electro-shield and semi-automatic sonic boomer gun."

| Strength | Intelligence | Speed | Endurance | Rank | Courage | Firepower | Skill |
|----------|--------------|-------|-----------|------|---------|-----------|-------|
| 10 | 9 | 9 | 8 | 6 | 7 | 7 | 7 |

MLC: **$75-115**, MIB: **$135-175**, MISB: **$300-500**

Apeface,
alternate
gorilla mode.

According to Dreamwave's *Transformers: More Than Meets The Eye* guidebooks (2003), Apeface's Tech Spec hides a secret the Decepticon triple-changer would not like made public. If you look at his Tech Spec ability scores, he gauges a "9" on intelligence: therefore, we can assume that Apeface's obnoxiousness (and noxiousness, for that matter) are a ruse put in place for him to "dominate all those around him through fear." And with tremendous strength, intelligence, speed, and endurance, he has no problems maintaining power through his terrifying appearance.

**ALTERNATE MODE:** Jet, gorilla.
**EASILY LOST WEAPONS AND ACCESSORIES:** Spasma pilot/robot head, electro-shield, sonic boomer gun.

Apeface,
robot mode.

## [DECEPTICON]
# HEADMASTER
# HORRORCONS

Like the Decepticon Triple Changers [see Astrotrain (1985), Blitzwing (1985) and Octane (1986)] who came before them, the Headmaster Horrorcons have three different modes: robot, jet, and animal. As an added bonus, they come equipped with Nebulan Headmaster partners that also have alternate "head" modes: Headmaster Horrorcon Apeface's partner, Spasma, can change from a Nebulan to a robot head to a gorilla head; Headmaster Horrorcon Snapdragon's partner, Krunk, transforms from a Nebulan to a robot head to dinosaur head. A great concept, well-executed, and although their animal and robot modes were a little weird-looking, they're still quite popular among Transformers fans.

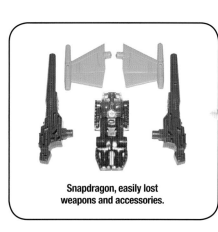

Snapdragon, easily lost
weapons and accessories.

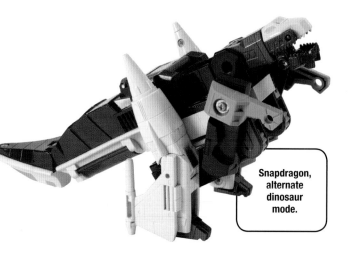

Snapdragon,
alternate
dinosaur
mode.

# SNAPDRAGON

**HEADMASTER** Horrorcons

**FUNCTION:** Interceptor
**MOTTO:** "If it doesn't get you dirty, it's not worth doing."

"Wading up to his neck in grease is his idea of a good time. Lazy, difficult to motivate, but has a hair-trigger temper. Binary bonded to Krunk, the vicious, vile bodyguard to the Nebulan leader, Lord Zarak. In jet mode, maximum speed 8800 mph… has 2 independent booster fins. In reptile mode, carbon-steel claws and teeth can cut through almost anything. Has 2 balance destroying gyro-guns in robot mode."

| Strength | Intelligence | Speed | Endurance | Rank | Courage | Firepower | Skill |
|----------|-------------|-------|-----------|------|---------|-----------|-------|
| 10 | 9 | 9 | 8 | 6 | 7 | 7 | 7 |

 MLC: **$75-115**, MIB: **$145-185+**,
MISB: **$350-550+**

Statistically, the two Headmaster Horrorcons are *exactly* the same, number for number, and it can be gleaned that they are exceedingly powerful Transformers, as their average Tech Spec ability score hover near an "8" out of "10." Snapdragon has a rather complex transformation mode, and can change from a streamlined winged jet to standard robot, to funky-awkward-looking dinosaur. Be careful of his dinosaur modes' pointy teeth (they're like little blades), and assume an aura of patience when transforming Snapdragon, as he is relatively fragile in all modes.

**ALTERNATE MODE:** Jet to dinosaur.
**EASILY LOST WEAPONS AND ACCESSORIES:**
Krunk pilot/robot head, 2 gyro-guns,
2 booster fins.

Snapdragon, robot mode.

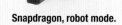

Snapdragon,
alternate
jet mode.

Scorponok, alternate scorpion mode, side view.

Scorponok, Headmaster close up (of Lord Zarak head mode).

# SCORPONOK

**HEADMASTER CITY**

Function: Headmaster Commander
**MOTTO:** "Kindness is no virtue…and cruelty is no vice."

"Despair and isolation are all that remain in his wake. Believes the poor should be exploited, the weak oppressed, and the noble corrupted. Others' pain is his sole pleasure. In scorpion mode, tail shoots 100,000 volt electric bursts, has twin pulse blasters, claws can crush mountains. In defense base mode, has over-the-horizon radar, communications center, anti-aircraft sonic cannon, repair bay, construction bay; semi-autonomous armored interceptor with dual photon cannons that patrol the base perimeter. In robot mode, has fusion-powered anti-gravity gun. Binary-bonded to Lord Zarak, leader of the evil Nebulans."

| Strength | Intelligence | Speed | Endurance | Rank | Courage | Firepower | Skill |
|---|---|---|---|---|---|---|---|
| 8 | 7 | 2 | 8 | 8 | 8 | 7 | 7 |

MLC: **$200-245**, MIB: **$285-345**,
MISB: **$800-1,200+**

One of the most-often demanded Decepticons on the secondary market, Scorponok is a force to be reckoned with. In Dreamwave's *Transformers: More Than Meets The Eye* (2003) guide books, it is suggested that this formidable force of terror is not as he appears on the surface. Although overtly cruel and destructive, Scorponok's *one-dimensional* personality is a calculated front which hides a deep despair about war. You see, Scorponok is actually, at heart, "…a noble warrior who hopes the (Autobot-Decepticon) conflict will eventually be resolved to the benefit of all Transformers."

As a toy, his huge amount of loose parts makes Scorponok difficult to obtain mint, loose, and complete, and collectors will see very high prices for MIB or MISB samples of the Headmaster Commander. With giant scorpion claws, great colors, imposing size, and an excellent city/defense base mode, Scorponok is one of the more popular Transformers. It should be noted that the two robots which are included with his toy are both transformable: Lord Zarak is a Nebulan who transforms into Scorponok's head; Fasttrack is a remote-controlled attack tank that converts to robot mode, whose function is to protect the larger robot's city mode.

As a final note, the statistics above are Scorponok's *revised* Tech Spec ability scores, which are modified from his *original* readout of Strength: 3; Intelligence: 4; Speed: 9; Endurance: 3; Rank: 3; Courage: 3; Firepower: 4; Skill: 4.

Scorponok, robot mode, left side view.

**ALTERNATE MODE:** Scorpion, defense base.

**EASILY LOST WEAPONS AND ACCESSORIES:** Lord Zarak trainer/robot head, anti-gravity gun, gun guard, Fasttrack mini attack tank/robot (with two removable right arms), 2 (Fasttrack) pistols, repair elevator, 4 (different) radar dishes, tower/shield, 2 mechanical repair arms (claw and gun), 4 dual photon cannons, 2 ramps, elevator platform, elevator connector, Scorponok helmet, 2 leg guards.

Scorponok, alternate scorpion mode, front view of Lord Zarak in the cockpit.

Scorponok, defense base left view.

Scorponok's assistants: Headmaster Lord Zarak and Fasttrack.

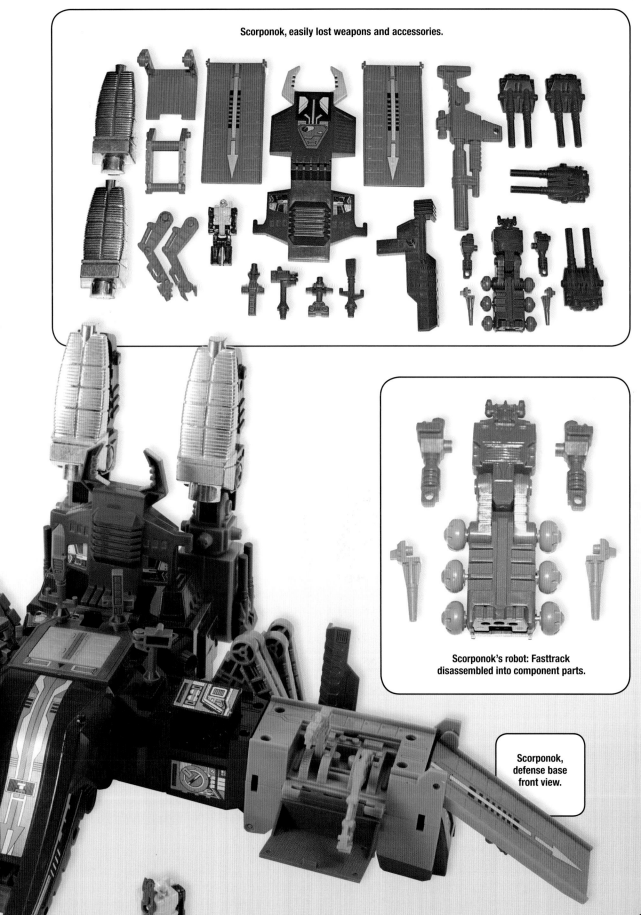

Scorponok, easily lost weapons and accessories.

Scorponok's robot: Fasttrack disassembled into component parts.

Scorponok, defense base front view.

# SERIES 5

In a way, Series 5 (1988, Generation One) was a precursor of things to come much later in the history of the Transformers license. It is with this year that Hasbro moved away from solely techno-organic characters, to some bio-organic beings in the form of Transformers Pretenders. Yes, the small action figure located inside of a Pretender's shell was indeed a Cybertronian robot, but the outer Pretender shell that housed this robot was humanoid in appearance. Furthermore, the days of Autobots and Decepticons mimicking Earth creatures, vehicles, and weapons with their alternate modes were nearly gone: now both robot and alternate mode were far more forward-looking and futuristic.

In 1988, the "second generation" of the Headmasters and Targetmasters were scaled down a bit—they were smaller, yet sometimes more intricate in detail. They also tend to cost a little more money on the secondary market than their first generation counterparts. To build off of the Headmaster (1987, 1988) and Targetmaster (1987, 1988) concept of a Nebulan transforming himself from small robot to either a Transformer's head or weapon, Hasbro created the "Powermasters"

motif in 1988. The Powermaster idea still used the Nebulans, but now these small humanoid aliens transformed into powerful engines for the Powermaster vehicles. According to Hasbro's flavor text, "Engine power is the key to every transformation. Each racing vehicle includes a Powermaster sidekick that converts to engine mode," boosting the Transformer's energy and power, and unlocking the process that allows these Transformers to change from vehicle to robot.

As with many other toy lines, however, when you deviate from the original concept too far (or when children think the toy line is played out), sales begin to fall, and they did in 1988 despite the excellent product Hasbro released. Some prime examples of their successes from Series 5 include the cassette combiners (Slamdance and Squawkbox); the formidable gestalt of Piranacon and his component parts, the Seacons; and the mercenary known as Doubledealer—one of the most intricate Transformers toys ever made.

<u>NOTE:</u> As of Series 5, Transformers no longer came with heat sensitive rub signs (from 1988-1990).

# FIZZLE

**SPARKABOTS**

**FUNCTION:** Military Strategist
**MOTTO:** "Planning a battle is ten times more important than fighting it."

"Overloads his circuits with grandiose schemes and cheap fuel. Acts as if his true worth is measured not by what he does, but how much he talks about doing it. If he could run on his own hot air, he'd go forever. In car mode, leaves trails of flame in his path. Capable of going from 0 to 200 mph in 8 seconds. Prone to stalling on left turns. Possesses superior logistics and geographical data banks."

| Strength | Intelligence | Speed | Endurance | Rank | Courage | Firepower | Skill |
|----------|--------------|-------|-----------|------|---------|-----------|-------|
| 6 | 7 | 6 | 2 | 6 | 6 | 1 | 8 |

💲 MLC: **$10-14**, MIP (opened): **$18-25**, MOC: **$40-80**

Fizzle, robot mode.

Fizzle, alternate mode.

As lower-price point Transformers, the Sparkabots (Fizzle, Guzzle, Sizzle) had simplified transformations, but because of their "push the (vehicle) and flames shoot out!" feature, they were fun and had some semblance of playability. Alas, they possessed no accessories to speak of.

**ALTERNATE MODE:** Baja buggy.
**EASILY LOST WEAPONS AND ACCESSORIES:** N/A.

Guzzle, robot mode.

# GUZZLE

**SPARKABOTS**

**FUNCTION:** Ground Assault
**MOTTO:** "It's better to have fought and lost than never to have fought at all."

"A battle-hardened survivor of the software wars of Polyhex. His hunger for combat is only equaled by his hunger for fuel. Tough, no nonsense, has few enemies and even fewer friends. He can thread a washer from 2.5 miles with a blast from his plasma cannon. Flame exhaust in tank mode incinerates on contact. Requires considerable fuel consumption."

| Strength | Intelligence | Speed | Endurance | Rank | Courage | Firepower | Skill |
|----------|--------------|-------|-----------|------|---------|-----------|-------|
| 7 | 6 | 2 | 7 | 5 | 8 | 7 | 4 |

💲 MLC: **$10-14**, MIP (opened): **$18-25**, MOC: **$40-80**

One of the three Autobot Sparkabots, Guzzle epitomizes his name: chugging through fuel like a champion. Even though he transforms into a realistic-looking tank, his prominent cannon in robot mode detracts a bit from his overall appearance.

Guzzle, alternate mode.

**ALTERNATE MODE:** ROF (Royal Ordnance Factories) Challenger 1 MBT (Main Battle Tank).
**EASILY LOST WEAPONS AND ACCESSORIES:** N/A.

Sizzle, robot
mode.

Sizzle, alternate
mode.

## SIZZLE

**SPARKABOTS**

**FUNCTION:** Interceptor
**MOTTO:** "Life in the fast lane is the only life worth living."

"Exceeds the speed limit and every other limit. Drives faster, uses more energy and gets into more fights than any other Autobot. A thrill-seeker. Enjoys life only when he's in danger. If he's not burning rubber, he's scorching Decepticons with his flamethrower exhaust. Maximum speed: 220 mph. Range: 550 miles."

| Strength | Intelligence | Speed | Endurance | Rank | Courage | Firepower | Skill |
|----------|--------------|-------|-----------|------|---------|-----------|-------|
| 4 | 7 | 6 | 7 | 5 | 7 | 6 | 5 |

MLC: **$10-14**, MIP (opened): **$18-25**, MOC: **$40-80**

Like the Decepticons' Firecons, the Autobots' Sparkabots have "spark shooting action," meaning that if rolled along the floor, their toys would shoot tiny sparks out of a designated opening. Sizzle's Tech Spec bio suggests he lives his life on the edge.

**ALTERNATE MODE:** Pontiac Firebird (3rd generation).
**EASILY LOST WEAPONS AND ACCESSORIES:** N/A.

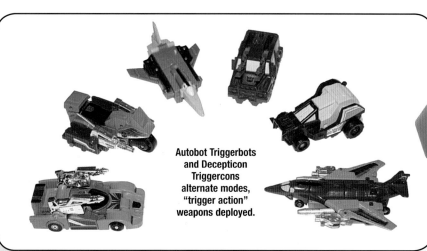

Autobot Triggerbots
and Decepticon
Triggercons
alternate modes,
"trigger action"
weapons deployed.

Dogfight, robot mode.

# TRIGGERBOTS

The following statement was included in the 1988 catalog, introducing the Triggerbots, "Quick-lever action and spring loaded weapons! These dynamic warriors are sure to send the Decepticons running!" With their flip-out weapons and lower price points, the Triggerbots were affordable replacements for Autobot Minicars (1984-1986) or Throttlebots (1987).

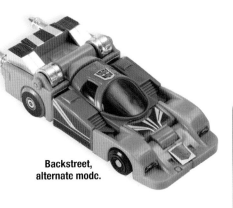

Backstreet,
alternate mode.

# BACKSTREET

**TRIGGERBOTS**

**FUNCTION:** Lookout
**MOTTO:** "A moment of indecision can be your last,"

"A temperamental, twitchy bundle of tightly-wound circuits. Jumps from one mode to another at the drop of a gasket. Constantly jumping to the wrong conclusions. Headlights equipped with high-intensity heat rays that turn enemy robots into molten steel. Fires 2 independent, targetable, laser-guided proton missile cannons. Able to accelerate up to 400 mph for 60 seconds, using rear rocket thrusters."

| Strength | Intelligence | Speed | Endurance | Rank | Courage | Firepower | Skill |
|----------|-------------|-------|-----------|------|---------|-----------|-------|
| 6 | 6 | 6 | 8 | 6 | 6 | 7 | 7 |

**$** MLC: **$10-15**, MIP (opened): **$20-25**, MOC: **$40-80**

Backstreet,
robot mode.

With the suggestion for kids to, "Push the button and weapons spring forward," emblazoned on Backstreet's package, his flip-up weapons were a neat trick, and he was a well-designed Transformer. His Tech Spec bio suggests a robot that is irritable and irrational (good qualities for a lookout?), well past the Autobots' appreciated cautiousness of Autobot Security Director Red Alert (1985).

**ALTERNATE MODE:** Porsche 962-based Le Mans race car.
**EASILY LOST WEAPONS AND ACCESSORIES:** N/A.

# DOGFIGHT

**TRIGGERBOTS**

**FUNCTION:** Aerial Combat
**MOTTO:** "Don't fire 'til you see the lights of their eyes."

"A wild, wicked street fighter of the skyways. Never met a Decepticon he didn't want to destroy immediately. Likes to go nosecone-to-nosecone with his opponents in a 'dance of doom' as he puts it. Equipped with rear-mounted fusion-powered blowtorch blasters in jet and robot modes. Also armed with serrated wingtips that cut through solid steel."

| Strength | Intelligence | Speed | Endurance | Rank | Courage | Firepower | Skill |
|----------|-------------|-------|-----------|------|---------|-----------|-------|
| 7 | 5 | 7 | 7 | 5 | 10 | 7 | 9 |

**$** MLC: **$10-15**, MIP (opened): **$20-25**, MOC: **$40-80**

Dogfight,
alternate mode.

As the lone jet on the Triggerbot team, Dogfight's dark blue colors and excellent Tech Spec characterization (where he seemed more like a Decepticon war criminal than an Autobot freedom fighter) made him a popular low-price point Transformer on the secondary market. If by definition, a "dogfight" is an aerial battle between fighter planes, it appears that Dogfight has a propensity toward this type of combat. His alternate mode, a Grumman X-29 concept aircraft, is capable of supersonic flight and has excellent control and maneuverability.

**ALTERNATE MODE:** Grumman X-29 fighter jet.
**EASILY LOST WEAPONS AND ACCESSORIES:** N/A.

Override, robot mode.

Override, alternate mode.

# OVERRIDE

**TRIGGERBOTS**

**FUNCTION:** Scout
**MOTTO:** "Let your actions do your talking and no one will misunderstand you."

"A proud, loud, two-wheeled fighting machine. Enjoys tearing up roads and shooting up Decepticons. Doesn't know the meaning of the word 'muffler.' Roars into battle with his guns blazing. Equipped with armored, reinforced windshield that's able to withstand direct enemy bombardment. Also armed with twin, side-mounted, armor-piercing, particle beam cannons."

| Strength | Intelligence | Speed | Endurance | Rank | Courage | Firepower | Skill |
|----------|-------------|-------|-----------|------|---------|-----------|-------|
| 5 | 8 | 5 | 8 | 6 | 9 | 6 | 8 |

MLC: **$10-15**, MIP (opened): **$20-25**, MOC: **$40-80**

The Triggerbots had "...trigger-action weapons! Push the button and weapons spring into action!" and Override was no exception. His endurance (combined with a near-impenetrable windshield) and courage makes him the perfect scout for the Autobot ranks. His fearlessness allows him to effectively gather the most recent information from any battle zone.

**ALTERNATE MODE:** Suzuki touring motorcycle.
**EASILY LOST WEAPONS AND ACCESSORIES:** N/A.

# GRAND SLAM

**CASSETTES**

**FUNCTION:** Audio Correspondence
**MOTTO:** "The sounds of war are history speaking."

"War-weary veteran of ten thousand battles on a hundred worlds. Dedicated his life to recording the sounds of the Autobot-Decepticon conflict: the nervous laughter, the cries of pain, the blistering explosions, the chilling quiets. Hopes his work will one day serve as a grim reminder of the awful price of war. Can audio-record up to 20 years of sound. Armament is purely defensive: smoke discharger combines with dual repulsors. With his partner Raindance, combines to form Slamdance."

| Strength | Intelligence | Speed | Endurance | Rank | Courage | Firepower | Skill |
|----------|-------------|-------|-----------|------|---------|-----------|-------|
| 6 | 8 | 3 | 8 | 4 | 9 | 3 | 7 |

MLC: **$18-32**, MIP (opened; two-pack w/Raindance): **$50-58**, MOC: **$200-300**

Grand Slam, easily lost weapons and accessories.

Grand Slam, alternate mode.

Grand Slam, robot mode.

Grand Slam records the audio of combat, while his partner, Raindance, provides the video components. Oddly enough, he is one of the few Transformers who had no robot or animal mode: his standard form was simply a tank, until he combined with Raindance to construct their gestalt robot mode: Slamdance.

**ALTERNATE MODE:** Olympus Type IV "Metal" MC60 Microcassette.
**EASILY LOST WEAPONS AND ACCESSORIES:** 1 smoke discharger, 2 dual repulsors.

# RAINDANCE

Raindance, alternate mode.

**CASSETTES**

**FUNCTION:** Video Correspondence
**MOTTO:** "Every picture tells a story."

"The death-defying daredevil of the skies. Willing to take any risk to record the best picture. With partner Grand Slam, he's covered thousands of battles. Entertains everyone with stories about each one of them. Witty and well-liked. Can video-record up to 20 years of pictures. Carries two self-defense air-to-air proton missiles. Combines with Grand Slam to form robot Slamdance."

| Strength | Intelligence | Speed | Endurance | Rank | Courage | Firepower | Skill |
|----------|--------------|-------|-----------|------|---------|-----------|-------|
| 4 | 8 | 6 | 5 | 4 | 9 | 5 | 8 |

**$** MLC: **$24-40**, MIP (opened; two-pack w/Grand Slam): **$50-58**, MOC: **$200-300**

Raindance's standard "robot" form is a futuristic jet, and so he must "hover" with the aid of antigravity projectors. See issue #5 of Dreamwave's *Transformers: More Than Meets The Eye* guide books (2003). When hovering, Raindance is awkward and relatively immobile, yet the speed of this mode in full flight is impressive. He combines with his partner Grand Slam to form the gestalt, Slamdance.

**Raindance, robot mode.**

**ALTERNATE MODE:** Olympus Type IV "Metal" MC60 Microcassette.

**EASILY LOST WEAPONS AND ACCESSORIES:** 2 proton missiles.

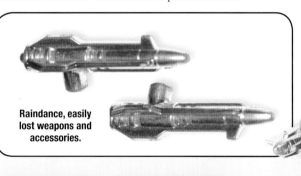

**Raindance, easily lost weapons and accessories.**

# SLAMDANCE

**FUNCTION:** Intelligence Coordinator
**MOTTO:** "Information is only as accurate as the being who gathers it."

**$** MLC (Grand Slam & Raindance): **$35-55**, MOC: **$200-300**

The above function and motto are from Dreamwave's 2003 *Transformers: More Than Meets The Eye* guide book, issue #6. His entry in this book is interesting, as it states that Slamdance's character expertly combines those personalities of his two component parts: Raindance and Grand Slam. Although Slamdance has an exaggerated opinion of his own self worth, his ability to organize and disseminate data and information are unparalleled.

**Slamdance, combined gestalt form of Grand Slam and Raindance.**

**ALTERNATE MODES:** Two Olympus Type IV "Metal" MC60 Microcassettes.

Landfill, easily lost weapons and accessories.

Landfill, robot mode.

# LANDFILL

**TARGETMASTERS**

**FUNCTION:** Materials Transport
**MOTTO:** "Adventure is found in unlikely places."

"A four-wheeled garbage site. Leaves a trail of decaying refuse wherever he goes. Friendly, cheerful, but a bit of a slob. His Nebulan partners are Silencer, a noiseless, recoilless proton rifle, and Flintlock, a heat-targeting stress pistol which induces metal fatigue and fractures in steel. Fellow Autobots dislike working with Landfill because he's filthy and smells so bad."

| Strength | Intelligence | Speed | Endurance | Rank | Courage | Firepower | Skill |
|----------|--------------|-------|-----------|------|---------|-----------|-------|
| 8 | 6 | 2 | 8 | 5 | 8 | 8 | 7 |

MLC: **$25-35**, MIP (opened): **$45-58**, MOC: **$100-200**

Landfill, alternate mode.

When Landfill's two Targetmaster weapons (Flintock and Silencer) are combined (one on top of another), these "second generation" Targetmaster weapons amplified one another. As with every other 1988 Targetmaster, whichever of the two weapons is used as the barrel of the combined Targetmaster weapon has its primary function/ability increased by the other.

**ALTERNATE MODE:** Dump truck.
**EASILY LOST WEAPONS AND ACCESSORIES:** Flintlock figure/Targetmaster weapon (heat-seeking stress pistol), Silencer figure/Targetmaster weapon (recoilless proton rifle).

# TARGETMASTERS

Scoop, alternate mode.

Hasbro scaled-down the size of both their Targetmaster and Headmaster lines (both Autobot and Decepticon) in 1988 to make price points for these items less prohibitive (see Headmasters, Targetmasters, 1987). As a result, the transformation processes of the main robots and the complexity of their accessories suffered. Particularly, it was the intricacy of the Transformers' Nebulan partners that was limited; Nebulans who changed into either a weapon (Targetmaster) or head (Headmaster) were much less sophisticated.

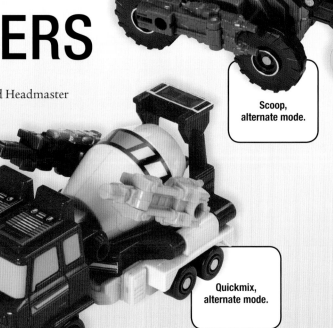

Quickmix, alternate mode.

Quickmix, easily lost weapons and accessories.

Quickmix, robot mode.

# QUICKMIX

**TARGETMASTERS**

**FUNCTION:** Chemist
**MOTTO:** "The faster it is, the better I like it."

"Impatient, short-tempered inventor. Always in a hurry. Constantly devising new formulas and developing new ways to defeat the Decepticons. Somewhat absent-minded. Too busy starting new projects to see his old experiments through to the end. Teamed with the mercurial Nebulan, Ricochet, who transforms into a submachine gun and the bombastic Boomer, who turns into a sonic pulse cannon. In vehicle mode, reaches maximum speed of 150 mph."

| Strength | Intelligence | Speed | Endurance | Rank | Courage | Firepower | Skill |
|---|---|---|---|---|---|---|---|
| 6 | 6 | 7 | 7 | 6 | 9 | 8 | 5 |

MLC: **$32-45**, MIP (opened): **$50-70**, MOC: **$100-200**

With a pretty cool transformation mode, Quickmix's character has a few odd characteristics: first, his impetuousness forces him to jump from new project to new project, without finishing what he initially started. Second, his short temper that stems out of defensiveness never allows him to admit when he's wrong. An interesting chemist indeed...

**ALTERNATE MODE:** Cement mixer.

**EASILY LOST WEAPONS AND ACCESSORIES:** Boomer figure/Targetmaster weapon (sonic pulse cannon), Ricochet figure/Targetmaster weapon (submachine gun).

# SCOOP

**TARGETMASTERS**

**FUNCTION:** Field Infantry
**MOTTO:** "Generosity has its own rewards."

"A gung-ho fighter who never gives up. Considered the best in the field. Uses cool headed logic and hardened battle tactics to outwit his enemies. Always ready to lend a helping shovel to his fellow Autobots, no matter how dangerous the situation. The kind of soldier you want around when you're pinned down in a slug swamp with no ammunition. Teamed with Tracer who transforms into a twin laser-guided ion blaster, and Holepunch, a former office manager turned military man who transforms into a steel-shattering dual compression cannon."

| Strength | Intelligence | Speed | Endurance | Rank | Courage | Firepower | Skill |
|---|---|---|---|---|---|---|---|
| 7 | 8 | 3 | 6 | 6 | 9 | 8 | 8 |

MLC: **$24-38**, MIP (opened): **$40-65**, MOC: **$100-200**

With a super-hardened shovel, two Targetmaster partners and a boundless optimism, Scoop is a dependable and loyal soldier in the Autobot army. Although his transformation mode is simple, he still looks formidable in robot form, with broad shoulders and intimidating Targetmaster weapons.

**ALTERNATE MODE:** Payloader.

**EASILY LOST WEAPONS AND ACCESSORIES:** Tracer figure/Targetmaster weapon (twin laser-guided ion blaster), Holepunch figure/Targetmaster weapon (dual compression cannon).

Scoop, easily lost weapons and accessories.

Scoop, robot mode.

# HEADMASTERS

With the introduction of the "second generation" of Headmasters (the smaller Headmasters), the Autobots fill up their ranks yet again. Although scaled down in terms of stature, these new Headmasters may have more accessories, poseability and detail than their first generation (see Autobot Headmasters, 1987) counterparts. Often, they even command more money on the secondary market than their larger Autobot Headmaster brothers as well.

These new toys have an attack mode as well. The smaller Headmasters' attack mode (for all three: Hosehead, Nightbeat, and Siren) similarly involves the incorporation of each robot's helmet, smaller dual lasers, main rifle, and driver/Nebulan figure. Each Headmaster possesses the same built-in "Tech Specs" meter as the earlier releases.

Small Autobot Headmasters in attack mode.

## HOSEHEAD

**HEADMASTERS**

**FUNCTION:** Emergency Rescue
**MOTTO:** "If at first you don't succeed, keep trying."

"A clear case of crossed cerebral circuits. Means well, but his good intentions often get him into trouble. Tends to do the right thing at the wrong time, like rescuing people after they're already saved. Eager to help in any situation. Binary-bonded to the Nebulan, Lug, a former all-star athlete. Armed with accelerator rifle which makes targets speed up uncontrollably. Range: 6 miles. Also equipped with two laser pistols."

| Strength | Intelligence | Speed | Endurance | Rank | Courage | Firepower | Skill |
|----------|-------------|-------|-----------|------|---------|-----------|-------|
| 8 | 6 | 5 | 8 | 6 | 9 | 5 | 2 |

💲 MLC: **$80-115**, MIB: **$140-165**, MISB: **$200-300**

Hosehead's vehicle mode is that of an excellent fire engine with extendable rescue ladder (with movable attachments), and his robot mode is fairly poseable. His character is well meaning but a bit of a lame brain: because of this, Hosehead simply can't accomplish tasks properly (note his low ability score in "Skill"). This is a poor distinguishing quality for an emergency rescue trooper. In the Japanese *Transformers: Masterforce* cartoon, he was known as "Cab."

**ALTERNATE MODE:** Fire engine.
**EASILY LOST WEAPONS AND ACCESSORIES:** Lug driver/robot head, 2 laser pistols (right and left), seat/helmet, accelerator rifle.

Hosehead, robot mode.

Nightbeat, easily lost weapons and accessories.

# NIGHTBEAT

**HEADMASTERS**

**FUNCTION:** Detective
**MOTTO:** "Truth is revealed in the smallest detail."

"Tough, no-nonsense type. Sometimes breaks rules in order to get what he wants. Works best when he works alone. As comfortable driving down a dark alley as he is on a well-lit, six-lane superhighway. Binary-bonded to Muzzle, a Nebulan private detective with an eye for detail. Carries two photon pistols and a plasma blaster with an infra-red sight. Also equipped with visual and audio sensors. Usually gets by with just cool-headed logic."

| Strength | Intelligence | Speed | Endurance | Rank | Courage | Firepower | Skill |
|---|---|---|---|---|---|---|---|
| 5 | 8 | 7 | 6 | 7 | 9 | 7 | 9 |

MLC: **$90-125**, MIB: **$150-165**, MISB: **$200-300**

Nightbeat, robot mode.

Nightbeat acted as a detective in Marvel Comics' *Transformers* comic book series, where he was prominently featured, and was also included in the Japanese cartoon, *Transformers: Masterforce*. As a toy, Nightbeat is similar in design to all the 1988 smaller Autobot Headmasters: seat as a head, pistols mount on head in robot mode, etc. Note that each of the new Headmasters' Nebulan partners had one simple hinge joint at the waist, a much less complex design than the small humanoids who were paired with the larger 1987 Headmasters.

**ALTERNATE MODE:** Porsche 959.

**EASILY LOST WEAPONS AND ACCESSORIES:** Muzzle driver/robot head, seat/helmet, 2 photon pistols, plasma blaster.

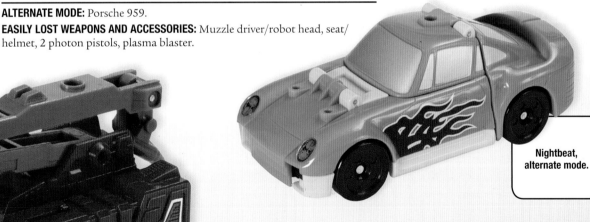

Nightbeat, alternate mode.

Hosehead, alternate mode.

Hosehead, easily lost weapons and accessories.

185

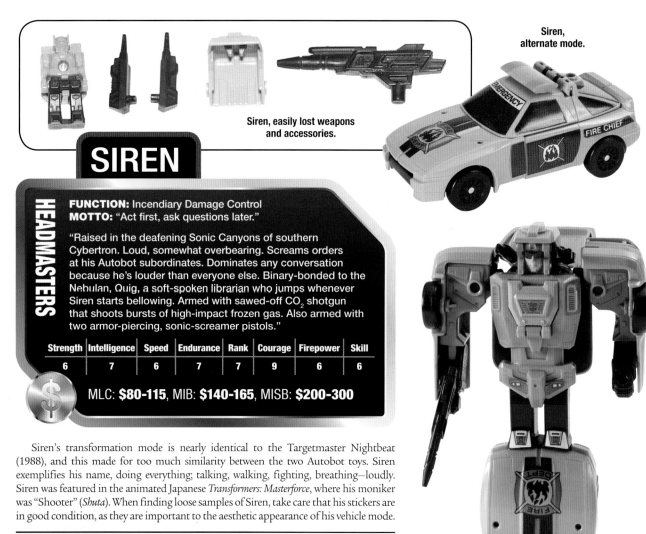

Siren, easily lost weapons and accessories.

Siren, alternate mode.

## SIREN

**HEADMASTERS**

**FUNCTION:** Incendiary Damage Control
**MOTTO:** "Act first, ask questions later."

"Raised in the deafening Sonic Canyons of southern Cybertron. Loud, somewhat overbearing. Screams orders at his Autobot subordinates. Dominates any conversation because he's louder than everyone else. Binary-bonded to the Nebulan, Quig, a soft-spoken librarian who jumps whenever Siren starts bellowing. Armed with sawed-off $CO_2$ shotgun that shoots bursts of high-impact frozen gas. Also armed with two armor-piercing, sonic-screamer pistols."

| Strength | Intelligence | Speed | Endurance | Rank | Courage | Firepower | Skill |
|---|---|---|---|---|---|---|---|
| 6 | 7 | 6 | 7 | 7 | 9 | 6 | 6 |

💲 MLC: **$80-115**, MIB: **$140-165**, MISB: **$200-300**

Siren's transformation mode is nearly identical to the Targetmaster Nightbeat (1988), and this made for too much similarity between the two Autobot toys. Siren exemplifies his name, doing everything; talking, walking, fighting, breathing—loudly. Siren was featured in the animated Japanese *Transformers: Masterforce*, where his moniker was "Shooter" (*Shuta*). When finding loose samples of Siren, take care that his stickers are in good condition, as they are important to the aesthetic appearance of his vehicle mode.

**ALTERNATE MODE:** Mazda RX-7 [as fire chief's car].
**EASILY LOST WEAPONS AND ACCESSORIES:** Quig driver/robot head, seat/helmet, CO2 shotgun, 2 sonic-screamer pistols.

Siren, robot mode.

# POWERMASTERS

In 1988, the Powermasters became the next evolutionary step in Cybertronian-Nebulan technology after the Headmasters (1987, 1988) and Targetmasters (1987, 1988). With this technological advance, Nebulans transformed into the engine of a vehicle's alternate mode, providing the Transformer with added energy.

**Note:** A Powermaster engine must be connected to the Transformers' vehicle/alternate mode in order for the robot to physically undergo a transformation (unless, of course, you can hit the little tabs with your fingers).

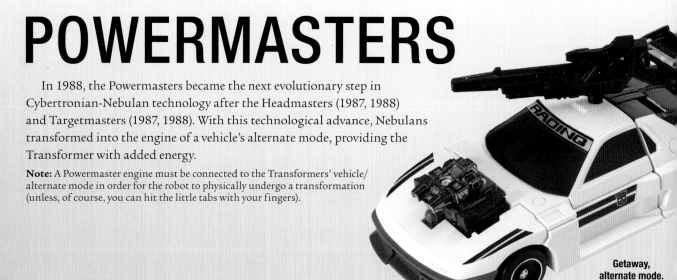

Getaway, alternate mode.

# JOYRIDE

**POWEREMASTERS**

**FUNCTION:** Warrior
**MOTTO:** "Enjoy each moment like it's your last."

"A reckless road-racing robot. Always drives faster than he should. Enjoys the thrill of racing at high speeds. Fights for the fun of it, which annoys many of his more serious-minded Autobots. Titanium-belted wheels secrete adhesives for pinpoint maneuverability on the road. Binary-bonded to the Nebulan, Hotwire, a reformed car thief and ace mechanic. Also armed with photon blaster that freezes internal mechanisms on impact."

| Strength | Intelligence | Speed | Endurance | Rank | Courage | Firepower | Skill |
|---|---|---|---|---|---|---|---|
| 6 | 7 | 6 | 10 | 5 | 9 | 6 | 7 |

MLC: **$58-75**, MIB: **$110-125**, MISB: **$200-300**

Joyride is the epitome of his name, as a joyride is "a pleasure ride in an automobile, especially when the vehicle is driven recklessly." Joyride's careless attitude is perhaps made more pronounced because of his ridiculously high "Endurance" ability score: a perfect 10. Why *not* drive with abandon if you're near invincible? Joyride appeared in the animated Japanese *Transformers: Masterforce* as the "Godmaster" known as "Ranger."

**ALTERNATE MODE:** Baja/dune buggy.
**EASILY LOST WEAPONS AND ACCESSORIES:** Hotwire figure/ Powermaster engine, laser (solar-powered blaster).

Joyride, easily lost weapons and accessories.

Joyride, robot mode.

Joyride, alternate mode.

# GETAWAY

**POWEREMASTERS**

**FUNCTION:** Warrior
**MOTTO:** "Run hot, but always keep your cool."

"An escape artist without equal. Uses finesse and logic to get out of any situation. Possesses expert tactical and strategic military skills. Binary-bonded to Rev, a smooth-running, 600 horsepower racing engine. Equipped with bulletproof windows and shell-resistant battle armor. Built-in onboard computers can be programmed for long-distance navigation. Armed with a double-barreled, plasma-shell shotgun."

| Strength | Intelligence | Speed | Endurance | Rank | Courage | Firepower | Skill |
|---|---|---|---|---|---|---|---|
| 4 | 8 | 6 | 10 | 7 | 10 | 6 | 8 |

MLC: **$70-90+**, MIB: **$125-140**, MISB: **$200-300**

Getaway, robot mode.

In Japan, the Powermasters were dubbed "Godmasters," and Getaway's name was changed to "Lightfoot." As a toy, Getaway is the most difficult of all Autobot Powermasters to find in good condition because of the toy's usually pronounced sticker wear, and its propensity toward yellowing—the white plastic that comprises Getaway is very prone to discoloration.

**ALTERNATE MODE:** Mazda RX-7 FC3S race car.
**EASILY LOST WEAPONS AND ACCESSORIES:** Rev figure/Powermaster engine, laser.

Getaway, easily lost weapons and accessories.

# SLAPDASH

POWEREMASTERS

**FUNCTION:** Interceptor
**MOTTO:** "Sometimes, if you wait long enough, problems solve themselves."

"Disorganized, neglectful, sloppy; Often goes to war without his weapon, or grinds to a halt for lack of fuel. Relies on others to pay the consequences for his mistakes. Often locked in vehicle mode because he's left behind his partner, the Nebulan, Lube, without whom he can't transform. Lube is meticulous, short-tempered, and usually at odds with Slapdash. Armed with a powerful electro magnetizer that drains Decepticon power sources."

| Strength | Intelligence | Speed | Endurance | Rank | Courage | Firepower | Skill |
|----------|-------------|-------|-----------|------|---------|-----------|-------|
| 5 | 5 | 5 | 7 | 4 | 8 | 6 | 5 |

MLC: **$65-90+**, MIB: **$120-135**, MISB: **$200-300**

Slapdash, easily lost weapons and accessories.

Slapdash, robot mode.

With the most complex transformation of the three medium-sized Autobot Powermasters, Slapdash has a formidable-looking robot mode. Unfortunately, as a character, because of Slapdash's disorganization and lack of competency, he must depend on his friends to bail him out of high-stress combat situations. In the Japanese animated program *Transformers: Masterforce*, he was known as the "Godmaster" "Roadking."

**ALTERNATE MODE:** Lotus 99T Formula-1 racecar.
**EASILY LOST WEAPONS AND ACCESSORIES:** Lube figure/Powermaster engine, laser, rear spoiler, yellow engine.

Slapdash, alternate mode.

# PRETENDERS

Cloudburst, inner robot's alternate mode.

"Pretenders hide the Transformers inside!"

Most collectors claim that the Pretenders were the last true innovation among Transformers G1, favoring this series over both the Micromasters (1989-1990) and the Action Masters (1990). The premise behind Autobot Pretenders was simple, yet effective: there was a transformable robot hidden inside an outer, armored, human-looking shell (a "synthoplasmic" shell according to the Marvel Comics). In 1988, the Autobot Pretenders' inner robots had fairly mundane transformations, yet are still innovative enough to warrant collectibility today on the secondary market. Following the cancellation of Sunbow's animated *Transformers* series, there was barely any media tie-in to the Transformers toy line besides the poor selling comic book and Hasbro's toy commercials.

Cloudburst, inner robot mode.

Landmine, outer shell mode.

Landmine, inner robot mode.

# LANDMINE

**PRETENDERS**

**FUNCTION:** Asteroid Miner
**MOTTO:** "The greatest treasures are found in the darkest places!"

"A hard-working hothead. Always concerned with getting the job done right. Outer shell constructed of high density Cybertronic alloy, impervious to most armaments. Outside his shell, transforms into all-terrain, exploration vehicle. Mining activities facilitated by electromagnetic, sonic, thermal, chemical and radiation scanners. Armed with laser saber and astro blaster that shoots concentrated bursts of incendiary explosives."

| Strength | Intelligence | Speed | Endurance | Rank | Courage | Firepower | Skill |
|---|---|---|---|---|---|---|---|
| 8 | 8 | 6 | 7 | 6 | 5 | 10 | 8 |

**MLC: $35-45, MIB: $50-55, MISB: $100-200**

Landmine, easily lost weapons and accessories.

His all-terrain vehicle mode was indeed a departure from most of the flying aircraft immortalized in Pretenders form, but still, he is one of the quickest Pretenders to obtain on the secondary market due to his lack of popularity and ease to find loose and complete.

**ALTERNATE MODE:** All terrain vehicle.
**EASILY LOST WEAPONS AND ACCESSORIES:** 2 "Landmine" figure shell halves, astro blaster, belt, helmet, laser saber.

Landmine, inner robot's alternate mode.

# CLOUDBURST

**PRETENDERS**

**FUNCTION:** Space Defense
**MOTTO:** "You can't tell a bot by his cover!"

"Aggressive, witty and charming, but only when hiding in his outer shell! Wary of everyone and everything, especially Decepticons. Uses his outer shell to disguise his dull personality as well as himself. Reluctant to leave his outer shell so he can transform into an interplanetary star cruiser, armed with particle beam cannon. Within shell, armed with lightning whip and thunderbolt laser pistol."

| Strength | Intelligence | Speed | Endurance | Rank | Courage | Firepower | Skill |
|---|---|---|---|---|---|---|---|
| 7 | 8 | 10 | 7 | 6 | 8 | 8 | 7 |

**MLC: $35-45, MIB: $55-60, MISB: $100-200**

Cloudburst, outer shell mode.

Cloudburst, easily lost weapons and accessories.

Dreamwave's *Transformers: More Than Meets The Eye* guide books (issue #1, 2003) suggest that Cloudburst was a boring, humdrum robot until he was granted the benefit of his outer Pretender shell. This event provided the Autobot with an opportunity to "reinvent himself and project an aggressive, charming attitude that is a complete turn around from his real personality." As an action figure, Cloudburst's interplanetary star cruiser alternate mode is similar in shape and model to nearly every other Pretender inner robot.

**ALTERNATE MODE:** Star cruiser.
**EASILY LOST WEAPONS AND ACCESSORIES:** 2 "Cloudburst" figure shell halves, belt, thunderbolt laser pistol, helmet, lightning whip.

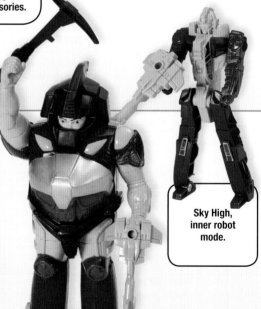

Groundbreaker, Mint in Box.

# GROUNDBREAKER

**FUNCTION:** Ground Trooper
**MOTTO:** "The first one in is the first to win!"

"A fast-moving fighting machine. Always the first to arrive and the first to start shooting. Brash, impulsive. Acts like someone with his foot on the accelerator. Built-in thermal and geological sensors in helmet home in on enemy installations and fuel supplies. High-density outer armor emits laser beam force field that can withstand direct enemy bombardment. Equipped with state-of-the-art, radar-targeting electron assault rifle. Also armed with laser-guided, programmable pulse blaster that flies and functions by remote control. Rocket car has all-terrain capabilities and can reach speeds of Mach 1."

| Strength | Intelligence | Speed | Endurance | Rank | Courage | Firepower | Skill |
|----------|--------------|-------|-----------|------|---------|-----------|-------|
| 7 | 6 | 6 | 8 | 5 | 10 | 8 | 7 |

**MLC: $45-58, MIB: $60-75, MISB: $100-200**

▲ Groundbreaker, inner robot mode.

◄ Groundbreaker, outer shell mode.

There are three Autobot Pretenders who have animal faces prominently featured on the armor of their outer shells: Groundbreaker (tiger), Sky High (bird of prey), and Splashdown (shark). Groundbreaker is the coolest of the three. As a toy, Groundbreaker is a high-demand piece due to his fabulous wealth of accessories.

**ALTERNATE MODE:** Rocket car.
**EASILY LOST WEAPONS AND ACCESSORIES:**
2 "Groundbreaker" figure shell halves, blaster, blaster base/wings, electron rifle, helmet, 2 pieces shoulder armor [left and right].

Groundbreaker, easily lost weapons and accessories.

Groundbreaker, inner robot's alternate mode.

# SKY HIGH

**FUNCTION:** Scout
**MOTTO:** "Imagination is the key that unlocks the chains of reality."

"A flying powerhouse of mechanical muscle. All brawn and no brains. Has trouble remembering where he is and why he's fighting. Leg-mounted energy beams temporarily burn out enemy visual sensors, rendering them sightless. Utility belt equipped with side-mounted, plutonium blasters with suborbital capabilities. Transforms to jet helicopter with long-range assault capabilities. Helicopter rotor also doubles as a molecular, bond-smashing, sonic scythe. Also armed with impulse-scrambling stun gun that jams enemy frequencies."

| Strength | Intelligence | Speed | Endurance | Rank | Courage | Firepower | Skill |
|----------|--------------|-------|-----------|------|---------|-----------|-------|
| 6 | 8 | 7 | 7 | 6 | 8 | 7 | 8 |

**MLC: $48-62, MIB: $70-78, MISB: $100-200+**

Sky High, inner robot mode.

Sky High, outer shell mode.

Splashdown, easily lost weapons and accessories.

Splashdown, inner robot's alternate mode.

Splashdown, inner robot mode.

# SPLASHDOWN

**PRETENDERS**

**FUNCTION:** Naval Commander
**MOTTO:** "Outflank your enemy and you won't have to outgun him."

"A hard-living, hard-hitting, wind-torn soldier. A veteran of battles on 10,000 oceans on 1,000 worlds throughout the universe. At home on water, mercury, even liquid lead. Outer shell armed with long-range, armor-piercing harpoon gun and electro-sword. Robot and hovercraft modes armed with photon blaster. Outer shell composed of high-density armor impervious to corrosive liquids and strong enough to withstand underwater depths of over 30,000 feet. Transforms to hovercraft with maximum speed of 210 mph."

| Strength | Intelligence | Speed | Endurance | Rank | Courage | Firepower | Skill |
|----------|--------------|-------|-----------|------|---------|-----------|-------|
| 7 | 8 | 6 | 7 | 8 | 9 | 7 | 8 |

💲 MLC: **$45-58**, MIB: **$62-80**, MISB: **$100-200**

Sporting an excellent Tech Spec biography, Splashdown truly captured the nature of the Pretenders concept by transforming from robot to hovercraft, and allowing his "human" shell to adapt to various environments on land or at sea. Perhaps his Tech Spec description is the reason so many loose samples of Splashdown have "hard-living, hard-hitting, wind-torn" wear on their stickers and paint.

**ALTERNATE MODE:** Hovercraft.
**EASILY LOST WEAPONS AND ACCESSORIES:** 2 "Splashdown" figure shell halves, harpoon gun, blaster, electron sword, helmet, belt, shield.

Splashdown, outer shell mode.

Sky High, easily lost weapons and accessories.

Because of his colors, accessories (a scythe!), stylized outer shell, and excellent jet helicopter mode, Sky High is one of the most popular (and hence, more expensive) of the first-year Pretenders. Although his Tech Spec biography states hes is slow and "all brawn" with "no brains," his intelligence ranks an 8 out of 10.

**ALTERNATE MODE:** Jet helicopter.
**EASILY LOST WEAPONS AND ACCESSORIES:** 2 "Sky High" figure shell halves, stun gun, scythe/(helicopter) rotor, belt, helmet.

Sky High, inner robot's alternate mode.

191

Waverider,
outer shell
mode.

Waverider,
inner robot
mode.

# WAVERIDER

**PRETENDERS**

**FUNCTION:** Naval Warfare
**MOTTO:** "Freedom for all starts with freedom
of navigation."

"A furious fighter and formidable adversary in battle. Prefers
exploring the ocean bottom for buried treasure over warfare.
Enjoys the 'out-of-body' experience of working side-by-side
with his humanoid shell. Without shell, transforms to aquatic
sea-skimmer capable of diving to a depth of 25,000 feet!
Armed for underwater combat with armored shell, energy-
spear gun and a thermal broad-axe!"

| Strength | Intelligence | Speed | Endurance | Rank | Courage | Firepower | Skill |
|----------|--------------|-------|-----------|------|---------|-----------|-------|
| 7 | 7 | 6 | 8 | 6 | 9 | 7 | 8 |

MLC: **$32-45**, MIB: **$50-62**, MISB: **$75-150**

One of the greatest criticisms of the Pretenders line (particularly
in 1988) was the lack of novelty that occurred with
the inner robots' vehicle modes, because each of the
inner robots' alternate modes looked very similar,
regardless if they were air, sea, or land vehicles.
Waverider's alternate mode as a "sea skimmer" is
no exception.

**ALTERNATE MODE:** Sea skimmer.
**EASILY LOST WEAPONS AND ACCESSORIES:**
2 "Waverider" figure shell halves, energy
spear gun, axe, helmet, belt.

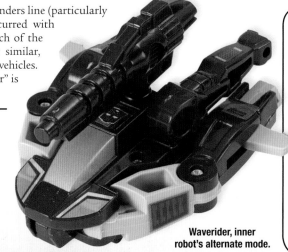

Waverider, inner
robot's alternate mode.

Waverider, easily lost
weapons and accessories.

# CATILLA

**PRETENDER BEASTS**

**FUNCTION:** Surveillance
**MOTTO:** "Stalk before you strike."

"Silent, yet vigilant. Enjoys stalking his victims and then moving
in to attack. Nothing escapes his cunning clutches. Battle
helmet equipped with infrared sensors, long range radar and
tracking systems. Whip-like tail can crush buildings with its iron
grip. Top-mounted turbo blaster provides phenomenal speed
and agility on the battlefield. Maximum speed: 150 mph. Armed
with air concussion cannon, durabyllium-steel alloy fangs and
claws that can slash through the thickest armor."

| Strength | Intelligence | Speed | Endurance | Rank | Courage | Firepower | Skill |
|----------|--------------|-------|-----------|------|---------|-----------|-------|
| 8 | 7 | 6 | 7 | 5 | 6 | 6 | 9 |

MLC: **$38-50**, MIB: **$72-70**, MISB: **$200-300**

The Pretender Beasts are curious incarnations
of the Pretenders line because both the inner
robots' alternate modes and their outer shells are
that of beasts/animals. The use of shell space is
also maximized by the Pretender Beasts, however
some collectors find it a challenge to put the
inner robots back in their Pretenders shells after
transforming them a few times.

**ALTERNATE MODE:** Sabertooth tiger.
**EASILY LOST WEAPONS AND ACCESSORIES:**
2 "Catilla" beast shell halves, concussion
cannon, tail, helmet.

# CHAINCLAW

**PRETENDER BEASTS**

**FUNCTION:** Ground Trooper
**MOTTO:** "The only thing for certain is uncertainty."

"A ferocious warrior. Usually too busy worrying to fight. Always afraid his outer shell won't unlock, that his fuel might be low, that his joints are rusting or almost anything imaginable. Sometimes appears inoperative because he worries himself to a standstill. Outer shell is equipped with serrated thermal claws that can sear through metal like paper. In robot mode, armed with a double-barreled, solid sonic energy blaster."

| Strength | Intelligence | Speed | Endurance | Rank | Courage | Firepower | Skill |
|----------|-------------|-------|-----------|------|---------|-----------|-------|
| 9 | 6 | 5 | 8 | 5 | 4 | 7 | 6 |

MLC $50.00, MIB $77.87, MISB $200-300

Chainclaw, outer shell mode.

Although his outer shell looks more like an angry beaver than a ferocious grizzly bear, it was still interesting to add this character to the Autobot ranks. Chainclaw is similar in transformation to the other Pretender Beasts (both Autobot and Decepticon), fitting compactly into his outer shell.

**ALTERNATE MODE:** Grizzly bear.

**EASILY LOST WEAPONS AND ACCESSORIES:**
2 "Chainclaw" beast shell halves, energy blaster, helmet.

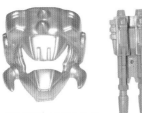
Chainclaw, easily lost weapons and accessories.

Chainclaw, inner robot mode.

Chainclaw, inner robot's alternate mode.

Catilla, inner robot's alternate mode.

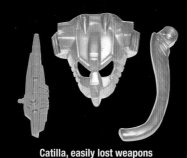
Catilla, easily lost weapons and accessories.

Catilla, inner robot mode.

Catilla, outer shell mode.

# GUNRUNNER

PRETENDER VEHICLES

**FUNCTION:** Squadron Leader
**MOTTO:** "The truth wrapped in a lie is still a lie."

"A super hero in reverse. Daring and defiant when inside outer vehicle, but shy and insecure when out on his own. Armored outer vehicle equipped with armored wheels and hydraulic lifters for all-terrain combat capabilities. Gunrunner transforms from robot mode to hypersonic jet with a maximum speed of Mach 5. Equipped with twin, turreted 8mm electro-static cannons with a range of over 60 miles. Also armed with two armor-piercing, energy-plasma missiles. Armor plating equipped with thermal generators that 'burn' through solid rock."

| Strength | Intelligence | Speed | Endurance | Rank | Courage | Firepower | Skill |
|----------|--------------|-------|-----------|------|---------|-----------|-------|
| 7 | 9 | 7 | 6 | 7 | 9 | 8 | 7 |

$ MLC: **$30-42**, MIB: **$55-68**, MISB: **$200-300**

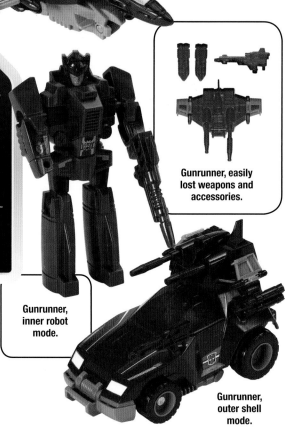

Gunrunner, inner robot's alternate mode.

Gunrunner, easily lost weapons and accessories.

Gunrunner, inner robot mode.

Gunrunner, outer shell mode.

The Pretender Vehicles were fascinating. Gunrunner's entire outer shell functioned as an armored attack vehicle, while his inner robot could transform into a decent-looking jet with the aid of his "dual electro-static cannons" accessory. There was a lot of versatile playability with the Pretender Vehicles, and in recent years, they have begun to slowly rise in demand.

**ALTERNATE MODE:** Assault cruiser, attack vehicle, jet.
**EASILY LOST WEAPONS AND ACCESSORIES:** "Gunrunner" outer shell, rifle, 2 energy plasma missiles, dual electro-static cannons.

Powermaster Optimus Prime, [smaller] robot mode with Powermaster HiQ.

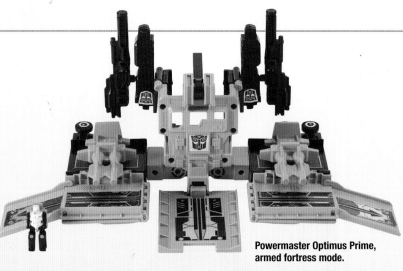

Powermaster Optimus Prime, armed fortress mode.

Powermaster Optimus Prime, attack truck, battle station, tractor trailer truck.

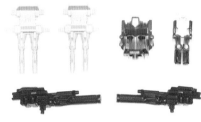

Powermaster Optimus Prime, easily lost weapons and accessories.

Powermaster Optimus Prime, alternate attack mode.

# OPTIMUS PRIME

**POWERMASTER LEADER**

**FUNCTION:** Commander
**MOTTO:** "Freedom is the right of all sentient beings."

"The beloved leader of all Autobots. Dedicated to protecting all life forms—mechanical, human, and otherwise. Willing to sacrifice anything in order to end the Autobot/Decepticon conflict. Wise and compassionate… the inspiration that fuels every Autobot. Binary bonded to the super intelligent Nebulan computer programmer, HiQ. In engine mode, HiQ handles all of Prime's power needs. Trailer transforms into armed fortress, complete with laser rifle, concussion blaster, and 2 twin particle beam cannons. Tractor and trailer combined construct Optimus Prime's new super-powered robot form."

| Strength | Intelligence | Speed | Endurance | Rank | Courage | Firepower | Skill |
|----------|--------------|-------|-----------|------|---------|-----------|-------|
| 10 | 10 | 6 | 10 | 10 | 10 | 9 | 10 |

💲 MLC: **$50-72**, MIB: **$90-125**, MISB: **$200-300**

Powermaster Optimus Prime super robot mode.

Whether in regular robot form, battle station mode, as the intimidating attack truck, or the imposing super-robot, Optimus Prime continues to be the most popular of Transformers regardless of incarnation—in original form (1984), or as a Powermaster. The wonderful thing about his new manifestation is that the tractor-trailer part of his truck still transforms into a robot reminiscent of his original alternate mode.

**ALTERNATE MODE:** Futuristic tractor trailer truck.

**EASILY LOST WEAPONS AND ACCESSORIES:** HiQ figure/Powermaster engine, super robot head, 2 particle beam cannons, 2 laser rifles.

Quickswitch, laser pistol.

# QUICKSWITCH

**SIX CHANGER**

**FUNCTION:** Assault Warrior
**MOTTO:** "A confused enemy is a defeated enemy."

"Completely unpredictable. Changes his mood as often as he changes his mode. Can be compassionate, merciless, friendly, hateful, happy, or angry, depending on what time of day it is. Equipped with 6 different modes: robot warrior, assault hovercraft cruiser, jet-propelled laser pistol, assault beast with stealth shielding, armor-piercing drill tank, suborbital fighter jet. Armed with twin photon blasters."

| Strength | Intelligence | Speed | Endurance | Rank | Courage | Firepower | Skill |
|----------|--------------|-------|-----------|------|---------|-----------|-------|
| 7 | 7 | 7 | 7 | 7 | 8 | 7 | 8 |

MLC: **$50-68**, MIB: **$75-105**, MISB: **$300-500**

Touting the following words on his packaging, Quickswitch, "Transform(s) from hovercraft to jet to drill tank to puma to laser pistol to robot and back!" Hasbro's Six Changers are very clever concepts (see Sixshot, 1987), yet with a very peculiar-looking robot mode, Quickswitch did not have the draw and allure of his Decepticon enemy, Sixshot. Quickswitch's colors are odd (teal green and red), and his various alternate modes are a bit stiff looking and boxy—not nearly as intimidating as the Decepticon Six-Changer. Still, what more could you want from a robot that transforms into six unique alternate modes?

---

**ALTERNATE MODES:** Robot, hovercraft, laser pistol, beast, drill tank, fighter jet.
**EASILY LOST WEAPONS AND ACCESSORIES:** 2 blasters.

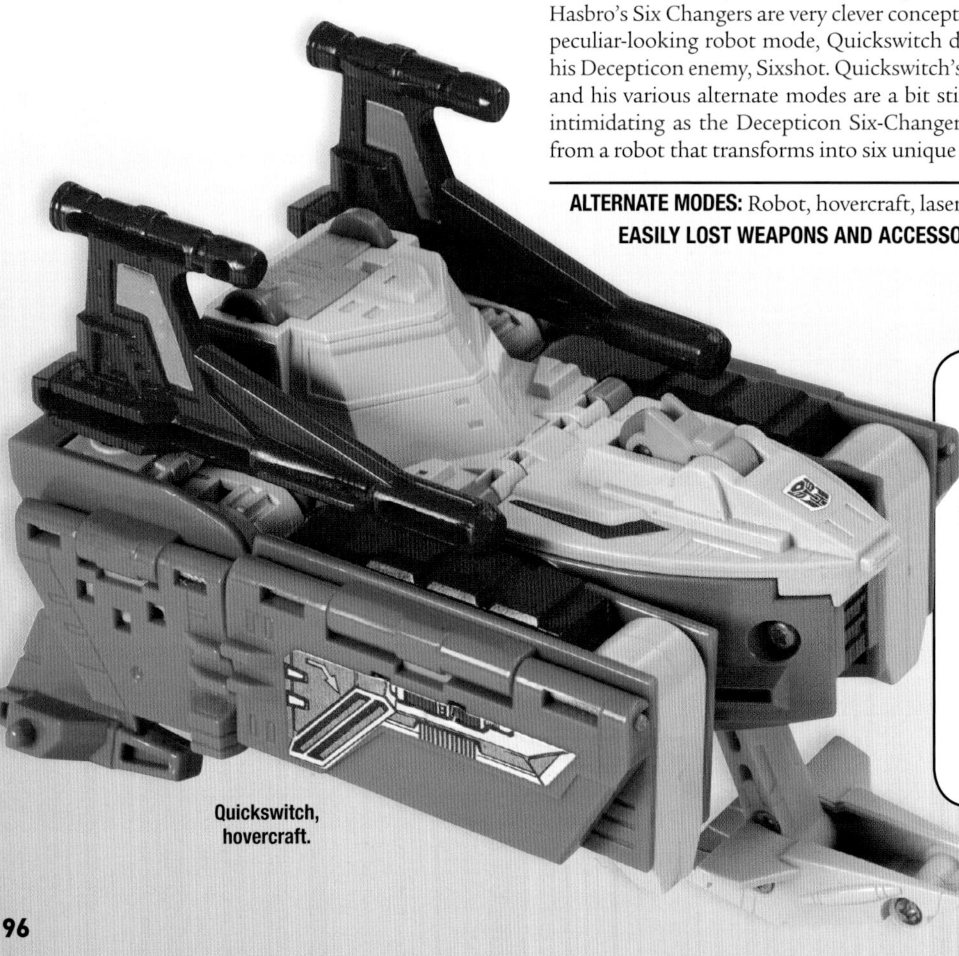

Quickswitch, hovercraft.

Quickswitch, easily lost weapons and accessories.

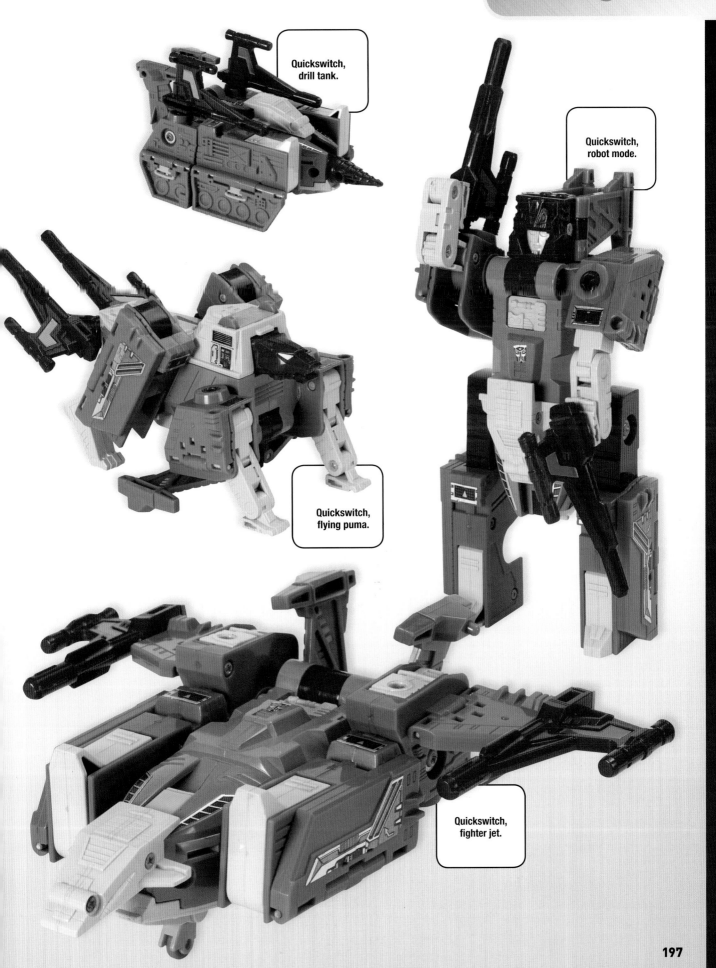

Quickswitch, drill tank.

Quickswitch, robot mode.

Quickswitch, flying puma.

Quickswitch, fighter jet.

# FIRECONS

The Firecons were, to some extent, the Decepticons' low-price point alternative to the Autobots' Monsterbots (1987), and are similar in basic design to the Sparkabots (1988). Unfortunately, they are some of the least popular and easiest Transformers to find on the secondary market due to their poor robot styling, overly simplistic transformations, and less than attractive alternate modes.

Cindersaur, robot mode.

## CINDERSAUR

**FIRECONS**

**FUNCTION:** Firestorm Trooper
**MOTTO:** "Crash and burn…and burn…and burn."

"Incinerates everything in his path so he can find his way home. Leaves a trail of charred ground wherever he goes. Probably fried some of his brain circuits from excessive smoke inhalation. Enjoys taking flame baths to soothe his aching joints. Equipped with fusion-powered flame breath that can be focused in a narrow stream or sprayed in a wide angle. His hobbies include barbecuing Autobots and drinking volcanic lava."

| Strength | Intelligence | Speed | Endurance | Rank | Courage | Firepower | Skill |
|----------|--------------|-------|-----------|------|---------|-----------|-------|
| 7 | 3 | 2 | 4 | 5 | 9 | 7 | 8 |

MLC: **$6-10**, MIP (opened): **$15-20**, MOC: **$50-100**

Cindersaur, alternate mode.

▶ Sparkstalker, robot mode.

As a character, Cindersaur is a dim-witted pyromaniac always rendering anything in front of him to rubble with his built-in fusion-powered flame-thrower. This destructive peccadillo comes in handy as he's the Decepticons' resident Firestorm Trooper. With loose samples of Cindersaur's toy, be careful not to transform him too much, as the silver paint on his nose is prone to rub off.

**ALTERNATE MODE:** [Firebreathing] dinosaur monster.
**EASILY LOST WEAPONS AND ACCESSORIES:** N/A.

## SPARKSTALKER

**FIRECONS**

**FUNCTION:** Cryptologist
**MOTTO:** "The smallest details reveal the largest secrets."

"His greatest talents are revealed in the tiniest structures. An expert at robbing banks, counterfeiting printed circuits, decoding binary messages. Meticulous, cautious, obsessed with minute details. Decepticons appreciate his appearance more than his other talents because he terrifies Autobots. Shoots flame from his mouth with limited accuracy. Better equipped to light campfires than melt Autobots."

| Strength | Intelligence | Speed | Endurance | Rank | Courage | Firepower | Skill |
|----------|--------------|-------|-----------|------|---------|-----------|-------|
| 5 | 9 | 2 | 6 | 6 | 6 | 4 | 9 |

MLC: **$6-10**, MIP (opened): **$15-20**, MOC: **$50-100**

Sparkstalker is the Decepticon's in-house cryptologist (a decoder skilled in the analysis of codes), who by looking at the small details in things, has amassed a wealth of knowledge that he applies to theft, crime, and profit. His high intelligence and skill combined with a truly horrifying alternate mode make him a powerful member of the Decepticon army.

**ALTERNATE MODE:** [Firebreathing] insect monster.
**EASILY LOST WEAPONS AND ACCESSORIES:** N/A.

Sparkstalker, alternate mode.

# FLAMEFEATHER

**FIRECONS**

**FUNCTION:** Warrior
**MOTTO:** "The only good Autobot is a deactivated Autobot."

"The only Decepticon ever thrown out of the Decepticon Military Academy for being too violent. Trashes entire car lots when there's nothing better to do. Usually works alone because his fellow Decepticons refuse to work with him. Flamethrower inside his mouth can fry a football field. Maximum flight speed: 90 mph. Greatest achievement: talking to someone for more than a minute before flying into a rage."

| Strength | Intelligence | Speed | Endurance | Rank | Courage | Firepower | Skill |
|----------|--------------|-------|-----------|------|---------|-----------|-------|
| 7 | 2 | 2 | 4 | 6 | 8 | 7 | 0 |

**$** MLC: **$6-10**, MIP (opened): **$15-20**, MOC: **$50-100**

Flamefeather, alternate mode.

Flamefeather, robot mode.

With the directions to, "Push the monster and flames shoot out of his jaws!", kids must have enjoyed the Firecons' spark-shooting action (they were not real flames, as the instructions suggested). Flamefeather's character is one of the most despicable and loathsome of all evil Decepticons as his Tech Spec suggests. Flamefeather's greatest triumph is delineated in Dreamwave's *Transformers: More Than Meets The Eye* guide books (2003, issue #2): "... the fact that he once talked to someone for .12 breems before flying into an unprovoked rage and running to go destroy something." In Cybertronian time, 1 breem = 8.3 minutes, .12 breems = .993 minutes, or approximately one minute straight!

**ALTERNATE MODE:** [Firebreathing] flying monster.
**EASILY LOST WEAPONS AND ACCESSORIES:** N/A.

# SEACONS

The Seacons were essentially the last combiner team produced in the G1 toy line apart from the Pretenders' Monstructor (1989), and their alternate modes were fascinating and unique. The team had a lot of playability, as each Seacon transformed from robot to sea creature, and then into a stand-alone (or Piranacon-held) Targetmaster weapon (with the exception of team leader, Snaptrap). The reason it appears that there is an "extra" robot in the Seacons' gestalt, is because one of the five smaller Seacons always transformed into Piranacon's weapon (usually the unpopular Nautilator). A truly great team, the amphibious Seacons provided an excellent swan song for Transformers combiners.

Seacons in attack modes.

# NAUTILATOR

**SEACONS**

**FUNCTION:** Underwater Excavations
**MOTTO:** "Blame someone else before they blame you."

"A stumbling, bumbling amphibious foul-up. Often gets caught in the undertow and has to be hauled out by his fellow Seacons. Quick to blame others for his mistakes. Equipped with geological sensors that register underwater fuel deposits. Armed with triple crusher cannon that shoots energon bands which trap their target and then tighten until the target has been reduced to rubble. Nautilator transforms to heat-seeking torpedo cannon in weapons mode. Combines with fellow Seacons to form Piranacon."

| Strength | Intelligence | Speed | Endurance | Rank | Courage | Firepower | Skill |
|----------|--------------|-------|-----------|------|---------|-----------|-------|
| 7 | 4 | 3 | 8 | 5 | 4 | 7 | 4 |

MLC: **$25-35,** MIP (opened): **$38-55,** MOC: **$75-150**

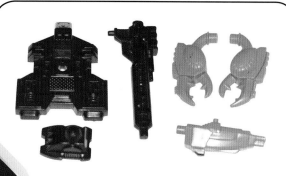

Nautilator, easily lost weapons and accessories.

Each of the Seacons were menacing in their own right, but Nautilator was the fiercest-looking lobster I'd ever seen. According to Dreamwave's *Transformers: More Than Meets The Eye* guidebooks (2003), Nautilator was the most unpopular of all the Seacons, and thus was used as Piranacon's Targetmaster weapon because the rest of the team refused to combine with him in gestalt mode.

---

**ALTERNATE MODE:** Lobster monster; Targetmaster heat-seeking torpedo cannon.
**EASILY LOST WEAPONS AND ACCESSORIES:** Triple crusher cannon, tripod rifle, connector, weapon stand base, removable claws (left and right).

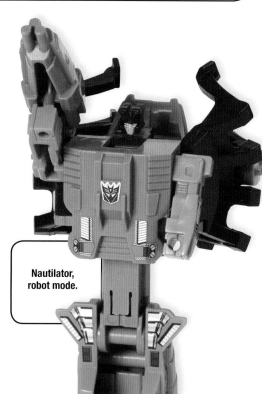

Nautilator, robot mode.

Nautilator, Piranacon's Targetmaster weapon mode.

Nautilator, alternate mode.

Overbite, Piranacon's Targetmaster weapon mode.

Overbite, robot mode.

Overbite, alternate mode.

# OVERBITE

**SEACONS**

**FUNCTION:** Undersea Terminator
**MOTTO:** "There are only two kinds of creatures: predator and prey."

"A menacing, mechanical monster. Prowls the ocean depths for his next victim. Unrelenting and unbeatable [in] underwater combat. Teeth and talons can tear through solid slabs of concrete and steel. Liquid-cooled, turbo-powered engine enables him to reach speeds up to 70 mph. In weapons mode converts to a double barreled tidal wave maker. In robot mode carries jawbreaker cannon that shoots metal eating, salt-based corrosives. Combines with fellow Seacons to form Piranacon."

| Strength | Intelligence | Speed | Endurance | Rank | Courage | Firepower | Skill |
|----------|--------------|-------|-----------|------|---------|-----------|-------|
| 7 | 7 | 5 | 7 | 6 | 7 | 6 | 8 |

**$** MLC: **$25-35**, MIP (opened): **$38-55**, MOC: **$100-200**

Overbite, easily lost weapons and accessories.

Simply remind yourself of Overbite's function as "Undersea Terminator," and you'll get the gist of how deadly this predator is when fighting underwater. Although his colors are less than intimidating (aquamarine, chartreuse, and purple), his alternate mode is still fierce and powerful: with an opening and closing jaw.

**ALTERNATE MODE:** Shark monster; Targetmaster double barreled tidal wavemaker.

**EASILY LOST WEAPONS AND ACCESSORIES:** Jawbreaker cannon, tripod rifle, connector, weapon stand base, removable claws (left and right).

# SEAWING

**SEACONS**

**FUNCTION:** Undersea Reconnaissance
**MOTTO:** "The darkest depths reveal the darkest secrets."

"Glides through the seas like a sinister steel specter. Enjoys surprising and then destroying his targets. Nothing escapes his notice... or his grasp. Equipped with electrical, chemical, and infrared sensors, long range sonar. Converts to dual proton blaster in weapons mode. Underwater, can detect and home in on anything living or moving within a 20 mile radius. Maximum speed: 110 mph. Armed with double venom lasers that paralyze on contact. Combines with fellow Seacons to form Piranacon."

| Strength | Intelligence | Speed | Endurance | Rank | Courage | Firepower | Skill |
|----------|-------------|-------|-----------|------|---------|-----------|-------|
| 7 | 8 | 6 | 4 | 6 | 8 | 6 | 9 |

($) MLC: **$18-26**, MIP (opened): **$30-42**, MOC: **$75-150**

Seawing, alternate mode.

Seawing, easily lost weapons and accessories.

Although his robot mode is not the most sturdy of the Seacons, Seawing's alternate mode is very interesting—a sort-of "attack manta ray." In Targetmaster mode, his two venom lasers are inserted into his manta ray's nosecone and they fit perfectly. As a character, he has high intelligence and skill, using his intimidating alternate mode to strike fear in both ally and adversary. He also has designs on a command position in the Decepticon army.

**ALTERNATE MODE:** Manta ray monster; Targetmaster dual proton blaster.

**EASILY LOST WEAPONS AND ACCESSORIES:** 2 venom lasers (that can combine), tripod rifle, connector, weapon stand base.

Seawing, Piranacon's Targetmaster weapon mode.

Seawing, robot mode.

# SKALOR

**SEACONS**

**FUNCTION:** Amphibious Assault
**MOTTO:** "I stink, therefore I am."

"A merciless, polluting parasite. So foul even his fellow Seacons avoid him. Leaves a trail of grease and toxic chemicals wherever he goes. Able to absorb fuel through the hull of any ship. In robot mode, equipped with dual crustation (sic) rifles that encase and immobilize the enemy with hard, sticky scales. Serrated, razor-sharp jaws are able to cut through any substance. In weapons mode, transforms into twin-barreled corrosive slime-shooter. Combines with fellow Seacons to form Piranacon."

| Strength | Intelligence | Speed | Endurance | Rank | Courage | Firepower | Skill |
|---|---|---|---|---|---|---|---|
| 7 | 5 | 3 | 8 | 4 | 7 | 6 | 6 |

**MLC: $20-28, MIP (opened): $35-42,
MOC: $100-200**

Skalor,
Piranacon's
Targetmaster
weapon mode.

With one of the most well written Tech Specs for a coelacanth/angler fish-type amphibious monster, Skalor is a sinister and stinky nightmare demon of the depths—despite his strange color scheme. Unlike fellow Seacons Overbite (1988) and Nautilator (1988), the two small monster arms on his toy are not removable and are permanently screwed into his body.

Skalor,
alternate
mode.

**ALTERNATE MODE:** Monster coelacanth; Targetmaster twin-barreled corrosive slime-shooter.

**EASILY LOST WEAPONS AND ACCESSORIES:** Dual crustation rifles (left and right), tripod rifle, connector, weapon stand base.

Skalor,
easily lost
weapons and
accessories.

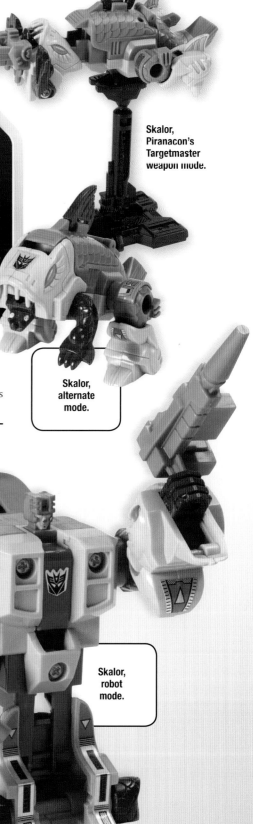

Skalor,
robot
mode.

Tentakil, alternate mode.

Tentakil, Piranacon's Targetmaster weapon mode.

Tentakil, robot mode.

# TENTAKIL

**SEACONS**

**FUNCTION:** Underwater Demolition
**MOTTO:** "Embrace your enemies...until they're terminated."

"Crushes submarines like they were soda cans. The more benevolent he appears, the crueler he becomes. Electromagnetic tentacles add super strength to his vise-like grip. Electrically-charged feelers short circuit and stun on contact. In robot mode, carries dual slime lasers that shoot globs of highly-adhesive gelatinous goo. In weapons mode, transforms to twin 50,000 volt lightning rifles. Also able to burst away in a cloud of viscous black grease that hinders his pursuers. Combines with fellow Seacons to form Piranacon."

| Strength | Intelligence | Speed | Endurance | Rank | Courage | Firepower | Skill |
|----------|-------------|-------|-----------|------|---------|-----------|-------|
| 8 | 6 | 6 | 6 | 6 | 7 | 7 | 5 |

MLC: **$25-35**, MIP (opened): **$38-55**, MOC: **$75-150**

From the description posited forth from his Tech Spec bio, at a distance, the amiable Tentakil is a well-meaning mechanoid. Yet, up close, he is destructive, cunning, and ruthless—physically one of the ugliest and most frightening of all Transformers. As a toy, his tentacles are a bit funny looking and can't technically "wrap" around enemies, but he was a nice addition to the Seacon forces.

**ALTERNATE MODE:** Monster squid; Targetmaster twin 50,000 volt lightning rifles.

**EASILY LOST WEAPONS AND ACCESSORIES:** Dual slime lasers (left and right), tripod rifle, connector, weapon stand base.

Tentakil, easily lost weapons and accessories.

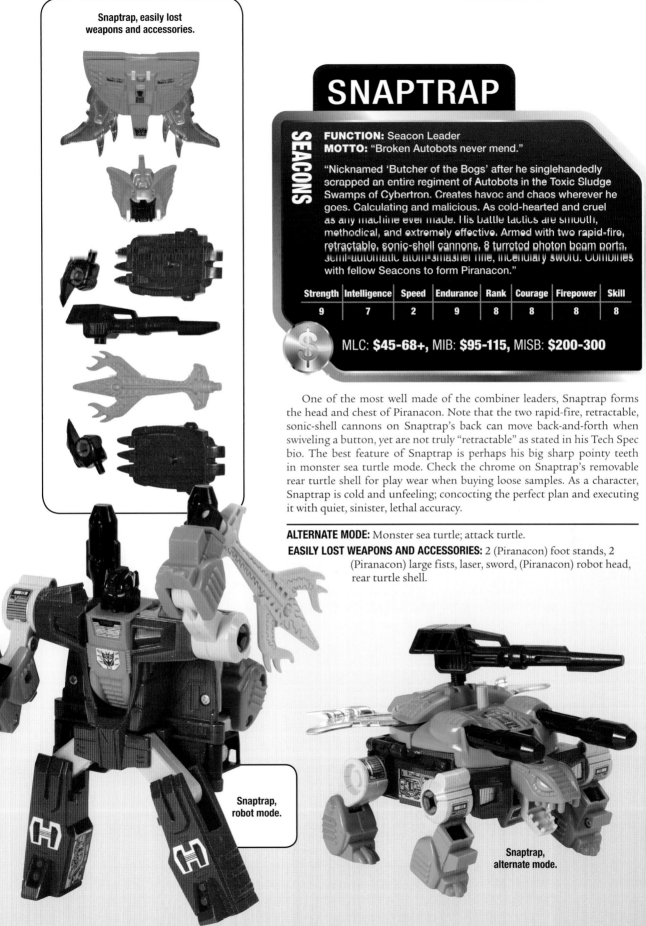

Snaptrap, easily lost weapons and accessories.

# SNAPTRAP

**SEACONS**

**FUNCTION:** Seacon Leader
**MOTTO:** "Broken Autobots never mend."

"Nicknamed 'Butcher of the Bogs' after he singlehandedly scrapped an entire regiment of Autobots in the Toxic Sludge Swamps of Cybertron. Creates havoc and chaos wherever he goes. Calculating and malicious. As cold-hearted and cruel as any machine ever made. His battle tactics are smooth, methodical, and extremely effective. Armed with two rapid-fire, retractable, sonic-shell cannons, 8 turreted photon beam ports, semi-automatic atom-smasher rifle, incendiary sword. Combines with fellow Seacons to form Piranacon."

| Strength | Intelligence | Speed | Endurance | Rank | Courage | Firepower | Skill |
|----------|-------------|-------|-----------|------|---------|-----------|-------|
| 9 | 7 | 2 | 9 | 8 | 8 | 8 | 8 |

MLC: **$45-68+**, MIB: **$95-115**, MISB: **$200-300**

One of the most well made of the combiner leaders, Snaptrap forms the head and chest of Piranacon. Note that the two rapid-fire, retractable, sonic-shell cannons on Snaptrap's back can move back-and-forth when swiveling a button, yet are not truly "retractable" as stated in his Tech Spec bio. The best feature of Snaptrap is perhaps his big sharp pointy teeth in monster sea turtle mode. Check the chrome on Snaptrap's removable rear turtle shell for play wear when buying loose samples. As a character, Snaptrap is cold and unfeeling; concocting the perfect plan and executing it with quiet, sinister, lethal accuracy.

**ALTERNATE MODE:** Monster sea turtle; attack turtle.

**EASILY LOST WEAPONS AND ACCESSORIES:** 2 (Piranacon) foot stands, 2 (Piranacon) large fists, laser, sword, (Piranacon) robot head, rear turtle shell.

Snaptrap, robot mode.

Snaptrap, alternate mode.

205

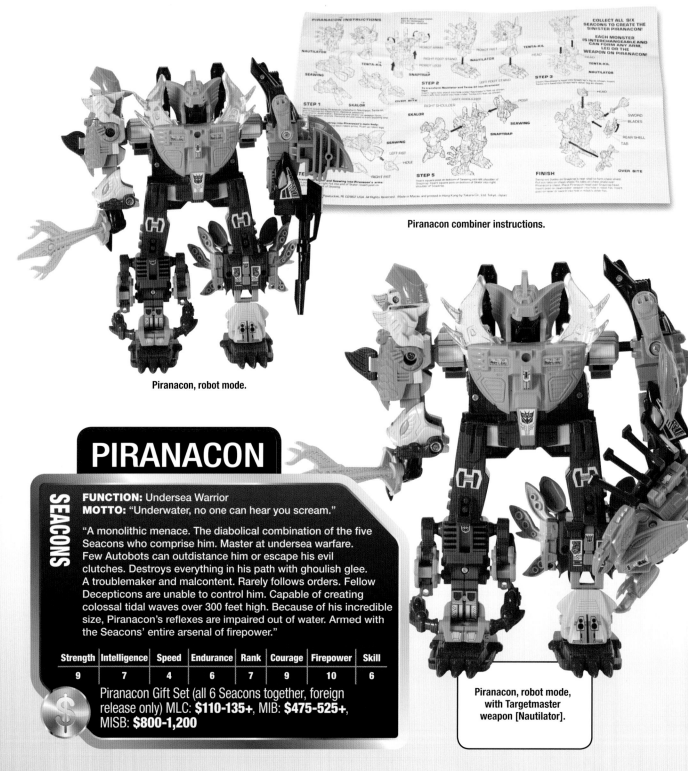

Piranacon combiner instructions.

Piranacon, robot mode.

## SEACONS

# PIRANACON

**FUNCTION:** Undersea Warrior

**MOTTO:** "Underwater, no one can hear you scream."

"A monolithic menace. The diabolical combination of the five
Seacons who comprise him. Master at undersea warfare.
Few Autobots can outdistance him or escape his evil
clutches. Destroys everything in his path with ghoulish glee.
A troublemaker and malcontent. Rarely follows orders. Fellow
Decepticons are unable to control him. Capable of creating
colossal tidal waves over 300 feet high. Because of his incredible
size, Piranacon's reflexes are impaired out of water. Armed with
the Seacons' entire arsenal of firepower."

| Strength | Intelligence | Speed | Endurance | Rank | Courage | Firepower | Skill |
|----------|--------------|-------|-----------|------|---------|-----------|-------|
| 9 | 7 | 4 | 6 | 7 | 9 | 10 | 6 |

Piranacon Gift Set (all 6 Seacons together, foreign
release only) MLC: **$110-135+**, MIB: **$475-525+**,
MISB: **$800-1,200**

Piranacon, robot mode,
with Targetmaster
weapon [Nautilator].

Although his gestalt robot mode looks a bit
stout, is still one of the most impressive-looking
combiners. Regardless of which Seacon Piranacon
uses as his Targetmaster weapon, his immense
firepower is obvious with a mere glance. Extremely
expensive to purchase mint loose and (entirely)
complete, as most retailers are unaware of the myriad
parts needed to construct a complete Piranacon
(particularly the 5 connectors, 5 tripod rifles, and
5 weapon stand bases for each smaller robot). His
boxed gift set is easily one of the most sought after
pieces of all boxed Transformers, and should be
priced accordingly. As a character, Piranacon is one
of the smoother-functioning gestalts, with a high
intelligence due to the "like mindedness" among his
Seacon combiners.

# CRANKCASE

**TRIGGERCONS**

**FUNCTION:** Data Collector
**MOTTO:** "Things are never as good as they seem."

"A wheezing, whining ingrate. As welcome as a rash of rust-rot. The worse things get, the happier he is. Enjoys complaining about everything. Equipped with vast memory storage capacity and shell-resistant armor. Also equipped with infrared probes that penetrate and analyze enemy circuitry. Armed with two high-impact laser blasters and a distortion modulator that scrambles enemy cerebral impulses."

| Strength | Intelligence | Speed | Endurance | Rank | Courage | Firepower | Skill |
|---|---|---|---|---|---|---|---|
| 8 | 6 | 3 | 9 | 7 | 7 | 8 | 8 |

MLC: **$12-15**, MIP (opened): **$25-30**, MOC: **$50-100**

Crankcase,
robot mode.

Crankcase,
alternate mode.

Crankcase's name truly exemplifies his personality as attested to by the Tech Spec: he is grouchy, ill tempered, aggravating, and annoyed. As a toy, his spring-loaded weapons mechanism emerges from the back of his SUV passenger compartment to lower above his hood.

**ALTERNATE MODE:** 4WD O.R.V.
(Off-road Vehicle).
**EASILY LOST WEAPONS AND ACCESSORIES:** N/A.

# RUCKUS

**TRIGGERCONS**

**FUNCTION:** Combat Assault
**MOTTO:** "I take a licking and keep on kicking."

"A rolling bucket of bolts. Always looks like he just lost a demolition derby. Willing to take big risks on the battlefield because he's in such a state of disrepair. A deadly, devastating warrior. Adept at ramming his enemies and then running them over. Nail-studded tires can tread over anything. Also able to emit viscous oil slicks that send his enemies into a tail spin. Armed with heavy-duty rocket launchers that fire mercury tipped explosives."

| Strength | Intelligence | Speed | Endurance | Rank | Courage | Firepower | Skill |
|---|---|---|---|---|---|---|---|
| 8 | 8 | 5 | 3 | 5 | 10 | 8 | 7 |

MLC: **$12-15**, MIP (opened): **$25-30**, MOC: **$50-100**

Ruckus,
robot mode.

Ruckus,
alternate mode.

Besides the two rocket launchers that flip out over his shoulders, Ruckus had one of the more fascinating biographies among Transformers and endeared himself (and his reckless attitude) to many die-hard toy collectors. According to his Tech Specs, he has a lot of different "features" as a warrior that helped to suspend our disbelief.

**ALTERNATE MODE:** Baja/dune buggy.
**EASILY LOST WEAPONS AND ACCESSORIES:** N/A.

# TRIGGERCONS

The Decepticon Triggercons are similar in function to the Autobots' Triggerbots, hence the phonetic similarity. The premise was cool for lower price-point Transformers, as their packaging touted, "With trigger-action weapons! Push the button and weapons spring into action!" This spring loaded function worked well and repeatedly, much to the pleasure of kids everywhere.

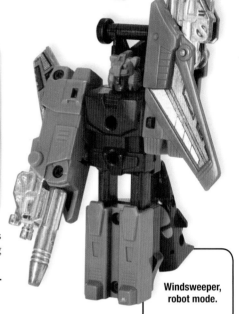

Windsweeper, alternate mode.

# WINDSWEEPER

**TRIGGERCONS**

**FUNCTION:** Air Defense
**MOTTO:** "Uninvited guests soon become smoldering wrecks."

"Malicious and meticulous. Feels the sky is his home and that it should be kept 'clean' of anything that flies. Notorious for shooting at anything, including his fellow Decepticons. High-intensity heat generators in wings enable him to tear through solid steel. Also equipped with long-range infrared scanners, sensitive enough to find a lug-nut in a junkyard. Armed with two, lock-target, long-range laser cannons."

| Strength | Intelligence | Speed | Endurance | Rank | Courage | Firepower | Skill |
|---|---|---|---|---|---|---|---|
| 8 | 4 | 7 | 7 | 6 | 9 | 8 | 6 |

MLC: **$25-35**, MIP (opened): **$35-42**, MOC: **$60-120**

As a fighter jet with flip-forward weapons in both modes, Windsweeper is one of the more popular Triggercons/Triggerbots. Be careful when transforming loose samples, as his chromed weapons are prone to chipping and rubbing.

**ALTERNATE MODE:** B-1B Lancer bomber.
**EASILY LOST WEAPONS AND ACCESSORIES:** N/A.

Windsweeper, robot mode.

# BEASTBOX

Beastbox, easily lost weapons and accessories.

**CASSETTES**

**FUNCTION:** Interrogator
**MOTTO:** "Speak now if you intend to ever speak at all."

"His violent temper often overcomes his natural curiosity. More willing to whittle down his captives with his fists than with his words. Few survive his interrogations long enough to reveal anything useful. Can record up to 6000 hours of testimony. Equipped with two compression cannons, which crush a target with tons of compressed air pressure. Combines with Squawktalk to form robot Squawkbox."

| Strength | Intelligence | Speed | Endurance | Rank | Courage | Firepower | Skill |
|---|---|---|---|---|---|---|---|
| 7 | 5 | 3 | 6 | 6 | 7 | 4 | 3 |

MLC: **$24-40**, MIP (opened; two-pack w/ Squawktalk): **$55-68**, MOC: **$200-300**

Beastbox is a well-designed smaller Decepticon, which is interesting because of his dual function as cassette and combiner. Like the Autobot cassette combiner Slamdance (1988), Beastbox and Squawktalk merge to form the gestalt Squawkbox. With a robot mode that approximates a small purple gorilla, and fairly good articulation (apart from his legs), Beastbox is a first-rate addition to the Decepticon ranks.

Beastbox, alternate mode.

**ALTERNATE MODE:** Olympus Type IV "Metal" MC60 Microcassettes.
**EASILY LOST WEAPONS AND ACCESSORIES:** 2 compressor cannons.

Beastbox, robot mode.

# SQUAWKTALK

**CASSETTES**

**FUNCTION:** Translator
**MOTTO:** "If you have nothing interesting to say, say it anyway."

"Never stops talking except to refill his fuel tank. Knows over 250 Earth and 6300 alien languages, but never has anything important to say in any of them. Other Decepticons often threaten to rip out his vocal circuitry and wrap it around his beak to shut him up. Carries two deafening high decibel sonic boomers. Combines with Beastbox to form robot Squawkbox."

| Strength | Intelligence | Speed | Endurance | Rank | Courage | Firepower | Skill |
|---|---|---|---|---|---|---|---|
| 3 | 5 | 6 | 5 | 6 | 6 | 5 | 8 |

**MLC: $24-40, MIP (opened; two-pack w/Beastbox): $55-68, MOC: $200-300**

Squawktalk, alternate mode.

Squawktalk, easily lost weapons and accessories.

Squawktalk, robot mode.

I have always considered the cancellation of the *Transformers* animated series to be one of the great tragedies perpetrated on popular culture in the 1980s because Transformers fans never got a chance to see the likes of Decepticons such as Squawktalk appear on the small screen. Combines with Beastbox to form the gestalt Squawkbox.

**ALTERNATE MODE:** Olympus Type IV "Metal" MC60 Microcassettes.

**EASILY LOST WEAPONS AND ACCESSORIES:** 2 sonic boomer cannons.

# SQUAWKBOX

**FUNCTION:** Battlefield Dissonance
**MOTTO:** "One being's noise is another's music."

MLC (Beastbox & Squawkbox): **$48-55**, MOC: **$200-300**

Squawkbox, robot mode, combined form of Beastbox and Squawktalk.

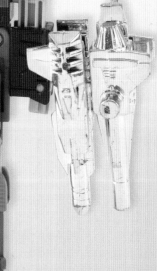

Squawkbox's function and motto are provided by Dreamwave's *Transformers: More Than Meets The Eye* (2003) guide books, where it states that this gestalt creatively uses both of his combined form's abilities in order to wreak sonic and audio havoc on the battlefield. Squawkbox is one of the most creative of Transformers, but has "little offensive capability." A terrific gestalt, he makes use of Beastbox's compressor cannons and Squawktalk's sonic boomer cannons in this combined mode.

**ALTERNATE MODES:** Two Olympus Type IV "Metal" MC60 Microcassettes.

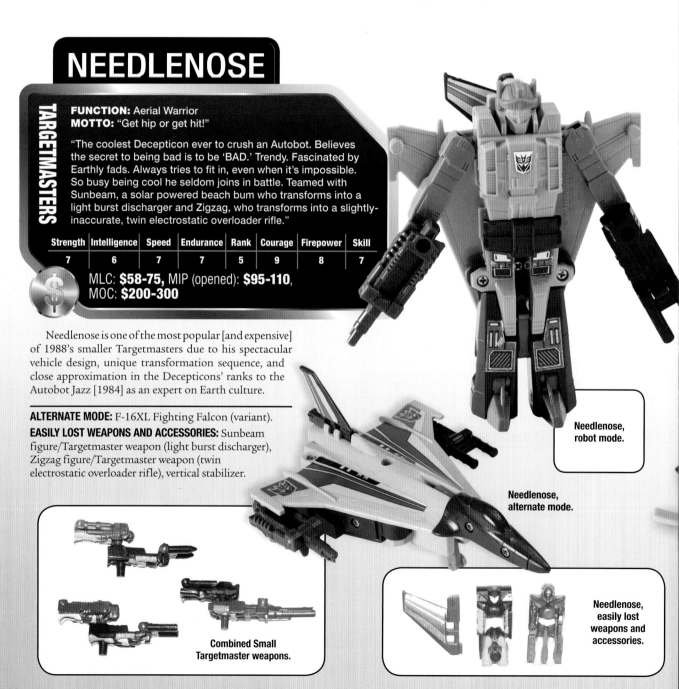

Quake,
alternate
mode.

## [SMALL DECEPTICON]
# TARGETMASTERS

Though similar in scale to the Small Autobot Targetmasters, the Small Decepticon Targetmasters were distinctly different in design, and were even unique among themselves. Needlenose, Quake, and Spinister did not share a similar motif like the Autobots (Landfill, Quickmix and Scoop all were similarly-colored construction vehicles), and each had a very sophisticated transformation process for smaller price point Transformers. These (small) Targetmasters are high demand pieces, and command decent money loose, but quite a bit more if carded (particularly Needlenose).

## NEEDLENOSE

**TARGETMASTERS**

**FUNCTION:** Aerial Warrior
**MOTTO:** "Get hip or get hit!"

"The coolest Decepticon ever to crush an Autobot. Believes the secret to being bad is to be 'BAD.' Trendy. Fascinated by Earthly fads. Always tries to fit in, even when it's impossible. So busy being cool he seldom joins in battle. Teamed with Sunbeam, a solar powered beach bum who transforms into a light burst discharger and Zigzag, who transforms into a slightly-inaccurate, twin electrostatic overloader rifle."

| Strength | Intelligence | Speed | Endurance | Rank | Courage | Firepower | Skill |
|----------|--------------|-------|-----------|------|---------|-----------|-------|
| 7 | 6 | 7 | 7 | 5 | 9 | 8 | 7 |

MLC: **$58-75**, MIP (opened): **$95-110**,
MOC: **$200-300**

Needlenose robot mode.

Needlenose is one of the most popular [and expensive] of 1988's smaller Targetmasters due to his spectacular vehicle design, unique transformation sequence, and close approximation in the Decepticons' ranks to the Autobot Jazz [1984] as an expert on Earth culture.

**ALTERNATE MODE:** F-16XL Fighting Falcon (variant).
**EASILY LOST WEAPONS AND ACCESSORIES:** Sunbeam figure/Targetmaster weapon (light burst discharger), Zigzag figure/Targetmaster weapon (twin electrostatic overloader rifle), vertical stabilizer.

Needlenose,
alternate mode.

Combined Small
Targetmaster weapons.

Needlenose,
easily lost
weapons and
accessories.

# QUAKE

**TARGETMASTERS**

**FUNCTION:** Ground Assault
**MOTTO:** "Nothing lasts forever…so why not destroy it now?"

"A destructive berserker. Attacks everyone and everything with a vengeance. Doesn't stop shooting until everything is in ruins. Capable of leveling an entire Autobot installation in minutes. Titanium-based treads are equipped with special adhesive that enables Quake to climb sheer cliff surfaces. Known for his somewhat 'off the wall' battle tactics. Teamed with Tiptop, a former circus strongman who transforms into a balance-altering, gyroscopic destabilizing weapon, and Heater, a smart-aleck street punk who transforms into a double photon pistol. Equipped with plasma cannon in tank mode."

| Strength | Intelligence | Speed | Endurance | Rank | Courage | Firepower | Skill |
|----------|-------------|-------|-----------|------|---------|-----------|-------|
| 8 | 4 | 3 | 9 | 5 | 9 | 9 | 6 |

MLC: **$48-65**, MIP (opened): **$75-100**, MOC: **$200-300**

Quake, robot mode.

Quake, easily lost weapons and accessories.

Smaller Targetmasters like Quake have the ability to combine their two Nebulan partners into a 'super-weapon'—whichever weapon is used as the barrel of the combined Targetmaster weapon has its primary function increased by the other.

**ALTERNATE MODE:** Leopard 2 M.B.T. (Main Battle Tank).
**EASILY LOST WEAPONS AND ACCESSORIES:** "Tiptop" figure/Targetmaster weapon [balance-altering, gyroscopic destabilizing weapon], "Heater" figure/Targetmaster weapon [double photon pistol], plasma cannon.

# SPINISTER

**TARGETMASTERS**

**FUNCTION:** Aerial Assault
**MOTTO:** "Respect your foes' abilities as you would your own."

"An eerie aerial adventurer. As much of a mystery to his fellow Decepticons as he is to his enemies. Talks little, reveals less. Spends most of his time off on his own. Enjoys scaring unwary Autobots and then attacking them while they're off guard. Equipped with infrared attack sensors in helicopter mode. Teamed with two Nebulans: Singe, who converts to a dual flamethrower and Hairsplitter, who turns into a twin lock-target laser rifle."

| Strength | Intelligence | Speed | Endurance | Rank | Courage | Firepower | Skill |
|----------|-------------|-------|-----------|------|---------|-----------|-------|
| 6 | 8 | 6 | 6 | 7 | 9 | 8 | 8 |

MLC: **$48-64**, MIP (opened): **$75-100**, MOC: **$200-300**

Spinister, robot mode.

Spinister, easily lost weapons and accessories.

His Targetmaster weapons were most appropriately placed on his helicopter's attack mode, as they attached onto a post under his side wings. Although Spinister's (a play on the word "sinister" and the "spin" of his rotor blades) colors were a bit much in blue, magenta, and purple, his transformation mode was complex and he looked intimidating as a vehicle.

**ALTERNATE MODE:** AH-64 Apache attack helicopter.
**EASILY LOST WEAPONS AND ACCESSORIES:** Singe figure/ Targetmaster weapon (dual flamethrower), Hairsplitter figure/Targetmaster weapon (twin lock-target laser rifle).

Spinister, alternate mode.

Horri-Bull, alternate mode.

## [SMALL DECEPTICON]
# HEADMASTERS

The designs of this second generation of Decepticon Headmasters were peculiar compared their larger, earlier iteration [see Decepticon Headmasters and Decepticon Headmaster Horrorcons (both 1987)]. However, these smaller Decepticon Headmasters toys are in very high demand on the secondary market. Regarding their alternate modes, as per usual, the Decepticon Headmasters transformed into animals while the Autobot Headmasters changed into vehicles.

Fangry, easily lost weapons and accessories.

Fangry, robot mode.

## FANGRY

**HEADMASTERS**

**FUNCTION:** Tracker
**MOTTO:** "Leaders are for fools who need to follow."

"A fearsome, foul-mouthed nightstalker. Rebels against authority in any form. Lashes out at anyone who even suggests his next course of action. His Decepticon superiors have more difficulty controlling him than the Autobots have fighting him. Binary-bonded to Brisko, a former Nebulan cartographer with a photographic memory. Shoots semi-automatic ion pulse gun. Tail converts to compressed air cannon that produces 200 mph gale force winds. Able to fly short distances in wolf mode."

| Strength | Intelligence | Speed | Endurance | Rank | Courage | Firepower | Skill |
|----------|--------------|-------|-----------|------|---------|-----------|-------|
| 6 | 8 | 6 | 8 | 6 | 8 | 6 | 8 |

MLC: **$72-105+**, MIB: **$135-155+**, MISB: **$200-400**

Although his alternate mode of a standing winged wolf is not as intimidating as his Tech Spec bio suggests, his tail and wings made up for these deficiencies in this form. His toy is not very poseable in either robot or wolf mode, yet it is still in demand on the secondary market due to its easily lost parts. And are those two things on Fangry's back protruding wolf legs? As a character, Fangry is one of the most offensive, rebellious, and reckless of Decepticon warriors (and he's up against some capable competition).

**ALTERNATE MODE:** [Winged] wolf.
**EASILY LOST WEAPONS AND ACCESSORIES:** Brisko trainer/robot head, ion pulse gun, wings/shield.

Fangry, alternate mode.

# HORRI-BULL

**HEADMASTERS**

**FUNCTION:** Ground Trooper
**MOTTO:** "Smash all that stands and trample the rest."

"A snorting, belching bully with a nasty temper. Drips grease and oil from his mouth and emits billowing black clouds of noxious black smoke from his nostrils. Enjoys destroying anything that stands in his way, particularly Autobots. In robot mode, uses flamethrower tail to incinerate his enemies. Also armed with a concussion blaster. Range: 12 miles. Binary-bonded to the Nebulan, Kreb, a former talk show host with obnoxious manners."

| Strength | Intelligence | Speed | Endurance | Rank | Courage | Firepower | Skill |
|----------|--------------|-------|-----------|------|---------|-----------|-------|
| 0 | 6 | 6 | 8 | 6 | 8 | 6 | 4 |

💲 MLC: **$100-130**, MIB: **$120-135**, MISB: **$100-200**

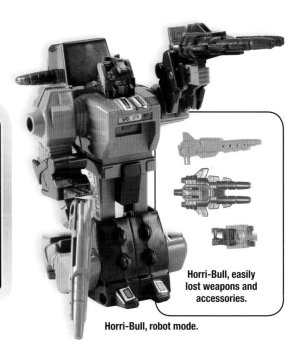

Horri-Bull, easily lost weapons and accessories.

Horri-Bull, robot mode.

As with all Headmasters, even the smaller toys released by Hasbro in 1988 had opening compartments that their respective drivers/trainers could fit into. And like their larger versions (1987), they still had built-in Tech Specs meters in their chests that could be read (showing the following abilities: Strength, Intelligence, and Speed) when their drivers/trainers were transformed into a robot head and inserted into the robots' shoulders.

Horri-Bull was indeed a bull, but a bull form of a buffalo (according to his instructions). Apart from his ridiculously awful color scheme, his jointed tail and intimidating fierce look makes him a popular catch in collectible stores and on the secondary market.

**ALTERNATE MODE:** Buffalo.
**EASILY LOST WEAPONS AND ACCESSORIES:** Kreb trainer/robot head, concussion blaster, flamethrower/tail.

# SQUEEZEPLAY

**HEADMASTERS**

**FUNCTION:** Saboteur
**MOTTO:** "Place brawn before brains and victory is yours."

"A raving, relentless, one-robot wrecking crew with slashing, crushing claws and needle-sharp, armor-piercing fangs. Rarely slows down. Never stops to think. Binary-bonded to Lokos, a Nebulan smuggler and hardened criminal. Armed with overrider rifle that overloads and blows out electrical circuits. In robot mode, uses tail as metal-rending mace. Titanium-reinforced claws can slice through almost any substance. An expert at underwater sabotage."

| Strength | Intelligence | Speed | Endurance | Rank | Courage | Firepower | Skill |
|----------|--------------|-------|-----------|------|---------|-----------|-------|
| 8 | 5 | 4 | 9 | 5 | 10 | 7 | 6 |

💲 MLC: **$68-92**, MIB: **$120-135**, MISB: **$200-400**

Squeezeplay, easily lost weapons and accessories.

Squeezeplay, robot mode.

With excellent poseability in both robot and "crab monster" mode (see his original instruction sheet—that's what he is), Squeezeplay is one of the more interesting looking of all Headmasters, large or small. Although his crab monster legs stick out of his back in robot mode, his tail-to-mace transformation and menacing monster face in alternate mode are well worth the price of admission.

**ALTERNATE MODE:** Crab monster.
**EASILY LOST WEAPONS AND ACCESSORIES:** Lokos trainer/robot head, overrider rifle, tail/mace.

Squeezeplay, alternate mode.

Darkwing, easily lost weapons and accessories.

Darkwing, alternate mode.

## DARKWING

**POWERMASTERS**

**FUNCTION:** Aerial Assault
**MOTTO:** "Things are never as bad as they seem—usually they're worse."

"Never has anything nice to say, but says it anyway. Believes that life is one long ordeal of pain and suffering and strives to insure that others experience more of it than he does. Binary bonded to the Nebulan, Throttle, a hot-headed burglar prone to over-heating while in engine mode. Armed with two laser-guided electro-kinetic blasters. Combines with Dreadwind to form the fearsome Dreadwing."

| Strength | Intelligence | Speed | Endurance | Rank | Courage | Firepower | Skill |
|---|---|---|---|---|---|---|---|
| 6 | 7 | 7 | 5 | 5 | 7 | 7 | 8 |

MLC: **$80-115+**, MIB: **$135-150**, MISB: **$300-500**

Great care must be taken with both Decepticon Powermasters when "unlocking the secret" of their transformations with their respective Nebulans/engines, as they are fairly difficult to manipulate into their vehicle modes. Particular care should be given to Darkwing, as tabs are frequently found snapped off of this toy when forced into vehicle mode, and when combining with Dreadwind to form Dreadwing, Darkwing is the rear of the gestalt.

**ALTERNATE MODE:** RAF [Royal Air Force] Panavia Tornado GR1 fighter jet.
**EASILY LOST WEAPONS AND ACCESSORIES:** Throttle figure/Powermaster engine, 2 (electro-kinetic blaster) lasers (left and right).

Darkwing, robot mode.

## [DECEPTICON]
# POWERMASTERS

Decepticon Powermasters Darkwing and Deadwind are slowly becoming some of the more high-demand and expensive of 1988 Transformers on the secondary market due to their intricate construction, superb detailing, first-rate accessories, and ability to combine into the gestalt super jet, Dreadwing. These two fearsome additions to the Decepticon armada spell doom for the Autobots' meager air force.

Dreadwind, easily lost weapons and accessories.

# DREADWIND

Dreadwind, robot mode.

**POWERMASTERS**

**FUNCTION:** Air Defense
**MOTTO:** "Fear is a friend whose presence is felt long after he's left."

"As ominous as a storm cloud and as chilling as a winter breeze. Grim and gloomy—always acts as if his best friend just became permanently inoperative. Binary-bonded to the Nebulan, Hi-Test, a thrill-seeking, over-achieving perfectionist, constantly striving to keep Dreadwind's morose mind on his evil work. Equipped with two thermal melters and two air-to-air missiles. Combines with Darkwing to form the fearsome Dreadwing."

| Strength | Intelligence | Speed | Endurance | Rank | Courage | Firepower | Skill |
|---|---|---|---|---|---|---|---|
| 6 | 8 | 7 | 8 | 6 | 7 | 7 | 8 |

MLC: **$85-110+**, MIB: **$140-155**, MISB: **$300-500**

As a character, Dreadwind seems much more "together" than his Powermaster partner Darkwing: although Dreadwind's moroseness combined with his teammate's negativity must adversely affect their combined mode of Dreadwing. Regardless, he is one of the more high-demand loose Transformers toys, and commands very high prices mint loose and complete, or even higher prices in MISB condition on the secondary market. Dreadwind forms the front part of the super-jet, Dreadwing.

**ALTERNATE MODE:** General Dynamics F-16 Fighting Falcon attack jet.
**EASILY LOST WEAPONS AND ACCESSORIES:** Hi-Test figure/ Powermaster engine, 2 (thermal melter) lasers.

Dreadwind, alternate mode.

# DREADWING

**FUNCTION:** n/a
**MOTTO:** n/a

MLC: **$130-165**, MIB: **N/A** [never sold <u>together</u>— only *separately* boxed], MISB: **N/A**

Dreadwing is the combined vehicle mode of Darkwing and Dreadwind, and has no robot mode, and therefore no function or motto. It is assumed that since his component robots' functions are Air Defense and Air Assault, that Dreadwing possesses the best of their abilities: perhaps Air Assault and Defense. In Dreamwave's 2003 *Transformers: More Than Meets The Eye* guidebooks, it is suggested that in this gestalt, both the firepower and speed of the two Decepticon Powermasters is doubled.

Dreadwing, combined form of Darkwing and Dreadwind, front view.

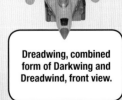

Dreadwing, combined form of Darkwing and Dreadwind, left view.

Dreadwing, combined form of Darkwing and Dreadwind, right view.

215

# DOUBLEDEALER

**POWERMASTER MERCENARY**

**FUNCTION:** Mercenary
**MOTTO:** "The price of victory is never too high."

"A ruthless, battle-ready robot for rent. A traitorous backstabber. Only loyal to the highest bidder. Valued by all, trusted by none. When binary-bonded to Knok, Doubledealer disguises himself as an Autobot robot. When binary-bonded to the bat creature, Skar, Doubledealer transforms into a Decepticon falcon. Armed with intercontinental ballistic missile that can travel 3,000 miles in 30 minutes. Equipped with enough explosives to flatten a mountain range. Uses solid light blaster in robot mode."

| Strength | Intelligence | Speed | Endurance | Rank | Courage | Firepower | Skill |
|----------|-------------|-------|-----------|------|---------|-----------|-------|
| 8 | 8 | 6 | 9 | 8 | 9 | 8 | 9 |

**$** MLC: **$60-85+**, MIB: **$125-150**, MISB: **$300-500**

Doubledealer, Powermaster engines.

Doubledealer, Autobot robot mode.

One of the single most fascinating toys of the 20th century, Doubledealer's mercenary ruthlessness, multiple transformation modes, two different Powermaster engines, and excellence of design makes him a high-demand Transformer on the secondary market, yet his price is not too prohibitive. Doubledealer switches from Autobot robot to missile trailer to winged Decepticon falcon with the aid of his Nebulan partners. With his Autobot Powermaster engine Knok, Doubledealer can unlock his *Autobot* robot mode. He uses his Decepticon Powermaster engine Skar to enable his *Decepticon* falcon mode.

His missile trailer vehicle form is used as a default mode between his robot modes and their factions, and it is an impressive-looking vehicle with its two-part inter-continental ballistic missile that transforms into a hand-held solid light blaster (bottom missile half) and shoulder cannon (top missile half) in his Autobot robot mode. He can carry this missile (both halves separately) in *Decepticon* falcon mode as well, along with his spare engine. Doubledealer is a Transformer to be feared, for sure.

---

**ALTERNATE MODE:** ICBM missile launcher trailer, falcon.
**EASILY LOST WEAPONS AND ACCESSORIES:** Knok Autobot figure/Powermaster engine, Skar Decepticon bat/Powermaster engine, engine holder/ chest shield, missile top, missile bottom.

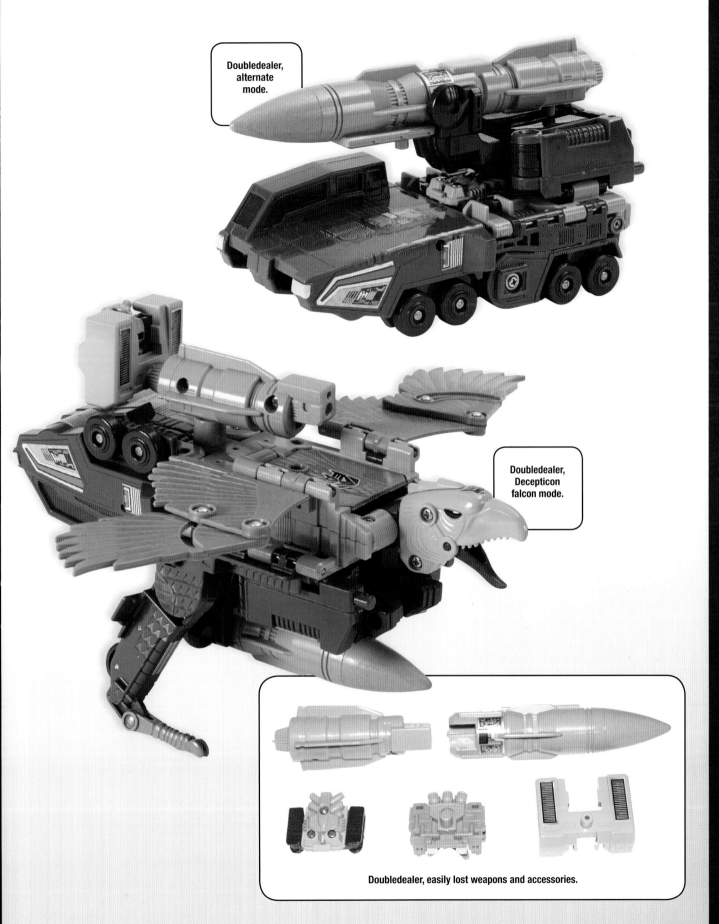

Doubledealer, alternate mode.

Doubledealer, Decepticon falcon mode.

Doubledealer, easily lost weapons and accessories.

## BOMB-BURST

**PRETENDERS**

**FUNCTION:** Predator
**MOTTO:** "The greater the foe, the sweeter his fuel!"

"A vicious, vile automated vampire! Enjoys swooping down on unsuspecting Autobots and using his serrated metallic fangs to drain the fuel from his victims. Specially-textured outer shell causes rust rash on contact. Blinded by bright sunlight. The ultimate terror in darkness. Without shell, transforms into a vertical take-off and landing hover jet with dual lasers. Within shell, armed with corrosive slime shooter and armor-piercing battle axe!"

| Strength | Intelligence | Speed | Endurance | Rank | Courage | Firepower | Skill |
|---|---|---|---|---|---|---|---|
| 8 | 8 | 7 | 4 | 7 | 9 | 7 | 8 |

 MLC: **$48-60**, MIB: **$70-85**,
MISB: **$200-300+**

Bomb-Burst, inner robot mode.

With a fearsome Pretender shell and a vehicle mode that utilizes his robot's lasers as wings, Bomb-Burst is the closest thing the Decepticon ranks have to a vampire—sorry, Ratbat (1986). Although his outer shell is limited in articulation (nearly every Pretenders' legs could not bend due to the room required inside the shell for a smaller robot), the colorful Bomb-Burst looks to be a fearsome opponent. Make sure that loose samples of this toy come with his oft-missing shoulder pads.

**ALTERNATE MODE:** VTOL (vertical take-off-and-landing) hover jet.
**EASILY LOST WEAPONS AND ACCESSORIES:** 2 "Bomb-Burst" figure shell halves, battle axe, 2 shoulder pads [right and left], belt, 2 wing/lasers [combine into corrosive slime shooter].

Bomb-Burst, inner robot's alternate mode.

Bomb-Burst, outer shell mode.

Bomb-Burst, easily lost weapons and accessories.

## [DECEPTICON]
# PRETENDERS

The main difference between the first generation of Autobot Pretenders and the first generation of Decepticon Pretenders is that the Autobots' outer shells assumed human [or humanoid] forms, while the Decepticons' shells were monster or alien-type creatures. Other than this distinct difference, the shells and inner robots possessed VERY similar design modes [if not transformations]: skinny-looking robots that changed into futuristic-looking vehicles that were housed inside a 'fat' Pretender shell.

Bugly, easily lost weapons and accessories.

Bugly, inner robot's alternate mode.

Bugly, inner robot mode.

# BUGLY

**PRETENDERS**

**FUNCTION:** Strategist
**MOTTO:** "The greatest power is the power to control."

"A deadly warrior with pinpoint maneuverability in the air. Intense, mystical, and very cruel. Practices the deadly martial art of Circuit-Su, which channels energy into one powerful electric blast. Electro-stingers in helmet deliver 3,000 volt charges that paralyze on contact. Also armed with 2 photon rifles. Transforms to lasered hover jet with built-in, forward-thrust turbo boosters. Also able to pilot outer shell by remote control."

| Strength | Intelligence | Speed | Endurance | Rank | Courage | Firepower | Skill |
|----------|--------------|-------|-----------|------|---------|-----------|-------|
| 6 | 9 | 6 | 7 | 7 | 8 | 7 | 9 |

MLC: **$62-78**, MIB: **$85-110**, MISB: **$200-300**

With Bugly, the Transformers canon was injected with the mysticism of the rarely practiced Cybertronian martial art of Circuit-Su. According to Dreamwave's *Transformers: More Than Meets The Eye* (2003) guidebooks, Circuit-Su's practitioners train their minds even more than they train their bodies. The end result of the mentally-challenging Circuit-Su is 1) bending others to your will, 2) turning attacks upon their initial aggressor, and ultimately 3) projecting your energy into physically manifested bolts, as does Bugly. The Transformers who follow this martial art are usually loners or solitary in nature.

**ALTERNATE MODE:** Hover jet.
**EASILY LOST WEAPONS AND ACCESSORIES:** 2 "Bugly" figure shell halves, 2 photon rifles, 2 electro-stingers, belt.

Bugly, outer shell mode.

# FINBACK

**PRETENDERS**

**FUNCTION:** Naval Assault
**MOTTO:** "Ashes to ashes, rust to rust."

"A freezing, wretched wreck in the making. Outer shell serves as container for his loose components. Enjoys making his enemies feel worse than he does. External, pressure-sensitive shell enables him to dive to a depth of 30,000 feet. Specially-reinforced scale armor is composed of 'living' mecha-organisms that regenerate spontaneously to protect inner circuitry. Equipped with metal-corroding stun rifle that ensnares the enemy in a layer of thick, vicious underwater slime. Transforms to high-speed hovercraft equipped with long range sonar and scanners. Also armed with jet-propelled, armor-piercing harpoon gun."

| Strength | Intelligence | Speed | Endurance | Rank | Courage | Firepower | Skill |
|----------|--------------|-------|-----------|------|---------|-----------|-------|
| 8 | 8 | 4 | 3 | 6 | 8 | 7 | 9 |

MLC: **$65-88**, MIB: **$95-120**, MISB: **$225-400+**

Finback, inner robot's alternate mode.

Finback, inner robot mode.

Finback, outer shell mode.

Finback, easily lost weapons and accessories.

Finback's hovercraft alternate mode is very similar in form to most other Pretenders' vehicle forms. His Tech Spec is descriptive and endearing: Finback is a mess, yet he functions well underwater with his outer shell comprised of living organisms. Once a fairly easy Pretender to obtain on the secondary market, yet his demand is increasing.

**ALTERNATE MODE:** Hovercraft.

**EASILY LOST WEAPONS AND ACCESSORIES:** 2 "Finback" figure shell halves, stun rifle, harpoon gun, belt.

Iguanus, easily lost weapons and accessories.

## IGUANUS

**PRETENDERS**

**FUNCTION:** Terror Trooper
**MOTTO:** "Sow the seeds of fear and victory is yours."

"A hideous, slithering monster. So in love with his loathsome, lizard-like outer shell that he rarely removes it. Shares misguided camaraderie with all reptiles. Equipped with super robotic strength. Able to crush cars with his reptilian claws. Hypno-beams in eyes penetrate enemy cerebro-circuits and override primary programming directives. Armed with hurricane air-blaster that shoots concussive blasts of pressurized air. Wheels in cycle mode equipped with spinning blades that tear through enemy armor. Built-in anti-gyrostators able to disrupt equilibrium of enemy robots."

| Strength | Intelligence | Speed | Endurance | Rank | Courage | Firepower | Skill |
|---|---|---|---|---|---|---|---|
| 8 | 6 | 4 | 9 | 7 | 9 | 7 | 8 |

MLC: **$48-60**, MIB: **$70-85**, MISB: **$200-300**

With Iguanus's textured skin, cool prehensile tail, and "cycle" mode (wasn't it just another Pretender hovercraft with attached wheels?), he was a bit more popular among collectors than some of the standard 1988 Pretenders. Iguanus's Tech Spec reflects what many other Pretender biographies suggest: that the Transformers' inner robot is more comfortable within its shell than without.

**ALTERNATE MODE:** Cybertronian motorcycle.

**EASILY LOST WEAPONS AND ACCESSORIES:** 2 "Iguanus" figure shell halves, hurricane blaster, wheels/blades, belt.

Iguanus, outer shell mode.

Skullgrin, easily lost
weapons and accessories.

Skullgrin, inner
robot mode.

Skullgrin,
outer shell
mode.

# SKULLGRIN

**PRETENDERS**

**FUNCTION:** Siege Warrior
**MOTTO:** "Those who stand against me shall soon
fall before me!"

"A brutal, uncontrollable engine of destruction! Doesn't stop
attacking until everything is destroyed! Never retreats from
danger. Usually communicates in a series of snorts and snarls.
In creature shell, wields a double slagmaker laser and metal-
rending vibro sword! Without shell, transforms into a shrapnel
blasting assault tank!"

| Strength | Intelligence | Speed | Endurance | Rank | Courage | Firepower | Skill |
|---|---|---|---|---|---|---|---|
| 9 | 9 | 4 | 9 | 6 | 10 | 8 | 5 |

**$** MLC: **$40-58**, MIB: **$65-78**, MISB: **$125-250**

Skullgrin is easily the most intimidating looking of all first-generation
Pretenders, and his absolutely huge "skull-head" on his semi-jointed neck is an
unforgettable feature. He appears to be a bit stouter than his like-minded-
bots, and his Tech Spec suffer from an infusion of overzealous exclamation
marks. His toy is a fairly easy find on the secondary market, but check and
make sure his belt (as with all Pretenders) is not broken along its buckle.

**ALTERNATE MODE:** Tank.
**EASILY LOST WEAPONS AND ACCESSORIES:** 2 "Skullgrin"
figure shell halves, vibro-sword, 2 lasers [combine to form
slagmaker carbine], belt.

Skullgrin,
inner robot's
alternate mode.

Iguanus, inner
robot's alternate
mode.

Iguanus,
inner robot
mode.

221

Submarauder,
inner robot
mode.

Submarauder,
outer shell
mode.

# SUBMARAUDER

**PRETENDERS**

**FUNCTION:** Undersea Warfare
**MOTTO:** "Conquer the seas and the rest will fall!"

"As silent and mysterious as the ocean depths. Sly and
sinister. Roams the sea in solitary contentment. Angers easily,
exploding into a furious frenzy. Serrated claws can shred
a battleship like paper. Transforms into deep sea attack
submarine, armed with proton cannon. Inside shell, wields
torpedo rifle and unbreakable, organic-steel sword that eats
metal on contact."

| Strength | Intelligence | Speed | Endurance | Rank | Courage | Firepower | Skill |
|----------|--------------|-------|-----------|------|---------|-----------|-------|
| 8 | 9 | 5 | 8 | 6 | 9 | 7 | 8 |

MLC: **$40-52**, MIB: **$65-75**, MISB: **$100-200**

Submarauder, easily lost
weapons and accessories.

Yet another amphibious Pretender like Finback, Splashdown,
or Waverider (all 1988), Submarauder didn't really deviate from the
standard Pretender formula: skinny robot inside larger shell; robot
transforms into spaceship/hovercraft-type vehicle. Although colorful,
Submarauder is one of the less popular Transformers from 1988, and
is found quite easily on the secondary market.

**ALTERNATE MODE:** Submarine.
**EASILY LOST WEAPONS AND ACCESSORIES:** 2 "Submarauder" figure
shell halves, sword, torpedo rifle, belt, shield.

Submarauder,
inner robot's
alternate mode.

# [DECEPTICON]
# PRETENDER BEASTS

The Decepticon Pretender Beasts were more vicious and colorful than their Autobot brethren, yet they followed the same basic schematic: organic beast shells with armaments on their backs, with a smaller robot lurked inside the shell. A thematic departure from the original Pretenders.

Carnivac, inner robot mode.

Carnivac, easily lost weapons and accessories.

Carnivac, inner robot's alternate mode.

# CARNIVAC

## PRETENDER BEASTS

**FUNCTION:** Hunter/Tracker
**MOTTO:** "A cunning smile is more devastating than the fiercest weapon."

"A growling, howling, mad dog destroyer. Commits abominable acts with unrelenting glee. Always smiling, even in battle. Outer shell has built-in hydraulic lifters that enable him to jump over 50 feet in any direction. High-intensity laser beams in eyes incinerate targets in seconds. In robot mode, armed with anti-thermal cannon with infrared scope that freezes targets on impact."

| Strength | Intelligence | Speed | Endurance | Rank | Courage | Firepower | Skill |
|----------|--------------|-------|-----------|------|---------|-----------|-------|
| 6 | 5 | 7 | 9 | 4 | 7 | 7 | 8 |

**$** MLC: **$38-50**, MIB: **$62-70**, MISB: **$200-300**

Carnivac's inner robot mode reflects his outer beast shell, and both are incorporated into the gist of his Tech Spec bio: he has all the characteristics of a wolf or hyena. His outer wolf/beast shell is quite formidable, sporting shoulder armor and an anti-thermal cannon. His inner robot's transformation is into a more recognizable wolf.

---

**ALTERNATE MODE:** Wolf.
**EASILY LOST WEAPONS AND ACCESSORIES:** 2
   "Carnivac" beast shell halves, anti-thermal cannon, tail, 2 pieces shoulder armor (left and right).

Carnivac, outer shell mode.

Snarler, easily lost weapons and accessories.

Snarler, inner robot alternate mode.

Snarler, outer shell mode.

Snarler, inner robot mode.

## SNARLER

**PRETENDER BEASTS**

**FUNCTION:** Assault Warrior
**MOTTO:** "Stealing isn't a crime, getting caught is."

"A selfish, obnoxious master of destruction. Does everything for himself. Refuses to follow orders. Transforms to boar with front-mounted, razor-tipped drill that drains enemy fuel supplies. Horns on outer shell equipped with sonar distorters that disrupt the flow of cerebral impulses and rupture enemy circuitry. Also equipped with armored hide on outer shell and a 30mm submachine gun in his tail. In robot mode, armed with programmable explosive shell rotary cannon. Range: 6 miles."

| Strength | Intelligence | Speed | Endurance | Rank | Courage | Firepower | Skill |
|----------|--------------|-------|-----------|------|---------|-----------|-------|
| 7 | 5 | 3 | 10 | 3 | 8 | 8 | 7 |

MLC: **$42-58**, MIB: **$68-78**, MISB: **$200-300**

Armed to the teeth, Snarler's outward appearance is one of the fiercest of all Pretenders. His inner robot's alternate mode is similar in design to that of his outer shell as well: that of a boar. With ludicrously high endurance and fantastic offensive capabilities, Snarler is a skilled warrior.

**ALTERNATE MODE:** Boar.
**EASILY LOST WEAPONS AND ACCESSORIES:** 2 "Snarler" beast shell halves, rotary cannon, tail, 2 pieces shoulder armor (right and left).

# ROADGRABBER

**PRETENDER VEHICLES**

**FUNCTION:** Gunner
**MOTTO:** "Destruction has a beauty all its own."

"A road-ripping demon of destruction. The cruelest of the cruel. Able to hide undetected inside his bulletproof protective shell and use its front-mounted claws to crush his enemies. Transforms from robot mode to fast attack hover jet with vectored thrusters for lightning-fast maneuverability. Built-in, turbo-powered boosters enable him to reach speeds over 3000 mph. Also equipped with subspace capabilities. Armed with dual pom-pom action freeze lasers that convert to flamethrower cannons."

| Strength | Intelligence | Speed | Endurance | Rank | Courage | Firepower | Skill |
|---|---|---|---|---|---|---|---|
| 7 | 7 | 7 | 7 | 6 | 8 | 7 | 8 |

MLC: **$36-52**, MIB: **$55-72**, MISB: **$100-200**

Roadgrabber, inner robot mode.

Roadgrabber, inner robot's alternate mode.

Another clever Pretender Vehicle, Roadgrabber's colors leapt out from toy store shelves, and his multiple transformation modes appealed to many Transformer fans. It should be noted that when rolled along a flat surface in assault vehicle mode, Roadgrabber's two mounted freeze lasers look like they are actually firing. In their instructions, Hasbro claimed that the two Pretender Vehicles (either Autobot Gunrunner or Decepticon Roadgrabber) could hold "any Pretender" within their respective shells.

**ALTERNATE MODE:** Assault cruiser, attack vehicle, hover jet.
**EASILY LOST WEAPONS AND ACCESSORIES:**
"Roadgrabber" outer shell, rifle, 2 freeze lasers.

Roadgrabber, outer shell attack mode.

Roadgrabber, outer shell mode.

Roadgrabber, easily lost weapons and accessories.

# 1989

## SERIES 6

Hasbro's 1989 Transformers pack-in catalog focused on two different Transformers sub-lines: the return of the successful Pretenders brand, and the introduction of the pint-sized Micromasters. Hasbro's final toy offerings of the 1980s truly capitalized upon the success of the alluring Pretenders concept offered one year earlier—soliciting 21 all-new Pretenders toys, while offering Transfans many lower price point alternatives which (at the time) were easier to obtain [and maintain] than their Pretenders brethren from 1988.

These twenty-one new Pretenders featured the following components: a team of soft-shelled Decepticon Monsters whose inner robots combined to form an impressive gestalt known as "Monstructor"; a half-dozen smaller-sized Pretenders who—although reduced in scale [similar in approach to the company's scaled-down Headmasters and Targetmasters of 1988]—possessed dynamic personalities; a quartet of Pretenders "Classic Characters" that allowed old school fans to witness their favorite Transformers (Autobots Bumblebee, Grimlock, and Jazz, and Decepticon Starscream) re-imagined as Pretenders; and finally, a trio of imposing Mega Pretenders and a pair of impressive Ultra Pretenders –deluxe toys that impressed collectors with their exceptional detailing. These pieces continue to elude even the most devoted Transformers collectors on the secondary market, whether mint, loose and complete, or MISB.

The flip side of the 1989 catalog focused on the Micromasters. Hasbro was reportedly trying to capitalize on the success of Galoob's Micro Machines toys [tiny automobile and assorted vehicles that averaged about 1-1/2 inches in length] in the late 1980s. So then, the Autobots and Decepticons were scaled down in size, while still retaining their basic ability to transform. In Dreamwave's *Transformers: More Than Meets The Eye* [2003, #8], the author describes the reason Cybertronians subjected themselves to the Micromaster Process. Apparently, during a period of time after Cybertron's resources were utterly depleted by a massive energy crisis, the planet's native life forms and its core functions began to shut down [dubbed "The Great Shutdown"], since there was no longer a battle for *territory* by the warring Autobots and Decepticons, the Transformers engaged in combat for mere survival.

Therefore, as a result of Cybertron's depleted resources following the Great Shutdown, Cybertronian scientists created newer, smaller, more energy-efficient bodies for the Transformers. The successful volunteers of this experiment were known as the Micromasters: reformatted Transformers who managed "... to maintain significant power levels despite their small size." Unfortunately, while the existing population wished the Micromasters to become their saviors, most Micromasters [both Autobot and Decepticon] chose to form "... violent, anarchic gangs that roamed the growing wastelands between Cybertron's rapidly diminishing cities

Battle Patrol, alternate modes.

# BATTLE PATROL

**MICROMASTER PATROLS**

**FUNCTION:** Rapid Deployment Strike Force
**MOTTO:** "It is better to strike first, than to not strike at all!"

"This tough-talking, battle-hardened foursome believes that the best offense is one that's fast, furious, and ferocious! They don't slow down until the enemy has been defeated and thrown into the scrap pile! With this in mind, Big Shot, Sidetrack, Flak, and Sunrunner use their brute force capabilities to hammer their Micromaster adversaries with devastating attacks!"

| Teamwork | Cooperation | Strength | Endurance | Speed | Intelligence | Courage | Skill |
|----------|-------------|----------|-----------|-------|--------------|---------|-------|
| 8 | 6 | 9 | 8 | 6 | 7 | 9 | 8 |

MLC (full set): **$10-18**, MOC: **$35-75**

Battle Patrol, robot modes.

**INDIVIDUAL MEMBERS AND THEIR ALTERNATE MODES:** Big Shot [Denel G-6 self-propelled gun], Flak [TOS-1 Buratino rocket system], Sidetrack [Roland missile launcher w/Marder IFV tank hull], Sunrunner [E-2C Hawkeye AEW (Airborne Early Warning) plane].
**EASILY LOST WEAPONS AND ACCESSORIES:** N/A.

# OFF ROAD PATROL

**MICROMASTER PATROLS**

**FUNCTION:** Covert Activities
**MOTTO:** "Don't follow orders, follow instincts."

"This quartet has an independence streak that runs as long as the Appalachian Trail. Experts at covert operations. Always work well together in any combat situation. Specialize in going where no one's ever gone and doing what no one's ever done. Continually caught up in some sort of enemy intrigue. Autobot Command trusts them to come up with brilliant counter-measures to be sprung on the Decepticons."

| Teamwork | Cooperation | Strength | Endurance | Speed | Intelligence | Courage | Skill |
|----------|-------------|----------|-----------|-------|--------------|---------|-------|
| 9 | 9 | 6 | 8 | 3 | 9 | 8 | 6 |

MLC (full set): **$8-12**, MOC: **$30-60**

Off Road Patrol, robot modes.

**INDIVIDUAL MEMBERS AND ALTERNATE MODES:** Highjump [Land Rover Defender], Mudslinger [monster truck], Powertrain ["sleeper truck" cab], and Tote [van].
**EASILY LOST WEAPONS AND ACCESSORIES:** N/A.

# MICROMASTER PATROLS

With the advent of Micromasters, the Tech Specs changed in Micromaster Patrol and Micromaster Squad sets: "Rank" was replaced with "Teamwork" and "Firepower" was replaced with "Cooperation."

Off Road Patrol, alternate modes.

Race Car Patrol, alternate modes.

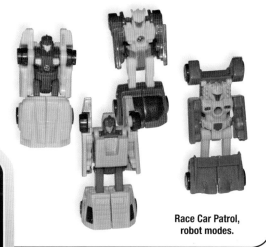

Race Car Patrol, robot modes.

# RACE CAR PATROL

**MICROMASTER PATROLS**

**FUNCTION:** Reconnaissance
**MOTTO:** "In confusion there is opportunity."

"The self-described 'tiny terrors of the turnpikes.' This frantic foursome's primary role is to reconnaissance battle sites before the Autobots' big guns arrive. Fast and fearless. Don't mind mixing it up with any early arriving Decepticons. A vital component in the Autobot ranks. Adept at using their superior maneuverability to harass the enemy."

| Teamwork | Cooperation | Strength | Endurance | Speed | Intelligence | Courage | Skill |
|---|---|---|---|---|---|---|---|
| 8 | 9 | 5 | 7 | 5 | 9 | 8 | 5 |

MLC (full set): **$10-18**, MOC: **$35-75**

**INDIVIDUAL MEMBERS AND THEIR ALTERNATE MODES (ALL ARE RACE CARS, COLORS INDICATED):** Free Wheeler [yellow Lamborghini Countach], Roadhandler [red Pontiac Firebird Trans Am], Swindler [gray Delorean DMC-12], and Tailspin [blue Porsche 962].
**EASILY LOST WEAPONS AND ACCESSORIES:** N/A.

Rescue Patrol, robot modes.

# RESCUE PATROL

**MICROMASTER PATROLS**

**FUNCTION:** Search and Rescue
**MOTTO:** "True victory can only lie in the ability to locate and mend the injured."

"This fearless foursome braves the heaviest combat fire on land and sea to perform their assigned tasks. Fully equipped to administer emergency aid under the most adverse conditions: Seawatch has over-the-horizon radar and towing capability; Stakeout has a state-of-the-air communications dashboard; Fixit is outfitted with repair bay and life-function monitors; Red Hot contains fire-retardant chemical foam."

| Teamwork | Cooperation | Strength | Endurance | Speed | Intelligence | Courage | Skill |
|---|---|---|---|---|---|---|---|
| 9 | 9 | 5 | 6 | 4 | 8 | 9 | 8 |

MLC (full set): **$10-18**, MOC: **$35-75**

Rescue Patrol, alternate modes.

**INDIVIDUAL MEMBERS AND THEIR ALTERNATE MODES:** Fixit [ambulance], Red Hot [fire engine with extendable ladder], Seawatch [hydrofoil], and Stakeout [Ford Taurus police car].
**EASILY LOST WEAPONS AND ACCESSORIES:** N/A.

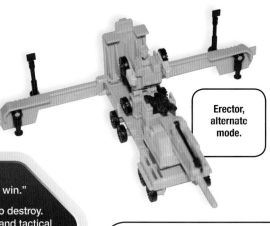

Erector, alternate mode.

# ERECTOR

**MICROMASTER TRANSPORTS**

**FUNCTION:** Construction Engineer
**MOTTO:** "Everyone loses if there's nothing to win."

"Programmed to build and preserve. Reluctant to destroy. Only fights when provoked. Often uses cunning and tactical maneuvering to ensnare his enemies. A brave, respected warrior. Equipped with titanium belted, bullet-proof tires and alloyed exterior that's impervious to most armaments. Crane hook with hydraulic swing can pierce enemy armor with deadly accuracy. Converts to battle station armed with devastating photon cannon and anti-aircraft machine gun battery."

| Strength | Intelligence | Speed | Endurance | Rank | Courage | Firepower | Skill |
|----------|-------------|-------|-----------|------|---------|-----------|-------|
| 7 | 8 | 2 | 7 | 6 | 8 | 7 | 9 |

MLC: **$12-20**, MOC (opened): **$20-25**, MOC: **$25-50**

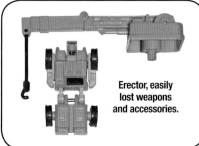

Erector, easily lost weapons and accessories.

**ALTERNATE MODE:** [Micromaster to] semi truck cab, [car carrier to] armored carrier.
**EASILY LOST WEAPONS AND ACCESSORIES:** Micromaster, crane hook, crane.

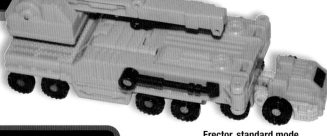

Erector, standard mode.

Overload, Micromaster robot mode.

# OVERLOAD

**MICROMASTER TRANSPORTS**

**FUNCTION:** Troop Transport
**MOTTO:** "Know your enemy and he's yours."

"A bold and daring soldier. Often breaks away from cargo-hauling missions to join his fellow Autobots on the battlefield. A tactical genius on the front line. Trailer converts to turbo-boosted, supersonic fighter jet armed with wing-mounted, double-barreled machine guns. Laser guided, lock-target scanners provide pinpoint firepower. Capable of reaching speeds in excess of Mach 2. Also equipped with hydrofoil capabilities."

| Strength | Intelligence | Speed | Endurance | Rank | Courage | Firepower | Skill |
|----------|-------------|-------|-----------|------|---------|-----------|-------|
| 5 | 8 | 7 | 8 | 5 | 8 | 7 | 6 |

MLC: **$12-20**, MOC (opened): **$20-25**, MOC: **$25-50**

**ALTERNATE MODE:** (Micromaster to) truck cab, (car carrier to) armored carrier.
**EASILY LOST WEAPONS AND ACCESSORIES:** Micromaster.

Overload, alternate mode.

Overload, standard mode.

Hot House,
Micromaster
alternate mode.

Hot House, easily lost weapons
and accessories.

# HOT HOUSE

Hot House,
standard mode.

**MICROMASTER BATTLE STATIONS**

**FUNCTION:** Long Range Defense
**MOTTO:** "Communication is the key that unlocks victory."

"A babbling brawler. Talks constantly, even in battle. His fire station is equipped with built-in siphons that draw water from soil to form a high-impact water jet that can blast through granite. In battle, his station's front ramp converts to high-speed battering ram. Also armed with rocket launcher and freeze missiles."

| Strength | Intelligence | Speed | Endurance | Rank | Courage | Firepower | Skill |
|----------|--------------|-------|-----------|------|---------|-----------|-------|
| 2 | 7 | 3 | 6 | 7 | 8 | 7 | 7 |

MLC: **$20-32**, MIB: **$35-50**, MISB: **$60-120**

**ALTERNATE MODE:** [Micromaster to] A-10 Thunderbolt II jet, [fire station to] battle station.
**EASILY LOST WEAPONS AND ACCESSORIES:** Micromaster, yellow-orange ramp, [removable] fire station tower.

Hot House,
alternate
mode.

# IRONWORKS

**MICROMASTER BATTLE STATIONS**

**FUNCTION:** Communications Bay
**MOTTO:** "Strong support needs a good foundation."

"A construction powerhouse. Capable of fixing just about anything. Converts his construction site to full-service repair bay equipped with hydraulic lifts, titanium rivet guns and searing iron forge. In battle mode, his station is armed with surface-to-air proton missile launcher and interstellar laser communicators."

| Strength | Intelligence | Speed | Endurance | Rank | Courage | Firepower | Skill |
|----------|--------------|-------|-----------|------|---------|-----------|-------|
| 3 | 7 | 1 | 7 | 6 | 8 | 7 | 9 |

MLC: **$24-38**, MIB: **$40-55**, MISB: **$75-150**

Ironworks,
standard
mode.

Ironworks, easily
lost weapons and
accessories.

**ALTERNATE MODE:** (Micromaster to) truck, (construction station to) radar station.
**EASILY LOST WEAPONS AND ACCESSORIES:** Micromaster, crane/rocket launcher, rocket, crane staging, ramp [gray].

Ironworks,
alternate mode.

Groundshaker, alternate mode.

# GROUNDSHAKER

**MICROMASTER BASES**

**FUNCTION:** Field Commander
**MOTTO:** "A life without risk is a life without reward."

"A rowdy, rebellious robot. Likes to be where the action is! At his best crashing his titanium-steel, self propelled cannon through enemy barricades, just so he can unload his x-ray laser cannon, sonic boomers and automatic machine gun at the Decepticons. Converts his ATV vehicle into a battle station and helipad. Also equipped with awesome ultra-violet radar that guards against Decepticon attacks!"

| Strength | Intelligence | Speed | Endurance | Rank | Courage | Firepower | Skill |
|----------|--------------|-------|-----------|------|---------|-----------|-------|
| 7 | 7 | 3 | 8 | 8 | 10 | 8 | 8 |

💲 MLC: **$35-55**, MIB: **$75-95**, MISB: **$100-200**

Groundshaker, standard mode.

Groundshaker, Micromaster robot mode.

**ALTERNATE MODE:** [Micromaster to] F-19 concept jet, [ATV (All-Terrain Vehicle) to] Autobot Base.

**EASILY LOST WEAPONS AND ACCESSORIES:** Micromaster, 2 missile launchers, large cannon, gun, figure stand, two different ramps.

Groundshaker, easily lost weapons and accessories.

Groundshaker, Micromaster alternate mode.

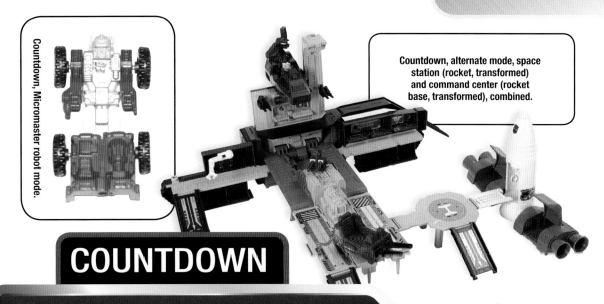

Countdown, Micromaster robot mode.

Countdown, alternate mode, space station (rocket, transformed) and command center (rocket base, transformed), combined.

# COUNTDOWN

**MICROMASTER ROCKET BASE**

**FUNCTION:** Aerospace Commander
**MOTTO:** "For a world without evil, you need a universe without evil."

"An intergalactic hero and space explorer. A legend to beings throughout the universe and an inspiration to his fellow Autobots. Fought 1000 battles and circled almost a million stars, defending the rights of the innocent. Transforms to lunar rover with com-link disk that enables him to control the entire defense base from up to 30,000,000 miles away. His interstellar rocket ship converts to mobile launch pad armed with two energy-zapping de-kineto cannons that freeze objects in mid-motion. Ship is also designed to use planetary orbits and gravitational pulls to 'slingshot' across entire galaxies in seconds. Command base equipped with laser blasters, high-tech repair bay, interstellar communications center, space-tracking radar, and high-speed launch pad."

| Strength | Intelligence | Speed | Endurance | Rank | Courage | Firepower | Skill |
|---|---|---|---|---|---|---|---|
| 8 | 10 | 10 | 9 | 9 | 10 | 8 | 10 |

MLC: **$72-105**, MIB: **$110-125**, MISB: **$150-300**

Countdown, standard mode, isometric view.

**ALTERNATE MODE:** (Micromaster commander to) lunar rover, (rocket and base to) space station.
**EASILY LOST WEAPONS AND ACCESSORIES:** Micromaster, large laser, mechanical arm, gunner pod, large double laser, 3 short ramps, 2 small double lasers, large ramp, platform, scout vehicle, rocket, helipad.

# MICROMASTER ROCKET BASE

Countdown was listed as follows in Hasbro's toy catalog: "The ultimate space complex! Powerful rocket and launcher convert to space station with interconnectible ramps and plenty of extras! Micromaster lunar vehicle also included!" Even if old school Tranfans were not enamored by the Micromaster concept, it is difficult not to be impressed by Countdown.

Countdown, easily lost weapons and accessories.

Countdown, standard mode, rear view [opened rocket].

Countdown, alternate mode, combined— with Autobot Micromasters.

234

Doubleheader, inner robot's alternate mode.

Doubleheader, easily lost weapons and accessories.

# DOUBLEHEADER

**PRETENDERS**

**FUNCTION:** Surveillance
**MOTTO:** "Burn, baby, burn!"

"Double trouble for the Decepticons! All functions and personality traits are divided between his two heads—the right head sees, smells and analyzes; the left hears, talks and makes decisions. Cool under pressure. Jet boosters in feet provide lightning-fast maneuverability in the air. Coil springs in legs also provide incredible jumping ability. Armed with semi-automatic, acid pellet pistol. Inner robot armed with rust-ray gun that corrodes metal on contact."

| Strength | Intelligence | Speed | Endurance | Rank | Courage | Firepower | Skill |
|----------|-------------|-------|-----------|------|---------|-----------|-------|
| 5 | 9 | 7 | 5 | 6 | 8 | 6 | 9 |

**$** MLC: **$75-100+**, MOC (opened): **$115-130**, MOC: **$200-300**

Part of the allure of second generation Pretenders like Doubleheader is the fact that the smaller robots fit precisely and snugly into their outer shells. Also, each inner robots' transformation mode, like Doubleheader, is unique. The double headed jet that is his alternate mode is small but looks effective.

**ALTERNATE MODE:** Futuristic jet.
**EASILY LOST WEAPONS AND ACCESSORIES:** 2 "Doubleheader" figure shell halves, double helmet, rust-ray gun, acid pellet pistol, wings/backpack.

Doubleheader, outer shell mode.

Doubleheader, inner robot mode.

## [SMALL AUTOBOT]
# PRETENDERS

Like all scaled-down second generation Transformer G1 motif-based lines ("Small" Headmasters, 1988; "Small" Targetmasters, 1988), 1989's "small" Pretenders were obviously stripped-down versions of the original designs (see Pretenders, 1988). However, there was one <u>major</u> difference between first and second generation Pretenders: most collectors prefer the smaller versions over their bigger "brothers." Characters like the well-defined Decepticon Bludgeon (thanks, Simon Furman for great Marvel Comics *Transformers* stories!) and the interestingly sculpted Autobot Doubleheader are quite popular with collectors, and command big money on the secondary market.

Longtooth, inner robot's
alternate mode.

Longtooth,
outer shell
mode.

# LONGTOOTH

**PRETENDERS**

**FUNCTION:** Undersea Defense
**MOTTO:** "The greatest truths lie at the greatest depths."

"Amphibious assault warrior. Patrols the murky ocean depths, defending underwater installations. Huge webbed feet enable him to swim at over 30 knots. Giant fang-like tusks can be used to shred metal like paper. Electronic eye equipped with advanced sonar, infra-red firing scope and heat and light sensors. Armed with searing ionic field generator. Also armed with plasma cannon in robot mode. Specially reinforced ecto-suit can withstand underwater depths up to 300 feet."

| Strength | Intelligence | Speed | Endurance | Rank | Courage | Firepower | Skill |
|----------|--------------|-------|-----------|------|---------|-----------|-------|
| 8 | 6 | 3 | 9 | 6 | 8 | 7 | 6 |

MLC: **$75-100**, MOC (opened): **$110-125**,
MOC: **$200-300**

Longtooth, inner robot mode.

Longtooth, easily lost
weapons and accessories.

Longtooth, example of an
inner Pretender robot fitting
into its outer shell halves.

The only Autobot Pretender who does not manifest a humanoid shell, Longtooth's outer shell is that of a large bipedal walrus, and he looks odd indeed next to the rest of the first and second generation G1 Autobot Pretenders. One of the least in-demand of the smaller Pretenders, Longtooth still sells fairly well on the secondary market.

**ALTERNATE MODE:** Armored carrier.
**EASILY LOST WEAPONS AND ACCESSORIES:** 2 "Longtooth" figure shell halves, plasma cannon, carrier wheels/backpack, ionic field generator.

Pincher, inner robot's
alternate mode.

# PINCHER

**PRETENDERS**

**FUNCTION:** Chemical Engineer
**MOTTO:** "Be humble of word, but great in deed."

"A mad scientist of sorts. Concocts metal-eating, corrosive acids, oxidizing agents and other powerful formulas. An over-achieving, unassuming genius. Venom coated stinger paralyzes on contact and can drill through metal to drain enemy fuel supplies. Also armed with 20 megavolt stun rifle that shoots short bursts of metal-fusing energon. Inner robot armed with laser torch. Serrated claws can pierce metal and emit circular force field in robot mode."

| Strength | Intelligence | Speed | Endurance | Rank | Courage | Firepower | Skill |
|----------|--------------|-------|-----------|------|---------|-----------|-------|
| 7 | 9 | 2 | 5 | 7 | 8 | 8 | 8 |

MLC: **$75-100**, MOC (opened): **$110-125**,.
MOC: **$125-250**

As with all of the second generation Autobot Pretenders, Pincher comes equipped with a backpack for his outer shell that attaches to his smaller robot's alternate mode, a large rifle for his outer shell, and a smaller laser for use by his inner robot that fits (or snaps) inside the shell when transformed. Apart from these similarities, each smaller Pretender's inner robot is unique in design and transformation, fueling their demand on the secondary market.

**ALTERNATE MODE:** Scorpion.
**EASILY LOST WEAPONS AND ACCESSORIES:** 2 "Pincher" figure shell halves, stun rifle, claws/backpack, backpack tail, helmet, laser torch [pistol].

Pincher, inner
robot mode.

Pincher, outer
shell mode.

Pincher, easily lost weapons
and accessories.

# PRETENDER CLASSICS

The Pretender Classics were released in order to capitalize on some of the more popular G1 Transformers characters from years past. Autobots Bumblebee (1984), Grimlock (1985), Jazz (1984), and Decepticon Starscream (1984) were re-released in smaller forms (with alternate modes similar to their originals), and all now fit nicely into their respective Pretenders shells. The inner robots of these Pretender Classics were then released as a Kmart retail exclusives without their Pretender shells, but with their inner robots' weapons, and marketed as "Transformers Legends."

Bumblebee, inner robot mode.

Bumblebee, outer shell mode.

## PRETENDER CLASSICS

# BUMBLEBEE

**FUNCTION:** Espionage
**MOTTO:** "The least likely can be the most dangerous!"

**NOTE:** The Pretenders text is the first paragraph below, and the Kmart Legends Tech Specs is the second paragraph below.

**PRETENDER:** "A free-wheeling, fun-loving Autobot. Recommissioned as a Pretender, this formerly tiny titan is now bigger and better than before. Outer shell equipped with Titanium armor, sonic blaster, and turbo-thrusted rocket pack. Reinforced helmet equipped with multi-band radio transmitter and thermal tracking meters. Inner robot armed with laser pistol. Car mode also equipped with X-ray lasers in headlights that can burn through solid rock. Entire frame, chassis and outer armor refortified for added endurance and fighting power on the battlefield."

**KMART LEGENDS:** "A free-wheeling, fun-loving Autobot. This formerly tiny titan is now bigger and better than before. Forged of reinforced Titanium armor and equipped with multi-band radio transmitter and thermal tracking meters. Also armed with X-ray lasers in headlights that can burn through solid rock. Entire frame and chassis refortified for added endurance and fighting power on the battlefield. Armed with laser pistol in robot mode."

| Strength | Intelligence | Speed | Endurance | Rank | Courage | Firepower | Skill |
|----------|-------------|-------|-----------|------|---------|-----------|-------|
| 7 | 8 | 4 | 8 | 8 | 10 | 6 | 7 |

Pretender Classics: **MLC: $32-45**, MIB: **$65-80**, MISB: **$100-200**

Transformers Legends [Kmart exclusive]: MLC: **$14-18**, MOC (opened): **$25-32**, MOC: **$40-80**

Bumblebee, inner robot's alternate mode.

**ALTERNATE MODE:** Volkswagen Beetle (Classic).
**EASILY LOST PARTS AND ACCESSORIES:** (Pretender) 2 "Bumblebee" figure shell halves, rifle, helmet, laser; (Kmart Legends) laser.

Bumblebee, easily lost weapons and accessories.

# GRIMLOCK

**PRETENDER CLASSICS**

**FUNCTION:** Lieutenant Commander
**MOTTO:** "Among the winners, there is no room for the weak."

**NOTE:** The Pretenders text is the first paragraph below, and the Kmart Legends Tech Specs is the second paragraph below.

**PRETENDER:** "A raging, reckless robot. The most fearsome and powerful Dinobot ever. Particularly nasty when he's reminded that he now resembles a human. Outer shell equipped with jet pack and atom smashing submachine gun that pierces all forms of armor and eats away enemy fortifications. Inner robot armed with double-barreled, self-propelled rocket launcher. In dinosaur mode, serrated steel jaws can tear through solid rock. Jet boosters in legs also provide flight capabilities."

**KMART LEGENDS:** "A raging, reckless robot. The most fearsome and powerful Dinobot ever. Very strong and very stupid. Easily angered. Power pistons in legs enable him to produce small earthquakes when he stamps his feet. Also armed with serrated steel jaws that can tear through solid rock. In robot mode equipped with double-barreled, self-propelled rocket launcher. Also armed with heat ray beams in eyes that can turn hardened steel into molten metal. Jet boosters in legs provide flight capabilities."

| Strength | Intelligence | Speed | Endurance | Rank | Courage | Firepower | Skill |
|---|---|---|---|---|---|---|---|
| 10 | 4 | 3 | 10 | 9 | 10 | 8 | 9 |

Pretender Classics: MLC: **$27-42**, MIB: **$55-72**, MISB: **$100-200**

Transformers Legends [Kmart exclusive]:
MLC: **$15-20**, MOC (opened): **$28-35**, MOC: **$40-80+**

**ALTERNATE MODE:** Tyrannosaurus Rex.

**EASILY LOST WEAPONS AND ACCESSORIES:** (Pretender) 2 "Grimlock" figure shell halves, rifle, laser/tail, helmet; (Kmart Legends) laser/tail.

Grimlock, outer shell mode.

Grimlock, inner robot mode.

Grimlock, easily lost weapons and accessories.

Grimlock, inner robot's alternate mode.

Jazz, easily lost weapons and accessories.

# JAZZ

**FUNCTION:** Special Operations, Saboteur
**MOTTO:** "Do it with style or don't bother doing it."

*NOTE:* The Pretenders text is the first paragraph below, and the Kmart Legends Tech Specs is the second paragraph below.

**PRETENDER:** "Optimus Prime's right-hand man. A danger-loving daredevil with a bottomless bag of tricks. Loves Earth culture, particularly rock n' roll. Outer shell armed with semi-automatic ion pulse gun and deflector shield. Inner robot armed with photon rifle and hydraulic lifters in legs that enable him to jump over fifty feet. In racecar mode, equipped with blinding, full-spectrum headlights and deafening 180 decibel speakers. Nitro-injected 12-cylinder engine allows him to reach speeds in excess of Mach 1. Thermal-sensitive windows also provide supplemental solar power."

**KMART LEGENDS:** "Optimus Prime's right-hand man. A danger-loving daredevil with a bottomless bag of tricks. Loves Earth culture, particularly rock n' roll. Equipped with photon rifle and hydraulic lifters in legs that enable him to jump over fifty feet. In racecar mode, equipped with blinding, full-spectrum headlights and deafening 180 decibel speakers. Nitro-injected 12-cylinder engines allow him to reach speeds in excess of Mach 1. Smoke ejector pack in tailpipe produces blinding smoke screen. Thermal-sensitive windows also provide supplemental solar power."

| Strength | Intelligence | Speed | Endurance | Rank | Courage | Firepower | Skill |
|---|---|---|---|---|---|---|---|
| 5 | 9 | 8 | 7 | 6 | 9 | 7 | 10 |

Pretender Classics: **MLC: $32-45**, MIB: **$65-80**, MISB: **$100-200**

Transformers Legends [Kmart exclusive]:
**MLC: $15-20**, MOC (opened): **$28-35**, MOC: **$40-80+**

**ALTERNATE MODE:** Porsche 935 Turbo.
**EASILY LOST WEAPONS AND ACCESSORIES:** (Pretender) 2 "Jazz" figure shell halves, rifle, laser, helmet; (Kmart Legends) laser.

Jazz, outer shell mode.

Jazz, inner robot mode.

Jazz, inner robot's alternate mode.

# MEGA PRETENDERS

The 1989 catalog description of these deluxe pretenders reads, "Double the excitement! Both the outer shell AND the inner robot convert into vehicles and back. Combine the two and form a super vehicle!" This concept was one of the most well executed of all new innovations by Hasbro, and the Mega Pretenders continue to be some of the most difficult and pricey Transformers to find on the secondary market.

Crossblades, mega vehicle mode
(combined inner robot and outer shell).

Crossblades, easily lost weapons and accessories.

Crossblades,
inner robot's
alternate
mode.

Crossblades,
deluxe robot
mode.

Crossblades,
inner robot
mode.

Crossblades, deluxe
vehicle mode.

## CROSSBLADES

**MEGA PRETENDERS**

**FUNCTION:** Ground Reinforcement
**MOTTO:** "A warrior is only as good as his weapons."

"A hyperactive, overheated sky jockey. Talks constantly. Patrols Autobot headquarter perimeters with lightning speed, searching for Decepticon infiltrators. Only stops long enough to refuel and check his weapons. Armed with automatic 35mm machine guns, air-to-air missiles, and a searing thermal cannon. Also equipped with mid-flight refueling capabilities and cloaking device that makes him invisible. Transforms to supersonic dragster, equipped with high-speed turbo boosters and electro-jammers that disrupt enemy circuitry. Outer shell chopper equipped with metal-eating roto-blades. Combines with dragster to form ultra-sonic helicopter equipped with front-mounted magneto-ray that magnetizes on impact."

| Strength | Intelligence | Speed | Endurance | Rank | Courage | Firepower | Skill |
|----------|--------------|-------|-----------|------|---------|-----------|-------|
| 6 | 8 | 5 | 6 | 6 | 9 | 8 | 9 |

MLC: **$75-100+**, MIB: **$115-125+**, MISB: **$200-400**

Mega Pretenders are noteworthy as both the outer and inner shells of the robots transform. Alas, if this innovation just caught on more, Hasbro may have produced more than just a handful. The intricacy of transformations (of both the shells) added astronomically to the play value of Crossblades, and all of his hard-to-find parts make him in high demand on the secondary market.

**ALTERNATE MODE:** (Inner robot) dragster, (outer shell) helicopter and deluxe helicopter.
**EASILY LOST WEAPONS AND ACCESSORIES:** "Crossblades" (opening and transformable) outer shell, 2 small lasers, wing/laser, 2 skis, 2 chopper blades, large laser/(helicopter) tail section, 2 leg vents (not listed on original instruction sheets).

# VROOM

MEGA PRETENDERS

**FUNCTION:** Saboteur
**MOTTO:** "Don't take a chance if you don't stand a chance."

"A drag racing daredevil. Learned his trade blowing up enemy fuel depots in the Asphalt Wars on Cybertron. Armed with two exterior 3000 rounds-per-minute ion pulse guns and magnetic repeller rifle. Also wields mind-altering illusionizer that distorts optic impulses. Transforms to rocket car made of rubber-coated armor that deflects and ricochets enemy shell fragments. Outer shell cycle equipped with oil slick and smokescreen ejection mechanisms, retractable tire spikes, hydraulic jumpers in suspension system, and rocket boosters in rear that provide short-term flight capabilities. Combines with rocket car to form super cycle equipped with digital fuel gauges and micronized turbo injectors."

| Strength | Intelligence | Speed | Endurance | Rank | Courage | Firepower | Skill |
|---|---|---|---|---|---|---|---|
| 6 | 9 | 5 | 6 | 7 | 9 | 7 | 10 |

**MLC: $125-165+**, **MIB: $165-185+**,
**MISB: $275-450+**

One of the most difficult of all Transformers to find complete on the secondary market, due to his rare and hard-to-obtain accessories, Vroom is also coveted in mint condition as his stickers are prone to wear.

**ALTERNATE MODE:** (Inner robot) attack car, (outer shell) motorcycle and deluxe motorcycle.

**EASILY LOST WEAPONS AND ACCESSORIES:** "Vroom" (opening and transformable) outer shell, large laser, small laser, small wheel, large rear wheel, sidecar/base.

Vroom, easily lost weapons and accessories.

Vroom, deluxe robot mode.

Vroom, deluxe vehicle mode.

Vroom, inner robot's alternate mode.

Vroom, mega vehicle mode (combined inner robot and outer shell).

Vroom, inner robot mode.

# ULTRA PRETENDERS

For Transformers fans, Ultra Pretenders hold "... surprises! Open the vehicle and reveal a poseable shell robot. Turn the robot shell into a vehicle and then open it to reveal another transformable robot." Although the concept and its delivery was ingenious, some of the plastic involved in the toys'

manufacture was either *originally fragile* or *turned brittle over time*—particularly gold-colored plastic. Dubbed "Gold Plastic Syndrome" (GPS), the fragile nature of Ultra Pretenders makes obtaining mint, loose specimens quite a challenge; MIB or MISB samples even more so.

## SKYHAMMER

ULTRA PRETENDERS

**FUNCTION:** Ground and Air Assault
**MOTTO:** "There is no disgrace in not succeeding, only in not trying."

"A valiant, vigilant warrior. Dedicated to defending the innocent. Automated high-tech sky cruiser ideal for defending against enemy attack. Thermal blasters in wings liquefy metal on impact. Front-mounted high-frequency modulators provide long-range audio and visual surveillance and tracking capabilities. Coolant vents in nose emit black clouds of sleep gas, and top-mounted turbo-fans can produce cyclonic wind funnels. Also armed with twin lightning bolt cannons and programmable, steel-shattering sonic overloader. Outer shell armed with photon pistol and converts to super-sonic hoverjet."

| Strength | Intelligence | Speed | Endurance | Rank | Courage | Firepower | Skill |
|----------|--------------|-------|-----------|------|---------|-----------|-------|
| 8 | 8 | 8 | 9 | 7 | 9 | 8 | 9 |

💲 MLC: **$85-125+**, MIB: **$150-175+**, MISB: **$300-500+**

Skyhammer, ultra vehicle mode (combined inner robot and outer shell).

Skyhammer, inner robot mode.

Skyhammer, inner robot's alternate mode.

Nearly impossible to find mint and loose (complete is even more rare) due to the chipping that occurs on his inner robot's gold feet, or on the protrusions on his larger jet mode, Skyhammer is a marvel of engineering. The gold inner robot's plastic is extremely fragile, and obtaining mint specimens loose are quite a challenge.

**ALTERNATE MODE:** (Inner robot) armored car, (outer robot) to jet, (outer shell) to attack jet.
**EASILY LOST WEAPONS AND ACCESSORIES:** "Skyhammer" (outer) jet, "Skyhammer" figure (outer) shell, "Skyhammer" (inner) robot, 2 missiles, wing laser, clear visor.

Skyhammer, ultra vehicle "attack" mode.

Skyhammer, deluxe robot mode.

Skyhammer, easily lost weapons and accessories.

Air Strike Patrol, alternate modes.

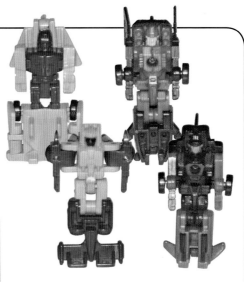

Air Strike Patrol, robot modes.

# AIR STRIKE PATROL

**MICROMASTER PATROLS**

**FUNCTION:** Espionage
**MOTTO:** "The more tightly you hold a secret, the more we like ripping it away."

"Spent years practicing in the mercury swamps of Cybertron. Perfected the 'fly, spy, and fry' teamwork technique of stealing info and blasting their targets. Rank among the most capable and savviest of Decepticons. Constantly fight among themselves to take credit for the group's successes. Always blame each other for its failures. Their inability to get along is their greatest weakness."

| Teamwork | Cooperation | Strength | Endurance | Speed | Intelligence | Courage | Skill |
|---|---|---|---|---|---|---|---|
| 2 | 2 | 4 | 6 | 8 | 8 | 8 | 7 |

MLC (full set): **$8-12**, MOC: **$30-60**

**INDIVIDUAL MEMBERS AND THEIR ALTERNATE MODES (ATTACK JETS):** Nightflight [gray Grumman F-14D Tomcat jet], Whisper [black F-19 concept jet], Tailwind [blue A-10 Thunderbolt II plane], and Storm Cloud [purple Dassault Rafale jet].
**EASILY LOST WEAPONS AND ACCESSORIES:** N/A.

Sports Car Patrol, robot modes.

# SPORTS CAR PATROL

**MICROMASTER PATROLS**

**FUNCTION:** Advance Assault
**MOTTO:** "It takes force to push back the enemy, but speed clears the way!"

"Detour, Hyperdrive, Blackjack, and Road Hugger are four of the meanest machines ever to hit the streets! Their primary purpose is to clear a route for Decepticon ground troopers, and they don't care how many wrecks they leave by the roadside! Known for their menacing clean-up tactics, it is 'speed' that is their true calling card, and it enables them to swiftly eliminate anything in their path!"

| Teamwork | Cooperation | Strength | Endurance | Speed | Intelligence | Courage | Skill |
|---|---|---|---|---|---|---|---|
| 7 | 5 | 8 | 7 | 9 | 7 | 8 | 6 |

MLC (full set): **$8-12**, MOC: **$30-60**

**INDIVIDUAL MEMBERS AND THEIR ALTERNATE MODES (RACE CARS):** Blackjack [black 1988 Ford Probe GT Turbo], Detour [yellow Chevrolet Corvette Indy sports car], Hyperdrive [light blue Mitsubishi X2S concept car], and Road Hugger [purple Ferrari 408 Intergale concept car].
**EASILY LOST WEAPONS AND ACCESSORIES:** N/A.

Sports Car Patrol, alternate modes.

Flattop, standard mode.

Flattop, alternate mode.

# FLATTOP

**MICROMASTER TRANSPORTS**

**FUNCTION:** Naval Warfare
**MOTTO:** "Terror is the ultimate weapon."

"The scourge of the seven seas. Prowls the oceans, sinking everything. Dreams of floating on a sea of burning Autobot fuel. Armed with torpedo launchers equipped with heat-sensitive tracking devices. Transforms into interstellar jet equipped with devastating X-ray laser cannons. Serrated wingtips in jet mode can cleave enemy warriors in two. Possesses superior maneuverability in the air. Reinforced, steel alloy fuselage ideal for mid-air dogfights."

| Strength | Intelligence | Speed | Endurance | Rank | Courage | Firepower | Skill |
|----------|--------------|-------|-----------|------|---------|-----------|-------|
| 5 | 8 | 7 | 6 | 6 | 7 | 8 | 8 |

MLC: **$12-20**, MOC (opened): **$28-40**, MOC: **$60-120**

**ALTERNATE MODE:** (Micromaster to) F4 Phantom jet, (aircraft carrier to) jet.
**EASILY LOST WEAPONS AND ACCESSORIES:** Micromaster, 2 laser cannons.

Flattop, Micromaster robot mode.

Flattop, easily lost weapons and accessories.

# ROUGHSTUFF

**MICROMASTER TRANSPORTS**

**FUNCTION:** Aerial Defense
**MOTTO:** "Shoot first, aim later."

"A trigger-happy sniper. Never aims, just starts blasting. Even Decepticons run for cover when he joins the battle. Trailer equipped with anti-aircraft, plasma-pulse gun battery and two heat-seeking proton missiles. Transforms to atomic-powered fighter jet and mobile battle platform with side-mounted gatling cannon. Nose cone emits high intensity heat ray that liquefies metal on contact. Also equipped with suborbital capabilities."

| Strength | Intelligence | Speed | Endurance | Rank | Courage | Firepower | Skill |
|----------|--------------|-------|-----------|------|---------|-----------|-------|
| 7 | 4 | 4 | 8 | 6 | 6 | 9 | 5 |

MLC: **$12-20**, MOC (opened): **$24-32**, MOC: **$40-80**

**ALTERNATE MODE:** (Micromaster to) truck cab, (military transport trailer to) jet.
**EASILY LOST WEAPONS AND ACCESSORIES:** Micromaster, double missile turret, 2 missiles.

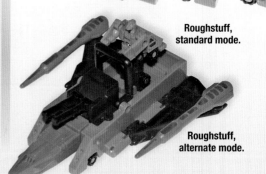

Roughstuff, standard mode.

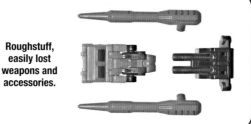

Roughstuff, alternate mode.

Roughstuff, Micromaster robot mode.

Roughstuff, easily lost weapons and accessories.

Airwave, standard mode.

Airwave, Micromaster robot mode.

Airwave, alternate mode.

Airwave, easily lost weapons and accessories.

# AIRWAVE

**MICROMASTER BATTLE STATIONS**

**FUNCTION:** Aerial Defense
**MOTTO:** "My price is too high and you're going to pay."

"A black market barbarian. His airport is equipped with retractable tire shredding spikes that prevent enemy invasions. In attack mode, airport converts to mobile, dual missile battery with a range of over 300 miles. Control tower armed with atomic panels that short out optic sensors."

| Strength | Intelligence | Speed | Endurance | Rank | Courage | Firepower | Skill |
|---|---|---|---|---|---|---|---|
| 1 | 6 | 7 | 5 | 6 | 9 | 8 | 8 |

MLC: **$22-32**, MIB: **$40-54**, MISB: **$60-120**

**ALTERNATE MODE:** (Micromaster to) Grumman F-14D Tomcat jet, (airport to) launch station.
**EASILY LOST WEAPONS AND ACCESSORIES:** Micromaster, ramp, 2 missiles.

# GREASEPIT

**MICROMASTER BATTLE STATIONS**

**FUNCTION:** Fuel Depot
**MOTTO:** "An engine is only as powerful as the fuel that runs it."

"A small-minded swindler. Siphons gas from the cars of humans to supply his Decepticon comrades. In battle mode, his station is armed with ionic cannons, rail-launched incendiary missiles and circuit-scrambling jammers. Tower-mounted sonic disruptor emits pressurized sound waves that can crush any target."

| Strength | Intelligence | Speed | Endurance | Rank | Courage | Firepower | Skill |
|---|---|---|---|---|---|---|---|
| 4 | 7 | 3 | 6 | 7 | 7 | 8 | 9 |

MLC: **$25-35**, MIB: **$42-54**, MISB: **$60-120**

**ALTERNATE MODE:** (Micromaster to) monster truck, (gas station to) assault tower.
**EASILY LOST WEAPONS AND ACCESSORIES:** Micromaster, sign post, short sign, missile, ramp, gas pumps, 4-phase laser, missile launcher.

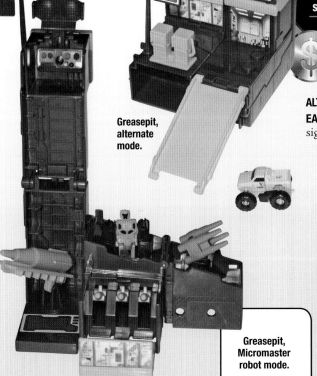

Greasepit, alternate mode.

Greasepit, Micromaster robot mode.

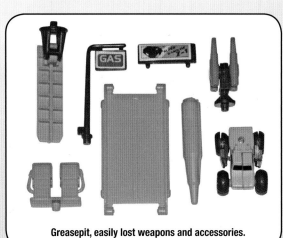

Greasepit, easily lost weapons and accessories.

Skyhopper, alternate mode.

Skyhopper, standard mode.

Skyhopper, easily lost weapons and accessories.

# SKYHOPPER

**MICROMETER BASES**

**FUNCTION:** Aerial Assault Commander
**MOTTO:** "The bigger the boom, the better I like it."

"Likes to watch things explode. Especially enjoys firing his helicopter's sonic cannon at anything associated with the Autobots. Transforms the copter into a battle base to use its powerful molecular disrupter gun to alter the Autobot's circuitry. Other Decepticons suspect all the explosions have rattled his brain circuits once to often!"

| Strength | Intelligence | Speed | Endurance | Rank | Courage | Firepower | Skill |
|----------|--------------|-------|-----------|------|---------|-----------|-------|
| 6 | 4 | 7 | 6 | 6 | 8 | 8 | 9 |

MLC: **$42-60**, MIB: **$72-85**, MISB: **$75-150+**

A fabulous addition to the Decepticon air forces, Skyhopper is the faction's resident Aerial Assault Commander, perhaps taking the job over from Starscream [1984, 1988] who served in a similar capacity [as Aerospace Commander]. One of the more ingenious Micromaster conversions—from "Attack Helicopter" to "Decepticon Base"—kids and collectors received a bargain when nabbing Skyhopper at retail.

**ALTERNATE MODE:** (Micromaster to) Dassault Rafale jet, (helicopter) to defense base.
**EASILY LOST WEAPONS AND ACCESSORIES:** Micromaster, 1 short ramp, 2 long ramps, 2 guns [right and left], rotor blade, radar dish, figure stand, front gun.

Skyhopper, robot mode.

Skyhopper, defense base mode.

Skystalker, assault base, left view: upper control panel and lower platform.

Skystalker, assault base, right rear view.

# SKYSTALKER

**MICROMASTER**

**FUNCTION:** Interstellar Assault
**MOTTO:** "Terror reigns from the skies, the hapless rule on the ground."

"Obsessed with power: acquiring it, keeping it and using it to tyrannize all who oppose him. Lives for the day when the Decepticons will rule the universe under HIS command. The meanest fighter to ever raid an enemy outpost. Rockets across galaxies in his fearsome space shuttle, destroying everything in his path. Shuttle and detachable jet pod armed with laser cannons, cluster bombs, accelerator beams, air-to-air missiles and nose cone modulator that emits earth-shaking sonic booms. Control panel armed with long-range aerial tracking devices and lock-target laser guidance systems. Lower platform equipped with atom scrambler that disintegrates objects in seconds."

| Strength | Intelligence | Speed | Endurance | Rank | Courage | Firepower | Skill |
|---|---|---|---|---|---|---|---|
| 4 | 9 | 7 | 9 | 9 | 8 | 10 | 9 |

MLC: **$60-85**, MIB: **$95-105**, MISB: **$125-215+**

**ALTERNATE MODE:** (Micromaster commander to) Porsche 959 sports car, (space shuttle) to assault base.

**EASILY LOST WEAPONS AND ACCESSORIES:** Micromaster, jet pod, 1 dual laser, 2 large lasers, 2 small lasers, 2 ramps, dual laser connector [hard-to-find].

Skystalker, robot mode.

Skystalker, easily lost weapons and accessories.

Skystalker, standard mode.

Skystalker, alternate mode.

Skystalker, dual laser connector, close-up view.

Birdbrain, inner robot's alternate mode.

## BIRDBRAIN

**PRETENDER MONSTERS**

**FUNCTION:** Aerial Attack Trooper
**MOTTO:** "Anyone who is not a predator is considered prey."

"This high-flying predator is as likely to swoop down on a poultry truck as it would on an Autobot. Incorporated with advanced 'eagle-eye' mechanisms, this fearsome flier can zone-in on Micromaster Autobot opponents over 300 miles away. His beak can snap a truck in half, while his talons lock onto an unsuspecting victim like a steel clamp! Birdbrain is armed with laser rifle."

| Strength | Intelligence | Speed | Endurance | Rank | Courage | Firepower | Skill |
|----------|-------------|-------|-----------|------|---------|-----------|-------|
| 6 | 6 | 6 | 7 | 5 | 9 | 6 | 4 |

MLC: **$35-48**, MOC (opened): **$50-65**, MOC: **$75-150+**

Birdbrain, inner robot mode.

From his outward appearance, Birdbrain's outer pretender shell is reminiscent of a cartoonish vulture-creature, and he appears to have adopted similar characteristics to this bird, according to his Tech Spec bio. His inner robot mode fits snugly into his shell, and the smaller robot (with included connector) forms the body of Monstructor.

**ALTERNATE MODE:** (Vulture) monster.
**EASILY LOST WEAPONS AND ACCESSORIES:** Pretender shell, small robot, (Monstructor's waist) connector, laser rifle, rear panel.

Birdbrain, easily lost weapons and accessories.

Birdbrain, outer shell mode.

# PRETENDER MONSTERS

The last of the Generation One combiners [other than 1990's two-'bot Micromaster Combiners], the Pretender Monsters have enjoyed a surge in popularity over the past few years, partly due to the fact that they weren't released in high numbers, compounded with the fact there were some exceedingly small, detailed parts that equipped each of the smaller, inner robots. Furthermore, finding *mint condition* loose samples of the soft-plastic Pretender Monster shells are well-

nigh impossible to locate due to the degradation [and discoloration] of the shells' soft plastic after 25+ years of exposure to air. The gestalt mode of the Pretender Monsters, Monstructor, is also difficult to obtain, and is—along with Piranacon [1988] and Predaking [1986]—one of the single most challenging super-robots to "build up" piece-by-piece. If you can find him for a reasonable (or even *unreasonable*) price, please don't pass up Monstructor.

# BRISTLEBACK

**PRETENDER MONSTERS**

**FUNCTION:** Ground Assault
**MOTTO:** "You can't tell a Decepticon by its cover."

"A bad-tempered, foul-mouthed malcontent made meaner by his decision to become a Pretender. While entering Earth's atmosphere, he discovered that his armor was corrosive to rust! This forced him to don the monstrous outer shell, causing him to lose his quickness. The spikes on the back of his outer shell secrete corrosive acid on contact. Bristleback is armed with rapid-fire, electrostatic pulse rifle."

| Strength | Intelligence | Speed | Endurance | Rank | Courage | Firepower | Skill |
|---|---|---|---|---|---|---|---|
| 7 | 6 | 2 | 8 | 6 | 9 | 6 | 7 |

MLC: **$42-58**, MOC (opened): **$62-70**, MOC: **$100-200+**

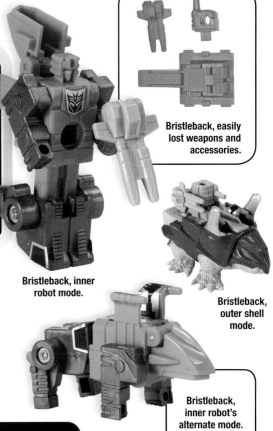

Bristleback, easily lost weapons and accessories.

Bristleback, inner robot mode.

Bristleback, outer shell mode.

Bristleback, inner robot's alternate mode.

Bristleback's alternate mode is reminiscent of a lizard-armadillo hybrid and looks effectively like a monster. His Pretender shell is quadruped, stands on all fours, and his compartment for his inner robot is in his back. Bristleback looks quite formidable in his shell or in his smaller robot's alternate mode. He forms the right arm of Monstructor.

---

**ALTERNATE MODE:** (Armored) monster.
**EASILY LOST WEAPONS AND ACCESSORIES:** Pretender shell, small robot, pulse rifle, cannon/robot hand (Monstructor's right fist), rear panel.

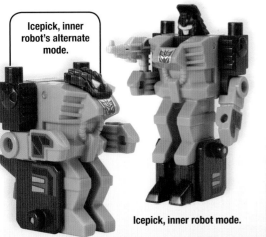

Icepick, inner robot's alternate mode.

Icepick, inner robot mode.

# ICEPICK

**PRETENDER MONSTERS**

**FUNCTION:** Demolitions
**MOTTO:** "From today's rubble-strewn fields shall emerge a new Decepticon world!"

"A fanatical follower of Planned Obsolescence, this metallic monster preaches about the destruction of things today, so they can be recycled into more advanced technologies tomorrow. His outer shell can withstand virtually any explosion. His claws can pierce through 12 inches of pure grade steel and he can crush a tank without even trying. Icepick has leaping range of 1.8 miles. Armed with fireball bazooka."

| Strength | Intelligence | Speed | Endurance | Rank | Courage | Firepower | Skill |
|---|---|---|---|---|---|---|---|
| 8 | 7 | 3 | 8 | 6 | 8 | 6 | 6 |

MLC: **$42-54**, MOC (opened): **$60-65**, MOC: **$75-150+**

Icepick's Pretender shell is bright orange, and he has two large protruding claws instead of hands. His robot mode is the standard Pretender Monster fare: a boxy robot body with very little poseability of the arms and legs. When forming Monstructor, Icepick functions as his right leg.

---

**ALTERNATE MODE:** (Ice) monster.
**EASILY LOST WEAPONS AND ACCESSORIES:** Pretender shell, small robot, backpack/(Monstructor) footstand, rifle, rear panel.

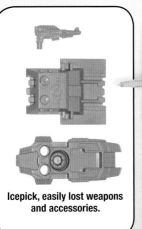

Icepick, easily lost weapons and accessories.

Icepick, outer shell mode.

◄ Scowl, inner robot's alternate mode.

Scowl, outer shell mode.

Scowl, easily lost weapons and accessories.

Scowl, inner robot mode.

# SCOWL

**PRETENDER MONSTERS**

**FUNCTION:** Sonic Saboteur
**MOTTO:** "Control sound, and the faintest whisper can be the fiercest weapon."

"A terrifying, merciless warrior who signed on as a Pretender when he realized he didn't scare anybody with his appearance! With his menacing new outer shell and his steel-shattering, hypersonic, stereophonic implants, his bark now matches his bite! His supersonic hearing capabilities enable him to pinpoint even the quietest sound! Scowl is armed with dual-sonic disrupter gun."

| Strength | Intelligence | Speed | Endurance | Rank | Courage | Firepower | Skill |
|----------|--------------|-------|-----------|------|---------|-----------|-------|
| 7 | 6 | 2 | 9 | 5 | 8 | 6 | 8 |

💲 MLC: **$42-58**, MOC (opened): **$62-70**, MOC: **$75-150+**

Scowl is an interesting looking monster whose outer shell's offensive capabilities function on sonic principles. As a combiner, joins with the rest of the Pretender Monsters' inner robots to form the left leg of Monstructor.

**ALTERNATE MODE:** (Sonic) monster.
**EASILY LOST WEAPONS AND ACCESSORIES:** Pretender shell, small robot, backpack/(Monstructor) footstand, dual disruptor gun, rear panel.

# SLOG

**PRETENDER MONSTERS**

**FUNCTION:** Combat Artist
**MOTTO:** "Destruction is the highest form of art."

"He has taken sculpture out of the art studio and transplanted it onto the battlefield. In his Pretender guise, he can whittle an Autobot warrior into an abstract wreck within minutes. He considers his carved-up conquests to be renowned masterpieces. His diamond-steel alloy talons can tear through any material known to man or robot. Slog is armed with a magnetic repellor-attractor which rips iron-bearing opponents into microscopic pieces."

| Strength | Intelligence | Speed | Endurance | Rank | Courage | Firepower | Skill |
|----------|--------------|-------|-----------|------|---------|-----------|-------|
| 5 | 8 | 2 | 8 | 7 | 7 | 7 | 10 |

💲 MLC: **$45-68**, MOC (opened): **$72-78**, MOC: **$85-175+**

Slog's Tech Spec is unique as it portrays the Decepticon as a combat artist: using his talents to render Autobots into aesthetically pleasing pieces of scrap metal. When combining to form Monstructor, Slog acts as the gestalt's chest and head.

**ALTERNATE MODE:** Monster.
**EASILY LOST WEAPONS AND ACCESSORIES:** Pretender shell, small robot, dual rifle, (Monstructor's) solar cannon, (Monstructor's) robot head, rear panel.

Slog, outer shell mode.

Wildfly, easily lost weapons and accessories.

# WILDFLY

**PRETENDER MONSTERS**

**FUNCTION:** Aerial Assault
**MOTTO:** "Strike fear into your enemy, and you've won half the battle."

"A flying fury of flashing fangs and tearing talons. He's a one-robot wrecking crew who has been known to reduce high-rise office towers into rubble within seconds, just for laughs! Also gets his kicks snapping wings off commercial airline jets. Wildfly is armed with a high-powered, laser-sighted, photon rifle for intense air-to-surface assaults!"

| Strength | Intelligence | Speed | Endurance | Rank | Courage | Firepower | Skill |
|----------|--------------|-------|-----------|------|---------|-----------|-------|
| 6 | 5 | 6 | 7 | 6 | 8 | 6 | 7 |

**$** MLC: **$35-48**, MOC (opened): **$60-70**, MOC: **$75-150+**

Wildfly, inner robot's alternate mode.

As an aerial warrior, Wildfly's apparent lack of wings in toy mode might ground him if they weren't so prominently featured on his stunning card artwork. If only the Pretender Monsters were designed to be twice their production size, perhaps they would have had more detailed inner robots and Pretender shells. Regardless, the Pretender Monsters are in extremely high demand and command high prices for MLC and MOC samples on the secondary market. Wildfly forms Monstructor's left arm.

**ALTERNATE MODE:** (Flying) monster.
**EASILY LOST WEAPONS AND ACCESSORIES:** Pretender shell, small robot, photon rifle, cannon/robot hand, (Monstructor's left fist).

Wildfly, inner robot mode.

Wildfly, outer shell mode.

Slog, inner robot's alternate mode.

Slog, easily lost weapons and accessories.

Slog, inner robot mode.

# MONSTRUCTOR

**PRETENDER MONSTERS**

**FUNCTION:** Super Warrior
**MOTTO:** "My touch is death."

"Six fearsome Pretenders combine to form this towering, metal-mashing menace! Monstructor's corrosive touch causes metal to decay, making it easier for him to use his incredible strength to crush his robotic foes! His solar fission cannon utilizes the power of the stars to obliterate anything in its sight!"

| Strength | Intelligence | Speed | Endurance | Rank | Courage | Firepower | Skill |
|---|---|---|---|---|---|---|---|
| 9 | 5 | 4 | 6 | 7 | 8 | 9 | 6 |

Monstructor (all 6 Pretender Monsters together)
MLC: **$275-350+** (no gift set available)

Monstructor, robot mode, front view.

Monstructor's completed gestalt mode is one of the most-requested Transformer G1 toys on the secondary market. According to Dreamwave's 2003 *Transformers: More Than Meets the Eye* guidebooks (where the above motto is gleaned from), standing in the shadow of this fearsome gestalt as it combines is a similar experience to watching an evil incantation being cast. To wit: "His very presence drains life, and an aura of palpable dread is his ever-present companion." When Monstructor is around, the life force of friend and foe alike appears to whither away.

Bludgeon, inner robot mode.

Bludgeon, outer shell mode.

# BLUDGEON

**(SMALL) PRETENDERS**

**FUNCTION:** Electric Warrior
**MOTTO:** "To know your own limits, you must first know your foe's limits."

"A merciless, emotionless master of Metallikato, the deadly Cybertronian martial art. Attacks his enemies' fracture points while remaining outside their line of fire. High-powered antennas produce electrical fireballs with a range of over 400 yards. Battle armor secretes odorous, mucus slime. Smoke generators in legs produce billowing clouds of black smoke that disorient the enemy. Inner robot armed with high-voltage electric cannon."

| Strength | Intelligence | Speed | Endurance | Rank | Courage | Firepower | Skill |
|---|---|---|---|---|---|---|---|
| 6 | 8 | 2 | 9 | 6 | 9 | 7 | 10 |

MLC: **$150-175+**, MOC (opened): **$190-210+**,
MOC: **$400-600+**

# OCTOPUNCH

(SMALL) PRETENDERS

**FUNCTION:** Salvage
**MOTTO:** "Anything that can sink is worth sinking."

"The terror of the deep. If he's not stealing sunken treasure or ancient artifacts, he amuses himself by smashing holes in submarines and cruise ships. Electrically-charged, razor-tipped harpoon gun momentarily short-circuits on contact. Also armed with vice-like tentacles that stick to any surface. So strong underwater, he can wrestle a whale to a standstill. Inner robot converts to metal-rending, deep-sea radar and acetylene torch gun."

| Strength | Intelligence | Speed | Endurance | Rank | Courage | Firepower | Skill |
|----------|--------------|-------|-----------|------|---------|-----------|-------|
| 8 | 5 | 1 | 9 | 6 | 8 | 5 | 7 |

MLC: **$90-120+**, MOC (opened): **$130-140+**,
MOC: **$150-250**

Octopunch's tentacled and helmeted outer shell (and the complexity of his inner robot's transformation mode) has drawn collectors to pick up this second generation Transformer in recent years. As with all of the smaller Pretenders, he's not a cheap buy loose, but well worth the money once you get him home.

**ALTERNATE MODE:** Crab.
**EASILY LOST WEAPONS AND ACCESSORIES:**
2 "Octopunch" figure shell halves, acetylene torch gun (pistol), harpoon gun (rifle), helmet, 2 claws.

Octopunch, outer shell mode.

Octopunch, inner robot mode.

Octopunch, inner robot's alternate mode.

Octopunch, easily lost weapons and accessories.

---

Looking like a skeleton inside heavy samurai armor, Bludgeon is one of the most popular of the later-issue G1 Transformers. This could be due to the fact that Simon Furman (the lauded Marvel Comics *Transformers* writer) carefully crafted the Decepticon's character into the Marvel Comics mythos, eventually making him Decepticon leader.

As a character, Bludgeon is a master of Metallikato, a Cybertronian martial art where the practitioners use their spiritual and physical training (and a strict ethical code) to achieve combat readiness and enlightenment, (see Dreamwave's *Transformers: More Than Meets The Eye* guide books, 2003). As toys, note that none of the second generation of smaller Pretenders ever came with sticker or a label sheets. Bludgeon is an excellent action figure, but why no sword?

**ALTERNATE MODE:** Cybertronian tank.
**EASILY LOST WEAPONS AND ACCESSORIES:** 2 "Bludgeon" figure shell halves, laser rifle, turret/shield, electric (tank) cannon, helmet.

Bludgeon, easily lost weapons and accessories.

Bludgeon, inner robot's alternate mode.

# STRANGLEHOLD

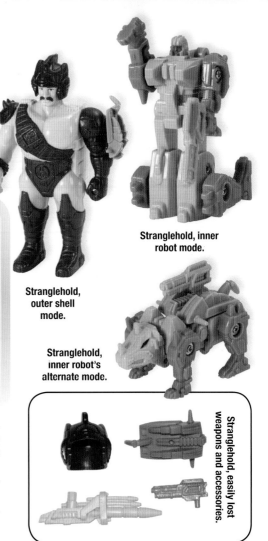

Strarnglehold, inner robot mode.

Stranglehold, outer shell mode.

Stranglehold, inner robot's alternate mode.

Stranglehold, easily lost weapons and accessories.

**(SMALL) PRETENDERS**

**FUNCTION:** Enforcer
**MOTTO:** "Rule one is: There are no rules!"

"A muscle-bound monster! Willing to do anything to win. Kicks, gouges and sucker punches his way to victory. The reigning Intergalactic Cybertronic Wrestling Federation Champ. A powerhouse of brute strength. All brawn and no brains. Enjoys bench-pressing houses and arm curling cars to stay in shape. Sends his opponents down for the count with his steel-smashing, ultra-suplex or a short-circuiting atomic piledriver. Armed with brawn blaster that drains his enemies' power. Equipped with concussion blaster in robot mode."

| Strength | Intelligence | Speed | Endurance | Rank | Courage | Firepower | Skill |
|---|---|---|---|---|---|---|---|
| 9 | 3 | 2 | 9 | 7 | 5 | 6 | 8 |

MLC: **$80-115+**, MOC (opened): **$125-138+**, MOC: **$150-250+**

Although his outer shell looks rather silly, as a second generation Pretender, Stranglehold's figure still sells well on the secondary market. But in regard to the appearance of both his outer shell and inner robot (and his Tech Spec, for that matter), the less said the better. "Ultra-suplex?"

**ALTERNATE MODE:** Rhino.
**EASILY LOST WEAPONS AND ACCESSORIES:** 2 "Stranglehold" wrestler shell halves, concussion blaster (pistol), brawn blaster (rifle), helmet, rhino top/backpack.

# STARSCREAM

Starscream, inner robot's alternate mode.

**PRETENDER CLASSICS**

**FUNCTION:** Aerospace Commander
**MOTTO:** "Conquest is made of the ashes of one's enemies."

**NOTE:** The Pretenders text is the first paragraph below, and the Kmart Legends Tech Specs is the second paragraph below.

**PRETENDER:** "A cheating, traitorous villain. Ruthless and cold-blooded. Always plotting another evil attack against the heroic Autobots. Determined to rule the universe with a fist of iron. Outer shell armed with methylial-powered jet pack and thermal carbine that can either freeze or melt metal on impact. Inner robot armed with null ray rifle that shorts out electrical impulses. Maximum speed: Mach 3. Also equipped with suborbital capabilities. Arrogance is Starscream's only weakness."

**KMART LEGENDS:** "A cheating, traitorous villain. Ruthless and cold-blooded. Always plotting another evil attack against the heroic Autobots. Determined to rule the universe with a fist of iron. A monstrosity of Cybertronic metal and complex circuitry. Armed with null ray lasers that short out electrical impulses. Maximum speed: Mach 3. Also equipped with suborbital capabilities. Arrogance is Starscream's only weakness."

| Strength | Intelligence | Speed | Endurance | Rank | Courage | Firepower | Skill |
|---|---|---|---|---|---|---|---|
| 7 | 9 | 8 | 7 | 9 | 9 | 8 | 8 |

Pretender Classics: MLC: **$45-68**, MIB: (opened): **$78-90**, MISB: **$125-250**
Transformers Legends [Kmart exclusive]: **MLC: $16-20**, MOC (opened): **$28-30**, MOC: **$40-80**

**ALTERNATE MODE:** McDonnel-Douglass F-15C Eagle.
**EASILY LOST WEAPONS AND ACCESSORIES:** (Pretender) 2 "Starscream" figure shell halves, rifle, helmet, 2 lasers/tail wings, 2 front wings; (Kmart Legends) 2 lasers/tail wings, 2 front wings.

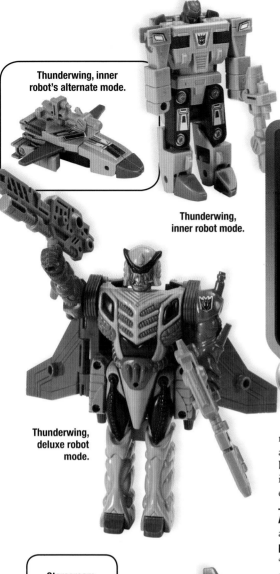

Thunderwing, inner robot's alternate mode.

Thunderwing, inner robot mode.

Thunderwing, deluxe robot mode.

# THUNDERWING

**MEGA PRETENDERS**

**FUNCTION:** Aerial Espionage
**MOTTO:** "Cover yourself with lies and no one will find you."

"A two-faced, lying, cheating, back-stabbing scoundrel. The ultimate Decepticon villain. Armed with power-enhancing, impenetrable exoskeleton. Also equipped with electrostatic gun ports in shoulders and metal-eating laser beam in forehead. Reserve fuel tanks in legs provide unlimited fuel supply and aerator hoses in chest emit noxious gases. Armed with cyclone cannon and transforms into inter-stellar jet that carries full payload of plasma charges. Outer shell jet equipped with neutron power pack that increases firepower by 50%. Combines with Jet pod to form super jet armed with heat-seeking laser blasters."

| Strength | Intelligence | Speed | Endurance | Rank | Courage | Firepower | Skill |
|----------|--------------|-------|-----------|------|---------|-----------|-------|
| 8 | 7 | 7 | 8 | 6 | 6 | 6 | 9 |

**$** MLC: **$160-210+**, MIB: **$245-270+**, MISB: **$400-600**

Thunderwing is a very sought-after Pretender toy. One of the most cruel and maliciously powerful of all Decepticons, he is a walking munitions factory in jet and robot modes. In Marvel Comics' *Transformers*, Thunderwing was possessed by a corrupt Matrix (see "The Matrix Quest" storyline, issues #62-66, written by scribe Simon Furman) that eventually led to his banishment and demise.

Thunderwing, mega mode (combined inner and outer robots).

**ALTERNATE MODE:** (Inner robot) jet, (outer shell) jet and deluxe jet.

**EASILY LOST WEAPONS AND ACCESSORIES:** "Thunderwing" (opening and transformable) outer shell, 2 large lasers, small laser.

Thunderwing, easily lost weapons and accessories.

Starscream, inner robot mode.

Starscream, easily lost weapons and accessories.

Starscream, outer shell mode.

Thunderwing, deluxe mode.

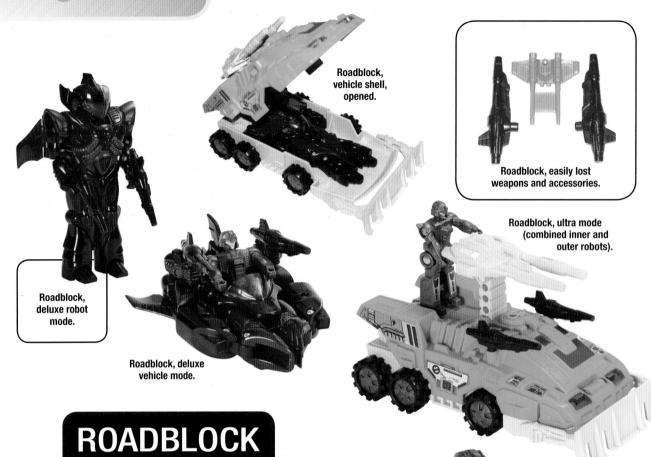

Roadblock, vehicle shell, opened.

Roadblock, easily lost weapons and accessories.

Roadblock, ultra mode (combined inner and outer robots).

Roadblock, deluxe robot mode.

Roadblock, deluxe vehicle mode.

Roadblock, inner robot mode.

## ROADBLOCK

### ULTRA PRETENDERS

**FUNCTION:** Ground Forces Commander
**MOTTO:** "To show fear is to admit defeat."

"The malevolent master of mayhem. Crushes everything in his path with his studded, iron-steel wheels. The front runner for the Decepticon army, and a locomotive of destruction. Armed with corrosive rust bombs that eat away enemy armor. Also equipped with high-intensity heat generators in exterior that provide thermal force field. Infra-red tracking and navigation systems and large scale fuel capacity ideal for remote controlled reconnaissance missions. Also armed with two proton shatter-cannons and hydraulic battle ram equipped with acetylene cutters. Outer shell transforms to subsonic windcruiser armed with two plasma blasters."

| Strength | Intelligence | Speed | Endurance | Rank | Courage | Firepower | Skill |
|----------|-------------|-------|-----------|------|---------|-----------|-------|
| 8 | 6 | 3 | 9 | 9 | 10 | 8 | 7 |

MOC: **$85-135+**, MIB: **$150-165+**, MISB: **$200-400**

Like the Autobot Ultra Pretender toy, Skyhammer, Decepticon Roadblock is a very fragile toy, most notably his inner gold robot's feet and hands—they become brittle (or have always been this way since coming off of the assembly line in 1989). Roadblock's colors are impressive, his outer tank shell is durable, and the simple fact that you can get him to transform from armored assault vehicle (inner robot), to jet/windcruiser (outer robot with smaller robot within), to attack tank (containing both the outer shell and inner robot) is a masterpiece of design. And hard-to-find in any condition.

**ALTERNATE MODE:** (Inner robot) armored assault vehicle, (outer robot) to jet/windcruiser, (outer shell) to attack tank.

**EASILY LOST WEAPONS AND ACCESSORIES:** "Roadblock" (outer) tank, "Roadblock" figure (outer) shell, "Roadblock" (inner) robot, 2 lasers, dual blaster.

Roadblock, inner robot's alternate mode.

# SERIES 7

During this last year of production, the Micromasters brand was continued and a new element was introduced: Micromaster Combiners. Now, two small Micromaster vehicles could form a longer vehicle mode. These Micromaster Combiners could attach to the front or back of any other Micromaster Combiner in order to create a brand new, unique vehicle form. This technology yielded even larger toys such as the Micromaster Combiner Squad trios, the deluxe Micromaster Combiner Transports, and the impressive Micromaster Combiner Playsets. From the Autobot Missile Launcher to the Decepticon Cannon Transport, from the Autobot Battlefield Headquarters to the Decepticon Anti-Aircraft Base, Micromaster toys that once languished on the secondary market are now in high demand for Generation One collectors.

Regardless, for most fans the straw that broke the camel's back was the addition of the Transformers Action Masters toys to the mix. Since Action Masters possessed no alternate modes and could not transform at all, collecting purists didn't accept these Transformers toys that were essentially "fully poseable" action figures with decent articulation and a Targetmaster weapon.

Although many diehards reviled these toys, some aficionados recognized the potential of these action figures: at long last collectors received a Megatron and Optimus Prime, a Bumblebee, and a Soundwave that looked and moved like their cartoon forms. Furthermore, all Action Masters were manufactured in exact scale with one another: Blaster didn't tower five body lengths over Bumblebee; Jazz no longer hid in Shockwave's shadow. Regardless of the endless debates over the relevance of the Action Masters to the Generation One lineup, these [non-transforming] Transformers sadly proved the end of the line in United States.

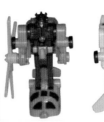

Air Patrol, robot modes: Tread Bolt, Eagle Eye, Sky High, and Blaze Master.

# AIR PATROL

**MICROMASTER PATROLS**

**FUNCTION:** Air Defense
**MOTTO:** "Keep your eye to the sky!"

"An elite corps of top-notch fliers. Considered the best aerial fighters to ever take to the skies. Revered by their fellow Autobots for their ability to neutralize enemy encampments without destroying the surrounding area. Fast, fierce, efficient fighters. Able to emit circular force field that's impervious to most armaments when flying in a 'V' formation. Also armed with high intensity heat lasers and long-range communications systems. All equipped with sub-orbital travel capabilities. Usually commissioned for the Autobot's most dangerous special air missions."

| Teamwork | Cooperation | Strength | Endurance | Speed | Intelligence | Courage | Skill |
|---|---|---|---|---|---|---|---|
| 8 | 6 | 8 | 8 | 9 | 10 | 8 | 10 |

 MLC (full set): **$14-24**, MOC: **$50-100**

Air Patrol, easily lost accessory.

Air Patrol, alternate modes.

Construction Patrol, robot modes.

# CONSTRUCTION PATROL

**MICROMASTER PATROLS**

**FUNCTION:** Ground Reinforcements
**MOTTO:** "The foundations of freedom are forged on solid ground."

"Powerhouses of metal and steel! Called to battle to fortify and reinforce the Autobots' front line. The first to roll in and the last to roll out. A formidable adversary when working as a team. Extremely smart and tremendously strong. Known for their ability to organize and build a towering fortress out of seemingly worthless junk. Each composed of high-density titanium steel for maximum resistance against enemy bombardment. Jet boosters under wheels provide short term flight capabilities."

| Teamwork | Cooperation | Strength | Endurance | Speed | Intelligence | Courage | Skill |
|---|---|---|---|---|---|---|---|
| 8 | 9 | 10 | 7 | 7 | 8 | 9 | 8 |

MLC (full set): **$14-34**, MOC: **$40-80**

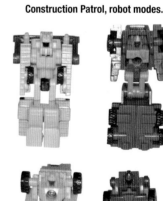

**EASILY LOST WEAPONS AND ACCESSORIES:** N/A.

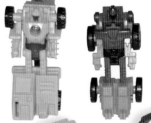

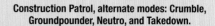

Construction Patrol, alternate modes: Crumble, Groundpounder, Neutro, and Takedown.

Hot Rod Patrol, alternate modes.

# HOT ROD PATROL

**MICROMASTER PATROLS**

**FUNCTION:** Highway Reconnaissance
**MOTTO:** "The essence of speed relies on our power to perform!"

"Each possesses 16 cylinders of carbonic Autobot muscle! High-performance avengers have more rubber-burning speed than the fastest squad of Decepticons. Usually seen cruising up and down Earth beaches and boardwalks. Highly mischievous and adventurous, sometimes mistaken for Decepticon punks. Though preoccupied with fun, still able to quickly respond to emergency roadway situations. Able to spot dangerous Decepticon highway marauders using telescopic, kelvar-energized, localizer radar. Each car is protected by a geometrical shield which deflects Decepticon photon disintegration beams. Courage and tenacity are the patrol's finest attributes."

| Teamwork | Cooperation | Strength | Endurance | Speed | Intelligence | Courage | Skill |
|---|---|---|---|---|---|---|---|
| 9 | 8 | 6 | 10 | 8 | 8 | 9 | 9 |

**MLC (full set): $18-27, MOC: $40-80+**

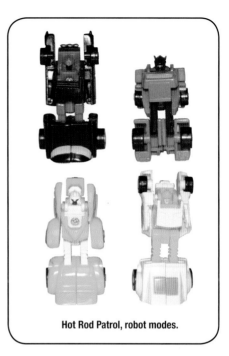

Hot Rod Patrol, robot modes.

**ALTERNATE CAR MODES:** Big Daddy (black), Greaser (orange), Hubs (mint green), and Trip-Up (white).
**EASILY LOST WEAPONS AND ACCESSORIES:** N/A.

# MONSTER TRUCK PATROL

**MICROMASTER PATROLS**

**FUNCTION:** Ground Transport
**MOTTO:** "We're a giant wall of Autobot Might!"

"Nothing stops them when they roll out! Hard driving road warriors travel fast and heavy! Incorporated with sophisticated auto-driver control systems and modulated weapons' stations. Quad-overhead cam, energon-ignited engine allows for travel at twice the speed of sound! Able to barrel through almost any obstacle. Unstoppable when roaring in full-throttle. Can utilize their massive strength for transporting wounded Autobots through the battle zone. Use their micro size and powerful engines to literally drag uncooperative Decepticons into the heat of the battle!"

| Teamwork | Cooperation | Strength | Endurance | Speed | Intelligence | Courage | Skill |
|---|---|---|---|---|---|---|---|
| 10 | 7 | 7 | 8 | 8 | 9 | 6 | 7 |

**MLC (full set): $14-24, MOC: $40-80**

Monster Truck Patrol, robot modes.

**ALTERNATE TRUCK MODES:** Big Hauler (green), Heavy Tread (orange), Hydraulic (blue), and Slow Poke (yellow).
**EASILY LOST WEAPONS AND ACCESSORIES:** N/A.

Monster Truck Patrol, alternate modes.

Astro Squad, robot modes.

# ASTRO SQUAD

**MICROMASTER COMBINER SQUADS**

**FUNCTION:** Interstellar Defense
**MOTTO:** "There's no speed like light speed!"

"Each Micromaster Combiner in the Astro Squad detaches from its main vehicle mode and can be re-attached with another Micromaster Combiner to create exciting new galactic special teams. Self-sufficient, metallized warriors. The Autobots' first line of defense against the Decepticons. Protected by an impenetrable coating of cyclonic steel for withstanding maximum enemy photon blasts. Able to travel at light speed and rocket across the galaxies in seconds. Equipped with an array of advanced, technological, micro-circuitry for defensive maneuvers and deep space exploratory operations. Also armed with an anti-gravitational device to counteract Decepticon tractor-beam attacks. Sometimes travel too fast and overshoot objective."

Astro Squad, alternate modes.

| Teamwork | Cooperation | Strength | Endurance | Speed | Intelligence | Courage | Skill |
|----------|-------------|----------|-----------|-------|--------------|---------|-------|
| 7 | 9 | 10 | 6 | 10 | 8 | 7 | 9 |

MLC: **$28-40**, MOC (opened): **$50-65**, MOC: **$100-200**

Astro Squad, alternate combinations.

**ALTERNATE MODES:** (Silver moon crawler) Barrage (front) and Heave (rear), (space shuttle) Phaser (front) and Blast Master (rear), (red missile carrier) Moonrock (front) and and Missile Master (rear).

**EASILY LOST WEAPONS AND ACCESSORIES:** Missile Master's missile (very hard-to-find).

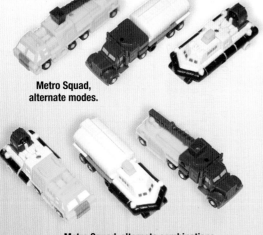
Metro Squad, alternate modes.

Metro Squad, alternate combinations.

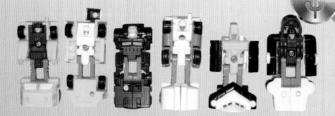
Metro Squad, robot modes.

# METRO SQUAD

**MICROMASTER COMBINER SQUADS**

**FUNCTION:** Urban Protection
**MOTTO:** "Protecting life is the most unselfish act of all!"

"As Micromaster Combiners, the Metro Squad's vehicles can separate in half and attach with other Micromaster Combiners to form different, specialized rescue vehicles. Commissioned to shield the streets from chaos and destruction! Reinforce Autobot defenses by clearing embattled area of debris and fallen Decepticons. Well-respected by fellow Autobots for their fearless courage in the face of danger. Possess an impeccable success ratio in protecting civilians during Decepticon attacks. Unwilling to accept awards for acts of heroism. Satisfied knowing they've helped the fight against evil! Eagerness to aid wounded is overshadowed by ability to get in each other's way. Combine to form fire truck, hovercraft, and tanker truck."

| Teamwork | Cooperation | Strength | Endurance | Speed | Intelligence | Courage | Skill |
|----------|-------------|----------|-----------|-------|--------------|---------|-------|
| 9 | 8 | 9 | 7 | 9 | 6 | 7 | 10 |

MLC: **$24-38**, MOC (opened): **$48-55**, MOC: **$50-100**

**ALTERNATE MODES:** (Yellow fire truck) Wheel Blaze (front) and Road Burner (rear), (tanker truck) Oiler (blue, front) and Slide (white, rear), and (hovercraft) Power Run (front) and Strikedown (rear).

**EASILY LOST WEAPONS AND ACCESSORIES:** N/A.

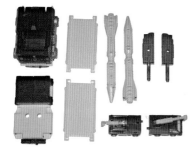

Missile Launcher, easily lost weapons and accessories.

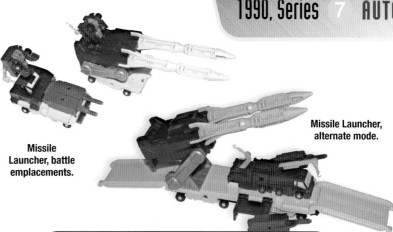

Missile Launcher, battle emplacements.

Missile Launcher, alternate mode.

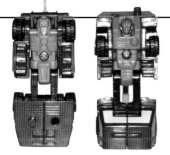

Missile Launcher, Micromaster robot modes — Retro and Surge.

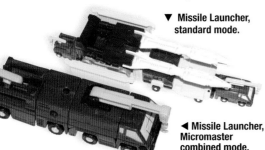

▼ Missile Launcher, standard mode.

◀ Missile Launcher, Micromaster combined mode.

# MISSILE LAUNCHER

**MICROMASTER COMBINER TRANSPORTS**

**FUNCTION:** Long Range Defense
**MOTTO:** "Perseverance leads to triumph."

"An awesome array of military might. In transport mode, able to easily scale steeply graded hills and rocky, brush-filled terrain. Converts into stationary battle platform for quick-strike, counterattack maneuvers. Platform equipped with dual gun emplacements, heavily protected Micromaster Combiner vehicle and hydraulic boarding ramps. Also changes into two cybernetically superior micro robots in Combiner mode. Specially programmed for Decepticon surveillance and Autobot infantry support. Retro and Surge, two tough tenacious fighters, command this hard-hitting battle unit."

| Strength | Intelligence | Speed | Endurance | Rank | Courage | Firepower | Skill |
|---|---|---|---|---|---|---|---|
| 10 | 6 | 8 | 5 | 9 | 9 | 9 | 6 |

$ MLC: **$55-75+**, MIB: **$80-90**, MISB: **$75-150**

**ALTERNATE MODE:** (micromasters combine to form) crane, (missile launcher to) battle station, battle emplacements.
**EASILY LOST WEAPONS AND ACCESSORIES:** "Retro" micromaster (front), "Surge" micromaster (rear), 2 missiles, missile launcher front, missile launcher rear, 2 ramps, 2 side guns.

# TANKER TRUCK/ TANKER TRANSPORT

**MICROMASTER COMBINER TRANSPORTS**

**FUNCTION:** Ground Defense and Counterattack
**MOTTO:** "Leave the enemy spitting dust and bolts."

"Headstrong heroes of armor and steel. Able to carry emergency reinforcements and fuel supplies to any area of confrontation. Combines to form fully equipped battle platform and heavy-hitting assault vehicle. Employs twin gun emplacements for defensive maneuvers that blast Decepticons into deep space. Utilizing the Micromaster Combiner feature, able to connect with other Micromaster Combiners to form fast-attack vehicles equipped with multi-functional, combat and transport capabilities. Commanded by Pipeline and Gusher, who spend more time fighting each other than fighting the enemy."

| Strength | Intelligence | Speed | Endurance | Rank | Courage | Firepower | Skill |
|---|---|---|---|---|---|---|---|
| 8 | 7 | 6 | 9 | 8 | 10 | 5 | 7 |

$ MLC: **$60-95**, MIB: **$100-110**, MISB: **$125-225**

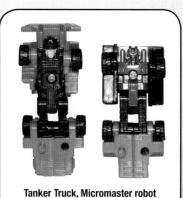

Tanker Truck, Micromaster robot modes—Pipeline and Gusher.

Tanker Truck, Micromaster combined mode.

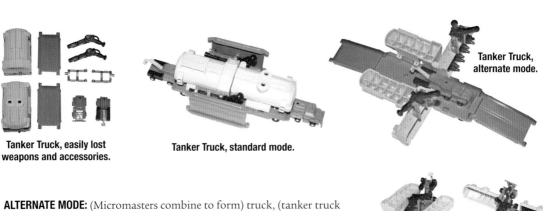

Tanker Truck, easily lost weapons and accessories.

Tanker Truck, standard mode.

Tanker Truck, alternate mode.

**ALTERNATE MODE:** (Micromasters combine to form) truck, (tanker truck to) battle station, battle emplacements.

**EASILY LOST WEAPONS AND ACCESSORIES:** "Pipeline" micromaster (front), "Gusher" micromaster (rear), 2 cannons, 2 ramps, trailer front, trailer rear, 2 cannon mounts.

Tanker Truck, battle emplacements.

# BATTLEFIELD HEADQUARTERS/
## Micromaster Combiner Autobot Headquarters

**MICROMASTER BASE**

**FUNCTION:** Regional Ground/Air Defense
**MOTTO:** "Speed and power are the driving force for victory!"

"Keeps the peace on land and in the air! Full-Barrel and Overflow use their overpowering size to rumble to victory over any Decepticon adversary. Highly mobile, stock-piled to the max with energon defense armaments, including twin wing-tip rocket launchers, pivoting high-intensity heat lasers and dual concussion mortars. Non-oxygenized, vacuum-sealed cybernetic computer system control all on-board weapons and energy output. Provides safety for Autobots under attack. Utilizing the Micromaster Combiner feature, tractor trailer separates to form two aerial defense crafts, then they combine to produce sub-orbital space station!"

| Strength | Intelligence | Speed | Endurance | Rank | Courage | Firepower | Skill |
|----------|--------------|-------|-----------|------|---------|-----------|-------|
| 10 | 6 | 7 | 5 | 7 | 9 | 10 | 7 |

MLC: **$82-118**, MIB: **$125-135**, MISB: **$145-250**

Battlefield Headquarters, smaller aerial defense craft.

**ALTERNATE MODE:** (Micromasters combine to form) tractor trailer, (attack battle truck to) attack jet, battlefield headquarters.

**EASILY LOST WEAPONS AND ACCESSORIES:** "Full-Barrel" micromaster (front), "Overflow" micromaster (rear), 2 scrambler guns (right and left), 2 air-to-air missiles, 2 laser machine guns, 2 cruise missiles.

Battlefield Headquarters, larger aerial defense craft, opened.

Battlefield Headquarters, easily lost weapons and accessories.

Battlefield Headquarters, standard mode, front view.

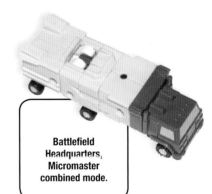

Battlefield Headquarters, Micromaster combined mode.

Battlefield Headquarters, Micromaster robot modes— Full Barrel and Overflow.

Battlefield Headquarters, sub-orbital space station, side view.

Battlefield Headquarters, standard mode.

Blaster, easily lost weapons and accessories.

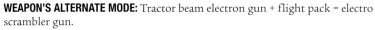

## BLASTER

**ACTION MASTERS**

**FUNCTION:** Communications
**MOTTO:** "When the music is rockin', I'm rollin'. "

"He loves all kinds of Earth music, but rock n' roll is his favorite because it's hard and loud, like him. Fights hard, plays hard, lives hard...and makes sure everyone knows it. In combat, routinely performs feats of courage and daring that would blow the fuses on other robots. As a communications center, his broadcast range is 4,000 miles. His energon-powered Flight-Pack can propel at airborne speeds in excess of 120mph. Backpack converts to a signal-jamming, electro-scrambler gun."

| Strength | Intelligence | Speed | Endurance | Rank | Courage | Firepower | Skill |
|---|---|---|---|---|---|---|---|
| 9 | 8 | 3 | 8 | 8 | 10 | 7 | 10 |

MLC: **$14-22+**, MOC: **$25-50**

Blaster, with combined Targetmaster weapon.

**WEAPON'S ALTERNATE MODE:** Tractor beam electron gun + flight pack = electro scrambler gun.
**EASILY LOST WEAPONS AND ACCESSORIES:** Tractor beam electron gun, flight pack.

Blaster, robot mode.

## BUMBLEBEE

**ACTION MASTERS**

**FUNCTION:** Espionage
**MOTTO:** "The least likely can be the most dangerous."

"By proving himself on countless missions, he has overcome his lack of size and strength to become the Autobot's top spy. Those who laughed at him, be it friend or foe, now treat him with respect. An eager, good-natured, daring warrior. His turbo-powered backpack, Heli-Pack, has a flying range of 1200 miles. Also serves as an aide in reconnaissance by transmitting pictures back to Bumblebee. It has a maximum speed of 280mph, and can convert to a high-powered air rifle."

| Strength | Intelligence | Speed | Endurance | Rank | Courage | Firepower | Skill |
|---|---|---|---|---|---|---|---|
| 3 | 8 | 5 | 7 | 9 | 10 | 5 | 10 |

MLC: **$18-26+**, MOC: **$30-60**

**WEAPON'S ALTERNATE MODE(S):** Astral exploder rifle + heli-pack = attack heli-pack, or air rifle.
**EASILY LOST WEAPONS AND ACCESSORIES:** Astral exploder rifle, heli-pack.

Bumblebee, easily lost weapons and accessories.

Bumblebee, robot mode.

Bumblebee, with combined Targetmaster weapon.

Grimlock, with combined Targetmaster weapon.

Grimlock, robot mode.

# GRIMLOCK

**ACTION MASTERS**

**FUNCTION:** Dinobot Commander
**MOTTO:** "Among the winners, there is no room for the weak!"

"A powerhouse of fighting muscle! Once rebellious, now one of Optimus Prime's most loyal and valiant warriors. Fearsome, powerful, virtually unstoppable on the battlefield. Thick-skinned and stubborn. Never concedes a victory to the enemy. Partnered with a combat-ready anti-tank cannon that fires concentrated bursts of flaming metal. Converts to long-range mortar launcher, equipped with 50-mile firing range. Smarter and more powerful than ever before, Grimlock is often called to lead the charge into battle."

| Strength | Intelligence | Speed | Endurance | Rank | Courage | Firepower | Skill |
|----------|--------------|-------|-----------|------|---------|-----------|-------|
| 9 | 7 | 2 | 10 | 9 | 10 | 8 | 9 |

MLC: **$12-18+**, MOC: **$30-50+**

**WEAPON'S ALTERNATE MODE:** Particle beam cannon + anti-tank cannon = long range mortar launcher.

**EASILY LOST WEAPONS AND ACCESSORIES:** Particle beam cannon, anti-tank cannon.

Grimlock, easily lost weapons and accessories.

# INFERNO

**ACTION MASTERS**

**FUNCTION:** Search and Rescue
**MOTTO:** "Where there's smoke, there's me."

"'The hotter things get, the better I like it!' is Inferno's motto, and he's not just talking about fires. Would rather fight Decepticons than fires, but his strength and ceramic-plated armored skin, [are] able to withstand temperatures as high as 14,000 degrees Fahrenheit, make him ideally suited for his job. His Hydro-Pack converts to a high-pressure cannon that can shoot any liquid substance from water to corrosive acid."

| Strength | Intelligence | Speed | Endurance | Rank | Courage | Firepower | Skill |
|----------|--------------|-------|-----------|------|---------|-----------|-------|
| 9 | 6 | 2 | 9 | 6 | 9 | 6 | 7 |

MLC: **$10-18**, MOC: **$20-40**

**WEAPON'S ALTERNATE MODE:** Magna-blast gun + hydro-pack = water laser.
**EASILY LOST WEAPONS AND ACCESSORIES:** Magna-blast gun, hydro-pack.

Inferno, robot mode.

Inferno, easily lost weapons and accessories.

Inferno, with combined Targetmaster weapon.

265

Jackpot, easily lost weapons and accessories.

# JACKPOT

**ACTION MASTERS**

**FUNCTION:** Strategist
**MOTTO:** "You can't win if you don't play."

"A boisterous, high-stakes do-gooder. Able to turn any situation into a wager and usually win. Once bet a Decepticon prison guard he could escape from the most fortified containment cell without being noticed. That guard is now serving time in his place. Good luck is part of his programming. His partner, Sights, always has his sonar locked into anything that can make Jackpot score big. Sights converts to hand-held, self-propelled photon cannon."

| Strength | Intelligence | Speed | Endurance | Rank | Courage | Firepower | Skill |
|----------|--------------|-------|-----------|------|---------|-----------|-------|
| 7 | 9 | 2 | 8 | 8 | 10 | 7 | 10 |

MLC: **$12-20**, MOC: **$24-48**

**TARGETMASTER WEAPON'S ALTERNATE MODE:** Heat induced photon rifle + Sights = photon cannon.

**EASILY LOST WEAPONS AND ACCESSORIES:** Heat induced photon rifle, Sights Targetmaster partner, Sight's feet (very difficult to find on loose samples).

Jackpot, robot mode.

**Jackpot, with combined Targetmaster weapon.**

# JAZZ

**ACTION MASTERS**

**FUNCTION:** Special Operations
**MOTTO:** Do it with style or don't do it at all!

"When this Earthen culture-lover isn't busy checking out the latest Rock 'n Roll reunion or Rap contest, he is usually on a secret mission for Optimus Prime. Gets a charge out of assignments involving incredible amounts of danger. His partner, Turbo Board, a hard-riding, rocket-powered skateboard, keeps Jazz rolling. This sidekick also converts into a dazzling destabilizer electromagnetizer gun."

| Strength | Intelligence | Speed | Endurance | Rank | Courage | Firepower | Skill |
|----------|--------------|-------|-----------|------|---------|-----------|-------|
| 5 | 9 | 4 | 7 | 8 | 9 | 6 | 10 |

MLC: **$16-26+**, MOC: **$30-60**

**Jazz, robot mode.**

Kick-Off, with combined Targetmaster weapon.

Kick-Off, robot mode.

# KICK-OFF

## ACTION MASTERS

**FUNCTION:** Security Expert
**MOTTO:** "Draw courage from defeat and you gain more than you lose."

"Trained as a gladiator in the grease pits of Polyhex while a Decepticon captive on Cybertron. A specialist in hand-to-hand combat who is without equal. Overheats in anticipation of using his skills on those who once imprisoned him. 'I want to show them what a good student I was,' he says vengefully. His Turbo-Pack can do 450mph while attached to Kick-Off. It also converts to an air-cooled, solar-powered flamethrower with pinpoint accuracy and heat beam attachment."

| Strength | Intelligence | Speed | Endurance | Rank | Courage | Firepower | Skill |
|----------|--------------|-------|-----------|------|---------|-----------|-------|
| 9 | 6 | 2 | 9 | 6 | 9 | 6 | 7 |

**MLC: $8-14, MOC: $20-40**

Kick-Off, easily lost weapons and accessories.

**WEAPON'S ALTERNATE MODE:** Sonic blaster + Turbo Pack = flamethrower.
**EASILY LOST WEAPONS AND ACCESSORIES:** Sonic blaster, Turbo Pack.

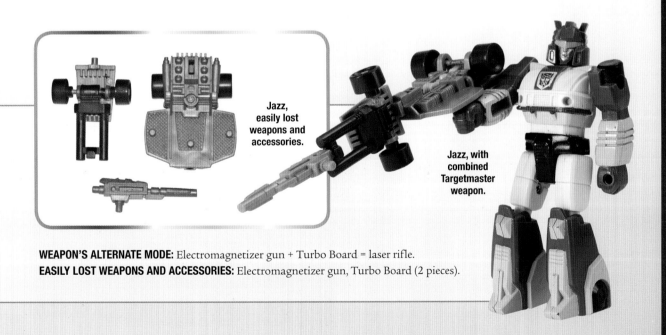

Jazz, easily lost weapons and accessories.

Jazz, with combined Targetmaster weapon.

**WEAPON'S ALTERNATE MODE:** Electromagnetizer gun + Turbo Board = laser rifle.
**EASILY LOST WEAPONS AND ACCESSORIES:** Electromagnetizer gun, Turbo Board (2 pieces).

# MAINFRAME

ACTION MASTERS

**FUNCTION:** Systems Analyst
**MOTTO:** "A program is only as good as its programmer."

"A walking, talking computer terminal. Would rather attack fourth order differential equations than Decepticons. Totally committed to his work. Views the galactic conflict as an inconvenience he must tolerate rather than a struggle in which he must participate. Is often compelled to flex his intellectual muscle, when needed. Equipped with 200,000 mega-byte capacity. His pugnacious partner, Push-Button, prefers converting to self-propelled proton rifle mode and disintegrating Decepticons over his assigned task of debugging Mainframe's various programs."

| Strength | Intelligence | Speed | Endurance | Rank | Courage | Firepower | Skill |
|---|---|---|---|---|---|---|---|
| 5 | 10 | 2 | 6 | 7 | 7 | 5 | 10 |

MLC: **$14-18**, MOC: **$20-35**

Mainframe, robot mode.

**WEAPON'S ALTERNATE MODE:** Vibro pulverizer + Push Button = Proton Rifle.
**EASILY LOST WEAPONS AND ACCESSORIES:** Vibro pulverizer, Push Button.

Mainframe, with combined Targetmaster weapon.

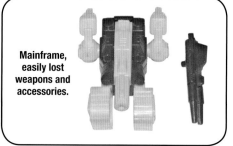

Mainframe, easily lost weapons and accessories.

Rad, with combined Targetmaster weapon.

# RAD

ACTION MASTERS

**FUNCTION:** Aerospace Engineer
**MOTTO:** "Think before you shoot, but shoot before you're shot!"

"With more moves than an all-pro halfback, this clever, cool-headed daredevil is equally adept at combating Decepticons or calculating the coefficient of friction for a rocket booster. Paired with Lionizer, a roaring raging bundle of overheated circuits who can change into an atom-smashing blaster at the drop of a microchip... unless Rad can cool his engines first."

| Strength | Intelligence | Speed | Endurance | Rank | Courage | Firepower | Skill |
|---|---|---|---|---|---|---|---|
| 6 | 9 | 2 | 8 | 6 | 9 | 7 | 9 |

MLC: **$12-18**, MOC: **$30-60**

# ROLLOUT

**ACTION MASTERS**

**FUNCTION:** Covert Operations
**MOTTO:** "The greater the weapon, the greater the power!"

"A super-charged fighting machine. Considered dangerous by his fellow Autobots because of his brash nature. Equipped with turbo backpack that can propel him to any position on the battlefield in seconds. Also equipped with electromagnetic rocket launcher that fires bursts of static electricity, shorting out enemy cerebral impulses. Launcher converts to Glitch, a short-burst, remote controlled, all terrain battle drone, armed with medium-range stun laser and photon gun. Often used for covert demolitions in battle."

| Strength | Intelligence | Speed | Endurance | Rank | Courage | Firepower | Skill |
|----------|--------------|-------|-----------|------|---------|-----------|-------|
| 8 | 7 | 7 | 8 | 7 | 10 | 9 | 8 |

MLC: **$16-24**, MOC: **$25-50**

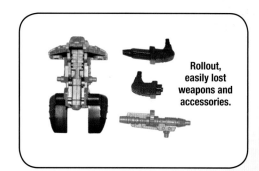

Rollout, with combined Targetmaster weapon.

**WEAPON'S ALTERNATE MODE:** Photon gun + Glitch = electromagnetic rocket launcher.
**EASILY LOST WEAPONS AND ACCESSORIES:** Photon gun, Glitch, 2 removable Glitch arms (different from one another).

Rollout, robot mode.

Rollout, easily lost weapons and accessories.

**WEAPON'S ALTERNATE MODE:** Thermal mortar gun + Lionizer = Atom-smashing blaster.
**EASILY LOST WEAPONS AND ACCESSORIES:** Thermal mortar gun, Lionizer.

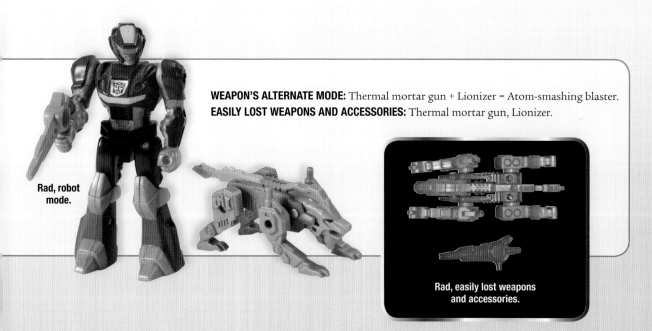

Rad, robot mode.

Rad, easily lost weapons and accessories.

# SKYFALL

ACTION MASTERS

**FUNCTION:** Weapons Engineer
**MOTTO:** "Flying is the ultimate freedom."

"Can change into anything from a construction crane to a can opener, then into a weapon in less time than it takes to plug in a phone jack. Even when he's battling on the ground, this former jet fighter has his head in the clouds, daydreaming about flying. His nagging partner, Top-Heavy, can change into a radar-guided, triple-barreled, electro-pulse machine gun."

| Strength | Intelligence | Speed | Endurance | Rank | Courage | Firepower | Skill |
|----------|--------------|-------|-----------|------|---------|-----------|-------|
| 6 | 9 | 2 | 7 | 7 | 9 | 6 | 9 |

MLC: **$14-26**, MOC: **$30-50**

Skyfall, robot mode.

# SNARL

ACTION MASTERS

**FUNCTION:** Desert Warrior
**MOTTO:** "Only in battle is there true happiness."

"An unhappy loner of few words and fewer opinions. Finds pleasure only in conflict. Otherwise, this stubborn, surly Dinobot is as welcome as a turboworm crawling up an exaust pipe. Solar-powered, his strength increases tenfold in sunlight. Paired with Tyrannitron, a tiny, temperamental terror who'd rather sink his teeth into his opponent's ankle assembly than convert into Snarl's metal-rendering shrapnel rifle."

| Strength | Intelligence | Speed | Endurance | Rank | Courage | Firepower | Skill |
|----------|--------------|-------|-----------|------|---------|-----------|-------|
| 9 | 6 | 2 | 9 | 5 | 8 | 7 | 5 |

MLC: **$13-19**, MOC: **$25-50**

Snarl, robot mode.

**WEAPON'S ALTERNATE MODE:** Intensity beam + Tyrannitron = shrapnel rifle.
**EASILY LOST WEAPONS AND ACCESSORIES:** Intensity beam, Tyrannitron, tail.

Snarl, with combined Targetmaster weapon.

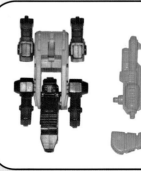

Snarl, easily lost weapons and accessories.

Skyfall, with combined Targetmaster weapon.

Skyfall, easily lost weapons and accessories.

**WEAPON'S ALTERNATE MODE:** Cloudbuster cannon + Top Heavy = machine gun
**EASILY LOST WEAPONS AND ACCESSORIES:** Cloudbuster cannon, Top Heavy.

Over-Run, robot mode.

Over-Run, attack mode.

# HELICOPTER WITH OVER-RUN

**ACTION MASTER BLASTERS**

**FUNCTION:** Air Defense
**MOTTO:** "I rule the skies with a heavy hand!"

"Over-Run takes orders from no one but himself. He pilots an advanced model Attack Copter, which has a maximum speed of 340mph, a flying range of 1200 miles, and is armed with air-to-ground magnetic missiles and a rotary photon pulse button. Also converts to a double-barreled concussion cannon emplacement."

| Strength | Intelligence | Speed | Endurance | Rank | Courage | Firepower | Skill |
|----------|--------------|-------|-----------|------|---------|-----------|-------|
| 6 | 8 | 5 | 7 | 7 | 10 | 8 | 8 |

MLC: **$26-38**, MIB: **$40-48**, MISB: **$50-100**

**ALTERNATE MODE(S):** Attack helicopter, battle roller.
**EASILY LOST WEAPONS AND ACCESSORIES:** Laser cannon, tail, rotor, landing skid, 2 side cannons, foot platform, 2 missiles, 2 landing skid rollers.

Over-Run, easily lost weapons and accessories.

◄ Over-Run, standard mode, with armed Autobot Helicopter.

**271**

Prowl, attack mode.

## TURBO CYCLE WITH PROWL

**ACTION MASTER BLASTERS**

**FUNCTION:** Military Strategist
**MOTTO:** "Logic is the ultimate weapon."

"A master with complex formulations. Equipped with sophisticated micro circuits, able to intake 30,000 bytes of information per micro second. Turbo cycle equipped with hydro-injected rocket engine, dual missile launcher and titanium belted tires. Converts to stationary battle emplacement armed with rocket bomb launcher."

| Strength | Intelligence | Speed | Endurance | Rank | Courage | Firepower | Skill |
|---|---|---|---|---|---|---|---|
| 7 | 8 | 6 | 7 | 9 | 9 | 8 | 6 |

MLC: **$26-38+**, MIB: **$40-48**, MISB: **$65-125**

**ALTERNATE MODE(S):** Attack cycle, gun emplacement.
**EASILY LOST WEAPONS AND ACCESSORIES:** Turbo cycle, small cannon, 2 missiles, 2 engine intakes (left and right), shield/gas tank cover, (removable) wheel assembly, (removable) engine side cover.

## ATTACK CRUISER WITH SPROCKET

**ACTION MASTER ACTION VEHICLES**

**FUNCTION:** Surface Surveillance
**MOTTO:** "Know your enemy and victory is yours!"

"Sprocket is programmed to take fast, forceful action and no prisoners. This fierce warrior doesn't withdraw from a battlefield until he's covered it with the smoking wreckage of Decepticons. He drives a rebuilt, all-terrain Attack Cruiser which has the standard supply of two photon rifles, metal-immobilizing magnetic rockets, and bumper energy shields. The Attack Cruiser converts into a vector-thrust hovercopter, armed with front-mounted plasma-pulse machine guns."

| Strength | Intelligence | Speed | Endurance | Rank | Courage | Firepower | Skill |
|---|---|---|---|---|---|---|---|
| 9 | 7 | 8 | 6 | 6 | 9 | 9 | 8 |

MLC: **$26-38+**, MIB: **$42-48**, MISB: **$50-100**

**ALTERNATE MODE(S):** Attack cruiser, attack helicopter.
**EASILY LOST WEAPONS AND ACCESSORIES:** Attack cruiser, rotor blades, 2 missiles.

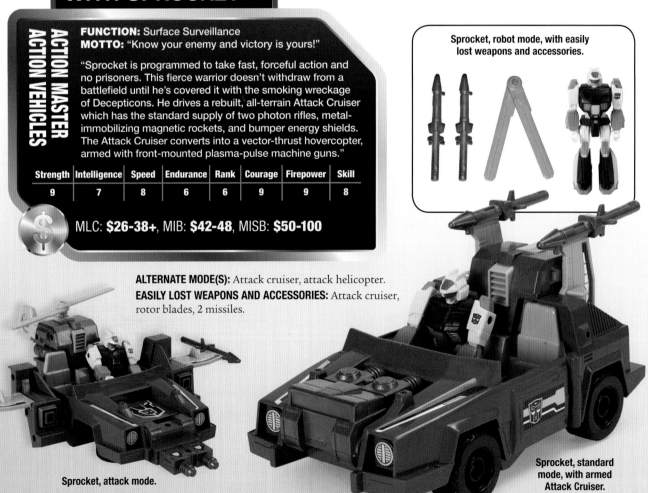

Sprocket, robot mode, with easily lost weapons and accessories.

Sprocket, attack mode.

Sprocket, standard mode, with armed Attack Cruiser.

Prowl, easily lost weapons and accessories.

Prowl, robot mode.

Prowl, standard mode, with armed Turbo Cycle.

Wheeljack, robot mode, with easily lost weapons and accessories.

Wheeljack, attack mode.

# TURBO RACER WITH WHEELJACK

**ACTION MASTER ACTION VEHICLES**

**FUNCTION:** Tactical Diversion
**MOTTO:** "Never do what your enemy expects you to do!"

"Wheeljack built and currently drives the Turbo Racer, the most versatile ground/air attack vehicle ever made. In car mode, its energon-injected, liquid nitrogen-cooled engine accelerates the craft from 0 to 250 mph in just 3 seconds. Armed with Laser-strafer rifle and a rear-mounted cannon that fires shrapnel and incendiary projectiles. Car instantly converts into jet fighter with nose mounted proton missile launcher."

| Strength | Intelligence | Speed | Endurance | Rank | Courage | Firepower | Skill |
|----------|-------------|-------|-----------|------|---------|-----------|-------|
| 8 | 8 | 6 | 9 | 8 | 9 | 6 | 7 |

MLC: **$28-40+**, MIB: **$50-60**, MISB: **$75-100**

**ALTERNATE MODE:** Attack turbo racer, turbo jet.
**EASILY LOST WEAPONS AND ACCESSORIES:** 2 missiles.

Wheeljack, standard mode, with armed Turbo Racer.

Optimus Prime, fortified battle headquarters with interceptor jet (left view).

Optimus Prime, Action Master, Mint in Box.

Optimus Prime, robot mode.

# ARMORED CONVOY WITH OPTIMUS PRIME

**ACTION MASTER COMMANDER**

**FUNCTION:** Autobot Commander
**MOTTO:** "Freedom is the right of all sentient beings."

"Philosopher, scholar, soldier, leader—Optimus Prime is all this and more. To peace-loving beings across the galaxy, he is the living symbol of freedom. A true beacon of hope that shines against the forces of darkness. To his followers, Optimus Prime represents a bottomless well from which they draw courage and strength. And to the evil Decepticons, he is the hero in the universe who can shatter their dreams of conquest. He drives the Armored Convoy, a trailer truck with communications, fueling and offensive capabilities. It divides into an interceptor shuttle and fortified battle headquarters equipped with a multitude of defense weaponry, including heat-seeking ballistic buzz bombs, a long-range photon cannon, rapid-fire disintegration laser and double-barreled pom-pom cannons."

| Strength | Intelligence | Speed | Endurance | Rank | Courage | Firepower | Skill |
|----------|--------------|-------|-----------|------|---------|-----------|-------|
| 10 | 10 | 7 | 10 | 10 | 10 | 9 | 10 |

MLC: **$95-120+**, MIB: **$125-140**, MISB: **$150-275**

**ALTERNATE MODE:** Armored convoy, space jet, battle headquarters.
**EASILY LOST WEAPONS AND ACCESSORIES:** Photon bazooka, 4 blaster cannons, 2 laser guns, 2 energon exhaust stacks, laser barrel.

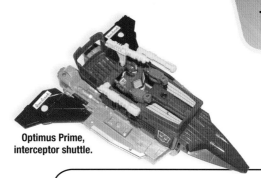

Optimus Prime,
interceptor shuttle.

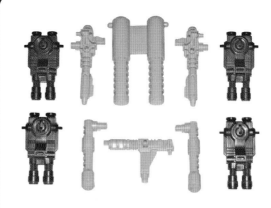

Optimus Prime, easily lost weapons and accessories.

Optimus Prime, standard
mode, top view.

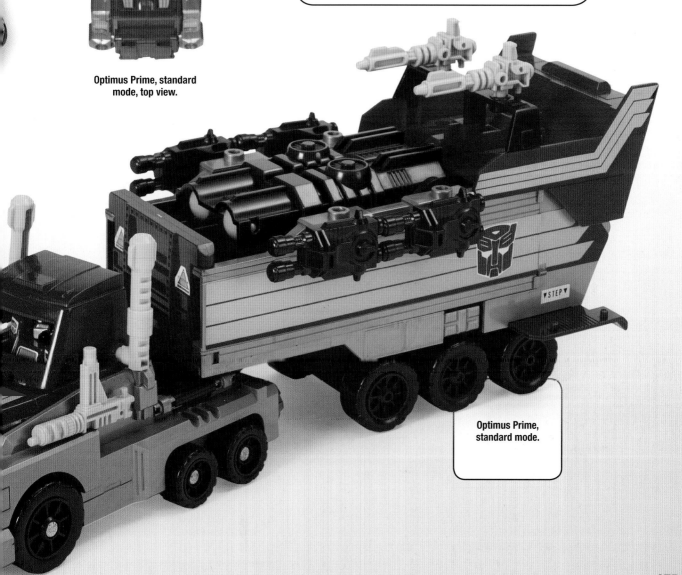

Optimus Prime,
standard mode.

Military Patrol, alternate modes.

# MILITARY PATROL

MICROMASTER PATROLS

**FUNCTION:** Front Line Assault
**MOTTO:** "The ultimate force is the force of destruction."

"The bullies of the battlefield. Learned to fight while terrifying the steel streets of Cybertron. As unmerciful and cold as solid ice. Feared by their Autobot enemies for their fierce and unrelenting attacks. Often circle their target, blasting it again and again until nothing but ashes remain. Each firmly convinced he should be the leader of the patrol. Often take potshots at one another out of spite. Constant bickering and refusal to work together make it impossible for them to complete a mission."

| Teamwork | Cooperation | Strength | Endurance | Speed | Intelligence | Courage | Skill |
|---|---|---|---|---|---|---|---|
| 7 | 7 | 10 | 6 | 9 | 7 | 9 | 9 |

MLC (full set): **$18-35+**, MOC: **$40-80+**

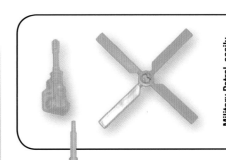
Military Patrol, easily lost accessories.

**ALTERNATE MODES:** Bombshock (green Leopard-1 tank), Dropshot (blue Armored Personnel Carrier), Growl (tan FMC XR311 combat support vehicle) and Tracer (black AH-64 Apache attack helicopter).
**EASILY LOST WEAPONS AND ACCESSORIES:** Tracer's propeller, Growl's top gun.

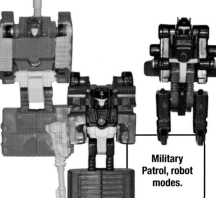
Military Patrol, robot modes.

# RACE TRACK PATROL

MICROMASTER PATROLS

**FUNCTION:** Mobile Assault
**MOTTO:** "There are two kinds of fighters, Decepticons and losers."

"The ultimate speed demons! Leaned to drive on Cybertron freeways with some of the meanest, nastiest drivers in the universe. Enjoy swerving in and out of traffic, cutting each other off, tailgating and sending each other into tail spins. All equipped with turbo-powered energon engines that can rocket them to speeds in excess of Mach 1. Often forget their mission and get side-tracked with their dangerous roadway antics. Extremely powerful when they work together as a team. Sometimes use their illegally-powered engines to win drag races and help finance the Decepticons' latest evil scheme."

| Teamwork | Cooperation | Strength | Endurance | Speed | Intelligence | Courage | Skill |
|---|---|---|---|---|---|---|---|
| 7 | 8 | 8 | 9 | 10 | 6 | 8 | 9 |

MLC (full set): **$18-28**, MOC: **$30-60**

Race Track Patrol, robot modes.

**ALTERNATE RACE CAR MODES:** Barricade (blue Ligier JS3 Formula-1 racecar), Ground Hog (purple Dodge Shelby Charger funny car), Motorhead (yellow 1987 Callaway Corvette [B2K]) and Roller Force (magenta Baja off-road buggy).
**EASILY LOST WEAPONS AND ACCESSORIES:** N/A.

Race Track Patrol, alternate modes.

# BATTLE SQUAD

Battle Squad, alternate modes.

**MICROMASTER COMBINER SQUADS**

Function: Aerial Counterattack
**MOTTO:** "The higher they fly, the faster they'll fall!"

"Utilizing the Micromaster Combiner feature, each micro robot of the Decepticon Battle Squad has the ability to connect with other Micromaster Combiners to form powerful, devastating vehicles of destruction! The nucleus of the Decepticons' off-radar defense system. Banded together by a cybernetic compressor to ignite the stratosphere with a magnitude of firepower! Equipped with sophisticated, visual tracking devices for high-definition, target-lock capabilities! Usually to blame when Autobot spacecrafts suddenly disappear from radar. Able to annihilate anything within a three mile radius. When separated, take pop-shots at each other for sport. Combine to form an armored assault vehicle, blast cannon transport, and high-spy jet."

| Teamwork | Cooperation | Strength | Endurance | Speed | Intelligence | Courage | Skill |
|---|---|---|---|---|---|---|---|
| 7 | 7 | 8 | 6 | 7 | 8 | 9 | 5 |

MLC: **$24-38**, MOC (opened): **$48-55**, MOC: **$50-100**

Battle Squad, alternate combinations.

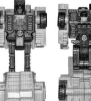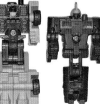

Battle Squad, robot modes.

**ALTERNATE MODES:** (Armored assault vehicle) Meltdown (front) and Half-Track (rear), (blast cannon transport) Direct-Hit (front) and Power Punch (rear), and (Blackbird jet) Fireshot (front) and Vanquish (rear).
**EASILY LOST WEAPONS AND ACCESSORIES:** N/A.

# CONSTRUCTOR SQUAD

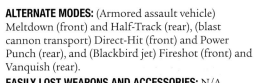

**MICROMASTER COMBINER SQUADS**

**FUNCTION:** Battlefield Fortification
**MOTTO:** "There's nothing like the feel of cold steel!"

"As part of the Micromaster Combiner force, each member of the Decepticon Constructor squad can be separated from its partner and re-combined with another Micromaster Combiner to form an incredible new Micromaster Combiner constructor! Can turn raw ideas into structural monsters of hard concrete! Known for constructing monuments at Decepticon headquarters after every Autobot conquest! Enjoy watching the destruction of something beautiful so they can build a frightfully ominous edifice in its place! Together they're unbeatable. When separated, too busy trying to out-design each other. They take pride constructing rather than destroying. Will build anything, anywhere, anytime for the highest bidder! Combine to form crane, dump truck, and ground digger vehicles."

| Teamwork | Cooperation | Strength | Endurance | Speed | Intelligence | Courage | Skill |
|---|---|---|---|---|---|---|---|
| 7 | 7 | 9 | 8 | 5 | 6 | 9 | 8 |

MLC: **$24-38**, MOC (opened): **$48-55**, MOC: **$40-80**

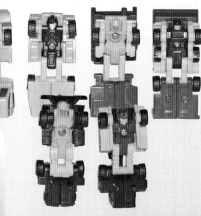

Constructor Squad, robot modes.

Constructor Squad, alternate modes.

**ALTERNADE MODES:** (Crane) Stonecruncher (front) and Excavator (rear), (dump truck) Sledge (front) and Hammer (rear), and (ground digger) Grit (front) and Knockout (rear).
**EASILY LOST WEAPONS AND ACCESSORIES:** N/A.

Cannon Transport, standard mode.

Cannon Transport, alternate mode.

# CANNON TRANSPORT

**MICROMASTER COMBINER TRANSPORTS**

**FUNCTION:** Demolitions
**MOTTO:** "We aim for nothing less than total victory!"

"The essence of Decepticon evil. Moves twin turret, high impact cannon into prime position to unleash earth crunching firepower. Able to change into all-terrain micro vehicle, ultra force battle platform, or two battle-ready micro robots. Micromaster combiner mode allows armored transport to fuse with other Combiners for fast attack capabilities. Equipped with state-of-the-art, cybernetic scanner that detects Autobot troop movements up to 20 miles away. Commanded by Cement-Head and Terror-Tread, two swaggering braggarts who enjoy trashing enemy installations."

Cannon Transport, Micromaster robot modes—Cement-Head and Terror-Tread.

| Strength | Intelligence | Speed | Endurance | Rank | Courage | Firepower | Skill |
|----------|-------------|-------|-----------|------|---------|-----------|-------|
| 7 | 10 | 9 | 9 | 7 | 8 | 9 | 6 |

MLC: **$50-75+**, MOC (opened): **$78-85**, MOC: **$125-250**

**ALTERNATE MODE:** (Micromasters combine to form) dump truck, (cannon transport to) battle station, battle emplacements.

**EASILY LOST WEAPONS AND ACCESSORIES:** "Cement Head" micromaster (front), "Terror Tread" micromaster (rear), 2 cannons, 2 ramps.

Cannon Transport, easily lost weapons and accessories.

Cannon Transport, Micromaster combined mode.

Cannon Transport, battle emplacements.

# ANTI-AIRCRAFT BASE

**MICROMASTER BASE**

**FUNCTION:** Ground Infantry
**MOTTO:** "Persistence is the cornerstone of victory."

"One of the most powerful Decepticon weapons ever. Commanded by Spaceshot and Blackout that combine to form a B-1 bomber jet. Able to plot a course of attack in the middle of battle, change maneuvers to match the enemy and emerge victorious. Often circles overhead during battle, surveying the battlefield and providing air and ground support when necessary. Tank armed with sophisticated all-terrain and underwater attack capabilities. Also armed with dual 50mm cannons for long range firepower. In battle station Mode, outfitted with 3-stage photon rocket launcher, heat-seeking stun laser and turret that converts to devastating gun emplacement. On-board computer radar guidance systems and automated repair bays provide additional ground support. Self-propelled scout vehicle fully equipped for short range reconnaissance missions, and can reach speeds in excess of Mach 1."

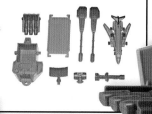

Anti-Aircraft Base, easily lost weapons and accessories with Micromaster combined mode.

| Strength | Intelligence | Speed | Endurance | Rank | Courage | Firepower | Skill |
|----------|-------------|-------|-----------|------|---------|-----------|-------|
| 8 | 7 | 9 | 7 | 8 | 6 | 6 | 9 |

MLC: **$58-75+**, MOC (opened): **$78-85**, MOC: **$100-200**

**ALTERNATE MODE:** (Micromasters combine to form) B-1 Bomber, (attack tank to) anti-aircraft base.

**EASILY LOST WEAPONS AND ACCESSORIES:** "Blackout" micromaster (front), "Spaceshot" micromaster (rear), tank/base, scout vehicle, ramp, missile launcher, radar drum, turret, 2 turret cannons, bazooka, communications dish.

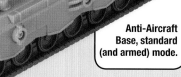

Anti-Aircraft Base, standard (and armed) mode.

Banzai-Tron, easily lost weapons and accessories.

# BANZAI-TRON

**ACTION MASTERS**

**FUNCTION:** Martial Arts Warrior
**MOTTO:** "To the victor go the profits."

"A master of Crystalocution, the Cybertronic martial art of defeating an opponent by attacking his metal fracture points. Usually reduces an enemy to spare parts in minutes and then sells what's left, if given the chance. Always willing to fight, for a profit. His partner, Razor-Sharp, is a lethal titanium-piercing crab that can tear through just about any kind of metal obstacle! Converts to a semi-automatic rifle that shoots plasma energy projectiles that explode on contact."

| Strength | Intelligence | Speed | Endurance | Rank | Courage | Firepower | Skill |
|---|---|---|---|---|---|---|---|
| 8 | 7 | 2 | 9 | 6 | 10 | 6 | 10 |

MLC: **$18-23**, MOC: **$30-60**

**WEAPONS'S ALTERNATE MODE:** Photon neutralizer + Razor-Sharp = semi-automatic gun.

**EASILY LOST WEAPONS AND ACCESSORIES:** Photon neutralizer, Razor-Sharp, 2 Razor-Sharp claws (left and right), 2 Razor-Sharp legs (both the same).

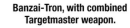

Banzai-Tron, with combined Targetmaster weapon.

Banzai-Tron, robot mode.

Anti-Aircraft Base, alternate mode with scout vehicle.

Anti-Aircraft Base, Micromaster robot modes—Spaceshot and Blackout.

Devastator, with combined Targetmaster weapon.

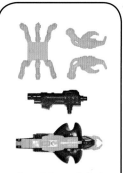

Devastator, easily lost weapons and accessories.

## DEVASTATOR

**ACTION MASTERS**

**FUNCTION:** Warrior
**MOTTO:** "Thinking and winning do not mix."

"Awesome and terrifying! Programmed for the sole purpose of crushing everything in his path. He is the embodiment of a life form which takes full advantage of his enemies' weaknesses and uses them for their destruction. His ferocious partner, Scorpulator, conducts attacks without reason and warning, ripping his victims to scrap metal with his razor sharp claws. Scorpulator's tail shoots twin pulse laser beams. Changes into an acid spray gun."

| Strength | Intelligence | Speed | Endurance | Rank | Courage | Firepower | Skill |
|---|---|---|---|---|---|---|---|
| 10 | 2 | 1 | 9 | 6 | 10 | 8 | 5 |

MLC: **$12-20**, MOC: **$20-40**

**TARGETMASTER'S ALTERNATE MODE:** Magnifier blaster + Scorpulator = acid spray gun.
**EASILY LOST WEAPONS AND ACCESSORIES:** Magnifier blaster, Scorpulator, Scorpulator's legs, 2 Scorpulator claws.

Devastator, robot mode.

Krok, robot mode.

## KROK

**ACTION MASTERS**

**FUNCTION:** Foot Soldier
**MOTTO:** "The road to conquest is best traveled one step at a time."

"Gets his kicks from kicking! One blow from his automatic-powered foot can send an Autobot into orbit. Centuries of playing all-star mecha-soccer on Cybertron has made him the terror that he is today. By taking a single-stomping step, he can create a mini earthquake with a scaled reading of at least 7.0. His faithful partner, Gatoraider, uses his vise-like jaws to crush any unfortunate being caught in the aftershocks. Converts to powerful concussion cannon."

| Strength | Intelligence | Speed | Endurance | Rank | Courage | Firepower | Skill |
|---|---|---|---|---|---|---|---|
| 9 | 6 | 2 | 10 | 5 | 7 | 6 | 8 |

MLC: **$12-20**, MOC: **$20-40**

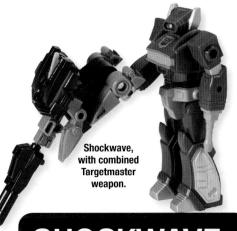

Shockwave, with combined Targetmaster weapon.

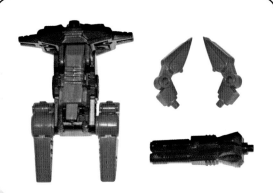

Shockwave, easily lost weapons and accessories.

# SHOCKWAVE

**FUNCTION:** Military Operations Commander
**MOTTO:** "Clarity of thought before rashness of action."

"An awesome warrior. Plots the destruction of the Autobots with the same cold, computer-like efficiency as in planning the overthrow of his Decepticon leader, Megatron. Believes that only one as logical as himself can lead the Decepticons to victory. Left arm shoots a wide range of electromagnetic armaments from explosive gamma rays to super-hot infrared particle beams. Paired with Fistfight, a loathsome terror droid who enjoys dissecting late model cars when he's not in his long range, laser-sighted, lightning rifle mode."

| Strength | Intelligence | Speed | Endurance | Rank | Courage | Firepower | Skill |
|----------|--------------|-------|-----------|------|---------|-----------|-------|
| 10 | 10 | 7 | 7 | 9 | 9 | 9 | 9 |

**MLC: $14-28**, MOC: **$40-80**

**TARGETMASTER'S ALTERNATE MODE:** Turbo rifle + Fistfight = lightning gun.
**EASILY LOST WEAPONS AND ACCESSORIES:** Turbo rifle, Fistfight, 2 Fistfight arms (right and left).

Shockwave, robot mode.

Krok, with combined Targetmaster weapon.

**TARGETMASTER'S ALTERNATE MODE:** Electro pulsator + Gatoraider = concussion cannon.
**EASILY LOST WEAPONS AND ACCESSORIES:** Electro pulsator, Gatoraider.

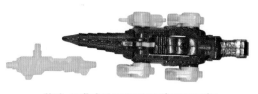

Krok, easily lost weapons and accessories.

Soundwave, with combined Targetmaster weapon.

# SOUNDWAVE

**ACTION MASTERS**

**FUNCTION:** Communications
**MOTTO:** "Cries and screams are music to my ears!"

"A smooth-talking opportunist who uses his eavesdropping abilities on friends and foes alike. Equipped with advanced radio wave and energy sensors, photographic memory and newly improved 2,000 mile range transmission capability. Wingthing, his loyal, lethal cohort, is all too eager to carry out Soundwave's every vengeful whim and diabolical scheme. Upon command, Wingthing turns into a metal-piercing concussion cannon. It's difficult to say which one is more despised by the other Decepticons."

| Strength | Intelligence | Speed | Endurance | Rank | Courage | Firepower | Skill |
|---|---|---|---|---|---|---|---|
| 8 | 9 | 2 | 6 | 8 | 5 | 6 | 9 |

MLC: **$16-28**, MOC: **$40-80**

Soundwave, robot mode.

Soundwave, easily lost weapons and accessories.

**TARGETMASTER'S ALTERNATE MODE:** Photon negator + Wingthing = concussion cannon.
**EASILY LOST WEAPONS AND ACCESSORIES:** Photon negator, Wingthing, 2 Wingthing wings (right and left).

# OFF-ROAD CYCLE WITH AXER

**ACTION MASTER BLASTERS**

**FUNCTION:** Bounty Hunter
**MOTTO:** "No prey is too large, no fee is too small."

"Axer learned his craft hunting down microchip smugglers in the slag swamps of Cybertron. His custom-designed all-terrain Turbo Cycle is equipped with heat-seeking proton missile batteries, quadriphonic sonic blasters and magnetic-lock targeting destabilizer rifle; and converts to a dual photon cannon battle station."

| Strength | Intelligence | Speed | Endurance | Rank | Courage | Firepower | Skill |
|---|---|---|---|---|---|---|---|
| 6 | 8 | 3 | 9 | 7 | 8 | 8 | 10 |

MLC: **$25-30**, MIB: **$45-50**, MISB: **$50-100**

Axer, easily lost weapons and accessories.

**ALTERNATE MODE(S):** Attack cycle, pom-pom cannon.
**EASILY LOST WEAPONS AND ACCESSORIES:** Cannon, seat rest, 2 missiles.

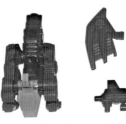

Axer, robot mode.

Axer, standard mode, with armed Off-Road Cycle.

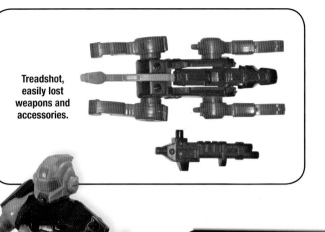

Treadshot, easily lost weapons and accessories.

Treadshot, with combined Targetmaster weapon.

Treadshot, robot mode.

# TREADSHOT

**ACTION MASTERS**

**FUNCTION:** Gunslinger
**MOTTO:** "A gun is only as good as the one who holds it!"

"When someone needs shooting, he's the one the Decepticons call to pull the trigger! Treadshot can outdraw and outshoot any robot this side of the galaxy. And his partner Catgut, is more than a willing weapon. This snarling, ferocious, 4-legged beast eagerly turns into a powerful, fusion-powered particle blaster with pulse demagnetizer attachment. Like Treadshot, Catgut gets a blast out of his job."

| Strength | Intelligence | Speed | Endurance | Rank | Courage | Firepower | Skill |
|----------|--------------|-------|-----------|------|---------|-----------|-------|
| 6 | 7 | 3 | 8 | 7 | 8 | 8 | 10 |

MLC: **$16-25**, MOC: **$25-55**

**TARGETMASTER'S ALTERNATE MODE:** Pulse demagnetizer + Catgut = particle blaster.
**EASILY LOST WEAPONS AND ACCESSORIES:** Pulse demagnetizer, Catgut.

Axer, attack mode.

Starscream, standard mode, with armed Turbo Jet.

Starscream, attack mode.

# TURBO JET WITH STARSCREAM

**ACTION MASTER BLASTERS**

**FUNCTION:** Assault
**MOTTO:** "Conquest is made of the ashes of one's enemies."

"Armed with null ray rifle that binds its target in bands of energized steel. Turbo Jet armed with wing-mounted missile launchers and twin turbo-fan boosters. Photon blaster on nose fires earth-shattering missile bombs. Converts to air-powered battle chariot, armed with force field and 4-stage rocket launcher."

| Strength | Intelligence | Speed | Endurance | Rank | Courage | Firepower | Skill |
|----------|--------------|-------|-----------|------|---------|-----------|-------|
| 10 | 9 | 9 | 8 | 5 | 8 | 7 | 7 |

MLC: **$35-48+**, MIB: **$50-55+**, MISB: **$65-110**

**ALTERNATE MODE(S):** Attack jet, mobile launcher.
**EASILY LOST WEAPONS AND ACCESSORIES:** Laser cannon, 2 missiles, steering bar, foot platform, engine cover.

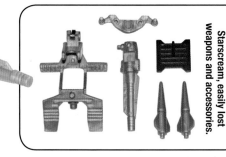

Starscream, easily lost weapons and accessories.

Starscream, robot mode.

# NEUTRO-FUSION TANK WITH MEGATRON

Megatron, standard mode, armed.

**ACTION MASTER ATTACK VEHICLES**

**FUNCTION:** Decepticon Leader
**MOTTO:** "Conquest of the universe rests upon the immediate termination of all Autobots!"

"Cybertron and Earth are not enough for this power-hungry Decepticon! Now he wants the whole galaxy! More ferocious and powerful than ever, this living engine of evil seeks the worlds throughout the cosmos and utterly crushes all those who dare defy him, especially the Autobots. In pursuit of these grisly goals, he drives the Neutro-Fusion Tank, a high-impact battle tank armed with fusion cannon, corrosive smoke shells, anti-aircraft photon machine guns, and heat-seeking mechano-sensors. The tank converts into a ground-to-air, wire-guided missile launcher, and search and destroy jet throne."

| Strength | Intelligence | Speed | Endurance | Rank | Courage | Firepower | Skill |
|----------|--------------|-------|-----------|------|---------|-----------|-------|
| 10 | 10 | 4 | 8 | 10 | 9 | 10 | 9 |

MLC: **$80-115+**, MIB: **$130-150+**, MISB: **$165-225**

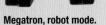

Megatron, robot mode.

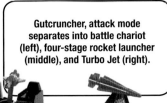
Gutcruncher, attack mode separates into battle chariot (left), four-stage rocket launcher (middle), and Turbo Jet (right).

Gutcruncher, easily lost weapons and accessories.

# STRATOTRONIC JET WITH GUTCRUNCHER

**ACTION MASTER ATTACK VEHICLES**

**FUNCTION:** Air-to-Ground Support
**MOTTO:** "Conquest of the Autobots begins with control of the sky!"

"Gutcruncher shares the Decepticons' dream of total defeat of the Autobots, but for his own reasons. He has a contract with Megatron to trade their remains to the Junkions and other interplanetary spare parts dealers for vast quantities of energon cubes. This cold, calculating capitalist views all opponents as potential profit. He pilots the space-faring Stratotronic Jet, which has a maximum speed of 40,000 mph and is armed with fusion bombs, two cruise missiles, particle beam, infrared laser guns and more. It converts into a devastating battle station with missile launcher and fusion blaster cannon. Also includes pilotless surveillance drone and one-man battle tank."

| Strength | Intelligence | Speed | Endurance | Rank | Courage | Firepower | Skill |
|---|---|---|---|---|---|---|---|
| 8 | 8 | 7 | 9 | 10 | 7 | 5 | 9 |

MLC: **$70-90+**, MIB: **$100-120+**, MISB: **$125-175+**

Gutcruncher, standard mode, armed.

Gutcruncher, robot mode.

**ALTERNATE MODE(S):** Stratotronic jet, surveillance drone and tank, battle cannon and missile base.
**EASILY LOST WEAPONS AND ACCESSORIES:** 2 laser cannons, 4 missiles, jet nose, 2 rear stabilizer fins, twin laser gun, scout tank, seat.

Megatron, easily lost weapons and accessories.

Megatron, attack mode separates into jet throne (left) and missile launcher (right).

**ALTERNATE MODE(S):** Neutro-fusion tank, missile base and jet throne.
**EASILY LOST WEAPONS AND ACCESSORIES:** Tank turret, turret barrel/fusion missile, 4 missiles, twin laser cannon.

# INDEX

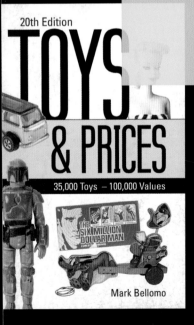
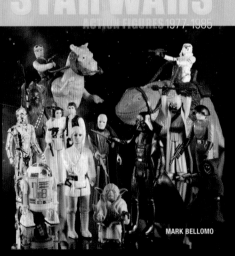
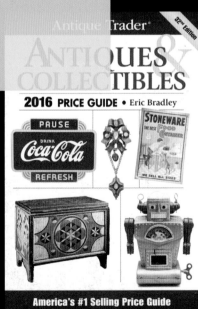